PENGUIN BOOKS

BASTIONS OF THE BELIEVERS

Yoginder Sikand did his M.Phil. in sociology from Jawaharlal Nehru University, New Delhi and his Ph.D. in history from the University of London. He completed his post-doctoral work on 'Islamic Perspectives on Inter-Faith Relations in Contemporary India' at the International Institute for the Study of Islam in the Modern World, Leiden, the Netherlands. He has written several articles on Islam and Muslims in contemporary India and has previously published *Sacred Spaces: Exploring Traditions of Shared Faith in India* (Penguin, 2003) and *Muslims in India since 1947: Islamic Perspectives on Inter-Faith Relations* (Routledge Curzon, 2004).

He is currently a freelance researcher based in Bangalore.

Bastions of the Believers

Madrasas and Islamic Education in India

YOGINDER SIKAND

PENGUIN BOOKS
An imprint of Penguin Random House

PENGUIN BOOKS

USA | Canada | UK | Ireland | Australia
New Zealand | India | South Africa | China | Singapore

Penguin Books is part of the Penguin Random House group of companies
whose addresses can be found at global.penguinrandomhouse.com

Published by Penguin Random House India Pvt. Ltd
4th Floor, Capital Tower 1, MG Road,
Gurugram 122 002, Haryana, India

Penguin
Random House
India

First published by Penguin Books India 2005

10 9 8 7 6 5 4 3

ISBN 9780144000203

Typeset in Sabon MT by Eleven Arts, New Delhi

Printed at Repro India Limited

www.penguin.co.in

FSC
www.fsc.org
MIX
Paper from
responsible sources
FSC® C047271

This is a legitimate digitally printed version of the book and therefore might not have certain extra finishing on the cover.

Dedicated to the sacred memory of victims of terror in the name of religion and nationalism in South Asia

Contents

Foreword

In recent years Yoginder Sikand has rapidly moved to the front rank of the coming generation of scholars of the Muslim world. Just ten years ago he came to me in London to begin research for his Ph.D. Since then he has published a prodigious body of research. This began with his Ph.D. thesis which was published as *The Origins and Development of the Tablighi Jama'at 1920–2000: A Cross-Country Comparative Study* (New Delhi, 2002). It has continued with *Sacred Spaces: Exploring Traditions of Shared Faith in India* (New Delhi, 2003), his book on Sufis in South Asia, their shrines, practices and constituencies, which was followed by a collection of essays published by the Royal Asiatic Society of Great Britain and Ireland, *Muslims of India since 1947: Islamic Perspectives on Inter-Faith Relations* (London, 2004). Since then two further collections of essays have been published in India, and now this major work on *madrasas*. In addition to these essentially academic contributions, Yoginder Sikand also writes frequently for the press, publishes a web magazine, *Qalandar*, which has a specific inter-faith agenda, and maintains his own email circulation list, which offers some fresh piece of research, or some comment, on aspects of contemporary Indian Islam almost every day. There is already a worldwide community of scholars which holds Yoginder Sikand in high esteem.

Yoginder Sikand is driven by a powerful desire to bring great harmony both to India and, by implication, to the world at large. 'The task before us, Muslims as well as others,' he states in his introduction, reflecting on his purposes over the past few years, 'is to seek to explore and promote more liberal and open understandings of Islam, and indeed, of all other faiths. If we are to learn to live together despite our differences, inter-faith dialogue, struggling together for a more peaceful, and at the same time just, social order is, I have come to believe, one of the principal duties confronting committed believers today.' In pursuing this end Yoginder Sikand has sought to use the outcomes of scholarly research to establish new levels of understanding about Muslim issues and thereby improve the quality of national and international discourse about them. This has of course meant that he has been increasingly concerned to do what many of the best scholars do, which is to liberate his learning from the narrow confines of scholarly publication, make it accessible to the general public, and make it work in the world. His one concern, following the spiritual traditions of the great faiths of South Asia, has been to be in the best possible position to enable his knowledge to create a better world for its peoples.

No one today, looking from an Indian or a global perspective, would question the importance of the task Yoginder Sikand has set himself. In a globalizing world in which, over the past thirty years, religious faiths have acquired a new significance, and their fundamentalist forms have seemed to become more widespread than ever before, there is no doubt that more bridges of understanding need to be built between the followers of the great religious traditions. For no faith is this more important than Islam, for whose followers the pains of adjustment to the demands of 'modernity' have seemed to be particularly acute. That this should be so is hardly surprising. For a thousand years, from the eighth to the eighteenth century, the Muslim world, which came to stretch from the Atlantic coast of Africa in the West to Indonesia in the East, saw itself at the leading edge of human affairs; indeed, its trading networks and the knowledge which was shared across continents made it the world system which preceded that of the West. Then, from 1800, everything changed. By 1920 almost all the Muslim world was under European colonial rule. From the mid-twentieth century the end of that rule made little difference because it was replaced ultimately by the global hegemony of the West which, to most Muslims, has seemed to exert increasing pressure on their lives and on their values. In these circumstances, with their backs against a wall, insulted by the arrogance of the West, and often feeling humiliated by their treatment at Western hands, Muslims have had to review the legacy handed down to them from their millennium of triumph to see how they might go forward in the present. This has not been easy. It is hard, in such circumstances of weakness, to cast away the institutions, the forms of knowledge and the ways of thinking which have served a civilization well for much of its existence.

The search for knowledge of all kinds was at the heart of early Muslim civilization. As that civilization developed, two distinct forms of religious knowledge came to be recognized. The first was spiritual knowledge, the techniques of spiritual development which enable Muslims to know God, and the meaning of His revelation to man through the Prophet, in their hearts. This knowledge, and these techniques, were passed on by spiritual masters known as *shaikh*s or *pir*s. The second form of knowledge was knowledge of the Qur'an, the traditions and the *shari'ah*, and all the skills that Muslims might need to make them socially useful, from Arabic grammar and syntax to logic, philosophy, rhetoric and mathematics. This second form of knowledge, the formal learning of Islam, was made to work for each generation, and transmitted to new generations, by scholars, *'ulama*. For most of Muslim history the spiritual and the formal traditions of learning have been seen as two sides of the same coin. Indeed, the best examples of both Sufis and 'ulama imbibed both spiritual and formal learning in good measure. While knowledge could be transmitted anywhere, typically Sufis might pass on their knowledge at the shrine complex of a saint in their order and 'ulama would pass on their knowledge in a madrasa.

Under British rule madrasas spread vigorously in South Asia. In doing so they reflected the many different responses of 'ulama to the challenges that rule presented, among them those of the Deobandis, the Barelwis, the Ahl-i Hadith and the Ahmadiyyas. Indeed, the Deobandi madrasas displayed a remarkable increase: in 1900 the Deobandis had established, or affiliated, just over thirty schools, but by 1967 they claimed nearly 9000 such schools worldwide. Arguably, the major reason for this development was a transformation of the function of the madrasas. No longer did they exist merely to train scholars and government servants. Now they were increasingly part of the frontline in defending Muslim society against both the pressures of colonial rule and Western culture, and the possibility of being absorbed into the wider Hindu world. Madrasas were no longer supported by the state, although the Muslim princes continued to play a role, but by public subscription. As part of their resistance to colonial rule, as well as being part of the process of Islamic revival and reform, madrasas, particularly in the Deobandi tradition, aimed to take Islamic knowledge to the people of India in languages they could understand, by translating key texts into Indian languages, and in cheap and widely available form, by the adoption of print. Thus, madrasas came to be rooted in the Muslim societies of India as bastions of Islam and Islamic culture. At the same time their ʻulama came, on the one hand, to see themselves increasingly as the champions of community interests and, on the other, to be an increasingly significant pressure group in the politics of British India, as demonstrated by their impact on public life in the Khilafat and Non-cooperation era and by their capacity steadily to assert the claims of the *shariʻah* over customary law, which had its crowning success in the Muslim Personal Law (Shariʻat) Application Act of 1937.

After independence the numbers of madrasas continued to multiply. In Pakistan, remittances from Pakistanis working in the Middle East, subsidies from the governments of Saudi Arabia and the Gulf states, and the Islamization policies of the government of General Zia ul-Haq led the number of madrasas to grow from c. 140 in 1947 to over 8000 by the 1990s. In India, the numbers of madrasas grew in part because of their continuing role, as under the British, of preserving an embattled Muslim identity, but in part too because they provided education, and often board and lodging, free, and because their role as carriers of Islamic revival and reform enabled them to mobilize funds at home and abroad for these purposes. There is considerable disagreement, as Yoginder Sikand indicates, over the number of madrasas in India by the late 1990s, but it is not unreasonable to suggest their number lies between the 12,000 identified by the home ministry and the figure of 30,000 which he prefers.

In recent years these madrasas have come to have a bad reputation. In Pakistan this has been because of their alleged association with a radicalization of Islam and sectarian violence. In Pakistan and India this has been because of the association of some Deobandi madrasas with the rise of the Taliban, the brutal and backward regime which these madrasa students imposed upon the peoples of Afghanistan, and post-9/11 an understanding of the close association between the Taliban and Osama bin Laden. Then, in India, especially in recent years, madrasas have been subject to Hindutva propaganda, being branded as 'dens of terror'.

Yoginder Sikand has set out to explain South Asian madrasas in a readily accessible fashion, and has done so well. He reminds us of the importance of the pursuit of knowledge in its widest sense in Muslim societies, the role that madrasas have played through time in transmitting knowledge, and the particular role they came to have in South Asia under British rule in being bastions of Islamic culture. He reminds us, most importantly, that madrasas differ—for instance, they follow different Islamic understandings, some are more open to incorporating 'modern' subjects than others, some are for girls alone, while there is a remarkable forward-looking madrasa system in Kerala, which has state recognition and from which madrasas in the rest of India could learn much. He tells us all that we need to know about traditional madrasas: student life, teachers and how they teach, and madrasa finances and management. He makes it clear that many 'ulama are aware of the need for madrasa reform—reform of the traditional texts taught and teaching methods, the expansion of the curriculum to include 'modern' subjects, the introduction of information technology, indeed the revision of the whole corpus of madrasa learning so that it can work more effectively in the world. But he also points out that in this matter, as in so many for the world's Muslims over the past 200 years, it is difficult to proceed with change when being vilified by powerful forces outside the community.

This said, he introduces us to some remarkable examples of progress—the Jami'at ul-Falah at Azamgarh with its 5000 students (2700 girls and 2300 boys), its inclusive admission policies, its wide-ranging curriculum, and its encouragement of its students to go on to universities; the system created by the Mumbai-based Maulana Badruddin Ajmal to enable madrasa graduates to find jobs in the wider world beyond mosque and madrasa; and the growing number of madrasas focusing specifically on the education of girls. And, finally, he confronts the accusations that madrasas are 'dens of terror'. Quite properly he reminds us that the Jami'at ul-'Ulama-i Hind and most of the 'ulama of Deoband were important supporters of the Indian nationalist movement. He points out that despite rhetoric to the contrary, most Pakistani madrasas have not been involved in militant activities. Indeed, these have been concentrated in the North-West Frontier Province and Baluchistan, where they served US interests in fighting the Russian invaders in the 1980s and Pakistani interests in gaining 'strategic depth' in Central Asia through their support of the Taliban in the 1990s. As far as India is concerned, he declares that 'there is probably no madrasa in India that, as an institution, is actively engaged in training terrorists' although there may be some individuals associated with madrasas who are doing so.

Yoginder Sikand has visited many madrasas, he has read many publications by and about them, and he has talked to many students and 'ulama. He is concerned with setting down the facts as he finds them in all parts of India. He approaches his subject from a background of deep knowledge and also from respect for 'ulama and what they do. Yet, he is not starry-eyed about his subject. While he recognizes an inclusiveness and a willingness to progress in harmony with the modern world in some, he does not ignore claims of religious exclusiveness when he finds them, the deep conservatism of many 'ulama, and the essentially slow pace of change.

This is a most important book, which should be read by all, whether policy-makers or the general public, who are interested in madrasas in particular and in Indian Muslims in general. Such is the range and depth of Yoginder Sikand's research that it should remain of value to scholars of modern Islam in South Asia for many years to come.

Royal Holloway
University of London
March 2005

FRANCIS ROBINSON

Preface

Writing about anything to do with Islam in times such as these is hazardous business. The simultaneous upsurge of militant Islamist movements, on the one hand, and fierce Islamophobia, on the other, has converted the entire terrain of Islamic studies into a sharply contested battlefield. Powerful forces are at work, dictating how Islam and Muslims are represented in academic and popular discourse, and the space for any reasoned comment on the subject is rapidly contracting. There has always been a strong association between politics and scholarship on Islam, as critics of the Orientalist project have so brilliantly illustrated, but in the writings of the classical Orientalists at least, that link was sought to be concealed, however clumsily, with the fig leaf of 'objectivity' and 'detachment'. Today, such pretensions are no longer regarded as necessary, as rivals furiously battle each other, seeking to impose their own claims to represent what Islam and its followers are actually all about.

It has become increasingly accepted practice for social scientists to state upfront where they are coming from and what their own normative preferences are. One's value orientations, and, linked to that, one's personal politics, inevitably influence what one chooses to write about and how one undertakes that task. Because of this I believe it is a moral obligation on my part to inform the reader of my personal history and ideological position.

I come from a middle-class Indian Punjabi family of mixed, indeed liminal, religious background. I experimented with various religions during my college days, searching for some sense of meaning and purpose in life. I was introduced to Sufism by Hasan, a Muslim friend, who took me to a Sufi shrine in Delhi which he regularly frequented. On my first visit to the shrine I was struck by the beauty of the throbbing music performed by itinerant *qawwal*s, the intricacy of the Arabic and Persian calligraphy scattered across the walls of the shrine, and the presence of people from different communities—Muslims, Hindus, Dalits and Sikhs—all worshipping together in a rare gesture of inter-communal camaraderie. At the same time, much that I saw also disturbed me, the stark poverty and squalor of the locality, open sewers overflowing with filth, and the rapacious, pot-bellied custodians of the shrine who pestered hapless pilgrims for donations.

Soon, I began regularly visiting the shrine, generally on Thursday evenings, when special *qawwali* sessions are organized and large crowds gather to beseech buried Sufi saints, whom they believe to be still alive, for blessings and favours. As my interest in Sufism developed, I began to learn Urdu, from a *maulvi* who insisted that Sufism was complete anathema and that it had nothing to do with 'real' Islam. He proudly identified himself as a 'Wahhabi', a follower of the eighteenth century Arabian purist, Muhammad ibn 'Abdul Wahhab, known for his fierce opposition to the cults of the saints. The *maulvi*'s regular diatribes against the Sufis later prompted me, once my Urdu was tolerably good, to embark on a study of the works of the 'Wahhabis' and of other '*ulama* (sing. '*alim*), or Islamic scholars, who were equally opposed to what they saw as 'un-Islamic' forms of Sufism. By this time I had enrolled for an M.Phil. course in Sociology at the Jawaharlal Nehru University, New Delhi, and I decided to work for my dissertation on one particular Islamic movement, the Tablighi Jama'at, known for its fierce hostility to popular Sufism. I chose to study the movement principally because I was concerned about the challenge that it appeared to pose to the sort of Sufism that I had begun to develop an interest in. Two years later, I managed a scholarship to study in Britain to do a doctoral thesis on the same topic.

As a consequence of my interest in things Islamic and my effort to know Islam as it is understood in diverse ways by Muslims, I became involved with groups working to promote inter-communal harmony and dialogue between different religious communities. It struck me how completely ignorant people were of the religions and practices of others, and how instrumental this was in bolstering deeply ingrained prejudices and hatred and in fuelling bloody conflicts that have taken such a heavy toll of innocent lives throughout history. Along with my academic pursuits, I sought, in my own small way, to reach out to a wider audience through writing for the popular press and participating in conferences and public lectures, pleading for a more nuanced and empathetic understanding of Islam and its followers. I was particularly concerned to stress the diversity of understandings of Islam and the point that essentialized images of Islam and Muslims were completely misplaced. Like any other religion, Islam, I felt it my duty to constantly reiterate, could be interpreted in a multitude of ways, progressive as well as reactionary. The task before us, Muslims as well as others, I stressed, was to seek to explore and promote more liberal and open understandings of Islam, and, indeed, of all other faiths, if we were to learn to live together despite our differences. Inter-faith dialogue, struggling together for a more peaceful, and, at the same time, just, social order was, I came to believe, one of the principal duties confronting committed believers today.

This led me to work on a post-doctoral project on Islamic perspectives on inter-faith relations in contemporary India. I travelled to different parts of the country to conduct interviews with leading Muslim scholars and activists, including advocates for inter-community amity, as well as those who spoke the language of conflict and revenge. In order to put across my own views on this vexed and extremely charged subject to a wider audience beyond the pale of academia, I, with the help of a friend, launched *Qalandar*, a monthly web-magazine[1] devoted to discussion of issues related to Islam and inter-faith relations in South Asia. We—I and the many contributors who, with their writings, helped get the magazine off the ground—saw *Qalandar* as a platform to help promote more open and progressive visions of Islam and other faiths and to counter religious extremism.

*

My interest in inter-faith relations and my limited involvement in initiatives for inter-faith dialogue enabled me to travel to various parts of India and visit numerous madrasas, Islamic seminaries, and to interact with ‘ulama of different schools of thought as well as their critics. The ‘ulama regard themselves as repositories and transmitters of the Islamic sciences and have played a central role in transmitting that knowledge from one generation to the next. This interaction helped me broaden my own understanding of Islam. At their madrasas and homes the ‘ulama received me with courtesy and hospitality, and from them I learnt a great deal. I found, I must admit, the self-righteousness and narrow-mindedness of many 'ulama greatly distressing, and so, too, their willingness to twist the teachings of their faith in order to bolster their own claims. The inordinate concern that many of them seemed to display with the minutiae of the law, to the neglect of its spirit, simply appalled me. In this, of course, I knew they were not unique, but, rather, quite typical of the class of professional religious specialists in any institutionalized form of religion. I soon came to the conclusion that such 'ulama were actually a major hurdle on the path of Muslim progress, and in that sense an even greater threat to Muslims themselves than to others. I was convinced that the juristic and literalist understanding Islam of many 'ulama represented a considerable departure, and to me, a degeneration, of the sublime message of the Sufis whose writings I had read and a few of whom I had personally encountered. The contrast between the many 'ulama I met and the Sufis I knew of could hardly have been more stark.

At the same time, however, I did meet numerous other 'ulama whose work I greatly appreciated. I recognized the immensely valuable contributions that they were making to maintain Muslim identity and to preserve the tradition of Islamic learning, which are today under threat from the growing influence of Hindu supremacist forces. I was also struck by the significant role of many madrasas in promoting literacy and social reform, particularly among poor Muslim families, victims of neglect and considerable discrimination.

*

Although my extensive interaction with the 'ulama led me to write several newspaper articles about the madrasas, the thought of devoting an entire book to madrasa education would not have struck me had it not been for the widespread vilification of the madrasas in the form of a veritable witch-hunt spearheaded by Hindutva groups, large sections of the Indian press and even key actors within the Indian state machinery. Madrasas have, as a rule, hardly enjoyed a good press in India, or elsewhere for that matter. Till a decade or so ago, the 'mainstream' Indian press hardly ever bothered to refer to them, despite the fact that they number several thousand and play a crucial role in the lives of many Muslims. As elsewhere, the 'ulama of the madrasas in India were generally depicted as survivors of an age long past who would disappear in the face of the onward march of modernity. They were regarded as of no more than nuisance value in perpetuating Muslim 'backwardness' and 'separatism'. Madrasas were routinely dismissed, if ever they were referred to, as dens of 'obscurantism', and as an obstacle to Muslim 'integration' into the 'national mainstream'. In large parts of the Muslim world, states closed down or took over and suitably 'modernized' the madrasas by integrating them into the university system. Traditional madrasas seemed to survive largely in South Asia, a fact noted with great pride by many of the region's leading 'ulama.[2] For their part, most outside observers seemed to think that here, too, they were doomed to final extinction. That probably explains why few scholars deemed the traditional 'ulama as worth studying at all. Instead, much scholarly effort was expended on seeking to understand and write about new types of Muslim intellectuals, including Islamists and Muslim modernists, who were thought to represent the direction in which the Muslim world was moving.

The myth of the marginality of the 'ulama was to be shattered with the outbreak of the Islamic Revolution in Iran in 1979, headed by Ayatollah Khomeini, a leading Shi'a cleric. The rise of Khomeini catapulted the 'ulama from obscurity into the limelight. Western academics and journalists suddenly began talking about the enormous clout of the 'ulama, whom they had earlier dismissed as of little or no consequence. The rise of Khomeini led to a number of studies on the 'ulama, but these focused almost entirely on Iran and the Arab world, completely ignoring the 'ulama of South Asia. The situation changed, however, with the attacks of September 2001, claimed by the Americans to have been masterminded by Islamists associated with Osama bin Laden's al-Qa'ida network. The attacks led to a sharp escalation in anti-Muslim sentiments across the world. Muslims were vilified as bloodthirsty monsters and Islam as a terrorist creed bent on the extermination of all 'disbelievers'. The attention of the global media now turned to the madrasas of South Asia. Although none of those involved in the attacks, not even bin Laden himself, had been trained in a traditional madrasa or was a qualified 'alim, the press routinely lambasted the South Asian madrasas as veritable 'dens of terror'. Since the Taliban regime in Afghanistan, which had provided sanctuary to bin Laden, owed its inspiration to the Deobandi school of thought, the madrasa at Deoband, a small, sleepy town in northern India, was now alleged to be the epicentre of a global Islamic 'terrorist' conspiracy. Some writers went so far as to assert that Deoband had emerged as the nerve centre of a plot, hatched in league with the dreaded Pakistani Inter-Services Intelligence (ISI), to dismember India. It was claimed that many, if not most, madrasas in India were secretly involved in training terrorists in the guise of providing students with religious education. Senior Indian government officials and bureaucrats, whose sympathy for Hindu supremacist organizations was an open secret, joined the press in insisting that the madrasas had now emerged as a major threat to 'national security'.

Scores of books and thousands of newspaper articles now began to appear on the Indian madrasas, most of them making sweeping generalizations. In doing so, the historical pattern of the evolution of the madrasas and the enormous diversity within the madrasa system itself, including conflicting and mutually opposed political stances of the 'ulama of different madrasas, were conveniently ignored. Targeting the madrasas was added ammunition to serve what can be described as an organized project of Islamophobia. Ignoring the fact that only a relatively small proportion of Muslim children actually study in madrasas, it was made to appear as if the entire Muslim community was somehow so mired in religious 'obscurantism' that Muslims simply refused to send their children to regular schools. In this way, it was sought to be argued that Muslims were themselves to blame for their educational and economic backwardness. In the process, the poverty that drives many Muslims to educate their children in madrasas instead of regular schools and the very real fact of discrimination that Muslims often face from an indifferent government and a hostile state bureaucracy, resulting in woefully minimal state provision for Muslim education, were glossed over.

Few journalists and 'scholars' working on the madrasas sought to empathetically listen to what Muslim parents, madrasa students, the 'ulama of the madrasas and Muslim social activists themselves had to say about the madrasas. In their writings on the madrasas, few cared to engage in any intensive field-based investigation. Highlighting cases of some isolated hate-spewing 'ulama, they presented them as speaking on behalf of the 'ulama as a class and as being somehow representative of the madrasa system as a whole. Facts that would forcefully challenge their thesis of madrasas being necessarily 'obscurantist' and 'communal' were ignored. Thus, the fact that till less than a hundred years ago in large parts of northern India the village *maktab* and the madrasa attracted both Hindu as well as Muslim children, providing them with valued linguistic and social skills, was left unmentioned. So, too, was the fact that numerous Hindu leaders, including none less than Raja Ram Mohan Roy, hailed as the father of the Indian renaissance, had received their primary education in madrasas. Likewise, in seeking to present the madrasas as 'anti-national' and as agents of 'pan-Islamism', the role of large sections of the 'ulama in opposing the Muslim League and in supporting the demand for a united India received but scant mention.

At the same time as the vilification of the madrasas assumed the form of an organized campaign, the Indian press, with some notable exceptions, remained largely silent on the hate propaganda being churned out of Hindutva-sponsored schools that routinely brand Muslims and Christians as 'enemies' of the nation, and openly vilify their religion, history and traditions. Such poisonous propaganda, which continues unabated, has played a crucial role in provoking and legitimizing violent attacks against Muslims and Christians, as the tragic case of Gujarat illustrates. In addition, while lambasting the madrasas for spreading 'obscurantism', few newspapers cared to critique textbooks prescribed by the state that, besides containing derogatory remarks about Muslims, are now filled with patently unscientific assertions, such as the claim that the Vedas are the fount of all wisdom, and assertions about the 'scientific' nature of Hindu astrology, and the supposed 'merits' of the caste system.

Having visited madrasas and interacted with 'ulama of

different schools of thought, it struck me how damaging were the allegations that were being heaped on the madrasas as a whole. While I recognized that much of what the madrasas taught was simply outdated (the Deoband madrasa, for instance, still insists that the sun revolves around the earth, and it has special seating arrangements for invisible *jinns*), to label all, or most, of them as 'dens of terror' was, I felt, completely fallacious. One may well argue that madrasas, as a rule, although with notable exceptions, represent a conservative form of theology and jurisprudence that is, in many ways, ill-suited to a modern, plural society. Muslim modernists would themselves dispute much of what the madrasas teach. Obscurantism, however, need not necessarily lead to militancy and physical hostility against others. For instance, in the decades leading to India's independence the Deobandis, representing an extreme form of religious conservatism, insisted on Hindu–Muslim amity and a joint struggle for a free and united India. Then again, obscurantism is not simply a monopoly of the Muslim 'ulama. A comparative study of religious schools in India—Muslim, Hindu, Sikh, Christian and other—would be sure to come up with the general conclusion that obscurantism flourishes almost everywhere where representatives of institutionalized religion dare to tread.

Given the fierce and continuing vilification campaign against the madrasas, I recognized the need for a detailed study of the Indian madrasas and of the 'ulama associated with them in order to present a more balanced perspective on the subject. As I began searching for material for this book, it struck me how little had actually been written in English about the madrasas of South Asia, despite the fact that some four-tenths of the world's Muslim population lives in the region. Indeed, I discovered, the entire field of South Asian Muslim studies remains sorely neglected. Scholars working on Islam have tended to focus largely on the Arab world, labouring under the misconception that Islam is somehow an Arab religion and that Arabs are somehow *the* 'true' Muslims. On the other hand, scholars specializing in religion in South Asia have generally dealt with Hinduism and Buddhism, treating Islam and Christianity as 'foreign' religions not deserving of serious attention.

Numerous works exist in Urdu, Persian and Arabic on various Indian 'ulama and the schools of thought they represent, from early medieval times to the present. Penned by their disciples or scholars who claim their legacy, they contain valuable insights and details, but, being largely hagiographic writings, their value as balanced historical accounts is limited. For the general English-language reader with no knowledge of the classical 'Muslim' languages but interested in knowing more about the Indian madrasas, hardly any works written in an easily accessible form are available. Some scholars, such as Francis Robinson,[3] Barbara Metcalf[4] and Muhammad Qasim Zaman,[5] have produced seminal works on the madrasas of South Asia, but these are geared to a somewhat specialized academic readership. Robinson deals with just one family of, admittedly vastly influential, Indian 'ulama, the scholars of Firangi Mahal in Lucknow, while Metcalf focuses on a single important Indian madrasa, the Dar ul-'Ulum at Deoband. Both limit their discussion to the colonial period and do not look at the significant transformations in the madrasa system in post-colonial India. Zaman's focus is on the ways in which sections of the 'ulama, in British India and then in Pakistan, sought to construct and maintain their own claims to authority, but he does not deal in detail with the post-1947 Indian situation. Although all three books add vastly to our limited knowledge of the South Asian 'ulama, they do not provide us with an overall view of the madrasa system as such, and tell us little about the 'ulama in contemporary India.

Some books do exist in English on madrasas in contemporary India, mainly written by Indian scholars, Muslims as well as others. These are, by and large, based on secondary sources and are not grounded in detailed empirical investigation. Many of them are poorly researched, often propagandist in tone and intent. Journalistic writings on the Indian madrasas penned by non-Muslim writers abound, being generally sensational accounts, often grossly exaggerated and sometimes even based on completely concocted stories. Some of them are useful, only in a limited way, for certain facts that they highlight rather than the conclusions that they make. Similar is the case of writings on the subject by numerous Muslim writers whose concern to defend the madrasas from charges levelled against them often leads them to highlight only what they see as their positive achievements. Given the lack of a single text that brings together perspectives from historical analysis, sociology, political science and Islamic studies, I felt the urgent need for a study that would combine insights from all these disciplines, supplemented with empirical field-based observations and buttressed by secondary sources.

My basic aim in writing this book is to provide for the general reader a broad overview of the madrasa system of education in India. Given the appalling ignorance that most people, even many Muslims themselves, have of madrasas and of the immense diversity within the madrasa system as a whole, this book has necessarily had to cover a wide range of subjects. I have had to deal with issues related to Islamic jurisprudence and theology at a very basic level, for most readers might not be familiar with these at all. However, since interest in the madrasas is generally related to contemporary concerns, including, and especially, their complex political stances, I have naturally given particular attention to how madrasas in India today seek to relate to present-day social realities. Overall, my concern has been to portray the roles and functions of the madrasa system in all their complexity and diversity.

Central to our understanding of the madrasa as an institution is the concept of *'ilm* or knowledge in the Islamic tradition. One of the tasks that this book seeks to undertake is to trace the evolution of this concept, from being a somewhat open-ended and fluid notion to one that has now become, at least as many traditionalist 'ulama see it, largely focused on matters related to the *shari'ah* or Islamic law. Together with this, I also look at how the concept of the *shari'ah* itself has undergone major transformation over the centuries. While in the early Islamic period the *shari'ah* generally denoted a broad Islamic way of life based on the Qur'anic ethical system, I show how it has now come to be seen by many 'ulama as a set of laws that need to be imposed on society, either through effective persuasion or force. This, in turn, is related to a complex process of the reification of Islam. I look at how these changing notions of Islam and Islamic knowledge have led over the centuries to new understandings of the roles of the 'ulama and their authority. Since the madrasa is the principal means for the 'ulama to constitute and assert their authority, I examine how the changing understandings of Islam and *'ilm* have impacted on the ways in which the madrasa itself is viewed. In the process, I also seek to critically interrogate the ways in which the 'ulama of the madrasas see their task and the roles of the institutions they manage. Finally, I try to show that if much of what the 'ulama regard as the received Islamic tradition is actually a historical construct, there are no insurmountable theological barriers to madrasa reform, which many, including numerous leading 'ulama themselves, today regard as a pressing necessity.

Since I believe it important for us to try to understand 'ulama self-perceptions I have sought to take into account the ways in which the 'ulama associated with the madrasas themselves see the world and the place of the madrasa in it. For this I have relied heavily on writings, mainly in Urdu, by Indian 'ulama. I see this as a corrective to much writing on the madrasas that tends to ignore the inner worlds of the 'ulama, thereby effectively silencing their voices. Besides writings by the 'ulama, I have drawn upon works penned by non-'ulama actors, including scholars, critics and activists, Muslims as well as others. Finally, in my account of the contemporary madrasas I have drawn upon a number of interviews with 'ulama and madrasa students, many of whom I have been forced to leave unnamed, or whose names I have changed, in order to protect their identity.

*

A few lines are in order about my fieldwork experiences, because the manner in which the 'ulama I met reacted to my presence and questioning inevitably influenced both the information I was able to gather and my own views of the madrasas and their roles. In the initial stages of fieldwork I was hesitant to enter the madrasas, obviously a stranger given my own external appearance and my name. I was afraid that the 'ulama would be reluctant to meet me, probably because I was not a Muslim. My fears were put to rest soon enough. In every madrasa but one I was warmly welcomed and treated as an honoured guest. 'The gates of the madrasas are always open to everybody, Hindu, Sikh, Muslim or whoever,' I was told wherever I went. If I had thought that the 'ulama would be unwilling to talk, I was grossly mistaken. 'We want that others should come to the madrasas and interact with us,' they insisted. 'Only in that way would they really come to know what madrasas are really all about.' They generously answered all my questions, even those that I thought rather sensitive, such as about finances and political leanings. In most madrasas I visited I was allowed to freely interact with the students without the presence of a watchful teacher carefully monitoring my doings. One madrasa even invited me to speak to a gathering of its teachers and students about my own views about the madrasas.

Some 'ulama and their students I met in the course of my fieldwork expressed their surprise and delight at my knowledge (admittedly limited) of Islam and of Urdu, and hoped that I would sooner rather than later convert to Islam. Others were cautious in their response, supposing, I was later informed by friends, that the fact that I had a fairly good understanding of Islam but had not become a Muslim, as they understood the term, proved that my intentions were dubious.

Yet, despite their willingness to speak to me, I was constantly aware of a certain distance that I could not cross. Behind the constant glorification of the madrasas I detected a painfully obvious defensive attitude, a struggle to defend the institution at all cost, to the extent of even excusing some of what were, to me, its obvious limitations. I was also aware that my presence often stirred up considerable suspicion. I must admit I met many 'ulama who struck me as being fiercely narrow-minded and who did not seem particularly pleased by my presence. Several 'ulama, I later came to hear, thought I was in the pay of Indian or even American intelligence. Others thought I had been sent in the guise of a do-gooder scholar by the militantly anti-Muslim, Hindu 'nationalist' Rashtriya Swayamsevak Sangh (RSS). Yet others were convinced that I was an agent of the dreaded Israeli Mossad! On the other hand, some, who were familiar with my writings on Islam and Indian Muslims, saw me as generally reliable and encouraged me to write this book in the hope that it would help clear the misconceptions that abound about the madrasas and about Islam in general. Naturally, the ways in which my own presence was understood determined the sort of material I was able to gather during my field visits.

Although at a time when such misunderstanding exists about the madrasas and any serious work on the subject is to be welcomed, it is important not to exaggerate the influence of the madrasas on Muslim society. There are several thousand madrasas in India today—figures are disputed—and although this might seem considerable in absolute numbers, it is not particularly impressive, given that Muslims in India number anywhere between 130 and 150 million. The number of Muslims studying at madrasas is much smaller than those enrolled in regular schools and colleges. Not all, or even most, parents who send their sons to study at madrasas to train to become 'ulama do so for purely religious reasons. Often, although they would wish to educate their children in modern, English-medium schools, they simply cannot afford their prohibitively expensive fees, and are instead forced, out of compulsion rather than choice, to send them to madrasas where education is generally provided free of cost.

Then again, one must constantly bear in mind that although the 'ulama of the madrasas claim to be religious specialists and authoritative spokesmen of Islam, not all Muslims take that claim seriously, and the worldly '*alim* remains a popular butt of jokes. Widespread distrust of and scorn for half-educated 'ulama, who are seen as 'ignorant troublemakers', are expressed in a number of popular proverbs. One such saying mocks the traditional *mullah* of the mosque as having little or no knowledge of the world around him thus: *mullah ki daur masjid tak* ('The journey of the *mullah* is only till the mosque'). Another proverb warns people that a *maulvi* with little knowledge is a dangerous being: *neem hakeem khatra-i jaan, neem mullah khatra-i iman* ('Your life is threatened by a half-baked doctor and your faith by a half-baked *mullah*'). It is rare for most Muslims to seek the advice of the 'ulama in all their affairs, although they might consult them in purely personal matters such as ritual worship and family relations. When it comes to wider issues, such as social and economic matters or political affairs, most Muslims, like everybody else, usually act out of simple pragmatism rather than in accordance with the strictures that the 'ulama seek to impose.

This work is based on the premise that the institution of the madrasa needs both to be normalized or naturalized as well as complicated. By 'normalized' or 'naturalized' I mean first, that the madrasa must be seen, at least in the initial stages of its history, as simply an institution for the imparting of knowledge. In Arabic-speaking countries, the word madrasa refers to any sort of school, and does not denote, as it does in India, a school specifically devoted to the teaching of religious subjects. 'Normalizing' or 'naturalizing' the madrasa also entails challenging the notion of a rigid distinction between 'religious' and 'secular' knowledge in Islam. Classical Islam knows of no such distinction. For the early Muslims, as indeed for the Prophet himself, knowledge was holistic, and all forms of beneficial knowledge were considered to be divinely sanctioned and a means for discovering the glory of God and winning His pleasure. Accordingly, many medieval Muslim madrasas provided education of what we would today consider 'secular' as well as 'religious' subjects.

'Complicating' the madrasa entails critically interrogating notions of Islam and Muslims and the madrasa system itself as being homogeneous or monolithic. It involves discovering and highlighting the internal divisions within the wider Muslim community that are often articulated by the madrasas themselves and are also reflected in the internal debates among the 'ulama associated with different schools of thought. It points to the fact, often ignored by outsiders, that Islam itself is a sharply contested terrain, with rival groups claiming to be the only 'authentic' Muslim community and condemning each other as virtual apostates, or, as is sometimes mildly put, as 'misled'. 'Complicating' the madrasas helps highlight the fact that they represent different, and often mutually opposed, understandings of theology and jurisprudence, and, linked to this, of wider community and political agendas. It also indicates the remarkable shifts that have occurred in the madrasa system as a whole over time, so that it makes little sense to speak of an unchanging, static form of education, impervious to external developments. In other words, to 'complicate' the madrasa is to illustrate the immense diversity within the institution and its changing historical forms and to resist the tendency to paint all madrasas with the same brush.

*

Chapter 1 of this book deals with the concept of knowledge in Islam, based on a reading of the Qur'an and the Prophetic Traditions or Hadith. Here I highlight the importance that these two primary sources of Islam place on knowledge, both 'worldly' and 'religious', with no rigid distinction being made between the two. I then go on to explore the origins of the institution of the madrasa as a specialized centre for the production and transmission of Islamic knowledge in eleventh century West and Central Asia, tracing its links to wider political and religious developments, including the emergence of various schools of jurisprudence. This digression is crucial, for much of what the madrasas in India today teach is based on subjects and texts developed by these early medieval madrasas. Chapter 2 looks at the development of madrasas in India, starting in the period of the Delhi Sultanate and leading up to the end of the colonial period. It provides a broad overview of significant changes and developments in the forms and curricula of Indian madrasas and of the complex web of links between sections of the 'ulama and social elites. It also looks at the fierce internal debates, starting from the late nineteenth century, between modernizing reformers and conservative 'ulama on the content of Islamic education, resulting in new forms of madrasas and the emergence of a dualism between madrasa education and the modern school system. Chapter 3 provides a general picture of traditional madrasas in contemporary India, dealing with such issues as curriculum, methods of organization and instruction, the social composition of students and teachers, and the career paths of madrasa students. This is, of necessity, a very rough sketch, and the notion of a traditional madrasa is used here simply for heuristic purposes. In fact, no madrasa can be said to be completely 'traditional' in the true sense of the word, since the tradition of Islamic education, as the preceding chapters suggest, is itself a historical construct and in the process of constant development and elaboration. Nor can one speak of a 'typical' madrasa, given the immense diversity within the madrasa system, a point that this and the next chapter indicate. Chapter 4 examines the discourse of madrasa reform and the different understandings and underlying political agendas of this project as articulated by a range of actors, including the 'ulama themselves, Islamic modernists, Islamists and the Indian state. Chapter 5 looks at new forms of Islamic education in India that are rooted in debates about madrasa reform. It examines crucial developments in contemporary madrasa education, such as the inclusion of modern subjects in the curriculum and the emergence of a number of girls' madrasas, examining what these mean for notions of religious authority and for the claims of the traditionalist 'ulama as spokesmen of normative Islam. Chapter 6 concludes the book with a discussion of the alleged links between the Indian madrasas and terrorism. It points out that militancy is not inherent in the madrasa system as such, and argues that there is no substantial evidence to suggest that Indian madrasas have been actively engaged in any form of militant activity. However, in examining the issue the chapter draws attention to the need to look at the diverse ways in which madrasas imagine the theological 'other' and the manner in which they envision Islamic law, for these can be powerful resources that can determine political choices and actions. The chapter also looks at how the Indian 'ulama have sought to respond to the accusations levelled against the madrasas, showing how, ironically, the anti-madrasa campaign, while fuelling an already deeply rooted insecurity among the country's Muslims, might actually be forcing madrasas towards greater openness and willingness to reach out to people of other faiths and to the Indian state.

*

In order to facilitate easier reading I have dropped diacritical marks for Arabic, Persian and Urdu words altogether, except in the case of the letter *ayn* (indicated by a single inverted comma). For the plural form of certain non-English terms I have simply added an 's' after the word in the singular form.

Thus, instead of *madaris* I use the term madrasas, or *fatwas* instead of *fatawa*. I have spelt several Arabic words used in Urdu in the manner in which they are generally spoken in colloquial Urdu. For instance, *mazhab*, instead of *madhhab*. However, in the case of some other terms I have employed the Arabic form that is more commonly used in English—for example, *shari'ah* instead of *shar'iat*.

Acknowledgements

This book is, in a sense, a collaborative venture, the result of the efforts and support of several people, too numerous to be mentioned here individually. Without the help of the many 'ulama and students of the various madrasas that I visited across India this book would never have been possible.

Special thanks are due to Waris Mazhari, Alauddin Khan and Zafrul Islam Khan for providing me with references and valuable contacts.

The International Institute for the Study of Islam in the Modern World, Leiden, the Netherlands, and the Hamdard University, New Delhi, afforded me the opportunity to work on the book, and for the help of their staff I am deeply grateful.

I must also acknowledge my gratitude to Francis Robinson, from whom I have learnt so much.

Kamini Mahadevan and Ravi Singh deserve the warmest thanks for giving me what I consider a major honour of doing a second book for Penguin.

I would not have been able to carry through this study had it not been for all the support that my mother gave me. Thanks to her, and to my best friends, Adu, Sizzie, Sona and Papita.

{1}

‘*Ilm* and Islam: The Early Islamic Scholarly Tradition

A madrasa, as the word is understood in South Asia today, is an institution geared to the preservation and teaching of the Islamic scholarly tradition. The term shares a common root with the Arabic word *dars* or ‘learning’. Thus, technically, any school or college where any sort of education, not necessarily simply religious, is imparted, can be called a madrasa. In common parlance in South Asia, however, the term generally refers to a school for the teaching of the various Islamic sciences. Hence, the prefix *dini* (‘religious’) is often used to denote a madrasa that is devoted specifically to the teaching of religious or Islamic subjects.[1] The madrasa has historically occupied a central role in Muslim civilizations, transmitting and further developing the Islamic scholarly tradition. The ‘ulama, scholars of the Islamic sciences, are products of the madrasas and, being the transmitters of the Prophet’s legacy, regard themselves as second only to him in authority.

*Maktab*s and madrasas exist in almost every city, town and village in India where Muslims live. Among poorer Muslim communities they may have no separate buildings, with classes being held inside mosques. Some, such as the Dar ul-'Ulum, Deoband, or the Jami'at ul-Ashrafiya, Mubarakpur, may be the size of universities, occupying sprawling campuses and including a number of separate buildings for classrooms, libraries, hostels, dining halls, guest houses, staff quarters, dispensaries, mosques and *shari'ah* courts. With large domes and graceful arches, often imitations of Mughal structures, the larger madrasas serve as crucial markers of identity and as a symbolic claim to space in a country where Muslims are a relatively small and marginalized minority.

In order to understand the worldview of the 'ulama of the madrasas in contemporary India and how they imagine their role and functions, an examination of the concept of knowledge in the Islamic textual tradition, as it has developed over time, is indispensable. This is because the madrasas see their principal task as transmitting the knowledge revealed by the Prophet and then passed down from one generation to the next by qualified 'ulama. The madrasas seek to sustain or recreate the general ethos of the early 'ulama, who are seen as the ideal model for Muslims to emulate as closely as possible. This extends even to matters such as methods of teaching, relations between teachers and students and many of the texts taught in the madrasas.

Knowledge in the Qur'an and the Hadith

The written word is central to Islam for it is a religion in which the holy book plays a crucial role. The Qur'an is regarded by most Muslims as the literal word of God. The word 'Qur'an' itself means 'recitation', and in Islam God is believed to communicate with humankind principally through the medium of revelations that take the form of books. The importance that Islam places on the acquisition of knowledge for every believer is clear in the Qur'an itself. The very first revelation given to Muhammad stressed the importance of knowledge and the written word thus:

> Read: in the name of thy Lord who createth,
> Createth man from a clot.
> Read: And thy Lord is the Most Bounteous,
> Who teacheth by the pen,
> Teacheth man that which he knew not.

A striking illustration of the importance that the Qur'an gives to knowledge is the fact that of the 6347 verses of the sacred text, the obligation to offer prayers is mentioned in about 200, while the verses exhorting the believers to ponder on the mysteries of nature, to reflect on God's creation and to use their reason are more than three times that number. The Qur'an repeatedly stresses the need to acquire knowledge, insisting that the knowledgeable are actually the truly God-fearing. It announces that God exalts those who have faith as well as knowledge, the two being seen as inseparable. It also refers to the superiority of human beings over the angels on grounds of knowledge.

The Hadith, the corpus of traditions attributed to the Prophet, also contains numerous exhortations of the Prophet that stress the importance of acquiring knowledge as a religious duty. In contemporary Muslim representations, the Prophet is presented as, above all, a teacher (*mu'allim*), and Islam as the first religion to enjoin universal literacy.[2] Reference is often made to Muhammad's assertion, 'I have been sent only as a teacher.' 'Knowledge is the life of Islam and a pillar of faith,' Muhammad is said to have remarked. A *hadith* relates that Muhammad declared it a duty binding on all Muslims, men as well as women, to acquire knowledge. 'Seek knowledge from cradle to grave and search for it even if you are to go to China,' another Prophetic tradition advises. The seeker of knowledge is regarded as one who strives in the path of God (*jihad*), and Muhammad is said to have declared, 'The ink of the scholar is more holy than the blood of a martyr.' Insisting on the need for all Muslims to acquire knowledge, the Prophet is reported to have said, 'Valueless is the Muslim who is not a teacher or student.' Another *hadith* says that the superiority of a scholar ('*alim*) over a worshipper ('*abid*) is like that of the Prophet over the least of his companions, or, as another report expresses it, like that of the moon over all the stars. 'To listen to the instructions of science and learning for one hour,' the Prophet announced, 'is more meritorious than attending the funerals of a thousand martyrs, and more meritorious than standing up in prayer for a thousand nights.'

In the Islamic tradition, acquisition of knowledge is not regarded as an end in itself or as a means for purely utilitarian purposes or materialistic pursuits. Rather, the aim is to understand the will of God and to lead one's life according to it. Only in this way can one acquire salvation in the life after death. True knowledge is said to be that which leads to piety, which, in turn, is expressed in the form of virtuous actions. On the basis of true knowledge alone can one's worship approach perfection and one's dealings with fellow creatures of God be conducted in accordance with the Divine Will. True knowledge is thus different from bookish learning, and need not be acquired by several years of studying various books. In fact, it is often pointed out that many of the Prophet's companions (*sahaba*, sing. *sahabi*) were themselves illiterate, but yet possessed great knowledge.

Because of this integral link between knowledge and practice (*'amal*), education (*ta'lim*) in the Islamic tradition is seen as inseparable from the 'training' (*tarbiyat*) of the self. This explains the great importance that continues to be given to the deep personal bond between teacher and student in the madrasas. The ideal teacher is not simply a means of transmission of knowledge, but rather, a living embodiment of that knowledge, a spiritual guide for the student, a representative of the Prophet and a model for the student to emulate. Hence the value of *sohbat*, or keeping the company of pious people as a means of acquiring true knowledge. Books of Islamic pedagogy, from the earliest times down to our own, repeatedly stress the centrality of *sohbat* and the inculcation by the student of appropriate moral values and normative behaviour patterns (summed up as *ikhlaq* and *adab*) through a close emulation of the teacher, this being seen as more important than mere textual learning. Without the former, the latter is hollow and meaningless. Knowledge without the appropriate practice is said to be a dangerous thing. It threatens to drive people away from the path of religion, tempting them to use religious knowledge for worldly gain and hence to ultimately lead them to Hell.

It is striking to note that in both the Qur'an and the Hadith knowledge is seen as one comprehensive whole, there being no rigid division between 'religious' (*dini*) and 'worldly' or 'secular' (*duniyavi*) knowledge, a distinction that was to emerge at a later stage in Muslim history. As the Qur'an sees it, to conduct one's worldly affairs in accordance with God's will is also a form of worship (*'ibadat*). This is why the Qur'an repeatedly asks believers to use their reason (*'aql*) to ponder on the wonders of nature, which are described as among the 'signs' (*ayat*) of God. As a *hadith* puts it, 'Knowledge is the friend of the true believer and reason is his guide.' In line with this dictum, the

Prophet went so far as to insist that his followers should acquire all manner of useful knowledge, for, as he said, 'A word of wisdom is the lost property of the true believer. Wherever he finds it he takes it.' At least partly because of this approach to knowledge, the early Muslims emerged as the torchbearers of science at a time when Europe was entering the Dark Ages and scientists were being put to the stake by the medieval Church.

In the Islamic tradition, knowledge is understood as God's gift that must be freely shared with others, this being seen as a religious duty in accordance with the Qur'anic commandment of 'commanding the good and forbidding the evil'. This explains, in part, the considerable investment that Muslim communities, in India and elsewhere, continue to make in setting up madrasas for promoting Islamic knowledge. The Qur'an and the Hadith are replete with references to the importance of spreading knowledge among others. The Prophet is said to have declared that the angels, all the creatures living in the skies and on earth and even the ants in their holes pray for the person who spreads knowledge of what is good. 'There is no better alms than giving knowledge to others,' a *hadith* quotes Muhammad as having said.

*

In Mecca, the Prophet and his companions were reviled and stiffly opposed by the leading tribe of the town, the Qur'aish. They found Muhammad's message of monotheism and egalitarianism a major challenge to their system of crude polytheism and a grave threat to their own social privileges. Faced with the opposition of the Qur'aish, the Prophet and his small band of followers would gather secretly at the house of one of the Prophet's companions, 'Arqam bin Abi 'Arqam, hidden in a valley outside Mecca. There they would pray together and listen to the Prophet recite passages of the Qur'an. This is said to have been the very first Muslim 'school'.

After suffering thirteen long years of persecution in Mecca, the Prophet decided to shift with a group of his followers to the town of Medina. The people of Medina welcomed him, and here the Prophet laid the foundation of a proto-state. One of the first ventures that he undertook in Medina was to construct a mosque for the community, which later came to be known as the 'Prophet's Mosque' (*masjid-i nabavi*). The mosque served as a prayer house for the Muslims of the town. Besides, it was here that the Prophet discussed the administrative affairs of Medina, decided legal disputes and planned military strategies. It was also in this mosque that he regularly imparted religious education to his followers, the *sahaba*. He would recite portions of the Qur'an, which the *sahaba* would then commit to memory. He would explain to them the import of the divine revelations that he had received and would answer their queries.

In Medina Muhammad is also said to have arranged for some of his disciples to teach others to read and write. Interestingly, after the Battle of Badr, two years after his migration to Medina, Muhammad agreed to release Meccan prisoners of war if they would each teach ten Muslims how to write. Some 600 Muslims are believed to have been educated in this way. Muhammad is also said to have commissioned some *sahaba* to learn foreign languages, such as Syriac, Hebrew and Coptic, and subjects such as mathematics and medicine. The remarkable impact of the educational *jihad* that Muhammad ushered in can best be appreciated if we recall that literacy was almost unknown among the Arabs in pre-Islamic times. It is said that there were only seventeen literate people in Mecca before the Prophet's birth.[3] Although the pre-Islamic Arabs had a rich oral tradition of their own, excelling in poetry and composing legends about the brave deeds of their ancestors, they seem to have paid little attention to the written word.

Since the Prophet stressed that knowledge was a religious duty binding on all believers, he also devoted his attention to the education of the Muslim women of Medina. In response to a complaint by women that he was paying more attention to the education of his male followers, the Prophet arranged to teach women in the mosque and allotted them one day a week. Muslim women would also regularly meet the wives of the Prophet, some of whom were themselves literate, and seek answers to their questions. The Prophet is said to have appointed a teacher for one of his wives, Hafsah, to learn how to write.[4] Of Ayesha, his youngest wife, Muhammad is said to have remarked, 'Seek half of the knowledge [of the faith] from her.' Ibn Zubayr, a companion of the Prophet, asserted that Ayesha knew more than all the *sahaba* put together.[5]

Post-Prophetic Developments

Islamic education in the Prophet's time was imparted in the mosque and people's homes, there being no separate institution for the transmission of learning. As Islam spread to neighbouring areas, delegations of various tribes flocked to the mosque in Medina to learn from the Prophet. On returning to their homes they set up mosques where they taught their people the Qur'an. A group of *sahaba*, mostly poor, some of them having renounced the world for a life of stern austerities, would sit on a platform (*suffa*) outside the mosque in Medina, spending their time in meditation, and reciting the Qur'an and teaching it to others. These pious men of God are referred to as the *ahl-i suffa* or the 'people of the platform', and are regarded as the progenitors of the Sufis as well as among the earliest Muslim 'teachers'.

During the Prophet's time, Islamic instruction consisted largely of the Qur'an. For his followers the divine text and narrations of his practice (*sunnah*) served as sources of guidance in proper Islamic behaviour. After his demise, Muslims were confronted with the need for answers to new situations for which they found no explicit guidance in the Qur'an. While the Prophet was still alive his companions could consult him for his opinion on any matter, but now he was no longer in their midst. This role was now assumed by the Prophet's immediate successors, the 'four rightly-guided' Caliphs for the Sunnis,[6] and the Imams for the Shi'as. The Caliphs and Imams ruled according to their own readings of the Qur'an and the example of the Prophet. On new issues confronting the community on which neither the Qur'an nor the *sunnah* provided any explicit instruction they resorted to *ijtihad*, the exercise of creative reflection on and exegesis of the Qur'an and the *sunnah*. The *ijtihad* of the 'rightly-guided' Caliphs and Imams is said to have been flexible, context specific and based on actual problems rather than hypothetical or imaginary ones, in contrast to the practice of many later *fuqaha*, scholars of Islamic jurisprudence.[7]

The need to seek instruction from the model of the Prophet, whether in the form of explicit instruction or analogy (*qiyas*), led to the collection of sayings and reports of the actions of the Prophet, or Hadith, which today forms a central component of the curriculum of the madrasas. In the absence of the Prophet the Hadith served as a guide for Muslims in the conduct of their lives. Many companions of the Prophet and others who came after them travelled widely in search of those who could provide them reports of the Prophet. Thus, for instance, Jabir ibn 'Abdullah is said to have undertaken an arduous month-long journey to Syria just to collect one *hadith* from 'Abdullah ibn Anas. Likewise, Abu Ayub Ansari travelled from Medina to Egypt to listen to a single *hadith* from Aqaba bin 'Amr.[8] The ninth century Imam Bukhari (810–870), compiler of one of the most authoritative compendia of Hadith, travelled sixteen years in search of *hadith* narrations, but selected only 7500 traditions out of over half a million that he collected.

Bukhari's sifting out of only a relatively small number of *hadith* reports as 'genuine' from among such a vast number suggests that already by his time a process of fabrication of *hadith* was well under way. Thousands of *hadith* reports were manufactured in order to suit a range of doctrinal and political positions. Rival theological schools and sects developed their own Hadith collections to justify their own stances and to condemn the others as 'un-Islamic'. The very corpus of Hadith as we know it today is thus, to a considerable degree, a product of a long period of historical development and of fierce political contestation, and, as such, cannot be said to represent completely the words or deeds of the Prophet himself. This corpus continues to be taught in the Indian madrasas, and many 'ulama take an uncritical view of it, using weak (*za'if*) and even concocted (*mauzu*) *hadith* reports to justify a range of stances that clearly go against established notions of rationality and justice.

The Qur'an lays down general principles for personal conduct and ethics and contains few legal pronouncements, which the corpus of Hadith deals with in greater detail.

However, with the passage of time, as Islam spread to new areas, Muslims were confronted with new situations for which neither the Qur'an nor the Hadith contained any specific advice. This led, from the middle of the eighth century onwards, to the founding of a number of schools (sing. *mazhab*, pl. *mazahib*) of Islamic jurisprudence or *fiqh*.

Exploring the nature of *fiqh* and the development of various *fiqh* schools is crucial for understanding the madrasa system in contemporary India, where *fiqh* remains the main pillar of the curriculum. The word *fiqh* literally means 'to understand' a particular matter properly, and in the Qur'an it is employed in the general sense of 'understanding in religion'.[9] Gradually, however, it came to be regarded in a more or less legalistic sense, as rules and laws derived through human interpretation of the Qur'an and the Hadith and deductions made from these sources. Often incorrectly translated as 'Islamic law', *fiqh* is much more comprehensive than law in the modern sense of the term, providing regulations for such personal matters as prayer, ablutions, diet and dress, as well as rules for public affairs, such as the conduct of government. Being the product of human effort, *fiqh* must be distinguished from the divine *shari'ah* ('the way'), the body of revealed laws contained in the Qur'an, although the 'ulama are often guilty of conflating the two. *Fiqh*, therefore, is derived from the *shari'ah*, and is not synonymous with it. While the *shari'ah* is regarded by many Muslims as fixed for all time, *fiqh*, in theory, is flexible and can be modified according to changing conditions. While the laws of the *shari'ah* tend to be general, *fiqh* prescriptions are specific, attempting to express, as best as is humanly possible, the requirements of the *shari'ah* in particular circumstances. No single school of *fiqh* can be said to express the *shari'ah* perfectly, for perfection is regarded as an attribute of God alone. The human element in the development of *fiqh* is readily apparent from the numerous contradictions between the different *fiqh* schools themselves, based as they are on different understandings of the Qur'an and the *sunnah* and reflecting the different social conditions in which they emerged and flourished.

Local conditions played an important role in the development of different Muslim sectarian groupings and *fiqh* schools in different regions. The process was gradual, spanning several generations, a product of accumulative doctrinal development and elaboration. Local customs were often accepted and incorporated into *fiqh*, as were Jewish, Persian and Roman usages, leading to sharp divergences in understandings of jurisprudence as well as the infusion of notions that had no validity in the Qur'an as such. Islam had, by now, spread into new cultural areas with highly developed civilizations with well-established traditions of authoritarian monarchy and patriarchy, such as Syria, Egypt, Iran and Iraq. The proto-democratic state of the Prophet had given way to a vast Muslim empire. The tribal egalitarianism of the Arabian desert was now a thing of the past. That the schools of *fiqh* should have been so deeply influenced by the authoritarian, hierarchical and patriarchal social context in which they developed is hardly surprising. Thus, from a general mandate for social justice and egalitarianism, *fiqh*, or the historical *shari'ah*, came to reflect and, in turn, uphold, monarchical authoritarianism and stern patriarchy. This was reflected, for instance, in harsh laws related to women, non-Muslims and slaves, and in injunctions that stressed obedience to ruthless rulers, all of which had no mandate in the Qur'an itself. Many of these *fiqh* rules continue to be taught in the madrasas in India today.

The Emergence of the 'Ulama as a Professional Class

The emergence and elaboration of the schools of *fiqh* led to a gradual transformation of the notion of the 'ulama. Tracing this fascinating process is crucial for understanding how the contemporary Indian 'ulama see themselves, their roles and privileges and the claims that they make of speaking for normative Islam on behalf of the entire Muslim community.

In earlier times, anyone who possessed knowledge (*'ilm*), in any particular field or subject, was considered to be an *'alim* or scholar. The category of 'ulama was loosely defined and hardly corresponded to the rigidly defined class of professional religious jurists or *fuqaha* that it was to later become. In the first two Islamic centuries the 'ulama were not clearly identified as a distinct social group, there being no systematic rules relating to the profession of scholarship. Indeed, several 'ulama pursued other professions, particularly trade, alongside religious teaching and instruction. Many of them refused payment for teaching, believing this to be a service in the cause of the faith. The third Islamic century witnessed the emergence of a professional class of *fuqaha* who earned their livelihood from teaching and scholarship. This must be seen in the wider context of the development of rival schools of *fiqh*, with elaborate rules governing inclusion and membership and complex linguistic skills and sartorial codes separating the *fuqaha* from the 'common' mass of Muslims. Although the schools of *fiqh* and the insistence on *taqlid*, blind following of jurisprudential precedent, probably developed as a means to safeguard the faith from interference from the rulers, soon the *fuqaha* were co-opted by political elites, a development that further worked to strengthen the professionalization of a separate class of religious specialists.

Several schools of *fiqh* emerged and flourished over the centuries. Within the Sunni fold, there are said to have at one time been over 500 schools or *mazhab*s. However, by the thirteenth century, only four remained, and today most Sunnis identify themselves with one of these, all of which are considered to be equally 'orthodox': the Hanafi (named after Abu Hanifa al-Nu'man [d. 767]), the Maliki (after Malik ibn Anas [d. 795]), the Shafi'i (after Muhammad ibn Idris al-Shafi'i [d. 820]) and the Hanbali (after Ahmad ibn Hanbal [d. 855]). Most Shi'as identified themselves with the Ja'fari school, named after Imam Ja'far as-Sadiq (d. 765). Each school of *fiqh* based itself on the *ijtihad* or creative interpretation of the primary sources of Islamic law as exercised by its putative founder and his students. Flourishing in different parts of the Muslim world, often in vastly different social and economic contexts, it was but natural that on a range of legal issues, from the most personal, such as physical postures during prayer or rules related to divorce and marriage, to the most public, such as the relations between the Muslim ruler and his non-Muslim subjects, they often voiced different opinions. These differences also reflected diverse readings of the Qur'an, as well as conflicting, weak and concocted *hadith* reports.[10]

The Imams who are credited with founding the different schools were clear that their understanding of the Qur'an and the *sunnah*, based on their own personal *ijtihad*, might not be free from error. Recognizing that they were fallible beings, they warned their disciples not to blindly accept their rulings. They advised them that on matters in which their opinions might inadvertently violate the Qur'an and the *sunnah* they must not accept them, but instead, should follow the instructions of the divine text and the Prophetic practice. The immediate followers of the founders of the *mazhab*s seem, likewise, to have been characterized by a fair degree of openness and a lack of dogmatism that was to become so characteristic of the later 'ulama. Often, followers of one Imam did not hesitate to seek instruction from followers of another. Some of the early *fuqaha* did not hesitate to overrule the opinions of their own teachers if they found them not to be in accordance with the Qur'an and Hadith.

Ijtihad thus provided an inherent dynamism to *fiqh* to enable it to meet the demands of changing conditions. Yet, the dynamic possibilities that *ijtihad* provided did not remain open for long. The gradual codification of *fiqh*, leading to the contracting of possibilities of *ijtihad*, gave Islamic jurisprudence a distinctly patriarchal and feudal stamp, one that lasts to this very day, as is evident in the curriculum in most Indian madrasas. The stress on the centrality of *fiqh* went alongside the crystallization of a class of *fuqaha* specializing in the details of jurisprudence. Qur'anic verses exhorting believers to seek the opinion of the knowledgeable were interpreted to suggest the need for Muslims to consult experts in *fiqh* on every matter, an insistence that is tirelessly repeated by the 'ulama of the madrasas even today. Suitable *hadith* reports were generated to argue that experts in *fiqh* had a special claim on the wider community in their capacity of 'successors of the Prophet'.[11] *Fiqh* thus came to be regarded as the highest form of knowledge, while 'worldly' knowledge, the cultivation of which the Qur'an had encouraged, came to be neglected or frowned upon. Naturally, this helped bolster the claims of the *fuqaha*, experts in Islamic jurisprudence, as representatives of what they came to regard as the 'authentic' Islamic tradition.

Islamic Learning and the Political Elite

In a short span after the demise of the Prophet, the Muslim state had transformed itself into a vast empire, stretching from the Atlantic in the west to Sind in the east. Under the Umayyad Caliphs, from the mid-sixth century to the mid-eighth century, Islamic education developed more organized forms. Scores of *sahaba* settled in the newly conquered territories outside the Arabian peninsula, setting up mosque-schools (*maktab*s) at various places. There were no full-time or professional teachers, however, at least to begin with. Those who taught the Qur'an, the Hadith and *fiqh* in 'learning circles' (*'ilmi halqa*s) in the mosques and in people's homes generally did so on a voluntary basis, as an expression of their religious commitment, earning their livelihood through other means. However, as time passed, the later Caliphs started the practice of paying teachers to teach the Qur'an to Muslim children.

With the spread of Islam outside the Arab peninsula, new subjects began to be studied and cultivated by the Muslims, and cities such as Kufa, Baghdad, Damascus, Cairo and Cordoba emerged as leading centres of Islamic learning. For neophytes who knew little or no Arabic there developed the disciplines of Arabic grammar, prosody and rhetoric. In the face of the challenge of Greek philosophy the discipline of *kalam* or theology emerged, using the tools of Greek philosophy and logic to refute the challenge of 'rationalists' such as the Mu'tazilites and the Isma'ilis. Other disciplines that developed at this time included literature, history, medicine, logic and biographies of the Prophet.[12] Although these subjects were taught, more or less, in all Muslim lands, there were significant geographical variations that reflected local particularities. However, travel, and especially the annual pilgrimage to Mecca where Muslims gathered from different regions, facilitated a considerable exchange of views, doctrines as well as texts that worked to develop a broadly shared Islamic scholarly tradition.

The Muslim Contribution to Knowledge

If pre-Islamic Arabia, as Muslims see it, was immersed in 'ignorance' (*jahiliya*), the revolution wrought by the Prophet led the Arabs to make great contributions to various sciences. The Muslim contribution to science is a fascinating chapter in the history of world civilization. Even as fierce a critic of Islam as Bernard Lewis was forced to recognize that early medieval Muslim society 'had achieved the highest level so far in human history in the arts and sciences of civilization'. As he went on to remark, 'In most of the arts and sciences of civilization, medieval Europe was a pupil and in a sense a dependent of the Islamic world [. . .].'[13] It was through the Muslims that paper reached Europe, and without the Muslim educational impact the European Renaissance may not have been possible or else would have taken a markedly different course.[14]

The period of Umayyad and Abbasid rule, from the eighth to the thirteenth century, was characterized by important developments in science and technology. This flowering of learning would not have been possible without the active support of the state. The Caliphs generously patronized scientists, Muslims as well as others, and some Caliphs themselves were authors of treatises on various sciences. With the establishment of the Umayyad Caliphate began a process of translation into Arabic of Greek, Coptic, Persian and Sanskrit works on a variety of subjects, from philosophy, science and mathematics to literature and history. The Abbasids were even more enthusiastic in their promotion of learning, establishing many schools and public libraries. The Abbasid Caliph al-Hakim II is said to have requisitioned a vast number of books from various countries, the combined catalogue of which filled forty volumes, and arranged for many of these to be rendered into Arabic. The renowned Harun al-Rashid (786–

809) established 'the House of Wisdom' (*bayt al-hikmat*) in Baghdad, through which numerous works were translated into Arabic by Jewish, Christian and Muslim scholars.[15] At the height of its glory, Abbasid Baghdad is said to have boasted of several schools and some seventy-two libraries. Most of these were destroyed in 1257 when the Mongols, under Hulaku Khan, destroyed the city, killed the Caliph and brought the Abbasid Caliphate to an end.[16]

The 'Rationalists' and the Development of Islamic 'Orthodoxy'

Soon after the death of the Prophet, as Islam rapidly spread to regions beyond the confines of the Arabian peninsula, Muslims came into contact with new cultures, many of which had been deeply influenced by Hellenic civilization. The influence of Greek philosophy on Muslim thinkers through translations of Greek works into Arabic led to the emergence of strong rationalist trends, exemplified by the Mu'tazilites from the eighth century onwards. Mu'tazilite rationalists stressed the importance of reason ('*aql*) and justice ('*adl*), arguing against those 'ulama who insisted that there was no scope for free thought in Islam. They asserted that the Qur'an was not the eternal word of God, for to assume this would violate God's uniqueness. Since the Qur'an was, therefore, the created word of God, they claimed, it could be interpreted variously over time through the use of reason, discovering new meanings of the holy text as human knowledge expanded. Opponents of the Mu'tazilites, later to be called the 'Asharites,[17] asserted that God's ways were beyond human reason and must be accepted without question. They argued that the Qur'an was indeed God's eternal word, which meant that there could be only one possible reading of the Qur'an, the fixed and literal interpretation that they championed. In contrast to the Mu'tazilites, they opposed the concept of free will and claimed that all acts of human beings, whether good or evil, were created and willed by God, thus leaving almost no scope for human choice. It was in response to the Mu'tazilite challenge that 'Asharite thinkers developed the science of theology (*'ilm al-kalam*), using the tools of Greek philosophy to combat the Mu'tazilites. Many 'ulama associated with the madrasas today consider themselves heirs of the 'Asharites, and continue to faithfully articulate the 'Asharite position in their writings, teaching their students the classical works of *kalam* that their detractors stridently critique as being hopelessly outdated.

After a brief period of state patronage, the Mu'tazilites fell into official disfavour and were actively persecuted for their beliefs. The Caliphate, now transformed from a simple tribal democracy into a hierarchical feudal state, saw in the 'Asharite position a powerful ideological weapon to bolster its own legitimacy. If all acts, good as well as evil, were predestined by God himself, the powers and privileges that the Caliphs had arrogated to themselves could also be said to be in accordance with the Divine Will. The nexus between the 'Asharites and the feudal Muslim state received further impetus with the large number of fabricated *hadith* reports purporting to represent the statements of Muhammad but calculated to promote conformity and stifle all dissent. Traditions were forged that forbade Muslims to rise up against unjust and tyrannical rulers on the specious grounds that injustice (*zulm*) was preferable to anarchy (*fitna*),[18] although the Qur'an is replete with exhortations to struggle against injustice.[19] Other *hadith* reports were manufactured in order to defame and condemn 'heretical' sects, some of which fiercely opposed the tyrannical rule of the later Caliphs. In this project of concocting *hadith* reports the ‘ulama closely linked with the state played a central role, in return for which they received the generous support of the rulers.

Because of their close connection with the state, ‘Asharite ‘ulama thus gradually came to be defined as representing Islamic ‘orthodoxy’. As a corollary, dissenting groups were condemned as ‘heterodox’, deserving to be forcefully stamped out. In popular memory the image is still deeply imprinted of unscrupulous ‘ulama who lived off imperial largesse, twisting the faith in order to suit the interests of the rulers by providing them with appropriate ‘Islamic’ sanction for their patently ‘un-Islamic’ behaviour. Such ‘ulama did not hesitate to instigate their patrons to attack their opponents, including Sufis and rival ‘ulama, some going so far as to sentence them to death for alleged heresy.[20] Yet, there were always pious ‘ulama who protested against the excesses of the Caliphs and refused to serve under them. Islamic history is replete with stories of how such ‘ulama boldly spoke out against the oppression of tyrannical rulers as well as the ‘worldly’ ‘ulama (*‘ulama-i su*), for which they had to undergo long periods of imprisonment and even death.

The absence of a well-defined priestly hierarchy in Islam meant that despite the efforts of the state and the ‘worldly’ ‘ulama to enforce their own vision of Islam, dissenting ‘ulama consistently sought to articulate competing understandings of ‘authentic’ Islam, as in the case of numerous Sufis and various groups among the Shi‘as. In fact, it appears that the emergence of Sufism in the form of regular spiritual brotherhoods owed much to a growing dissatisfaction among the ‘pious’ ‘ulama with the close nexus between the ‘worldly’ ‘ulama and the state. As they saw it, the ‘worldly’ ‘ulama had drained Islam almost completely of its spiritual content, reducing it to a bundle of external (*zahiri*) laws and rules. In contrast, the Sufis, also known as *'ulama-i batin* ("ulama of the esoteric sciences'), insisted that the external laws of the *shari'ah* were not an end in themselves, as the 'ulama who stressed simply the exoteric aspects of the faith (*'ulama-i zahir*), believed. Rather, they argued, these laws were merely a means to the final goal of *haqiqat* ('Truth'), variously described as establishing closeness with God, meeting Him or even uniting with Him.[21] This conflict between Sufis and strict literalist 'ulama is still alive today, and numerous madrasas associated with the latter carry on in the tradition of fiery denunciations of Sufism.

Taqlid *and the Decline of* Ijithad

The tradition of *ijtihad*, as we have seen, provided an inherent dynamism to *fiqh*, enabling it to respond to the challenges of changing social conditions. However, by the late twelfth century many 'ulama had come to argue that the 'gates of *ijtihad*' (*bab ul-ijtihad*) had been firmly closed, although there is no evidence of this having actually been the case. In practice, *ijtihad* continued, but in an attenuated form. It was confined to providing answers to questions that had not been addressed by the consensus of earlier 'ulama, while on issues that the schools had already reached an agreement new answers were generally ruled out. *Ijtihad* was now largely restricted to adaptations within each established school of *fiqh*, and that too only on minor matters (*furu'i masa'il*). In place of innovative research and writing, great stress now began being laid on penning commentaries and super-commentaries on works by earlier 'ulama, and to rote learning of texts rather than expertise in particular disciplines.[22] Many Indian madrasas faithfully carry on in this tradition today, and the nitty-gritty of *fiqh*, as developed by the medieval *fuqaha*, continues to remain the core of their curriculum. The stress on strictly following the rules laid down by what they describe as their 'pious predecessors' (*salaf-i salihin*) explains why the Indian madrasas, with notable exceptions, are averse to any form of radical legal innovation.

The enormous destruction wrought by the marauding Mongols who swept across large swathes of Muslim territory, destroying the capital of the Abbasid Caliphate, Baghdad, in 1258, led to tremendous insecurity among the 'ulama, aghast at the loss of Muslim power and prestige. This further strengthened the hands of the conservative 'ulama who saw in free-ranging *ijtihad* a threat to the integrity of Islam. It was feared that if the possibilities of *ijtihad* were left open, with recourse to it being allowed to all and sundry, it might open the doors to ruthless rulers to interfere in matters of Islamic jurisprudence in order to serve their own interests. Hence, many 'ulama now began to enjoin rigid *taqlid*, arguing that individual Muslims must strictly abide by the rulings of one or other of the established schools of *fiqh*. This continues to remain the position of the vast majority of the Indian 'ulama even today.

The insistence on the *taqlid* of the established *mazhab*s or schools of jurisprudence received a fillip with the compiling of books of *fiqh* detailing the opinions of the Imams of the *mazhab*s and their followers on a range of issues. While the Imams and their immediate disciples had stressed that their opinions were tentative and were not binding on all Muslims, the later 'ulama argued for rigid conformity to one of the established *mazhab*s. Some 'ulama insisted that such conformity was binding even on matters where the books of *fiqh* conflicted with the explicit commands of the Qur'an and Hadith.[23] Some even went to the extent of concocting stories to the effect that Muhammad himself had predicted the appearance of the Imams and their *mazhab*s, arguing, therefore, that anyone who tried to go beyond the boundaries of the established *mazhab*s was a heretic or even an apostate.[24]

Naturally, the insistence on *taqlid* worked to further strengthen the hands of the *fuqaha*, with their detailed books of *fiqh* being considered as normative sources guiding all aspects of personal as well as collective behaviour. This guaranteed their privileges as guardians of what came to be seen as the 'authentic' Islamic tradition. The centrality that law came to occupy in the minds of the 'ulama meant that for many Muslims Islamic education now became more or less synonymous with knowledge of the intricate details of *fiqh*, ranging from the most personal matters of hygiene, worship and sex, to matters of the state. This tradition remains deeply ingrained in the madrasas of today, where the teaching of the rules of *fiqh* forms the core of the curriculum.

The pervasive concern with legal issues, coupled with the advocacy of strict *taqlid*, led to a heightening of rivalries between advocates of different schools of jurisprudence as they competed with each other for the patronage of ruling elites and for public support. Such conflicts continue to be played out, in different forms, in the madrasas to this day. The degree of inter-*mazhab* conflict that prevailed at some places can be gauged by the fact that the Shafi'i founder of the Madrasa Rawahiya in Damascus is said to have considered the followers of the Hanbali *mazhab* to be 'as much outside the bounds of Islam as the Jews and Christians were'.[25] Such disputes gave birth to the notion of the established *mazhab*s as 'completely distinct and oftentimes antagonistic entities', characterized by what Philips calls fierce 'fanaticism and sectarianism'.[26] From merely different approaches to the question of Islamic jurisprudence, they soon grew into, for all practical purposes, separate communities and political interest groups. Often, Muslims belonging to one school would refuse to pray behind an Imam belonging to another school. This led to the construction of separate prayer niches in mosques located in areas where Muslims belonging to more than one *mazhab* lived. In the mosque at Mecca separate niches were built around the Ka'aba for the different *mazhab*s, and this continued till the early years of the twentieth century. Some scholars were of the opinion that if a Muslim of one *mazhab* followed the ruling of an Imam of another *mazhab* he should be punished at the discretion of the local judge. '*Ulama* of rival schools entered into *fatwa* wars, each seeking to win the favour of ruling elites, many of whom, in turn, actively sponsored heated debates among the 'ulama, leading to further inter-*mazhab* conflict. Conflicts between followers of different *fiqh* schools even led to incidents of rioting in some cases.[27]

Discussions between the 'ulama of different *mazhab*s also led to their splitting hairs on hypothetical issues completely divorced from real-world concerns, a practice that is characteristic of many madrasas even today. These debates were sometimes used by ruling elites for their own purposes in order to procure legal opinions that suited them. Often, what one '*alim* from a particular school declared as 'permissible' would be condemned by another '*alim* from another school as 'forbidden', and rulers generally chose the opinion of the scholar who met their interests best. *Fiqh* texts even began including separate sections on 'pious ruses' (*hiyal*) in order to circumvent what were seen as inconvenient provisions of the *shari'ah*, which rulers were quick to take advantage of. Each ruler sought to patronize a particular *mazhab* as the official school of the state, providing its 'ulama with suitable posts as judges and bureaucrats, thereby seeking to win them over to gain the legitimacy they needed. Naturally, this worked to promote inter-*mazhab* rivalry and competition, which received further impetus with the establishment of the institution of the madrasa.

The Origins of the Madrasa

As we have seen, at the time of the Prophet education was imparted in mosques. However, as Islam began to rapidly spread outside the Arabian peninsula, the need for a more organized educational system to meet the administrative needs of the empire was increasingly felt. This gave birth to the madrasa as an institution separate from the mosque. Although religious education continued to be imparted in mosques, Sufi lodges (*khanqah*s), literary salons, the homes of the 'ulama, and even in caves and under trees in makeshift structures, the madrasa emerged as a major institution for formal education.

The period between 950, marking the conquest of the Abbasid capital of Baghdad by the Shi'a Buyids, and 1258, the year the Abbasid Caliphate was destroyed by the Mongols, was a time of rapid transformation in Muslim society. The growing influence of the Shi'as, the rapid expansion of the Isma'ili Fatimids in Egypt, who were looked upon by the Sunni 'ulama as dangerous heretics, and the challenge posed by Isma'ili missionaries in Syria and Iran led to what Ephrat calls a 'Sunni revival', manifesting itself in more institutionalized forms of religious organization and education in order to sustain the Sunni communitarian identity which was seen as under grave threat.[28] It was at this time that the institution of the madrasa, as we know it today, was born.

There is no unanimity on when the first madrasa, as the

term is understood today, was established. Some believe that the honour goes to the Madrasa Nizamiya in the Iranian town of Nishapur, founded in the eleventh century. However, it seems that some madrasas existed even prior to that. According to one source, the first madrasas were established in the eighth century in northwest Africa by two sisters. Fatima bint Muhammad is said to have set up the Jami'a Kairawan in Tunisia, and her sister Maryam reportedly founded the Jami'a Andalus in Fez, Morocco. A century later, the grand Jami'a al-Azhar, the oldest surviving university in the world, was established in Cairo by the Fatimid Caliph al-Mu'izuddin billah to train Isma'ili missionaries and to counter the Sunnis who were seen as both religious as well as political rivals. The Turkish ruler Sultan Mahmud (971–1030) is said to have established a madrasa at Ghazni in present-day Afghanistan in the early eleventh century, a few years prior to the establishment of the Nizamiya madrasa in Nishapur.[29]

Whatever be the case, the Nizamiya madrasa at Nishapur, one of the earliest state-sponsored madrasas in the Muslim world, is regarded as the model that many later madrasas elsewhere followed. The madrasa was named after its founder, Khwaja Abu 'Ali Hasan, more popularly known as Nizam ul-Mulk Tusi (1018–1092).[30] Born in a village near Mashhad in Iran, Nizam ul-Mulk rose to become the prime minister of the Seljuq Turk Sultan Alp Arslan (r. 1063–1072).[31] Although he functioned as a deputy of the Abbasid Caliph, the Sultan wielded the power behind the throne of the vast Abbasid Empire. Nizam ul-Mulk also served for several years as *wazir* of Alp Arslan's son, Malik Shah (r. 1072–1092).

After the madrasa at Nishapur, Nizam ul-Mulk later set up similar institutions in other places in the Abbasid Empire, such as Baghdad, Balkh, Herat, Isfahan, Basra and Khorasan, all of which were named after him. A range of disciplines was taught at these schools. The Qur'an and the Hadith formed a central component of the syllabus, but, increasingly, *fiqh* began to receive greater attention, given that one of the major functions of the madrasas was to train a class of judges to staff the imperial courts. Besides, the madrasas also taught mathematics, astronomy and various human sciences. Several teachers in these schools functioned as Sufi preceptors for their students, seeking to combine the mystical path with the *shari'ah*.

The precise political roles of the Nizamiya madrasas and the other schools that they later inspired has been the subject of considerable debate. George Makdisi contends that these madrasas were relatively autonomous of the state, with the state having no control over their curriculum. Hence, he argues, to consider them as having served as instruments of state policy is misleading.[32] Other scholars disagree, pointing out that state patronage to the madrasas and their fierce opposition to 'heretical' groups made these institutions a powerful means of providing the Sunni state with the legitimacy it needed. After all, several graduates of the madrasas went on to join the administrative services as judges (*qazi*s), legal specialists (*mufti*s) and censors of public morals (*mustahib*s). The Nizamiya madrasas generally devoted themselves to teaching and popularizing the Shafi'i school of *fiqh* and 'Asharite 'orthodoxy'. In turn, 'Asharism reflected the needs and interests of the rulers, preaching as it did obedience to those in authority and opposing dissenting groups such as the Isma'ilis and Mu'tazilites who were also regarded as political threats. In this sense, then, it is likely that these madrasas did play crucial political roles, contrary to Makdisi's claim.

The most famous of Nizam ul-Mulk's madrasas was the

Madrasa Nizamiya in Baghdad which began functioning in 1067 during the reign of the Abbasid al-Qasim bi 'Amrillah. It was housed in a grand building and was endowed with vast properties by Nizam ul-Mulk, from whose income it sustained itself. A large market was set up outside the madrasa to cater to its 6000 students who were drawn from different parts of the Caliphate. Its library contained several hundred thousand books on a variety of subjects. The madrasa continued to function for some 300 years, and among its more famous teachers and students were the historian Imam Tabari, and the renowned Sufi masters Imam Ghazali, Shihabuddin Suhrawardi and 'Abdul Qadir Jilani.[33]

Following Nizam ul-Mulk's example, later Muslim rulers, nobles and wealthy traders also set up madrasas in different lands, endowing them with estates and providing them with large libraries. They liberally rewarded leading 'ulama for composing books on a variety of subjects, religious as well as others, in the belief that through such pious deeds they would earn for themselves merit in the eyes of God. Leading 'ulama of some madrasas even entered into matrimonial alliances with the nobility. Not all madrasas were directly linked to the state, however, and there were several schools, led by renowned 'ulama, who consciously eschewed association with rulers and the nobility.[34] Such 'ulama were often contrasted with the 'ulama associated with the royal courts. While the former were generally regarded by the public as true men of God, the latter were often seen as corrupt and willing to trade their faith for worldly trifles. 'Ulama who consciously distanced themselves from the rulers were often Sufi masters, serving as spiritual guides and helping the poor through acts of charity.

Madrasa education was provided free of cost for all, and students were drawn from virtually all social classes. Students often came from far-off lands, attracted by the fame of certain renowned teachers. Madrasas thus provided a remarkable channel for upward social mobility for poor students, and helped shape a common cultural world in which all social classes could participate. They also facilitated the development of a broadly defined Islamic civilizational unity from the Atlantic coast to India and beyond. The fluidity of the early madrasa system was conducive to a wider circulation of ideas, including normative Islam, leading to the gradual creation of the 'ulama as a more clearly defined and organized group, linked by a complex web of ties and allegiances and a common world-view shaped by a shared set of texts and expertise in the nitty-gritty of Islamic jurisprudence.

Although the madrasas represented a more organized form of education than the earlier study circles in the mosques, madrasa education remained largely informal and flexible. The primary loyalty of the students was to individual teachers, that is, it was the particular teacher who was the centre of the educational system, rather than the institution of the madrasa as such. This explains the high mobility among madrasa students, who travelled from one madrasa to another in search of leading teachers.

Medieval madrasas had no rigid rules of admission, system of examinations or age requirements. Often, after spending some time in the 'learning circle' or *halqa* of one teacher at a particular madrasa, a student would go on to another madrasa, perhaps in a different country, for further instruction in the same or a different subject. Students of varying ages studied together under the same teacher, and there was no fixed period within which one was expected to complete one's studies. The general practice was to study a particular book on a particular subject under a teacher noted for his expertise in it. Then, when the student had completed the book, he would receive a certificate (*ijaza*, *sanad*) from his teacher certifying that he had studied the book from him and allowing him to teach it to others. The *sanad* was considered reliable only when it clearly specified that the student had learnt the book from a particular teacher, who, in turn, had learnt it from his own teacher, and so on, the chain leading back to the author of the book, with all links in the chain being named. A student's knowledge was thus judged by the number of texts he had read and the scholars he had studied under.[35]

There does not seem to have been any fixed syllabus in these early madrasas which, although sometimes patronized by the state, were generally left free to teach the books they wanted. Often, what a particular madrasa taught was conditioned by local factors as well as the predilection of particular teachers. The Qur'an and the Hadith formed the core of medieval madrasa education. It was considered a matter of great pride and spiritual achievement if a student memorized the entire Qur'an and large numbers of *hadith* reports. Since many madrasa graduates went on to join the administrative apparatus of the state, detailed matters of Islamic jurisprudence or *fiqh* came to occupy a particularly important place in the curriculum. In a departure from the past, most madrasas restricted themselves to the teaching of the views of just one legal school, the particular school to which its patrons and teachers adhered. This led to further elaboration of the schools of *fiqh* and also to a sharpening of their differences. Besides the 'transmitted' sciences (*'ulum al-naqaliya*), such as Qur'anic commentary, Hadith and *fiqh* that were transmitted from one generation to the next, medieval madrasas also taught a number of 'rational' sciences (*'ulum al-'aqaliya*) such as grammar, poetry, philosophy, medicine, mathematics and astronomy.

After spending years at a madrasa a student had a variety of career options before him. He could join the state bureaucracy, take up teaching in a madrasa or set up one of his own, preach in a mosque, or else go in for higher education, either at a madrasa specializing in the 'transmitted' sciences if he wanted to become a religious specialist, or at a school specializing in the 'rational' sciences. There was thus no rigid distinction between 'religious' and 'secular' education in medieval Muslim societies, although the two were gradually growing distinct from each other, and many *fuqaha* had begun speaking out against what they saw as the 'irreligious' influence of Greek rationalism and the 'worldly' sciences.[36]

*

The system of Muslim education and the various 'rational' and 'transmitted' sciences developed by medieval Arab and Iranian 'ulama were to have a profound influence on Muslims elsewhere. The development of the Islamic scholarly tradition and the classical madrasa in West Asia and Iran occurred at a time when Turkish rule had begun consolidating itself in India. Soon, India was to emerge as a leading centre of Islamic learning with the establishment of a number of important madrasas, many of them patronized by Muslim rulers. The following chapter looks at the origins and development of the madrasa system in India during the period of the Delhi Sultanate and then the Mughal Empire, followed by the British period.

{2}

Madrasas in India: Historical Evolution

Madrasas in contemporary India see themselves as carrying on in the tradition set by past generations of 'ulama. In several respects, many madrasas today consciously seek to replicate medieval models of madrasa education, in such matters as teaching methods, styles of argumentation, relations between teachers and students, and key texts that form the core of the madrasa curriculum. Contemporary Indian madrasas share much with their medieval counterparts, but they also depart significantly from them in other respects. Understanding the madrasa system in India today thus necessitates a historical analysis, looking at the evolution of and changes in Islamic education in the country over a period spanning more than a thousand years, from the establishment of the Delhi Sultanate to the period of British rule.

*

India emerged as a major centre for Islamic scholarship and learning during Turkish and Mughal rule. Islamic education in India, as elsewhere in the Muslim world, took several forms, being imparted in formal institutions as well as informally in learning circles in mosques, the homes of 'ulama, nobles and merchants and the lodges of the Sufis. The first madrasas in India were established not long after Islam first made its advent in the region. In the wake of the invasion of Sind by an Arab army led by Muhammad bin Qasim in the early seventh century, some Arab scholars settled down in the towns of Ucch, Thatta, Debal and Mansura, where they are said to have established small madrasas.[1] Of the early madrasas of Sind and Multan we know little. It appears that they played a major role in combating the influence of the Isma'ili Shi'as, who had by this time set up a strong centre in the region and had won many converts to their faith. With the establishment of Turkish rule in Delhi, numerous madrasas were constructed in different parts of the country. According to available records, the first of these was established in 1191 at Ajmer by Muhammad Ghori after his capture of the town.[2] In the reign of Muhammad bin Tughlaq (1324–1351) there were reportedly 1000 madrasas in Delhi alone.[3] The collapse of the Abbasid Caliphate, along with the devastating attacks by the Mongols on leading Islamic centres in West and Central Asia, brought scores of Muslims to India seeking refuge. Among these were 'ulama and Sufis, who were to go on to play a major role in the development of the Islamic tradition in India. Most of these refugees were Hanafi Sunnis, and they brought along with them the books of Hanafi *fiqh* that were to become standard texts in the majority of Indian madrasas.

Muslim kings and nobles in India took an active interest in the promotion of learning, of both the 'transmitted' as well as the 'rational' sciences, and some of them were notable scholars in their own right.[4] The sultans of Delhi, and, later, the rulers of various regional kingdoms such as Gujarat, Bengal, Jaunpur, Gulbarga, Bidar and Bijapur, and the Mughals who followed them, generously patronized the 'ulama, endowing vast properties to madrasas in various parts of the country. Some of them arranged for leading 'ulama from Iran, Central and West Asia to settle down in their kingdoms where they set up madrasas as well as Sufi lodges.[5]

As elsewhere in the Muslim world in the same period, there seems to have been no fixed system of classes or syllabi in the medieval Indian madrasas. In general, each madrasa had considerable freedom in its choice of books and subjects. Different books were used by teachers at different madrasas and these often changed over time, lending the system a certain flexibility. Hence, rather than speak of a general syllabus employed in the medieval Indian madrasas it is more appropriate to talk in terms of a wide range of books that were used in the schools, from which individual teachers could select certain texts.[6] Subjects that were taught in madrasas in other parts of the Muslim world, such as Qur'anic recitation and commentary, Hadith and Arabic grammar, were also included in the course of teaching in the Indian madrasas, as were calligraphy, poetry, alchemy, astronomy and geography.[7] Both 'transmitted' as well as 'rational' sciences were taught at the madrasas, for the notion that the two were somehow opposed to each other or that there was a clear distinction between religion and the secular world was, as in other contemporary Muslim societies, quite foreign to the medieval Indian Muslim educational system.

Common to other parts of the Muslim world at the same time, medieval Indian madrasas tended to place inordinate stress on Islamic jurisprudence, a requisite for many of their students who would later take up posts in the judiciary and administration. Since the vast majority of the Central Asian 'ulama who settled in India were Hanafis, most medieval Indian madrasas laid particular stress on the teaching of books of the Hanafi school. Although many Indian 'ulama had a large number of books to their credit, most of these were commentaries upon commentaries or footnotes on texts prepared by earlier Hanafi 'ulama from elsewhere.[8] This meant, as a modern Indian Muslim scholar laments, that because of their insistence on *taqlid* of the earlier Hanafi 'ulama, they failed to develop a system of jurisprudence grounded in the particular context of India, where Muslims were a small minority.[9] This complaint continues to be made even today by critics who see the contemporary 'ulama as clinging to certain medieval *fiqh* formulations that are not relevant to the Indian situation. Instead, the task of formulating understandings of Islam more attuned to the Indian context was left to several Sufis, many of whom were also 'ulama in their own right.

Women and the 'Low' Castes

Although most madrasas were meant for males, Muslim elites also made arrangements for the education of their girls in their own homes, and special female tutors (*ustanis*) were employed for the purpose. Several rulers of the Mughal dynasty (1525–1857) were known for encouraging the education of women of the Muslim nobility. Some Mughal princesses were patrons of learning, and several of them were great poets and writers in their own right. Gulbadan, daughter of Babur, the founder of the Mughal dynasty, was the author of the *Humayun Namah*, a valuable source of our knowledge of the reign of Humayun. Salima Sultana, niece of Emperor Humayun and one of Akbar's wives, was a well-known poetess. Siti un-Nisa, a woman well versed in medicine and tutor to Jahanara, daughter of Emperor Shahjahan, received the title of 'Prince of Poets' at Jahangir's court. Jahanara was an accomplished writer, and penned a book on the life of her Sufi preceptor, Hazrat Pir Mullah Shah Badakhshani, and another on the renowned Khwaja Mu'inuddin Chishti of Ajmer. Jana Begum, daughter of 'Abdur Rahim Khan-i Khanan, wrote a commentary on the Qu'ran for which she earned a reward of 50,000 dinars from Akbar.[10] Several Mughal noblewomen also established and patronized madrasas.

While madrasas were open to all Muslims, in general it appears that the leading 'ulama, as well as Sufis, were drawn almost entirely from the *ashraf*, Muslims of Iranian, Central and West Asian extraction, who considered themselves superior to the indigenous converts. Access to the Islamic scriptural tradition was sought to be kept a closely guarded preserve of the *ashraf*, for it was a crucial means to guarantee their own claims to higher social standing. Thus, Ziauddin Barani, the thirteenth century court historian of Delhi, wrote in his *Fatawa-i Jahandari* that the Sultan should make sure that the 'low born' (*razil*, *ajlaf*), by which he meant Muslims of Indian, particularly 'low' caste, origin, should be denied all posts in the government services. He suitably misinterpreted the Qur'an to argue that God, in His wisdom, had appointed the *ashraf* as leaders, political as well as religious. Hence, he stressed, the sultans should ensure that the *razil* be kept bereft of education, save basic knowledge of the faith that would suffice for them to know how to say their prayers and keep their fasts. Sultan Ghiyasuddin Balban (1200–1287) is said to have acted faithfully on Barani's advice. Once, a certain Kamal Mahyra, a Muslim of 'low' caste origin, appeared before him and requested him for a job. When the sultan learnt of his *razil* status he was so enraged that he issued an order that the caste background of all government officials be investigated, and those found to be of 'low' caste be immediately removed from their posts.[11]

Barani's was not a lone voice. Rather, several other *ashraf* scholars argued on similar lines. It is not surprising then that there are very few references to leading 'ulama or leading Sufis from among the *razil* in the literature from the Sultanate and Mughal periods. This does not, however, mean that all medieval Muslim scholars shared Barani's contempt for the *razil*, or that accomplished Islamic scholars of *razil* origin were completely unknown. Thus, for instance, the leading Chishti Sufi of Delhi, Khwaja Nizamuddin Auliya, himself a Sayyed, claiming descent from the Prophet, is said to have learnt how to recite the Qur'an from a Hindu slave convert.[12]

The 'Ulama and the Sultans

Graduates of medieval Indian madrasas were employed in the state bureaucracy in various capacities, as judges, experts in offering legal opinions, censors of public morals, preachers and teachers. Leading 'ulama thus enjoyed close relations with the state. Most Muslim kings kept up the pretence of ruling by the *shari'ah* on the advice of the 'ulama attached to their courts. However, no Muslim ruler in India ever ruled fully in accordance with the *shari'ah*, contrary to what many 'ulama expected of them, although many styled themselves as 'protectors of the *shari'ah*' (*muhafiz-i shari'ah*) and 'servants of the faith' (*khadim-i din*). Many of these rulers are remembered for having openly flouted the *shari'ah* themselves; for instance, in consuming wine, indulging in 'improper' sexual activities and wrongly killing fellow Muslims, acts which the court 'ulama often chose to conveniently overlook. Thus, for instance, Sultan Ghiyasuddin Balban, noted for his fondness for the 'ulama, followed a strict policy of denying Muslims of 'low' caste origins any posts in his administration. He also spilt Muslim blood on a large scale, inflicting on Muslim nobles who dared to challenge him gruesome punishments that the *shari'ah* clearly forbade. He defended his actions by claiming that in administrative affairs he was guided simply by political interests and not by the *shari'ah*.[13]

At best, then, the *shar'iah* guided the dispensation of justice in matters of criminal law and personal affairs, although even here popular custom seems to have played a greater role. The 'ulama associated with the courts served as a crucial tool for legitimizing political power, not hesitating to offer *fatwa*s to suit the interests of the rulers, even if this sometimes meant violating the *shari'ah* itself. Muslim rulers looked to the 'orthodox' 'ulama to provide them with the support and legitimacy that they needed. In turn, they lavished their patronage on leading 'ulama, offering them landed estates and high posts in the bureaucracy. Naturally, this symbiotic relationship opened the way for corruption on a large scale. Numerous 'ulama associated with the courts were known for their willingness to provide suitable *fatwa*s to justify patently un-Islamic policies of their patrons.[14] Often, the court 'ulama were requested to issue *fatwa*s against rebels, condemning them as apostates and, therefore, as fit to be killed. As Zia ul-Hasan Faruqi argues, the 'ulama associated with the courts were content to let the monarchs rule much as they liked, even if they flouted the rules of the *shari'ah*, as long as they did not renounce formal allegiance to Islam and continued to patronize the 'ulama. 'No longer did the 'ulama insist,' Faruqi remarks, 'that, as in the period of the Prophet's companions, the ruler should be acceptable to the community at large.'[15]

Not all 'ulama associated with the courts were amenable to royal blandishments. Some of them are remembered for their willingness to confront royal authority and even to criticize the rulers for their 'un-Islamic' ways. For instance, Qazi

Mughisuddin is said to have rebuked Sultan Alauddin Khilji (1296–1316) for violating the *shari'ah*, pointing out that the vast sums of money that he was spending from the public exchequer on his harem was contrary to Islamic teachings. The enraged sultan is said to have threatened him, saying, 'Are you not scared of my sword?', to which the pious *qazi* boldly replied, 'I fear only the sword of God.'

A similar story is told of Sultan Sikander Lodi (1488–1517). While still a prince, he considered destroying an old pond in the town of Kurukshetra, which the local Hindus considered as particularly sacred. He organized a debate among the 'ulama before taking a decision. Miyan 'Abdullah Ajodhani, one of the 'ulama present on the occasion, vigorously opposed his plan, arguing that it was not allowed by the *shari'ah*. This enraged the prince, who accused the *'alim* of supporting the 'disbelievers', and threatened to kill him before destroying the 'idol-house'. To this the *'alim* replied, 'If you don't respect the *shari'ah* then why did you ask me for my opinion?'[16]

Admittedly, however, such bold 'ulama were rare, and on the whole the 'ulama associated with the courts, in contrast to many Sufis, were an integral and important pillar of the medieval feudal establishment.

The Tradition of Hanafi Fiqh *in Medieval India*

In his study of Islamic 'orthodoxy' in India, Zia ul-Hasan Faruqi writes that almost all the 'ulama associated with the Delhi Sultanate, and, later, the Mughal court, hailed from Central and West Asia or claimed descent from immigrants from these regions. He argues that they made little effort to adapt their understanding of theology and jurisprudence to the vastly different Indian context where Muslims were a relatively small, albeit dominant, minority. Instead, they advocated strict following of the rules of *fiqh* as developed by the Hanafi 'ulama in Transoxiania and West Asia. Accordingly, in the medieval Indian madrasas, *fiqh* remained throughout the main pillar of the educational system and, in theory, rigid adherence to the Hanafi school was stressed.[17] Yet, it must not be supposed that in actual practice the argument that the 'gates of *ijtihad*' were closed meant that the medieval 'ulama responded to new conditions or challenges by simply reiterating traditional *fiqh* prescriptions in all cases. Rather, their readings of the traditional legal texts often entailed considerable reinterpretation so that their application was not always rigid, being shaped by specific local contexts and local customary laws.

The teaching of *fiqh*, as suggested earlier, seems to have been given even more importance than the Qur'an and Hadith in medieval Indian madrasas.[18] Most Muslims in India were and remain Hanafi Sunnis, and the Hanafi *fiqh* acquired the status of the official school of jurisprudence during the reign of all Sunni rulers in the country. Experts in Hanafi *fiqh* were eagerly sought by Muslim kings to advise them. In medieval India, Zafar ul-Islam Islahi writes, 'the bazaar of *fiqh* thrived'. Many sultans organized discussions in their courts where leading 'ulama talked about the intricacies of Hanafi jurisprudence. Before taking decisions on issues of particular importance the more *shari'ah*-minded of the sultans would often seek the collective opinion of the 'ulama by organizing special debates or *mazhar*s.[19]

Their minority status in India meant that many Muslims were constantly aware of the threat of the 'corrupting' influence of 'idolatrous' Hinduism and of the impact of local customs and beliefs. Clearly setting Muslims apart from the non-Muslim populace by exaggerating points of difference and potential conflict thus served to protect and promote a sense of Muslim identity and superiority, and in this the 'ulama seem to have played a leading role. In medieval India the 'ulama were confronted with a novel situation for which Islamic jurisprudence, as it had developed by then, offered little guidance. The vast majority of Indians followed various religious traditions (later labelled indiscriminately together as 'Hinduism') that received no mention in the Qur'an, unlike, for instance, Christianity or Judaism. Beginning with Muhammad bin Qasim, Muslim rulers adopted a pragmatic path, accepting Hindus as akin to the 'People of the Book' (*ahl-i kitab*), at par with Christians and Jews, and thus as 'protected citizens' (*zimmis*).[20] Many Hanafi 'ulama acquiesced in this decision, for to treat Hindus as akin to the idolaters and polytheists of pre-Islamic Arabia (*mushrikun*) and to give them the choice between Islam or death would have been impossible, given the sheer size of the Hindu population.[21] This did not settle the debate on the legal position of the Hindus, however, and throughout the centuries of Turkish and Mughal rule in India, several 'ulama are known to have insisted that the sultans should embark on a large-scale massacre of the 'idolaters' and 'polytheists', whom they saw as inveterate 'enemies of the faith'. Few rulers, if any, took their advice seriously.

Numerous Hanafi 'ulama associated with the courts were at pains to stress the degradation of Hindus, this being seen as a means to preserve and promote Muslim supremacy. For this purpose recourse was taken to the books of traditional *fiqh*, and sometimes these were given novel interpretations in order to stress the point that, as non-Muslims, Hindus needed to be constantly reminded of their inferior status. For instance, Mullah Mughis, the Qazi of Bayana, advised Sultan Alauddin Khilji to prohibit Hindus from riding horses in public on the grounds that this was a Muslim prerogative. He suggested that 'extreme force' should be employed to collect taxes from Hindus in order to demean them. He insisted that 'If the collector of dues want[s] to spit in his [the Hindu taxpayer's] mouth, he [the Hindu] should without any hesitation open his mouth so that the collector might spit in it, and [even] under such conditions he must serve him.' The *mullah* adduced elaborate theological arguments for his advice. 'Degradation of the incorrect religion,' he said, 'is the proper manner of honouring Islam. God has ordered that they [non-Muslims] should be kept in degradation.' It was particularly necessary to demean Hindus, he argued, because they were the 'worst enemies of the Prophet', who, he claimed with no firm support, had 'clearly ordered that Hindus should be killed or be kept as booty and made to serve [Muslims]'. The sultan, we are told, conveniently ignored the *mullah*'s advice, not because he did not agree with his views on Hindus, but because it would have been virtually impossible to act upon it, threatening the very foundations of his own empire.[22]

Changes in the Madrasa System

A noticeable shift in the focus of Indian madrasas occurred in the early sixteenth century. Prior to this, madrasa education had centred on *fiqh*, Arabic grammar and Qur'anic commentary. Hadith received relatively little attention, often being restricted to the teaching of one book, the *Mashariq al-Anwar*.[23] In the reign of Sultan Sikander Lodi of Delhi, two brothers from Multan, Shaikh 'Abdullah and Shaikh 'Azizullah, introduced new books in the madrasas on various 'rational' sciences such as logic, mathematics, literature and philosophy. These subjects were considered essential for aspiring civil servants. The reign of Emperor Akbar witnessed further developments in the madrasa system in the direction of the 'rational sciences'. From his reign onwards, a significant number of 'upper' caste Hindus, too, began enrolling in madrasas, the education that they received there enabling them to take up a range of occupations in government service in both Muslim as well as Hindu kingdoms.

At the end of the sixteenth century, an Iranian Shi'a scholar, Mir Fatehullah Shirazi (d. 1588), joined Akbar's court. Shirazi was a learned scholar of the 'rational' sciences and he introduced books on ethics, mathematics, astronomy, physiognomy, medicine, logic, the natural and exact sciences, history and theology.[24] He had a large number of disciples who later settled down in different parts of the country where they introduced the new books and disciplines that they had learnt from their master.[25] Shirazi is credited, among other things, with interesting inventions, including a portable cannon, an instrument for cleaning gun barrels and a self-driven corn mill.[26] He also worked with Akbar's finance minister Todar Mal to organize the Mughal land revenue policy along more rational and efficient lines.

With the arrival of Shirazi, the 'rational' sciences received considerable impetus, much to the chagrin of many 'orthodox' 'ulama. Abul Fazl, Akbar's court historian, writes in his *'Ain-i Akbari* that the emperor, probably under Shirazi's influence, issued the following decree:

> [E]very school boy should first learn to write the letters of the alphabet, and also learn to trace their several forms [. . .] Every boy ought to read books on morals, arithmetic, the notation peculiar to arithmetic, agriculture [. . .], geometry, astronomy, physiognomy, household matters, the rules of government,

> medicine, logic [. . .] and history; all of which may be gradually acquired [. . .] No one should be allowed to neglect those things which the present time requires.[27]

This is not to suggest that the 'transmitted' sciences were totally marginalized under Shirazi's influence. *Maktab*s and madrasas continued to teach these, while Akbar is also said to have made arrangements for Hindu pupils to study books of Vedanta and Sanskrit grammar. However, overall, this period witnessed a remarkable ascendancy of the 'rational' over the 'transmitted' sciences, fuelling the suspicion held by many 'orthodox' 'ulama that Akbar was bent on the destruction of Islam, for it fitted in with his more tolerant religious policies *vis-à-vis* the Hindus.[28]

Opposition on the part of influential sections of the 'ulama to what were seen as Akbar's 'un-Islamic' policies ushered in an 'orthodox' reaction. Voices of protest now began to be heard, stressing the importance of following as closely as possible the path of the Prophet as laid down in the books of Hadith. A number of 'ulama emerged who went on to play a significant role in popularizing the study of Hadith, which had hitherto received relatively little attention in India. Several of these 'ulama are regarded by today's Indian 'ulama as brave crusaders against 'irreligiousness', and their writings continue to exercise a powerful influence.

Among the most well-known 'ulama who led the opposition to Akbar's policies was a Naqshbandi Sufi, Shaikh Ahmad Sirhindi (1564–1625). Shaikh Ahmad preached a reformed Sufism that stressed the compatibility of the Sufi path and the *shari'ah*. He called on Muslims to strive to follow strictly the Prophetic model, and vehemently combated what he saw as widespread Hindu and Shi'a practices and beliefs among his fellow Sunnis. He stressed the need for the revival of Hadith learning, and the 'transmitted' sciences in general, which he, like many other 'ulama, believed had been marginalized in Akbar's reign. Like him, the sixteenth century Shaikh 'Abdul Haq Muhaddith Dehlawi who, as his name suggests, was a leading scholar of Hadith, also sought to popularize the study of Hadith in India, seeing this as an antidote to Akbar's 'irreligious' policies.

The Dars-i Nizami of Mullah Nizamuddin

The last great Mughal emperor, Aurangzeb 'Alamgir (d. 1707), is said to have been a staunch defender of the *shari'ah*, and many Sunni 'ulama of today lionize him as a 'defender' of Islam, setting him in contrast to his 'irreligious' grandfather, Akbar. Aurangzeb is remembered for his generous patronage of the 'ulama, seeking their advice in the conduct of the affairs of the state. In order to guide the dispensation of justice in accordance with the *shari'ah*, Aurangzeb authorized the collection of a number of *fatwa*s issued by different Hanafi *mufti*s on a variety of subjects. These *fatwa*s were put together in the form of a massive encyclopaedia, the *Fatawa-i 'Alamgiri*, suitably named after Aurangzeb himself.

Involved in preparing this compendium of Hanafi law was a renowned '*alim*, Mullah Qutubuddin Sihalwi, a resident of the town of Sihali near Lucknow. He hailed from a family of Sufis and 'ulama long known for their piety and scholarship,[29] and was himself an expert in the 'rational' sciences, tracing the chain of his teachers to Mir Fatehullah Shirazi. In 1692, he lost his life in a land dispute between his fellow Ansaris and the rival 'Usmani clan.[30] To compensate for this loss, Aurangzeb offered his sons a mansion that had formerly belonged to a European (*firangi*) merchant, the Firangi Mahal, in Lucknow.

Under Mullah Qutubuddin's third son, Mullah Nizamuddin (d. 1748), Firangi Mahal grew into a leading centre of Islamic learning in India, with Lucknow taking the position that Delhi had once enjoyed.[31] Numerous Sunni and even Shi'a families from across India sent their sons to study there. This tradition carried on till long after Mullah Nizamuddin's death. While there was no madrasa as such at Firangi Mahal till 1905, students would study with leading scholars of the family in their homes, taking up residence in nearby mosques.[32]

Mullah Nizamuddin is credited with having prepared a syllabus of studies based on a set of carefully selected texts for the students of Firangi Mahal. Named after him as the *dars-i nizami*, it was heavily skewed in favour of the 'rational' sciences, providing students with the sort of education they needed for a job in government service.[33] Although the Firangi Mahal family was Sunni, the Shi'a rulers of Awadh generously patronized them for the valuable services that they rendered in training would-be government bureaucrats, judges and *mufti*s, many of whom joined the service of the Lucknow court.[34] Over time, the family went on to produce leading 'ulama, many of whom served as Sufi masters,[35] others as government servants, and yet others as doctors and teachers.[36] Together, they trained hundreds of students who settled in various parts of India, teaching or working as bureaucrats in various Muslim courts.[37]

Today, the syllabi of almost all madrasas in South Asia follow the basic structure of the *dars-i nizami*, albeit with significant modifications. In Mullah Nizamuddin's own time and even after, the *dars-i nizami* was not a rigidly defined curriculum, and additions and subtractions were continuously made in it by different 'ulama at different times, while leaving the basic framework relatively untouched.[38] Many of the texts included by Mullah Nizamuddin in his syllabus had been employed in

South Asian madrasas centuries before. Some of them dated as far back as the ninth century, and most were authored by Iranian and Central Asian Hanafi 'ulama. Given Mullah Nizamuddin's own training in the tradition of Mir Fatehullah Shirazi, the *dars-i nizami* was heavily biased in favour of the 'rational' sciences. Subjects like logic, philosophy and mathematics occupied an important place. The syllabus included fifteen books on logic and several books on Greek philosophy, mathematics, history, medicine and engineering, as also texts on Persian literature and Arabic grammar, rhetoric and literature. Students were also instructed in skills of official letter writing and calligraphy, which they would need as prospective civil servants. On the other hand, the 'transmitted' sciences were given less importance. Thus, only two books of Hadith, *Masharaq al-Anwar* and *Mishkat*, and two books on Qur'anic commentary, *Jalalayn* and *Bayazavi*, were included in the syllabus. *Fiqh* received more attention, being useful for would-be judges in Muslim courts. In all, the syllabus consisted of seventy-nine books.[39] This does not mean, however, that Mullah Nizamuddin or his successors were opposed to the 'transmitted' sciences as such. After all, Mullah Nizamuddin and several of those who followed after him in the Firangi Mahal line were themselves leading Sufis. Despite its 'rational' bias, the *dars-i nizami* enabled several students who studied with the 'ulama of Firangi Mahal to become leading Islamic scholars in their own right. The focus on the 'rational' sciences also made it possible for non-Sunnis, including Shi'as as well as Hindus, to study with the 'ulama of Firangi Mahal.[40]

*

The growing popularity of the 'rational' sciences, inaugurated by Mir Fatehullah Shirazi and then carried forward by Mullah

Nizamuddin, was seen by some sections of the 'ulama as a 'threat' to Islam as well as to their own authority as experts in the 'traditional' sciences. As mentioned earlier, 'ulama such as Shaikh Ahmad Sirhindi and Shaikh 'Abdul Haq Muhaddith Dehlawi sought to revive the 'traditional' sciences, particularly Hadith, while decrying what they saw as the inordinate importance that was given to the 'rational' sciences. Yet, as long as the study of the 'rational' sciences continued to be a principal means for securing employment in the Muslim courts their protests fell on deaf ears. Things began to change from the early eighteenth century, however. The reign of Aurangzeb witnessed the growing power of various non-Muslim powers, such as the Jats, the Marathas, the Sikhs and the British. This promoted a tremendous sense of fear and insecurity as political power began slipping out of Muslim hands and the Mughal Empire increasingly showed signs of crumbling. Islam, many began to feel, was now under grave threat. Only by going back to 'true' Islam, many 'ulama insisted, could the Muslims recover their political supremacy. The most well known of these revivalist 'ulama, who is today recognized as a powerful source of influence and inspiration by most South Asian 'ulama, was Shah Waliullah of Delhi.

The Waliullahi Tradition

Shah Waliullah was born in Delhi in 1703 towards the end of the tumultuous reign of Aurangzeb. His father, Shah 'Abdur Rahim (1644–1719), was a leading '*alim* of his times and taught at a madrasa, later to be known after him as the Madrasa Rahimiya, which he had set up in Delhi. Shah 'Abdur Rahim is remembered as a leading scholar of the 'transmitted' sciences. This, and his hostility towards the 'rational' sciences, left an indelible influence on his son. After spending twelve years teaching at his father's madrasa, Shah Waliullah set off on a journey to the holy cities in Arabia. He spent two years there learning Hadith and other subjects from renowned Arab scholars. He returned to Delhi in 1732 and began holding classes in a mansion gifted to him by the Mughal emperor Muhammad Shah. He exercised a major influence on the Delhi of his days, and students from far-flung places in India flocked to his school to study under him. His primary concern was the revival of the 'transmitted' sciences, and he is credited with popularizing the six canonical collections of Hadith of the Sunnis (*sihah sitta*) which were relatively unknown in the country before him. He also wrote on a variety of subjects such as Sufism, Qur'anic commentary and Hadith, stressing the need for Muslims to abide by the model of the Prophet in their daily lives. In order to popularize his message of Islamic reform, he translated the Qur'an into Persian so that the literate classes of the Muslims could understand the holy scripture. Later, his sons Shah Rafiuddin (1749–1817) and Shah 'Abdul Qadir (1753–1827) rendered the Qur'an into Urdu, enabling wider access to the meaning of the text. This effort was stiffly opposed by several 'ulama who regarded the Qur'an as untranslatable.

Considered by almost all Sunni schools of thought in South Asia today as the pioneer of Islamic reform, Shah Waliullah set in motion a process of revival of Islam that was to have far-reaching implications. He bitterly critiqued the practice of blind *taqlid*, arguing instead that Muslims of one school of Sunni *fiqh* could adopt the prescriptions of another school if the situation so demanded, because, he stressed, all four schools were equally acceptable. Furthermore, he insisted that the 'gates of *ijtihad*' had never been closed and that to meet changing demands *fiqh* had to be dynamic, allowing for *ijtihad* by qualified *mujtahid*s who need not be bound by past jurisprudential example, but could, instead, directly approach the Qur'an and Hadith for guidance. He was opposed to what he saw as the inordinate stress placed in the madrasas of his time on the 'rational' sciences, arguing that it was enough if they taught just one book, the *Shara-i Mulla Qutbi*, for the purpose. Likewise, he was critical of the influence of Greek philosophy among the 'ulama, which, he claimed, tended to promote scepticism. Of particular concern to him was what he saw as the widespread 'un-Islamic' customs practised by his fellow Muslims. He critiqued what he regarded as 'wrongful innovations' (*bida'at*), including 'Hindu' and 'Shi'a' practices that many Sunni Muslims had adopted, such as prostration before the tombs of the Sufis and participation in Shi'a rituals of mourning for Imam Husain.

This attack on popular custom was also aimed at drawing clear boundaries, setting 'true' Muslims apart from others. This was seen not only as mandated by Islam itself but also as a means to create a powerful sense of Muslim unity. Faced with the growing challenge of non-Muslims to Mughal power, Shah Waliullah insisted that Muslims needed to close their ranks in order to combat their foes. Faithfully abiding by the *shari'ah*, consciously distinguishing themselves from others and fiercely condemning popular customs that Muslims were seen to share with or have borrowed from their non-Muslim neighbours acted as powerful symbolic means of stressing Muslim superiority, even as it helped create a sense of community, uniting Muslims against others.

Reform of popular customs, Shah Waliullah believed, needed to be combined with practical efforts to reinstate Muslim political power. Thus, in 1760 he is said to have invited the Afghan warlord Ahmad Shah 'Abdali to invade India to rid it of what he saw as the Maratha menace. 'Abdali did act on this advice, but he hardly proved the Islamic *mujahid* or Islamic warrior that Waliullah had presumed he would be. He is said to have massacred Hindus and Muslims indiscriminately and to have only further diminished any real prospects for the revival of Muslim political power in India.

*

At the same time as the wave of Islamic reform was spreading in parts of India, new intellectual influences were also penetrating from Europe, mainly in the realm of the natural sciences. This came in the wake of the growing presence of European trading companies from the late fifteenth century onwards. The impact of the West on many Indian Muslims at this time, although not considerable, is worth noting. The sixteenth century 'Abdus Sattar Qasim, governor of Gujarat in the reign of Akbar, studied Latin from Catholic priests and then wrote a book on Greek philosophy. A century later, in the reign of Aurangzeb, the Mughal nobleman Muhammad Khan travelled to Portugal to study, where he translated a Latin book on mathematics into Arabic. The seventeenth century Maulvi 'Abdul Qadir bin Khairullah of Jaunpur penned two books on Western philosophy. Allama Tafassul Husain Kashmiri, ambassador of the Nawab of Awadh in Calcutta, learnt several European languages, wrote texts on engineering and logarithms and translated Newton's *Principia*. Hakim Azhar 'Ali Khan of Delhi prepared a long essay in English on elephantiasis which was published in a journal in London in 1792, the first article in English to have been written by an Indian Muslim. French and Muslim scholars worked together to translate European scientific treatises at the Jami'a ul-'Umoor, a college set up at Srirangapatnam by Tipu Sultan

(1750–1799), the Muslim ruler of Mysore. Several Muslims worked as translators at the Fort William College, established by the British in Calcutta in 1800, rendering works by European scholars into Persian.

The willingness on the part of some sections of the Muslim nobility at this time to accept Western scientific learning is particularly striking. At least till the late eighteenth century, since European powers posed no significant political challenge to the Muslim elites, Western scientific thought could be appropriated without any major opposition. Things were to change, however, with the decline of Muslim political power from the early nineteenth century onwards. With the British replacing the Mughals as rulers of the country, growing numbers of Muslims, including leading 'ulama, saw the British and the forms of knowledge that they represented as a major threat to Islam. It is to the responses of the 'ulama to the challenges that the establishment of British rule so starkly posed before them that we now turn.

Madrasas Under British Rule

By the end of the eighteenth century the Mughal Empire began to crumble as new powers appeared, challenging its might. The Jats, the Sikhs and the Marathas occupied large territories that were once ruled by the Mughals. But a far more formidable foe rapidly emerged in the form of the British East India Company. Soon, the Company was effectively ruling vast parts of the Mughal Empire, albeit in the name of the Mughals themselves. For the 'ulama, particularly those associated with the Mughal court, the rise of British power was seen as heralding the collapse of *dar ul-islam*, the abode of the faith. For centuries the 'ulama had regarded the existence of a Muslim sultan as a guarantor of the supremacy of Islam, although, as we have seen, no Muslim emperor of India ever ruled entirely in accordance with the *shari'ah*. The powers and privileges of the court 'ulama were inextricably linked to the state. Muslim emperors had generously patronized them to win their support by providing them regular stipends, offering them lucrative posts in the bureaucracy and judiciary, and extensive land grants for the maintenance of madrasas. The rise of the British was seen as threatening the entrenched privileges of the 'ulama, and hence as particularly menacing.

At the height of Turkish and Mughal rule, the court 'ulama seem to have displayed little concern for the vast majority of Indian Muslims who were of 'low' or *ajlaf* origin. Their close relations with the royal courts ruled out any strong links with the larger community outside the pale of the *ashraf* elite. They wrote and spoke Persian and Arabic, languages almost completely foreign to the *ajlaf*. They tended to look down upon the *ajlaf*, who remained rooted in the 'un-Islamic' traditions of their ancestors, regarding them as Muslims in name alone. The near monopoly over the cultural capital of scripturalist, *shari'ah*-centred Islam that the *ashraf* exercised created an almost unbridgeable barrier between them and the *ajlaf*, thereby serving to bolster their own claims to higher social status.

Since the authority of the *ashraf* rested on, among other things, their claim of representing 'Islamic' culture and knowledge, it is hardly surprising that Muslim rulers as well as the *ashraf* 'ulama associated with the courts took little or no interest in the 'proper' Islamization of the *ajlaf*, being content simply with their formal acceptance of Islam. Things began to change, however, with the coming of the British. To the British impact, in fact, we owe the creation of the notion of a unified, homogeneous and well-defined pan-Indian Muslim, as well as Hindu, community. As Thomas Metcalf rightly notes, 'Only with the coming of the British, from the late eighteenth century onwards, did the notion that there existed distinct "Hindu" and "Muslim" communities in India take on a fixed shape.'[41] The pan-Indian Muslim 'community', then, was very much an 'invented' and 'imagined' identity, like its alter ego, the pan-Indian 'Hindu' community, against which it sought to define itself. As we shall see, the chain of madrasas that began to be set up in the aftermath of the failed revolt of 1857 against the British had a central role to play in the construction of this identity.

Rise of 'Ulama Activism

The rapid collapse of Mughal power brought in its wake a growing shift in the focus of the *ashraf* 'ulama. Over time, with effective power increasingly slipping into non-Muslim hands, no longer could the Muslim ruler be regarded as effectively guaranteeing the supremacy of Islam. In this changing political context, the 'ordinary' Muslim emerged as the symbol of the faith, taking the place earlier occupied in the minds of the court 'ulama by the Muslim ruler. The 'ordinary' Muslim, fired with a passionate zeal for and commitment to *shari'ah*-centred Islam, was to be promoted to the status of the defender of the faith. This, in turn, was to have crucial implications for the understanding of what it meant to be Muslim. No longer would it suffice to be a Muslim by having been born into a Muslim family or possessing a 'Muslim' name. Rather, it was now stressed, one's 'Muslim-ness' was to be a self-conscious decision that was to be based on knowledge of the demands of the faith. This meant that all customs that were seen as 'un-Islamic' were to be shunned and that the individual believer was to consciously strive to mould himself on the Prophetic model.

The collapse of Muslim political authority, a valuable source of patronage for the ‘ulama, ironically strengthened the claims of the ‘ulama as representatives and leaders of the community. Faced with the territorial expansion of the East India Company, charismatic leaders arose from among the *ashraf* ‘ulama, seeking to mobilize ordinary Muslims, including the *ajlaf*, against encroaching non-Muslim powers. These reformist movements and the efforts of the ‘ulama to reach out to the *ajlaf* helped rally mass support for efforts to recover the fast-declining political power of the *ashraf* elite. For the ‘ulama involved in these movements the *ajlaf* increasingly provided new sources of patronage, now that support from earlier patrons such as Muslim rulers and landlords had considerably declined. For many *ajlaf* who enthusiastically participated in these movements for reform, the access that they provided to the valued symbols of *ashraf* ‘high’ culture opened up a new channel for upward social mobility. Abiding by the dictates of the *shari‘ah* was a means to claim a higher social status, and also represented a symbolic challenge to established elites whose lifestyles were often condemned as ‘un-Islamic’ by the reformists. These movements must not be seen as purely religious. For instance, the uprisings led by Titu Mir and Dudu Miyan in early nineteenth century Bengal had a strong class element. In Bengal, scores of peasants and weavers ruined by the policies of the East India Company, abject victims of a new breed of largely ‘upper’ caste Hindu landlords whom the British had helped set in place, enthusiastically supported the Islamic reformists. If they were to strictly observe the commandments of the *shari‘ah*, they were told, divine intervention would put an end to their worldly woes.

The rise of Islamic reform movements seeking to reach out to the masses of 'ordinary' Muslims was thus one of the principal outcomes of the rapid spread of British power. The most dramatic of these Islamic movements, and one that is deeply etched in the memory of many South Asian Islamic reformists till today, was the uprising of the *mujahidin* in the Pathan borderlands in the early nineteenth century. The movement traced its origins to the reformist message of the renowned '*alim* of Delhi, Shah Waliullah. It was also inspired by the teachings of one of his sons, Shah 'Abdul 'Aziz (1746–1822) who, in the face of British expansion, issued a *fatwa* declaring India to be a *dar ul-harb* ('abode of war'). Led by one of Shah Waliullah's grandsons, Shah Isma'il (1781–1831), and his charismatic preceptor, Sayyed Ahmad of Rae Bareilly (1786–1831), a student of another of Shah Waliullah's sons, Shah 'Abdul Qadir, the *mujahid* movement with its messianic appeal attracted numerous Muslims, including those of humble *ajlaf* origins. Gathering a large band of followers from across northern India, Shah Isma'il and Sayyed Ahmad travelled to the Afghan borderlands where they set up a proto-state of their own which they sought to rule in strict accordance with their understanding of the *shari'ah*, with Sayyed Ahmad styling himself as the 'Commander of the Faithful' (*amir ul-mu'minin*). For the Pathan tribesmen of that area, however, the stern puritanical zeal of the *mujahidin* was a gross violation of their own well-established traditions. This led to bloody clashes between the *mujahidin* and the tribesmen. When the *mujahidin* sought to win popular support for their cause by launching a *jihad* against the Sikhs, under whose rule the Muslims of the Punjab were subjected to discrimination, several Pathans joined the Sikhs to oppose the *mujahidin*. In 1831, in a gory battle in the village of Balakot, Shah Isma'il, Sayyed Ahmad and several other leading *mujahidin* were slain and the short-lived *mujahidin* state came to an abrupt end.[42]

Following this abortive *jihad*, few Islamic activists seriously contemplated military means to re-establish Muslim power in India. Sporadic attempts by the followers of Sayyed Ahmad and Shah Isma'il to take to arms to reinstate Muslim rule carried on till the 1860s, but were finally crushed by the British. However, the legacy of the *mujahidin* movement lived on, spawning new efforts at reforming Muslim religious practice and working for the eventual setting up of what their leaders and followers regarded as a truly Islamic society. Many madrasas in India today, particularly those associated with the Deobandi and the Ahl-i Hadith traditions, see themselves as carrying on in the tradition of Shah Isma'il and his followers, albeit through different means.

Intra-Muslim Disputes

The movement launched by Shah Isma'il and Sayyed Ahmad proved to be a major watershed in the history of the Muslims of South Asia. Till then, they were divided into two broad camps, the Sunni majority and the minority Shi'as, although among the latter there were several sectarian groupings. The *mujahidin* movement did not win the support of all, or even most, Sunnis. For many Sunnis associated with various Sufi orders, the theological underpinnings of the movement appeared suspect, or worse still, heretical. The movement was seen as an offshoot of the Wahhabis, followers of the Arabian puritan Muhammad ibn 'Abdul Wahhab (1703–1792), who violently decried popular Sufism and the *taqlid* of the schools of *fiqh*. Shah Isma'il penned two tracts modelled on ibn 'Abdul Wahhab's *Kitab ul-Tauhid* ('The Book of Monotheism'): the

Taqwi'at ul-Iman ('Strengthening of the Faith') and the *Sirat ul-Mustaqim* ('The Straight Path'). In these books, he insisted that Muslims must strictly abide by the commandments of the *shari'ah* and seek to emulate the Prophetic model. He stressed the absolute transcendence of God and was critical of the Sufis and their followers whom he accused of 'un-Islamic' beliefs and practices that compromised the Islamic principle of monotheism. These included prostrating before the graves of Sufis, sacrificing animals in their honour, and regarding Sufis and prophets as able to intercede with God to have one's requests met. Shah Isma'il even went so far as to insist that the Prophet Muhammad was a mere human being, although a particularly pious one, denying the unseen powers that many Sufis attributed to him. Such beliefs and practices were condemned as *shirk*, the sin of associating partners with God, and as innovations leading away from the Prophetic path. Predictably, this occasioned a virulent protest from Sufi circles and many 'ulama who were also Sufis wrote tracts against Shah Isma'il, issuing *fatwa*s condemning him as an apostate and as an enemy of Islam.[43] Not all members of Shah Waliullah's family supported Shah Isma'il and his theological views. Some of them, including his uncles Shah 'Abdul 'Aziz and Shah 'Abdul Qadir, are reported to have fiercely opposed the contents of the *Taqwi'at ul-Iman*.

The *mujahidin* movement thus led to sharp divisions within the broader Sunni community. These divisions continue to be deeply rooted in India today, and the madrasas, as we shall see, play a crucial role in sustaining them. Some supporters of the *mujahidin* who were bitterly opposed to all forms of Sufism and to *taqlid* of the schools of *fiqh* went on to form the Ahl-i Hadith ('The People of the Prophetic Tradition'), as they called themselves. They insisted that Sufism was an 'un-

Islamic' and post-Prophetic development, and argued that the schools of *fiqh* had appeared considerably after the death of the Prophet. The founders of the schools were not infallible and, therefore, their prescriptions, if they went against the express commandments of the Qur'an and Hadith, had no validity. To their opponents, the Ahl-i Hadith were seen as challenging the Islamic tradition as it had developed over time, as well as undermining their own position as religious experts, whether as Sufis or *fuqaha*.

Other Muslims who also drew inspiration from the *mujahidin* did not go as far as the Ahl-i Hadith in their critique of traditional understandings of Islam. Gathered together in the form of the Deoband school, they accepted the validity of the four schools of Sunni *fiqh*, arguing that ordinary Muslims should strictly abide by *taqlid* and that only the 'ulama could undertake *ijtihad* if the school of *fiqh* that they followed did not make any provision for a particular matter. They claimed that Shah Waliullah and Shah 'Abdul 'Aziz, whom the Ahl-i Hadith also accepted as their spiritual forebears, had not opposed Sufism and the schools of law as such, but had, instead, advocated reforms within them along what they described as proper 'Islamic' lines.

Yet another group emerged out of the heated controversy that the *mujahidin* movement had generated. It was led by a leading '*alim* from the town of Bareilly, Imam Ahmad Raza Khan (1856–1921), founder of what are today known by their opponents as the Barelwis.[44] The Barelwis bitterly castigated the Ahl-i Hadith and the Deobandis as heretics and enemies of Islam, issuing a number of *fatwa*s against them. Ahmad Raza Khan went so far as to argue that his opponents were apostates, who thus deserved to be killed (*wajib ul-qatal*), insisting that those who doubted their being non-Muslims had themselves gone out of the pale of Islam.[45] The Barelwis branded both the Deobandis as well as the Ahl-i Hadith as fronts of the 'Wahhabis' and even as agents of the Devil in his war against the true faith. They insisted on the centrality of Sufism in Islam, and defended some practices associated with the cults of the saints. Yet, they critiqued some other popular practices such as prostration before the graves of the Sufis or music at their shrines which they saw as having no proper 'Islamic' sanction. The Barelwis also argued for the necessity of *taqlid* and denounced calls for *ijtihad* as a cover-up to establish a new *shari'ah* in opposition to the law of the Prophet.[46]

In addition to these three groups, which later emerged as full-fledged movements with organizations and madrasas of their own, there remained vast numbers of Muslims affiliated with the cults of local Sufis, following a range of practices that were condemned, to varying degrees, by advocates of reform. They did not formally create organizations of their own, being locally based and linked to individual shrines and Sufi preceptors. For want of a better term, they could be called, as they often are, *dargah wale*, followers of the cults of the shrines (*dargah*s) of the Sufis. Reformist groups competed with each other to make inroads into this vast unorganized section of the community with varying degrees of success.

The sharp differences that characterized these groups began to crystallize within the broader fold of the Sunni community and led to heightened intra-community debates which sometimes took violent forms. Each group insisted that it alone represented the authentic Sunni Muslim tradition. The Prophet is said to have remarked that after his death his community would be splintered into seventy-three factions. Only one of these, the one that truly followed the Qur'an and his practice or *sunnah*, would be saved on the Day of

Judgement, the rest being consigned to Hell. Rival Sunni groups insisted that they alone represented this one chosen group (*firqa al-najiya*) and branded the others as heretics. These intra-Sunni conflicts occasioned by the *mujahidin* movement were to take on more strident forms with the establishment of new types of madrasas under British rule.

New Forms of Madrasa Organization in Colonial India

The establishment of British rule had momentous consequences for the system of traditional Islamic learning in India. Many of the distinctive features of madrasas today can be attributed to the colonial impact. These include the narrow focus on *fiqh* related to personal issues and the stress on what are seen as 'religious', as opposed to 'secular', subjects. These also include new forms of madrasa organization, a fixed syllabus, regular examinations and so on. Understanding the colonial impact is thus crucial to properly appreciate the madrasa system in contemporary India.

Almost a century before the formal incorporation of India into the British Empire in 1858, the East India Company had introduced new forms of land revenue management which had serious implications for the madrasas. In Bengal, from the late eighteenth century onwards, large-scale resumption by the East India Company of lands endowed by Muslim nobles and rulers to madrasas led to a virtual collapse of the traditional educational system in the province, which once boasted of several thousand madrasas, many of which provided free education to the poor. Writing about the devastation of the Muslim schools in Bengal caused by the expropriation by the British of rent-free endowments, Hunter, a colonial officer, remarked:

> At an outlay of 800,000 pounds upon Resumption Proceedings, an additional revenue of 300,000 pounds a year was permanently gained by the State, representing a capital at five per cent of six million sterling. A large part of this sum was derived from lands held rent free by Musalmans or by Muhammadan [*sic*] foundations [. . .] [T]he educational system of the Musalmans, which was almost entirely maintained by rent-free grants, received its death-blow. The scholastic classes of the Muhammadans [*sic*] emerged from the eighteen years of harrying absolutely ruined.[47]

Several other British officials acknowledged their culpability in seriously undermining indigenous institutions of education. Ludlow, an early nineteenth century colonial officer, remarked that before the arrival of the British, most Indian children could read and write, but, as in Bengal, the extension of British rule had resulted in the almost total destruction of indigenous systems of education.[48] As Lord Minto (1806–1813), the Governor General of India, himself admitted:

> It is a common remark that science and literature are in a progressive state of decay among the natives of India. From every enquiry which I have been enabled to make on this interesting subject, that remark appears to me but too well founded. The number of learned is not only diminished but the circle of learning, even among those who still devote themselves to it, appears to be considerably contracted.[49]

Till the end of the eighteenth century at least, however, the British rarely attempted to directly interfere with the system of Muslim education. Often, in fact, they worked closely with 'ulama, employing them in various departments in their administration, particularly in the judiciary. Although in contemporary 'ulama accounts of British rule the 'ulama are portrayed as having always been vociferously opposed to colonialism, the actual course of 'ulama–British relations was far more complex. For instance, in 1781, Warren Hastings, the first British Governor General of India, established the Madrasa-i 'Aliya in Calcutta, whose expenses were met entirely by the East India Company. It employed the *dars-i nizami* as its basic curriculum and its graduates went on to staff various posts in the revenue and judicial departments in the province.[50]

Yet, as the British consolidated their rule over large parts of India, *qazi*s and *mufti*s were increasingly dispensed with, and many areas of the legal system that had previously been under the *shari'ah* came to be governed by British law. Consequently, *qazi*s were replaced by British judges, and soon the only realm left under the *shari'ah* was that of personal affairs such as marriage, divorce, inheritance and endowments, and even in these matters, unlike the past, non-Muslim judges could decide cases. In addition, laws governing these issues underwent a significant transformation under colonial influence and interpretation. They departed in many ways from classical *fiqh* and hence were appropriately referred to as 'Anglo-Muhammadan Law' instead. Furthermore, in certain provinces such as Punjab, customary law was upheld as overriding the prescriptions of the *shari'ah*.

Yet, in some ways, the confinement of the *shari'ah* to the private sphere actually helped the 'ulama bolster their claims to authority. By defining the private sphere as governed by 'religious' law, and by codifying this law on the basis of their own reading of the texts of classical *fiqh*, the British acknowledged the claims of the 'ulama by giving them the authority to interpret that law. In the past the reach of the *shari'ah* had been limited, for customary laws were widely followed, particularly by Muslim communities that still retained many of their pre-Islamic practices and beliefs. By now extending Anglo-Muhammadan law to cover almost all Muslims in India, and by expanding the scope of that law to include areas previously governed by custom, the British created new opportunities for the ‘ulama to extend their influence by recognizing them as authorities in mediating the private sphere. The same development occurred in the case of Hindus who were increasingly sought to be governed by Brahminical law codes.

The codification of Muslim law, seen as necessary for efficient bureaucratic dispensation of justice according to European norms, had the ironical effect of freezing the law, sapping it of its inherent dynamism and of its ability to creatively respond to changing social conditions. The defining moment came in August 1772 when Warren Hastings issued the following decree:

> [I]n all suits regarding inheritance, marriage, caste and other religious uses and institutions, the laws of the Koran with respect to the Mohammedans [*sic*] and those of the Shaster with respect to the Gentoos [Hindus] shall be invariably adhered to; on all such occasions the Moulvies or Brahmins shall respectively attend to expound the law, and they shall sign the report and assist in passing the decree.[51]

Overall, British rule seriously narrowed the roles of the ‘ulama while, ironically, at the same time enabling them to assert more forcefully their claims to leadership of the Muslim community. Since vast sections of the law rapidly came to be administered without any reference to the *shari‘ah*, opportunities for the ‘ulama in government service were sharply curtailed. Striking a further blow to the influence of the ‘ulama, new forms of education were gradually introduced by the British. In 1837,

Persian was replaced by English as the language of official correspondence, and knowledge of English now became an essential requirement for government jobs. In 1844, the Governor General of India, Lord Hardinge, announced a policy that effectively debarred madrasa students from government employment.[52] The government now embarked on a deliberate policy of promoting Western-style schools, aimed at cultivating a class of Indian elites who would collaborate with the colonial regime.

English-medium education went on to create a sharp dualism within the Muslim community, between products of traditional madrasas and those who had studied in the schools that the British, and Christian missionaries, had started setting up. In earlier times, as we have seen, the madrasa provided the only available avenue for formal education for Muslim children. Leading *ashraf* families who aspired for their sons to gain employment in government service generally sent them to madrasas for training. Now, however, the link between madrasa education and 'respectable' employment was effectively undermined. Consequently, growing numbers of *ashraf* began sending their sons to English schools. Increasingly, and this was to grow more pronounced as the years went by, the madrasas began catering to Muslims from the lower classes instead, a marked departure from the past.

This educational dualism represented a major departure from tradition and led to the emergence of new conceptions of the place of religion in society as well as new understandings of 'Islam' and 'Islamic knowledge'. The notion that religion was a distinct sphere of life and activity, neatly separate or separable from other similarly defined spheres, was one that was completely foreign to classical Islam. With the advent of colonialism, however, religion came to represent a clearly demarcated zone, relegated to what came to be defined as the private sphere. This reflected a post-Reformation Western Christian notion of religion as set apart from the secular realm, one that colonial administrators sought to impose on their Indian subjects. India was regarded as somehow too religious, and reform was seen as possible only if religion was restricted to the personal realm, leaving other spheres of life open to the influences of Western-inspired 'progress'. If religion was allowed to play a role in guiding or controlling the public domain, it would have posed, it was widely recognized, a serious challenge to the colonial project of domination that was couched in the garb of guiding India on the path of 'reason' and 'civilization'.

The emergence of new forms of education under colonial rule and the development of the notion of religion as simply a private matter had significant consequences for the 'ulama and the madrasa system of education that continue to be felt even today. It meant, in effect, that the madrasas would no longer provide a general sort of education but would increasingly restrict themselves to what was to be narrowly defined as 'religious' (*dini*) or 'Islamic'. This, in turn, led to a marked shift in the ways in which Islam itself came to be understood: as a set of clearly defined beliefs and laws governing the private sphere, thereby tying in with a more general process of the reification of religion as colonial administrators sought to define each religion in terms of specified doctrines and ritual practices. As noted earlier, the notion of a rigid separation between religion (*din*) and the secular realm (*duniya*) was alien to the early Muslim tradition. While a distinction was indeed made between 'transmitted' and 'rational' sciences, the two were regarded as parts of a single whole, which explains why early madrasas often taught both sets of subjects and why experts in both could be considered as 'ulama in their own right.

The rigid compartmentalization between the 'religious' and the 'secular' that colonialism brought in its wake resulted in a distinct shift in the understanding of what constituted 'Islamic' education. Increasingly, in the minds of many 'ulama 'religious' education (*dini ta'lim*) came to be limited simply to the 'transmitted' sciences, while the 'rational' sciences came to be seen as 'secular' (*duniyavi*) or 'modern' (*'asri*, *jadid*), often as distinct from, if not in opposition to, the former, partly because many of the theories of the new Western 'rational' sciences challenged deeply held Muslim beliefs and assumptions. While earlier madrasas taught a range of subjects, they were to now focus almost entirely on what came to be narrowly defined as 'religious' disciplines, such as the Qur'anic sciences, Hadith, *fiqh* and Arabic. Students who wished to study what were now considered 'non-religious' subjects turned instead to schools set up by the colonial authorities or Christian missionaries.

This narrowing of the focus of the madrasas, caused by the imposition and acceptance of a sharp *dini–duniyavi* divide, led to a growing stagnation in the madrasa system of education, with students now largely limited to studying strictly 'religious' subjects. This development also meant a major shift in the concerns of the 'ulama. Since religion was effectively relegated to the private sphere, the authority of the 'ulama was, in significant respects, sharply curtailed. In the absence of Muslim political authority, and the applicability of *fiqh* restricted to personal affairs, the role of the 'ulama was now confined to governing the private lives of individual Muslims. This was also reflected in their teachings, in their writings, and in the contents of the *fatwa*s that they issued which now centred essentially on the rules of personal piety and conduct, ignoring larger issues of state and polity. In this way, colonial rule considerably narrowed the 'ulama's authority and it was in this limited sphere that they strived to establish their credentials of an Islam that was increasingly defined in colonial terms as largely having to do with individual believers' personal lives and divorced from larger social concerns. Consequently, the madrasas that the 'ulama began to establish in the colonial period were geared essentially to protect the private sphere from outside interference or attack, whether from the colonial state, Christian and Hindu missionaries or 'modernist' Muslims or Muslims of other sectarian persuasions. Overall, this meant that these madrasas came to differ considerably in their curriculum, focus and roles from their pre-colonial counterparts.

Madrasas Under the British

The revolt of 1857 against the British represented, in a sense, the last major effort on the part of sections of the Hindu as well as Muslim elite to retain their increasingly threatened privileges in the face of the expansion of the East India Company. It appears that at several places leading 'ulama participated or even led the fighting, considering this as a *jihad* against the infidels. After the British forcibly crushed the revolt they embarked on a bloody campaign against Muslim elites whom they saw as primarily responsible for the uprising. Some 200,000 Muslims are said to have been killed by British troops in Delhi alone. 'Ulama accused of having participated or instigated the revolt were sent to the gallows.[53] Several more had to endure long spells of imprisonment in the Andaman Islands.[54]

The formal incorporation of India into the British Empire in 1858 meant that madrasas now had to function under a very different political regime. The chain of schools that the British had begun setting up, along with the institutions established by Christian missionaries, were seen as motivated by the desire to convert Indians, Muslims as well as Hindus, to Christianity, and to instil in them a hatred for their own traditions. Large tracts of land granted to 'ulama and their schools by Muslim nobles were resumed by the British, and several other forms of patronage were suddenly withdrawn. Consequently, many 'ulama regarded the British as enemies of Islam for having overthrown the Mughals and for patronizing Christian missionaries. Islamic identity and the tradition of Islamic learning were seen to be in grave danger under the new rulers. Many 'ulama stiffly opposed these new forms of education which they saw as calculated to lead Muslims astray from their faith, to abandon Islam for Christianity or irreligious rationalism. In their opposition to the British, some 'ulama even went to the extent of issuing *fatwa*s of apostasy and heresy against Muslims who supported British education. So far did they go in their 'religious war' against 'modern, Western views', says a Muslim writer, probably with some exaggeration, that 'if in someone's house they found an English book, they would consider the house to have been rendered impure'.[55]

Yet, British rule opened up new spaces and opportunities for the 'ulama to carry on the work of preaching the message of Islamic reform among the Muslim masses. The printing press, in particular, provided a new means for the 'ulama to propagate their views to a wider audience. Inexpensive literature on a range of Islamic issues could now be printed in vast quantities and made accessible to 'ordinary' Muslims on a scale unimaginable before. *Fatwa*s were readily available and broadcast widely through printed collections, guiding

Muslims in the conduct of their lives in accordance with the commandments of the *shari'ah*. New methods of bureaucratic organization were also borrowed from the example of Christian missionary schools. Thus, the chain of madrasas that began to be established after the 1857 revolt, some of which still exist today, adopted a system of paid teachers, a clearly marked hierarchy of administrators, a fixed syllabus, separate classes for different levels, a well-defined academic year, annual examinations and hostels for their students. All these represented a clear departure from the pattern of the medieval madrasas.

The New Madrasas

By far the most significant of the madrasas to emerge in the aftermath of the revolt of 1857 was the renowned Dar ul-'Ulum, set up in 1866 in the town of Deoband in the Saharanpur district of the then United Provinces. Among the founders of the school were leading reformist 'ulama such as Maulana Qasim Nanotawi (1832–1880) and Maulana Rashid Ahmad Gangohi (1828–1905), who are said to have participated in the 1857 uprising. In setting up the madrasa the founders of the school saw themselves as engaged in an 'educational *jihad*', having realized the futility of armed struggle against the country's new masters. Islam, they believed, was under threat from the British who were bent on the extirpation of Islam. Although the founders of Deoband pragmatically accommodated themselves to the reality of British rule, they considered their school as a training ground for 'ulama who would take revenge on the British for having overthrown the Mughals.

Deoband represented a curious fusion of religious conservatism and political pragmatism. Within half a century, leading Deobandi 'ulama were to take an active part in India's freedom movement, most of them supporting the Indian National Congress and vociferously opposing the Muslim League and the British. Yet, this opposition to the British did not, at least till the second decade of the twentieth century, translate into active resistance against the colonial power. As Metcalf observes, the Deobandi 'ulama treated political affairs on a primarily secular basis, identifying religion with the personal sphere, in practice if not in theory, thus allowing them to enter into pragmatic political adjustments unhindered by rigid ideological constraints.[56] For their part, the British did not necessarily see the Deoband madrasa as a major threat, at least not till leading Deobandi 'ulama began getting directly involved in anti-British politics from the first decade of the twentieth century onwards.

To the founders of the Deoband school it was not only the British who appeared as a menacing threat to Islam. Rather, a perhaps even greater danger, as they perceived it, was posed by Western-influenced modernist Muslims as well as Muslim groups that opposed the traditional Hanafi insistence on *taqlid*. Accused of virtual infidelity, they were seen as a major challenge to the claims of the Deobandis as authoritative spokesmen of Islam. Islam, for the Deobandis, was regarded as largely synonymous with the established Hanafi tradition as they narrowly interpreted it,[57] and they went so far in their insistence on *taqlid* that they even condemned inter-scholastic eclecticism, the borrowing from other schools of Sunni *fiqh*, although they accepted these schools as equally 'orthodox'. In practice, however, they did allow for a limited *ijtihad* within the tradition of Hanafi jurisprudence, but only in matters on which there existed no clear consensus or '*ijma*. They claimed that they had been instructed by the Prophet himself to establish the school, seeing their endeavours as working to bring back to life the days of the *sahaba*. Yet, despite these claims of working to 'protect' Islam from the British, the Deobandis appear to have unwittingly accepted and worked on the colonial assumption that religion was a private matter, set apart from the secular world. It was this privatized form of Islam that the Deobandis sought to protect, and it was in this sphere that they sought to establish their claims as authoritative spokesmen of the faith. The necessity to protect or control the private sphere remains the major concern of most Indian 'ulama even today.

Shortly after it was founded, Deoband emerged as a leading centre of Islamic learning. It began to attract an ever-growing number of students from northern India and even from other countries such as Afghanistan and from Central Asia. For some years Hindu students also enrolled at the madrasa in order to study Persian and mathematics. They apparently stopped coming to the madrasa when the government made it compulsory for applicants for government jobs to have a certificate from a government school. Seeing itself as the protector of the Islamic tradition, the school played a major role in consolidating a pan-Indian Islamic identity. Its use of Urdu as a medium of instruction helped it to establish a countrywide constituency and, along with other madrasas that came to be established in the late nineteenth century, it played a major role in establishing Urdu as the language of communication of the Muslim elite in most parts of India. This, in turn, helped bolster a strong sense of Muslim communal identity, particularly from the mid-nineteenth century onwards, following the outbreak of the Hindi–Urdu controversy between competing Hindu and Muslim elites. Earlier, instruction in the madrasas was largely in Persian, and for students training to become 'ulama, in

Arabic. By adopting Urdu as its medium of instruction and dissemination, Deoband helped democratize access to the Islamic scripturalist tradition and to draw increasing numbers of Muslims into its reformist project.

The founders of the Deoband madrasa did not see themselves as simply managing a school. Rather, along with the later Deobandis, they took a leading role in community affairs, seeking to transmit the Islamic reformist message to a wider society using novel means such as publishing tracts and tomes, training missionaries to debate with theologians of other religions and other Muslim groups, and working among local Muslim communities. Another means that the Deoband madrasa used in this regard was the *fatwa*, through which it sought to provide guidance to individual Muslims in 'correct' belief, ritual practice and social behaviour in the light of the classical texts of the Hanafi school. In 1892 the madrasa launched a full-fledged department of *fatwa*s (*dar ul-'ifta*). Requests for *fatwa*s came from Muslims from all over India and abroad, from countries such as Afghanistan and Burma. The sheer number of *fatwa*s issued by the madrasa indicates how, through its *fatwa* department, it came to exercise a far wider influence than it would have had if it had restricted itself simply to teaching. The first *mufti* of the madrasa, 'Aziz ur-Rahman, is said to have issued a total of 37,561 *fatwa*s in a span of seventeen years.[58] The *fatwa*s of the 'ulama of Deoband were later put together and published in collected volumes for wider circulation. Many seekers of *fatwa*s requested guidance on intricate matters of belief, ritual, worship and dress, and issues such as marriage, divorce and inheritance. Others sought the opinion of the 'ulama on how to conduct their dealings with other Muslim groups or with Hindus. Yet others wanted advice on how to deal with new questions that colonial rule had brought in its trail, such as the method of praying while journeying on a train, the legality of using money orders and of subscribing to government bonds. The subjects that the *fatwa*s dealt with reflected the overall trend under the British to increasingly confine religion to the private sphere, the only area where the *shari'ah* had some legal recognition and where the 'ulama could express and assert their authority. The contents of the *fatwa*s indicated how the 'ulama were having to turn their attention from matters of the state and public law to issues of personal law and private behaviour in the new colonial setting.

The syllabus adopted at Deoband represented a slight modification of the *dars-i nizami* of Mullah Nizamuddin, combining with it an emphasis on the Qur'an and Hadith and other 'transmitted' sciences that drew upon the legacy of Shah Waliullah.[59] Certain books on Aristotelian philosophy and logic and other 'rational' sciences considered 'unnecessary' were removed, although many other 'rational' texts continued to be taught.[60] Deoband laid greater stress on the 'transmitted' sciences, teaching all the six Sunni canonical collections of Hadith, in contrast to pre-colonial madrasas that generally taught only one. *Fiqh* formed the core of the curriculum, and the Deobandis insisted on rigid conformity to the Hanafi school.[61] This stress on the 'transmitted' sciences reflected Deoband's wider reformist concerns, in particular its opposition to 'un-Islamic' or 'Hindu' customs among many Muslims.

This does not mean that the Deobandis were wholly opposed to the 'rational' sciences, particularly the new forms of scientific knowledge associated with the British. It would be wrong to accuse them of being completely against the learning of modern sciences or what they called *'asri 'ulum*. In fact, from a close reading of the writings of Deobandi 'ulama it appears that what many of them were opposed to was not modern education as such, but what they regarded as the 'anti-Islamic' culture associated with the schools set up by the British, which they saw as inevitably leading Muslim children away from Islam towards Christianity, scepticism or atheism. The fact that the British appeared to be vehement foes of the Muslims, from whom they had snatched political power, naturally made the 'ulama apprehensive of the possible impact of Western education on the community. Because the Deobandis saw the British as bent on the destruction of Islam, they consistently refused to allow the inclusion in their school of any form of knowledge associated with the British that, as a Deobandi graduate puts it, 'might create a soft corner in the hearts of the Muslims for them'.[62]

That the Deobandis did not condemn all forms of modern knowledge as such is apparent from some of the statements and *fatwa*s that they issued. For instance, they invoked a *fatwa* of Shah 'Abdul 'Aziz that allowed Muslims to study English in schools run by the British. Maulana Rashid Ahmad Gangohi issued a *fatwa* suggesting that Muslims could study English provided it did not dilute their faith in Islam. He asserted that it was, in fact, better for the Muslims to study English rather than traditional logic and philosophy because by mastering the English language they could improve their worldly fortunes.[63] Another leading Deobandi elder, Maulana Ashraf 'Ali Thanwi, believed that there was no harm in Muslims learning English provided they remained aloof from 'English culture' and did not allow 'modern' education to 'dominate' religious education.[64] Maulana Qasim Nanotawi, one of the founding fathers of the Dar ul-'Ulum, is said to have expressed the desire to introduce the teaching of English in the school on returning from a journey abroad, when it struck him that had he known the language he could have more effectively preached Islam to the non-Muslims with whom he had come into contact.[65] He had planned to travel to Europe to study English, realizing its value in Islamic missionary efforts, but died before he could embark on the journey.[66] He also recognized the importance and worth of modern scientific knowledge, and his opposition to its inclusion in the madrasa syllabus is said to have been only because he believed that Muslims who wanted to learn modern subjects could enrol in the schools which the government had established. Since government schools did not teach Islamic subjects, he decided that Deoband should focus on these alone.[67] At the graduation ceremony of the madrasa in 1873–74 he reportedly remarked that there was no harm if graduates of Deoband took admission in government schools to study modern subjects. In fact, he added, 'this would be only to their credit'.[68] However, few Deobandi graduates were to go on to take that step.

Since the doors to government service were largely closed for madrasa graduates under the British, students who passed out from Deoband and the other madrasas that were set up in this period increasingly turned to the community for support and employment. Some set up madrasas of their own, others taught in existing madrasas. Some adopted medicine as a profession, 'Greek' medicine (*unani tibb*) being taught at Deoband in its early years. Yet others functioned as professional *muftis*, offering guidance to ordinary Muslims on how to conduct their personal affairs in accordance with the *shari'ah* and the rules of Hanafi *fiqh*. Several emerged as writers and debaters, penning tracts and organizing lecture series to counter what were regarded as 'heretical' Muslim groups such as the Barelwis and the Ahmadis, as well as the Christian and Arya Samaj missionaries. Yet others took to missionary work as a profession, spending their lives preaching 'proper' Islamic faith and observance among scattered Muslim communities and bitterly attacking local customs which they saw as 'un-Islamic'.

The other major educational initiative undertaken in the immediate aftermath of the 1857 revolt was the setting up in 1875 of the Mohammadan Anglo-Oriental High School at Aligarh, not far from Deoband. Two years later it was upgraded to the status of a college, and in 1921 it received the status of a university. Its founder, Sir Sayyed Ahmad Khan, was born in Delhi in 1817 in a family that had for long served the Mughals. As a child he had attended the lectures of Shah Isma'il and developed a great regard for the reformist efforts of Shah 'Abdul 'Aziz. He later went on to enrol at the Delhi College where he studied under Maulana Mamluk 'Ali Nanotawi (d. 1850), who was also the teacher and uncle of Qasim Nanotawi, one of the founders of the Deoband madrasa. Sayyed Ahmad witnessed the gruesome events of 1857 and the terrible destruction wrought by the British thereafter. Realizing the futility of opposing the British through armed force, he argued that in the changed political context Muslims must be loyal to the new rulers and should seek to take advantage of the opportunities that British rule offered.

Appealing to the Muslims to abandon their opposition to the British, Sayyed Ahmad stressed the need for them to take to modern education. In 1869 he sailed for England, where he spent almost two years studying the educational system there. On his return to India he set about laying the foundation of a grand scheme of reform of Muslim education on modern lines. He saw his school as a means of revamping Islamic education, training a new generation of young Muslims equally well versed in modern as well as the Islamic sciences. He criticized the conservative 'ulama for what he saw as their unrepentant obscurantism. He sought to develop a new Islamic theology by reconciling Islam with the 'facts' of science. He also spoke out against the traditional 'ulama for their insistence on *taqlid*, arguing that Muslims should engage in *ijtihad* to develop new ways of understanding jurisprudence in accordance with the needs of the changing times.

Sayyed Ahmad had to face sharp criticism from the 'ulama, including the Deobandis, some of whom even went to the extent of branding him a *kafir*.[69] Their opposition to him was not only because of his advocacy of modern education. In fact, almost none of the *fatwa*s issued against him mentioned his advocacy of modern education or the learning of the English language as grounds for his being declared an apostate. What particularly incensed Sayyed Ahmad's opponents were his religious views which they branded as 'naturalism' (*nechariyat*), considering this a complete misreading of the Qur'an and opposed to the consensus of the 'ulama. Faced with the opposition of the 'ulama, Sayyed Ahmad was forced to relent, allowing the 'ulama to control the department of theology and Islamic studies in his college and announcing that he would not interfere in its functioning. Satisfied with his assurances, Qasim Nanotawi, rector of Deoband, sent his son-in-law, Maulana 'Abdullah Ansari, to Aligarh, and Sayyed Ahmad appointed him as head of department. Soon, Deoband and Aligarh entered into a compromise of sorts. Deobandi teachers were employed at Aligarh to teach Islamic studies, a compulsory subject for the Muslim students of the college. Later, an arrangement was reached whereby students from Aligarh could attend lectures at Deoband, although the number of students who did so was negligible. Conversely, Aligarh later began allowing Deobandi graduates to enrol in order to learn English. Yet, on the whole, Aligarh remained a modernist bastion, and the 'ulama continued to regard it with suspicion.

The growing educational dualism, as exemplified by Deoband on the one hand, and Aligarh on the other, spurred several efforts at reconciling traditional Islamic and modern education. These were also inspired, in part, by colonial critiques of 'native' education as 'irrelevant' and 'outdated'. One of the boldest attempts in this regard was the Nadwat ul-'Ulama (The Council of the 'Ulama), which was set up in 1892 on the occasion of the annual meeting of the Madrasa Faiz-i 'Am at Kanpur.[70] The Nadwa began as a group of 'ulama from different schools of thought, Muslim philanthropists, journalists, lawyers and government servants, who came together once a year to discuss issues relating to the education of the Muslim community and to promote a semblance of unity between different Muslim groups.[71] In a letter dispatched to various 'ulama introducing the organization, Maulana Muhammad 'Ali Mungeri (1846–1927), the first president of the Nadwa, wrote:

> Because it is seen that graduates of Arabic madrasas have little knowledge of the affairs of the world around them, and because they can do little else at their age, they remain dependent on the people of the world (*ahl-i duniya*) and are considered useless in the eyes of the public. They also do not possess the level of religious knowledge that they should. This organization [the Nadwa] seeks to bring about appropriate reforms in this regard in all madrasas [. . .] Further, today the internal differences among our 'ulama are creating severe problems, giving rise to great strife over little issues, because of which the 'ulama of Islam and even our pure faith are lowered in the eyes of others. This organization shall strive to ensure that these differences do not arise, and if they do, it shall seek to resolve them.[72]

Mungeri then went on to elaborate the aims and objectives of the Nadwa. These included reforms in the madrasa syllabus and methods of teaching, and improving the moral character of the students. The Nadwa would, he stressed, seek to unite different Muslim groups on issues of common concern, such as what was widely seen as a grand European 'conspiracy' against Islam.[73] It would strive to promote Islamic awareness among scattered Muslim groups in the country who still continued to practise various 'un-Islamic' customs. It would also promote Islamic missionary work among non-Muslims, training 'ulama in various languages for this purpose. Finally, in order to guide Muslims in the conduct of their daily lives it would establish a *dar ul-'ifta*, providing *fatwa*s on matters of religious import.[74]

To begin with, the annual meetings of the Nadwa attracted representatives of all major strands of Muslim opinion, including the Deobandis, the Aligarh 'modernists', the Ahl-i Hadith, 'ulama from the Firangi Mahal family and even Barelwi and Ithna 'Ashari Shi'a scholars. Shortly after, however, the Barelwis distanced themselves from the venture, and their leader, Ahmad Raza Khan, who had himself attended the inaugural sessions of the Nadwa, issued a number of *fatwa*s branding the initiators of the Nadwa, as well as the Deobandis and Sayyed Ahmad Khan, as *kafir*s, penning numerous tracts to back his claims.[75] Although some Shi'as did attend the early meetings of the Nadwa, later the Nadwa confined itself only to the Sunnis, thus effectively ruling out any significant Shi'a participation.[76]

At its annual meeting in 1898 the Nadwa decided to set up a madrasa in Lucknow, the Dar ul-'Ulum Nadwat ul-'Ulama, in order to train a new breed of 'ulama who would combine the best of Deoband and Aligarh. Maulana Muhammad 'Ali Mungeri suggested that along with the classical Islamic disciplines, the students at the new school should be trained in the Sufi path and should be made to study selected Sufi texts.[77] Departing from the pattern of traditional madrasas, he advocated that the students should also be made to take part in sports and various physical exercises, including horse riding, shooting and swimming.[78] He envisioned the students as going on to become scholars-cum-social activists, writing on religious issues in popular journals and learned magazines, and working to combat intra-Muslim dissensions. They would, he hoped, also play a leading role in opposing what he described as 'un-Islamic' practices among the Muslims, exhorting them to follow faithfully the commandments of the *shari'ah*.[79]

The newly established Dar ul-'Ulum Nadwat ul-'Ulama, or Nadwa for short, represented a pragmatic compromise on the part of the 'ulama with the exigencies of colonial rule. Although Nadwa did not go as far as Aligarh in courting British support, and some leading Nadwis were ardent supporters of the Congress, Nadwa did not hesitate from accepting government patronage. Thus, the foundation stone of the new building of the madrasa was laid by the lieutenant-governor of the United Provinces in 1908, and in that year the madrasa accepted a monthly grant of Rs 500 from the government to teach certain modern subjects. The madrasa also received generous financial support from rulers of various Muslim princely states, as well as from the Aga Khan, the leader of the Nizari Isma'ili Shi'as, in addition to donations by individual Muslim supporters.[80]

Over the years, Nadwa managed to attract some of the leading Islamic scholars of north India. The noted '*alim* Shibli Nu'mani (1857–1914), who had served at Aligarh as professor of Persian for sixteen years, joined the madrasa in 1905.[81] Shibli was fired with a passionate zeal for reforming the madrasa system, and he put forward bold proposals for modernizing it. Shibli's concern for madrasa reform was influenced by his experiences at Aligarh and his close association with Sir Sayyed.

He claimed that Islam was capable of coming to terms with the demands of changing times, arguing that this itself signified the truth and eternal validity of the faith. In contrast to conservative 'ulama who saw the West as wholly evil, Shibli advocated a middle path, exhorting Muslims not to shun those aspects of modernity that did not go against Islam. He pointed out that in the past Muslims had not hesitated to take advantage of the knowledge of people of other faiths, such as the Greeks, Persians and Hindus. He therefore recommended that madrasas also include modern subjects in their curriculum, including English, social and natural sciences and mathematics, without this affecting their religious character. 'This is the time to acquire the knowledge of both the West and the East,' he insisted.[82] He argued that it was necessary for the contemporary 'ulama to keep abreast of contemporary developments in various fields of knowledge, including 'anti-Islamic' polemical writings by Christian and Arya Samaj missionaries, so that they could defend Islam from the challenges that it was seen to be facing. He pleaded that madrasas should move away from the teaching of footnotes in classical texts, of commentaries upon commentaries and of the intricacies of grammar and syntax, so that their students actually understood the subjects that they were meant to be studying. He also suggested that new books be taught, and those texts that were difficult to comprehend and which contained, as he put it, 'many useless verbal duels and puzzles' be discontinued.[83]

Despite Shibli's efforts, the pace of reform spearheaded by Nadwa remained slow and halting. Nadwa replaced several books of Greek philosophy and logic with more texts of the 'transmitted' sciences, and introduced texts on economics and political science in its curriculum. It also placed greater stress on the teaching of modern Arabic. Yet, it retained the basic structure of the *dars-i nizami*. Despite the intentions of some of its founders, there was stiff resistance within Nadwa to Shibli's suggestion that English and modern social and natural sciences be taught, these being viewed by Shibli's rivals as 'worldly' subjects and hence to be excluded from the syllabus. Likewise, Shibli's appointment of a Hindu pundit to teach the students Hindi and Sanskrit in order to equip them to counter the propaganda of the Arya Samaj raised the hackles of many conservative 'ulama. To them Shibli's proposals appeared as moving, as a Nadwi scholar puts it, in the direction of 'interference or even as a change in religion itself'.[84] Opposed by the conservative 'ulama for allegedly spreading 'irreligiousness' among the students, Shibli left Nadwa in 1913. His resignation sparked off the first ever strike by the students of the madrasa, angered by the management's treatment of such a renowned scholar. The strike lasted for almost three months. Shibli spent the rest of his life engaged in other educational projects, managing the English-medium 'National School' that he had earlier established in 1883 and the Dar ul-Musannifin research centre at his hometown of Azamgarh.

Although Deoband and Nadwa emerged as the largest and most influential madrasas in north India at this time, many other madrasas were also established in order to propagate the teachings of particular schools of Islamic thought (*maslak*s). These madrasas saw themselves as defending their own *maslak*s from rival Muslim groups as well as preserving and promoting the Islamic tradition as they variously understood it. Thus, the Ahl-i Hadith set up a chain of madrasas in different parts of the country, although it continued to be looked upon with considerable hostility by most other Muslim groups.[85] In contrast to Deobandi madrasas, these schools did not follow any particular legal school in matters of *fiqh*, but laid greater stress on the Hadith. Yet, they also followed in the main the structure of the *dars-i nizami*. Likewise, the Barelwis set up a number of madrasas in north India, one of whose major functions was to defend their interpretation of Islam from attacks by Muslim reformist groups opposed to popular Sufism. Similarly, the Shi'as set up a number of schools, such as the Madrasat ul-Wa'izin, the Jami'a Nizamiya and the Sultan ul-Madaris in Lucknow, among whose aims was to prepare preachers and religious scholars to defend the Shi'a tradition from attacks by the Sunni 'ulama.

Some madrasas were also established in the years leading up to Partition that sought to foster a broad-based Sunni Muslim unity rising above inter-*maslak* differences. Most of these were founded by activist 'ulama who saw the focus on *taqlid* of the Hanafi *fiqh* in traditional madrasas as having contributed to Muslim decline. They pleaded for the 'ulama to revive the tradition of *ijtihad* so that Islamic jurisprudence could effectively meet the serious challenges posed by the forces of modernity. Many of them went beyond the conservative 'ulama's concern with personal behaviour and advocated a vision of Islam as an all-embracing ideology, providing guidance in all matters of personal as well as collective life.

One such effort was the establishment in 1909 of the Madrasat ul-Islah at Sarai Mir, near Azamgarh, in eastern Uttar Pradesh.[86] Its founder, Allama Hamiduddin Farahi, was a close friend and relative of Shibli Nu'mani.[87] Farahi envisaged his school as a training centre for what he called 'broadminded' 'ulama who would be 'liberated from stagnation and obscurantism' as well as inter-*maslak* rivalries.[88] The madrasa sought to position the Qur'an at the centre of its curriculum, in place of medieval *tafsir* and *fiqh*. Instead of Hanafi *fiqh* it taught what it called 'Islamic *fiqh*' (*fiqh al-islami*), based on the legal opinions of all the four accepted Sunni *mazhab*s, carefully selecting from each what it thought most closely approximated the teachings of the Qur'an and the Hadith. In a marked departure from traditional madrasas, it did not teach any of the medieval Qur'anic commentaries, arguing that all commentaries bore the mark of their age. Instead, students were encouraged to understand the Qur'an directly with the help of dictionaries. It opened its doors to all Muslims, not just Hanafis, and in its early years it even had a few Shi'a students on its rolls.[89]

Islah attempted to depart from the traditional form of madrasa education in yet other respects. It focused on the teaching of particular disciplines rather than of particular books. It sought to improve the teaching of Arabic, and many of its graduates later emerged as renowned scholars of the language. It also made arrangements for the teaching of mathematics, history, geography, English and Hindi. Several leading graduates of the madrasa went on to join the Islamist Jama'at-i Islami, some assuming senior positions in the organization.[90] Yet, as a graduate of the madrasa laments, the school did not live up to the expectations of its founder. While it did depart from 'blind imitation' of traditional *fiqh* and freed its students from inter-*maslak* rivalries, it ended up unwittingly promoting the *taqlid* of Farahi's own understanding of the Qur'an.[91]

Madrasas and the Freedom Struggle

By the end of the nineteenth century a class of English-educated Indians had begun to emerge, demanding representation in the government services. By the second decade of the twentieth century, the Indian National Congress had begun speaking in terms of self-rule, and soon after, of full independence. Seeing the Congress's demand as a ploy to impose 'upper' caste Hindu hegemony, the Muslim League, established in 1906, sought special guarantees for the Muslims and opposed the Congress. The history of Congress–League politicking that finally led to the partition of India has already been extensively written about and need not detain us here. But it is significant to remember that neither the League nor the Congress effectively represented the majority of 'Hindus' and 'Muslims' who, at this time, did not possess the right to vote.

As in the case of the Congress and the Hindu Mahasabha, feudal lords, industrialists and English-educated professionals were disproportionately represented in the leadership of the League. The League was to later emerge as a champion of Muslim nationalism, spearheading the demand for a separate Muslim-majority state of Pakistan. However, as its leader, the London-trained lawyer Muhammad 'Ali Jinnah, repeatedly stressed, Pakistan was to be a secular and democratic state and not one ruled strictly in accordance with the 'ulama's understanding of the *shari'ah*. Jinnah, at least in the early years of his political life, consistently opposed the intrusion of religion into politics. This, in fact, was one of the main reasons for his rift with Gandhi and the Congress. He also often spoke out against the conservative 'ulama, blaming them for the backwardness of the community.

For its part, the Congress under Gandhi actively sought to court various religious leaders, including the Deobandi 'ulama, in its campaigns. Although a significant section of the Deobandis were to closely ally themselves with the Congress, leading Deobandis had begun working for Indian independence much before Gandhi appeared on the scene as a popular leader.

In 1909, Maulana Mahmud ul-Hasan, head of the Deoband madrasa, set up the Jami'at ul-Ansar, an association of Deoband graduates, and deputed one of his most trusted students, a Sikh convert to Islam, Maulana 'Ubaidullah Sinḍhi (1872–1944), to head it. In 1915, Mahmud ul-Hasan directed Sindhi to go to Afghanistan, where he set up a provisional government of free India along with several Indian Hindu and Muslim revolutionaries associated with the Ghadr Party and the Congress. Meanwhile, in 1916, in order to mobilize Turkish support for his programme of an independent India, Mahmud ul-Hasan left for the Hijaz. However, Arab nationalists opposed to Ottoman rule betrayed him to the British who then arrested him and some of his associates in Mecca and imprisoned them in Malta. Soon after his release, Mahmud ul-Hasan issued a *fatwa* supporting the Non-Cooperation Movement launched by the Congress, appealing to Muslims to wholeheartedly participate in it. The *fatwa* was later endorsed by almost 500 'ulama.[92] Soon after, he issued another *fatwa*, declaring it sinful for Muslims to work for the British government.[93] This marked the beginning of a close and long relationship between a major section of the Deobandis and the Congress in the anti-colonial movement.

Following the end of the First World War, Indian Muslim leaders launched the Khilafat Movement seeking to protect the Ottoman Caliphate from attack by the victorious allies and to prevent the holy cities of Mecca and Medina from falling under European control.[94] The Khilafat movement provided a new lease of life to the 'ulama, who had, by this time, been increasingly marginalized by Western-educated Muslims as leaders of the community. An influential section of the Deobandis, fiercely opposed to what they saw as the 'secular', 'irreligious' and 'pro-British' Jinnah and his Muslim League, willingly joined hands with Gandhi, whose religious appeals they could easily identify with. These 'ulama sensed that modernist Muslims and those, many of whom were in the League, who employed Islam as a tool for their own secular interests were a major challenge to their own authority, while Gandhi's willingness to work with them and accept them as 'representatives' of Islam would strengthen their own claims to speak for the Muslim community as a whole.

In 1919 a group of 'ulama, mostly Deobandis, set up the Jami'at ul-'Ulama-i Hind (The Union of the 'Ulama of India). The immediate reason for the formation of the Jami'at was to work to protect the Ottoman Caliphate from the threat of dismemberment at the hands of rival European powers, particularly the British. Jami'at leaders insisted that the Caliphate was an integral part of Islam, linking Muslims all over the world as members of a universal *ummah*. They exhorted Muslims to actively struggle to safeguard the Caliphate, appealing to them to sacrifice their all for what they described as a central pillar of the faith. Some even went to the extent of declaring India under the British to be an 'abode of war', calling for Muslims in government service to quit their jobs and appealing to Muslims in general to migrate to Afghanistan. Khilafat committees were set up all over the country, organized by 'ulama in collaboration with modern educated Muslims. Taking advantage of the growing anti-British sentiment among the 'ulama, Gandhi and other senior Congress leaders lent their support to the Khilafatists, much to the dismay of Jinnah as well as the Barelwi 'ulama who fiercely opposed the movement, principally because of its association with their Deobandi rivals. Soon, Gandhi had emerged as the leader of the Khilafatists, spearheading the cause of the Caliph and insisting that self-rule and the Caliphate were inseparable. Leading Deobandi ʻulama issued a series of *fatwa*s declaring that in worldly matters, such as protecting the Caliphate and freeing India of the British, Muslims were permitted to cooperate with Hindus, provided this did not violate any principles of the *shariʻah*.

The close collaboration between the Deobandi ʻulama and activists from Aligarh in the course of the Khilafat Movement brought Muslim traditionalists and modernists together for the first time. This inevitably resulted in a sharing of views between the two, leading to some creative efforts to bridge the dualism that had developed in the Muslim educational system. Once a sturdy pro-British bastion, Aligarh began resounding with voices calling for independence, and many of its students now spoke the language of pan-Islamism and anti-colonialism. On the other hand, influenced by new links established with Western-educated Muslims in the course of the Khilafat agitation, numerous ʻulama seriously raised the issue of madrasa reform. One outcome of this encounter between Aligarh and Deoband was the establishment in 1920 of the Jamiʻa Millia Islamia in Delhi, inaugurated by the rector of Deoband, Maulana Mahmud ul-Hasan. The Jamiʻa was supported by leading anti-British activists from Aligarh and Deoband, besides senior Congress leaders. It saw itself as playing a major role in preparing a new class of Muslims, educated in both modern as well as traditional Islamic subjects. It was also envisaged as a training ground for activists struggling for India's freedom and for Hindu–Muslim collaboration.[95]

The movement to protect the Caliphate failed miserably, however, after the Turks themselves, under Mustafa Kemal Attaturk, abolished the post of Caliph in 1924 and declared Turkey a republic. Yet, the movement had provided the Deobandi ʻulama access to hitherto unreached Muslim groups all over the country and an opportunity to spread their reformist message to an increasingly wider audience. It also whetted their political appetite, encouraging them to take a more active role in politics, countering the claims of the Muslim League and Western-educated Muslims to be representatives of the community. Consequently, the Deobandis, with some notable exceptions, increasingly moved closer to the Congress. As many Deobandis saw it, the Muslim League's politics were neither 'Islamic' nor in the best interests of the Muslims themselves. Deobandi scholars disputed the League's 'two-nation' theory and what they saw as the irreligiousness of the leaders of the party, particularly Jinnah. The rector of the Deoband madrasa, Maulana Sayyed Husain Ahmad Madani (d. 1957), wrote a lengthy polemical tract targeting the Muslim League, arguing that in Islam nationality (*qaumiyat*) was determined by common homeland and not by religion. He sought sanction for this view from the example of the Prophet, quoting early Islamic history to stress his point.[96] The state set up by the Prophet in Medina, he wrote, gave equal rights to Muslims, Jews and pagan Arabs, and they were all regarded as members of one *ummah* or community. Accordingly, Madani argued, the Hindus and Muslims of India were members of a common nation. Like many of his fellow Deobandis, Madani believed that in a free and united India, Muslims would be able to lead their personal lives in accordance with the *shari'ah*, while also cooperating with people of other faiths in matters of common concern.[97]

This does not mean, however, that the pro-Congress Deobandis accepted the principle of secularism in the sense of a strict division between religion and the state. Although staunch conservatives in matters of religion, they were pragmatists in politics, realizing the impossibility of establishing an Islamic state in India as long as Muslims remained a minority. The immediate task before the Muslims, as they saw it, was to join hands with the Hindus to free the country from British rule. Once India won independence, they believed, Muslims would be able to work for the propagation of Islam, and then, finally, a day might dawn when it could even be possible to establish an Islamic state in the country if the majority of Indians became Muslim. Till such time, they insisted, Muslims must remain content with having their personal affairs governed in accordance with the *shari'ah*, while in other affairs being dutiful citizens of a joint Hindu–Muslim state. Relations between the different communities would be governed by a pact ensuring peaceful and friendly ties to the extent permitted by the *shari'ah*. As long as the other parties abided by the terms of the pact, Muslims would remain loyal citizens of the state and would even defend the country from external Muslim aggression. The free India that the pro-Congress Deobandis envisioned would be a federation of a number of culturally autonomous religious communities. Each community would administer its own internal affairs in accordance with its religious laws. The federal government, which would have adequate Muslim representation, would pass no laws that might seem injurious to the religious interests of any community.

Deobandis thus went on to play a crucial role in the struggle for India's independence as allies of the Congress party. They were not the only 'ulama to support the Congress, however. The renowned reformist *'alim*, Shibli Nu'mani, an ardent supporter of the pan-Islamic cause, also welcomed the Congress and its demand for a broad-based unity among the various religious communities in India. He was critical of the Muslim League for its 'narrowly conceived political base', dismissing it as 'a poor imitation of the House of Lords'.[98] Shibli managed to win the support of some other Nadwi ‘ulama in his opposition to the British. Several Nadwa students joined local Khilafat committees, and Sayyed Sulaiman Nadwi, one of Shibli’s favourite students, went so far as to declare that if Muslims wanted to liberate the Ka‘aba they should liberate India from the British first.[99]

Although the Congress won the support of many leading ‘ulama, there were others that fiercely opposed it. ‘Ulama associated with the Barelwi school declared the Congress to be anti-Muslim. They opposed the Khilafat Movement, supported the British and lent wholehearted support to the Muslim League. Their opposition to the Congress, which they condemned as a ‘Hindu’ organization, seems also to have been impelled by the close links that their rivals, the Deobandis, had established with senior Congress leaders, especially Gandhi. The Ahl-i Hadith and the Shi‘a ‘ulama were divided in their political stances, some supporting the Congress and others the League. For its part, the Jama‘at-i Islami, founded in 1941 by the scholar-activist Sayyed Abul ‘Ala Maududi, opposed the Congress as well as the Muslim League, seeing both as advocating nationalism, which it regarded as wholly ‘un-Islamic’.

*

In August 1947, British India was divided, with the coming into being of the two independent states of India and Pakistan. Partition caused the division of leading madrasas and families of ‘ulama. Several ‘ulama from parts of the country where Muslims were in a minority chose or were forced to migrate to Pakistan. Many others decided to stay on in India, acutely aware of the challenges of living as a threatened minority in a Hindu-dominated country. To the ‘ulama and madrasas in post-1947 India we turn in the chapters that follow.

{3}

Madrasas in Independent India

*Maktab*s and madrasas exist in almost every city, town and village in India where Muslims live. Among poorer Muslim communities they may have no separate buildings, with classes being held inside mosques. Some, such as the Dar ul-Ulum, Deoband, or the Jami'at ul-Ashrafiya, Mubarakpur, may be the size of universities, occupying sprawling campuses and including a number of buildings for classrooms, libraries, hostels, dining halls, guest houses, staff quarters, dispensaries, mosques and *shari'ah* courts. With large domes and graceful arches, often imitations of Mughal architecture, the larger madrasas serve as crucial markers of identity, and as a symbolic claim to space in a country where Muslims are a relatively small and marginalized minority.

Given the size and diversity of India, it is difficult, if not impossible, to generalize about all madrasas in the country. In that sense, it is misleading to speak in terms of *the* Indian madrasa system. Nor can one speak of a 'typical' India madrasa as they vary considerably across regions. For instance, a madrasa in Calicut, Kerala, might have little in common with a madrasa in rural Purnea, Bihar. Different *maslak*s or schools of thought have different approaches to Islamic education, as also different curricula, methods of teaching and organization. To consider all madrasas as identical, and to make conclusions based on this assumption, is misleading.

This chapter examines some aspects of madrasas in contemporary India, looking at such issues as curriculum, methods of teaching, teacher–student relations, sources of finance, organizational patterns, and career opportunities for madrasa students. These issues are discussed based on a broad survey of two categories of madrasas. The first set is what, for want of a better term, could be called 'traditional' madrasas, as in the case of the Dar ul-'Ulum, Deoband, and similar madrasas in northern India. The word 'traditional' is used here with caution, for, in actual fact, no contemporary Indian madrasa can be said to be 'traditional' in the true sense of the term. A 'traditional' madrasa as the term is used here, is one that restricts itself to the teaching of 'religious' subjects and is geared to the training of professional 'ulama. The second type of madrasas that this chapter looks at is the range of Islamic schools in the state of Kerala. They provide interesting points of contrast to the 'traditional' madrasas in many other parts of the country, highlighting the importance of understanding the madrasas in contemporary India as a very diverse phenomenon.

Growth of Madrasas in Post-1947 India

No reliable estimates exist as to the actual number of madrasas in India today.[1] In the absence of a comprehensive survey, conflicting figures are provided by different sources. The problem is further complicated by the fact that different sources use different definitions of what a madrasa is, some confining themselves to higher-level institutions of Islamic learning, while others include *maktab*s as well. Thus, according to the Centre for the Promotion of Science at the Aligarh Muslim University, in 1985 there were 2890 madrasas in the country. A decade later, the Union Minister for Human Resources Development put the figure at 12,000.[2] In 2002 the Union Minister for Home claimed that the number stood at 31,857.[3] In 2003, a leading Muslim paper claimed that there were some 1,25,000 madrasas in India, catering to around 30,00,000 students, and with a combined annual budget of approximately Rs 14 billion.[4]

The sheer numbers of madrasas might appear, at first sight, to be staggering. However, one should be careful not to exaggerate their influence. Given the vast Muslim population in India, estimated in the range of 130 to 150 million, some 30,000 madrasas are not particularly remarkable. Only a small proportion of Muslim students actually study full time in madrasas in order to train as professional 'ulama. The number of Muslims studying in regular schools, both private as well as government, far exceeds the number of madrasa students. The stereotypical image of the average Muslim student as one who dons a pillbox cap and has a scraggly beard, spending long years bent before a low-lying table in a dingy room memorizing ancient texts, to the exclusion of anything else, is thus entirely misplaced.

Yet, it cannot be denied that madrasas continue to play a central role in Muslim community life in India today. Both supporters as well as opponents of the madrasas agree that their number has steadily grown, particularly in recent years. This development cannot be properly understood without taking into account the vexed issue of Muslims living as an increasingly threatened and marginalized minority. The partition of India in 1947 proved to be a major watershed for

Muslims in the subcontinent. More than two million people, Hindus, Muslims, Sikhs, Dalits and others, lost their lives in bloody rioting that erupted in large parts of the country. Many more were expelled from their ancestral homes and forced across the border that now divided the independent states of India and Pakistan. Many Muslims sought refuge in Pakistan fearing Hindu persecution or in search of greener pastures. Millions of other Muslims, mainly from poor, artisan and peasant backgrounds, remained in India. Widespread rioting in the years after partition, in which inevitably Muslims were the major victims, rapidly drove the community into squalid ghettos. For many Muslims, Islam was seen as under grave threat. Hindu 'nationalists' claimed that Muslims were traitors and should be sent off to Pakistan. If they were to stay on in India, they insisted, they would have to effectively renounce their faith and live as 'Muhammadi Hindus', accepting the status of second-class citizens or worse. Only a Hindu, they argued, could be a true Indian, and in the eyes of many Hindus the loyalty of the Muslims to the country was greatly suspect.

Partition had major consequences for many larger madrasas, particularly in north India. The larger madrasas, such as Deoband and Nadwa, remained in India, and Pakistan inherited few of the notable madrasas set up under British rule. Several leading teachers from the madrasas in the north chose or were forced to migrate to Pakistan. In the years immediately after 1947 numerous Indian madrasas witnessed a sharp decline in the number of students, many of whom, prior to partition, hailed from areas that had now become part of Pakistan. Land reform legislation in some provinces soon after independence led to resumption of estates and endowed properties which hit some madrasas particularly severely. The integration into the Indian Union of Muslim princely states such as Hyderabad,

Bhopal and Rampur meant a sharp decline in the income of several madrasas that had earlier depended heavily on Muslim royal largesse. In large parts of north India, properties belonging to madrasas, mosques and Sufi shrines were forcibly taken over by local Hindus or by Hindu migrants from Pakistan. The large-scale flight of Muslim elites to Pakistan meant that many madrasas were now bereft of crucial sources of patronage.

In the years following partition, literacy rates grew, albeit at a slow pace, as government and private schools began to be established in towns and villages. Like other communities, Muslims, too, began taking to modern education, although they lagged far behind most other groups. Several factors were responsible for continued Muslim backwardness in education. There is enough evidence to suggest considerable discrimination against Muslims in matters of educational provision, with proportionately fewer schools being set up by the government in Muslim localities. Urdu, the language of the north Indian Muslim and many Hindu elites and the main vehicle for the transmission of Islamic knowledge in the subcontinent, was rapidly eclipsed by Hindi as the official language of the central and many state governments. Urdu was wrongly denigrated as a 'Muslim' language with 'Pakistani' associations, while Hindi was projected as somehow more 'Indian'. For their part, some 'ulama still viewed 'modern' education as 'un-Islamic', particularly for girls. They were also concerned that the lack of moral education in government schools and the increasing Hinduization of the textbooks would gradually lead to Muslims abandoning their faith. The government did little to set these fears at rest. Rather, over time, school textbooks became increasingly blatant in projecting negative images of Islam and Muslims and in glorifying Brahminical Hinduism. Naturally, this led many Muslims to look upon government schools with suspicion, as part of what some believed to be a grand conspiracy to destroy Islam in India and the separate identity of the Muslims, and as calculated to absorb the Muslims into the Hindu fold.[5] Further, many Muslims saw little point in sending their children for higher education in schools, because pervasive discrimination against Muslims meant that few of them could aspire for jobs in both the public as well as private sectors. For Muslims belonging to artisan and peasant families it was believed to be enough to provide their children with basic literacy, after which they could take to some sort of petty employment.

Over time, however, a small class of modern educated Muslims began to emerge in some pockets, particularly in the south, where Muslim traders still existed in considerable numbers. The Gulf boom attracted large numbers of Muslims, mainly from Kerala, as also smaller numbers from the rest of the country, leading to a certain degree of upward social mobility among some Muslim families. Muslim artisan groups, such as the weavers of Varanasi, the locksmiths of Aligarh and the coppersmiths of Moradabad, experienced a limited improvement in their fortunes with growing demand for their products. However, Muslims struggling to improve their conditions constantly ran the risk of being ruined in bloody pogroms, euphemistically called 'communal riots'. At several places where Muslims had witnessed a degree of economic prosperity that threatened to undermine monopolies hitherto enjoyed by Hindu traders and middlemen, violent attacks resulted in great loss of Muslim life and property, a phenomenon that seems to be accelerating and spreading to newer areas in contemporary India.

Since 1947 the number of madrasas in India has rapidly multiplied. This owes to a complex interplay of several factors. Often, families want to carry on in the tradition of their ancestors and get at least one son, often one of the less bright or promising of them, to become an '*alim*, sending the rest to regular schools. Children suffering from some form of physical disability are often sent to madrasas in the hope that after graduation they would at least be able to support themselves as Qur'an reciters or madrasa teachers. For many Muslims from poor families the madrasas provide the only access to any form of education, and, consequently, the vast majority of madrasa students come from low and lower-middle class backgrounds. At the madrasas poor children receive free education, board and lodging. On graduation they are generally assured of a job, albeit low-paying, as an Imam in a mosque or a teacher in a madrasa or *maktab*.[6] More enterprising graduates can set up madrasas of their own. For Muslims from 'lower' caste families, an '*alim* in the family is often a source of pride, enabling them to claim a higher status in the local social hierarchy. Overall, then, the increasing number of madrasas reflects the growing desire on the part of many Muslims to educate their children and to improve their fortunes in life, and cannot be attributed to an imagined 'global Islamic conspiracy' as is so readily alleged.

As Islamic reformist movements have spread to new areas of the country, critiquing popular 'Hinduistic' customs and appealing to Muslims to abide by the teachings of their faith, increasing numbers of Muslims are today sending their children to madrasas. The widespread perception of Islam and Muslims being under grave threat in India at the hands of Hindu chauvinists and the Indian state has accorded the madrasas the status of defenders of Islamic identity and tradition in the eyes of many. As a Deobandi '*alim* puts it, 'Today, madrasas are the forts of Islam (*islam ke qile*), guaranteeing the existence of the faith, and the future of Islam and Muslim identity in India depends particularly on them.'[7] This widely held conviction serves to mobilize funds and other forms of resources for the madrasa system and to reinforce the claims of the ‘ulama as representatives of Islam and leaders of the community. Owing to the widespread and not entirely misplaced feeling that government schools are deliberately being used to indoctrinate Muslim children in Hinduism and denigrate their faith and history, Muslim organizations are now increasingly turning their attention to setting up *maktab*s and madrasas so that Muslim children can be properly socialized in their faith and traditions.

‘Traditional’ Madrasas in Contemporary India

‘Traditional’ madrasas account for the majority of the madrasas in contemporary India. In contrast to a small, yet growing, number of other madrasas, these schools make very limited provision for the teaching of ‘secular’ subjects. In turn, this has given rise to heated controversies about the usefulness of such schools, leading to considerable debate about curricular reform.

Given the fact that in the majority of cases each ‘traditional’ madrasa is an autonomous institution, there is no single syllabus employed at all the various ‘traditional’ madrasas throughout the country. The managers of each madrasa frame their own syllabus and select the books that are to be taught to their students. The syllabus in most ‘traditional’ madrasas continues to conform to the basic structure and scholarly standards of the *dars-i nizami*. However, in almost all such schools several books of philosophy and logic that were included in the original *dars-i nizami* have been removed. Almost all ‘traditional’ madrasas continue to be affiliated with one of the many rival schools of thought, each claiming to represent the one true

Islamic community and tradition. Hence, the rebuttal of rival *maslaks* still remains a function of most 'traditional' madrasas and is also reflected in the structure of their curricula.[8]

The ways in which influential sections of the Indian 'ulama have approached the vexed problem of the curriculum is well illustrated in the case of the Dar ul-'Ulum Deoband, the most influential 'traditional' madrasa in India today, and probably the largest of its kind in the whole world.[9] There are several hundred smaller madrasas owing affiliation to the Deoband *maslak* in India as well as in Pakistan, Bangladesh and Afghanistan. Twenty-eight different subjects, consisting of a range of 'transmitted' and 'rational' sciences are included in the madrasa's syllabus.[10] These are taught through some 100 books, wholly or in part, in the course of eight years of study.[11]

In 1995 the madrasa adopted a slightly modified syllabus based on a five-year 'Urdu and Farsi' primary course and an eight-year 'Arabic' course, leading first to the '*alim* and then to the *fazil* degree. After the *fazil* level, selected students can go on to specialize in a particular discipline. The structure of these courses is as follows:

Urdu and Persian Course (*Shoba Diniyat Urdu-o-Farsi*)

Basic Level (*Darja Atfal*): Persian alphabet; memorization of the first creed of confession (*kalima*); basic religious beliefs (*aqa'id*); counting till 100; basic written Urdu.

Class 1 (*Darja Avval*): memorization of parts of the Qur'an; memorizing the first three *kalimas*; Urdu grammar; written Urdu; basic religious beliefs and practices; multiplication tables; prayers and ablutions.

Class 2 (*Darja Doum*): memorization of parts of the Qur'an; memorizing five *kalimas*; basic religious beliefs and practices;

Urdu grammar; Hindi alphabet; basic geography; basic mathematics; prayers and ablutions.
Class 3 (*Darja Saum*): memorization of parts of the Qur'an; basic Islamic history; religious beliefs and practices; Urdu grammar; Hindi grammar; Persian; English alphabet; local geography; basic mathematics; memorizing six *kalima*s; prayers and ablutions; methods of supplication (*du'a*) and burial (*janaza*).
Class 4 (*Darja Chaharum*): memorization of parts of the Qur'an; Urdu grammar; Persian literature; Islamic history; religious beliefs and practices; local geography; basic English; Hindi; basic mathematics; basic science.
Class 5 (*Darja Panjam*): Persian literature and grammar; Urdu literature; basic Hindi; basic English; Indian history; history of the founders of the Dar ul-'Ulum, Deoband; geography of India; basic mathematics; basic science; general knowledge.

Arabic Course (*Darja Arabiya*)

Year One (*Sal Avval*): biography of the Prophet; Arabic grammar; recitation of the Qur'an; memorization of parts of the Qur'an.
Year Two (*Sal Daum*): Arabic grammar; *fiqh* (*Qaduri*);[12] logic; *tajwid* (Qur'anic recitation); calligraphy.
Year Three (*Sal Saum*): Arabic grammar; translation (*tarjuma*) of parts of the Qur'an; *fiqh* (*Qaduri*); Hadith; morals and manners (*akhlaq*); logic; *tajwid*; history of the four righteous Caliphs.
Year Four (*Sal Chaharum*): translation of parts of the Qur'an; *fiqh* (*Sharh-i Wiqaya*);[13] principles of *fiqh* (*'usul al-fiqh*); *tajwid*; rhetoric; logic; history of the Ummayyad, Abbasid and Ottoman Caliphs; world and Arabian geography.
Year Five (*Sal Panjam*): translation of the Qur'an; *fiqh*; *'usul*

al-fiqh; *adab*; beliefs (*aqa'id*); *tajwid*; logic; history of the Muslim rulers of India.

Year Six (*Sal Shasham*): Qur'anic commentary (*Jalalayn*);[14] *fiqh* (*Hidaya*); principles of *tafsir* (*'usul-i tafsir*); principles of *fiqh*; *tajwid*; biography of the Prophet; Arabic literature; philosophy.

Year Seven (*Sal Haftam*): Hadith; *fiqh* (*Hidaya*); *aqa'id*; different schools of Islamic law.

Year Eight (*Sal Hashtam*, also called *Daura-i Hadith Sharif*): specialized study of Hadith (Bukhari, Muslim, Tirmidhi, Abu Da'ud, Nisa'i, Ibn Maja, Tahavi, Shama'il Tirmidhi, Muwatta Imam Malik, Muwatta Imam Muhammad).

Specialized Course (*Takmil/Takhsus*)

The following options are available for specialized study after the *fazilat* level, and each year a maximum of twenty-five students are admitted to each branch:

1. *Tafsir* 2. Comparative Religions 3. *Fiqh*
4. Arabic Literature 5. *'Ifta* (delivering *fatwa*s).[15]

The course of study at the Dar ul-'Ulum, Deoband and the other madrasas affiliated to it in the rest of the country still revolves around the teaching of Hanafi *fiqh*. Most of the texts employed in *fiqh* are well over 500 years old, some having been penned more than a thousand years ago. These texts are taught with the help of commentaries and super commentaries and footnotes penned by medieval Hanafi 'ulama. The main text of Hanafi *fiqh*, which is still used in Deoband and other higher-level madrasas in India, is the four-volume *Hidaya*, prepared in the twelfth century by the Central Asian Hanafi *faqih* Shaikh Burhanuddin Abul Hasan 'Ali al-Marghinani (b. 1117). It deals with a variety of subjects, ranging from the rules of ritual worship, alms and pilgrimage to marriage, divorce, inheritance, commercial transactions and punishments, providing detailed guidance on these matters from a strictly Hanafi perspective. Much of its contents deal with issues of specific relevance to the medieval world that have lost their significance today, such as detailed rules for the manumission of slaves and the legal rights of hermaphrodites. It is said to contain a large number of weak (*za'if*) *hadith*, some of which may have been concocted and wrongly attributed to the Prophet.[16] Several 'ulama have, down the ages, committed the entire text of the *Hidaya* to memory, this being seen as a mark of great piety and scholarship.[17] Scores of commentaries and glosses on the *Hidaya* have been written by Indian and other 'ulama. Many of these are still taught at Deoband, as well as 'traditional' madrasas of other *maslak*s in India.

Another major aspect of the course of studies at Deoband and affiliated madrasas is the teaching of *ikhtilafiyat* or the science of disputation, in which students are taught how to rebut other Muslim groups who are seen as 'un-Islamic' and sometimes even as 'enemies of the faith'. Thus, displayed at the entrance to the madrasa at Deoband are students' wall magazines devoted almost entirely to glorifying the Deobandi *maslak* as the only true Muslim group, and labelling Muslim opponents, such as the Jama'at-i Islami, the Ahl-i Hadith, the Barelwis and the Shi'as as heretics. Much of the literature produced by the madrasa is geared to the denunciation (*radd*) of ideological opponents, fellow Muslims as well as Christians and Arya Samajists. Students are trained in the fine art of religious debate (*munazara*) in order to combat rival *maslak*s. Every Thursday evening a grand debate is held in the sprawling Dar ul-Hadith hall, in which students divide themselves into two groups, one representing the Deobandis, and the other, one of their opponents. A heated discussion ensues, and in the end the Deobandi side is, of course, declared victorious, but not before suitably humbling the rival group.

Rebutting other Muslim groups is thus regarded by many madrasa students and teachers as one of their principal tasks. A young student at Deoband, not yet fifteen years of age, describes his mission in life as follows:

> At the madrasa we are taught that our main work, once we graduate, must be to combat un-Islamic ideologies. Now, as far as people who do not call themselves Muslim are concerned we all know where they stand and what they believe, so there is no need to oppose them. But we must combat all those groups that claim to be Muslim but are actually Zionist creations designed to destroy Islam from within. These include the followers of Maududi, Qadianis, the so-called Shi'as, the Barelwis and so on. We have to tell the Muslims to stay away from these people, because they are all agents of the Devil.

In 'traditional' madrasas such as Deoband, 'modern' subjects receive but little attention. As seen in the details of the syllabus, the present five-year 'Urdu and Persian' course at Deoband makes some provision for the teaching of such disciplines as history, geography, general science, and basic English and Hindi. However, these subjects are taught till the level of the fifth grade, and are thereafter completely discontinued in the eight-year *fazil* course. As a result, many students who pass through the five-year primary course receive only a very basic minimum exposure to these subjects, the teaching of which is not taken very seriously, being considered unimportant. Further, not all students who enter the first grade of the *fazil* course actually pass through the primary course. Many of them directly enrol for the course after having memorized the Qur'an at a *maktab*, which means that they would have not studied any of these subjects in their entire educational careers.

The authorities of the madrasa believe that the modicum of teaching of 'worldly' subjects provided in the primary course is sufficient for the needs of their students, whose main concern is expected to be the studying of the texts of the *dars-i nizami* in the form that it has been adapted by Deoband. Thus, the vast library of the madrasa is said to contain almost no books on 'modern' subjects penned by contemporary writers. Students are encouraged to study only the texts written or approved of by the Deobandi 'ulama. Teachers at Deoband are said to frown on their students for reading literature produced by other Muslim groups, fearing that this would weaken their commitment to the Deobandi vision. Some teachers insist that students should not read newspapers and magazines or watch television on the grounds that this might dilute their faith and divert their minds in the direction of worldly affairs. One argument often put forward is that newspapers generally contain tantalizing pictures of women, which might tempt the children away from the path of the faith. Consequently, after they graduate, many Deobandi students know little or no English or Hindi, and often find themselves faced with an alien world of which they have little knowledge.

Student Life in 'Traditional' Madrasas

While in the period of Turkish and Mughal rule in India, as we have seen, madrasas attracted people from all social classes, including ruling elites, today 'traditional' madrasas cater essentially to children of the lower-middle classes, the peasantry and the poor, albeit with significant exceptions. This shift in student composition owes largely to the fact that education in a 'traditional' madrasa is no longer seen as providing its students with skills needed for a lucrative occupation. Well-off Muslims might send their children to a part-time *maktab* as well as a regular school, or, more commonly, might arrange for an '*alim* to come to their homes to teach them the Qur'an, the Islamic rituals and Urdu, but few send them to full-time *maktab*s or madrasas. However, some of the larger madrasas, such as the Nadwat ul-'Ulama, Lucknow, and the Jami'at ul-Falah and Madrasat ul-Islah in Azamgarh where there is some arrangement for the teaching of 'modern' subjects as well, do have a small, yet significant, number of students from fairly prosperous families engaged in trade or government service. Yet, it is important not to exaggerate the rigid dualism that is seen as characterizing Muslim education, setting the madrasa neatly apart from the 'modern' school. In actual practice, many families who send their children to 'traditional' madrasas do have children studying in a modern school as well. It is common for families to send one of their sons to a madrasa and the rest to regular schools. Some families known for their Islamic scholarship also carry on in an ancestral tradition by having at least one son trained as an '*alim*, while the others are educated in schools and colleges. Often, 'ulama teaching at 'traditional' madrasas send their own sons to regular schools and even to universities.

Students studying at 'traditional' madrasas generally come from families that follow the particular *maslak* that the madrasa represents. This is because each *maslak*, as we have seen earlier, regards as one of its principal tasks the repudiation of its rivals, and therefore it is unlikely that parents would wish their children to study under 'ulama opposed to their own *maslak*. However, in the case of several madrasas that are not officially affiliated to any *maslak*, and seek instead to bridge the divide between the different *maslak*s, students may come from families associated with various *maslak*s. Smaller madrasas often attract students from towns and villages in their vicinity, and once they graduate they are encouraged to enrol in higher-level madrasas elsewhere. In the larger madrasas such as Deoband, students are drawn from various parts of India. In this way, these institutions play a crucial role in promoting and sustaining a pan-Indian Islamic tradition based on a set of classical texts, reverence for the 'ulama of their particular *maslak*, and commitment to a specific understanding of Islam. In this sense, the madrasa helps promote a sense of Muslim unity and community identity that transcends local and regional barriers, while at the same time reproducing internal divisions based on differences of *maslak*.

Admission to a 'traditional' madrasa is relatively informal. While some have entrance examinations and fixed quotas at each level, others are more flexible. Larger madrasas have specific dates for application for admission, usually soon after the fasting month of Ramzan. Applications are invited through advertisements placed in Urdu newspapers and magazines, and through leaflets and wall posters. Smaller madrasas generally have less formal admission procedures and students can often join at any time of the year. They may not be able to afford to issue advertisements, in which case news of admissions is spread simply by word of mouth. Most madrasas have somewhat open admission policies with no rigid entrance requirements. Madrasas such as Deoband charge no fees from their students for their education, but students from relatively well-off families are expected to make some contribution, whether in cash or kind, towards their board and lodging expenses. Children from poorer families are, in addition to free education, also provided food, hostel accommodation and books free of cost, and, if the resources of the madrasa permit, might also receive a monthly stipend, a medical allowance and clothes.

Student life in 'traditional' madrasas is closely regulated and students are expected to faithfully observe detailed rules of conduct or *adab*. Western clothes are frowned upon, and students must wear what is seen as 'Islamic' dress—a long *kurta* and loose pyjamas and skullcap. Students are expected to grow their beards when they come of age, in imitation of the Prophet. Violation of the dress code inevitably results in punishment or even expulsion from the madrasa. Students are encouraged to abide as closely as possible to the Prophetic model in their own lives, even eating, drinking, laughing and sleeping as he did. Likewise, they are expected to spend much time in prayer and remembrance of God (*zikr*).

This is, however, as far as theory goes, with elaborate rules detailing normative conduct being spelled out in manuals and tracts which students are often expected to read. In actual practice, however, conditions might be remarkably different. Thus, the 'ulama often complain of what they see as the rapidly declining moral, spiritual and intellectual standards of their students. As one '*alim* writes, echoing the views of many of his colleagues, most madrasa students actually lack commitment to their studies and a desire to work for the 'cause of Islam'. Instead, like students in regular schools and colleges, many of them are only concerned with 'acquiring money and fame'. This trend, he laments, has been greatly exacerbated by the new opportunities for employment available in the Arab world, leading to a tremendous brain drain, especially of the brightest madrasa graduates, leaving less intelligent students or those from poorer families to staff the madrasas. This, in turn, has led to a further decline in madrasa standards. He claims that the vast majority of madrasa students 'do not actually follow the rules of Islam', and, somewhat exaggeratedly, argues that in fact they 'lose their respect for religious values and laws'. The fault is not their own entirely, however. Teachers, he says, show little interest in the spiritual and moral training of their students, looking upon their work as simply a job and not as a divine mission.[18]

Graduates of 'traditional' madrasas take up a range of occupations. Many go on to teach in their own or another madrasa, or might set up one of their own. They might train to become *mufti*s or work as *qazi*s in *shar'iah* panchayats or else work as specialists in various Islamic organizations. Some might join their family business or set up a small shop or a Unani medicine clinic. Even after they graduate from the madrasa, students often maintain some sort of link with their alma mater. They might return to their school to teach, or else teach in another madrasa belonging to the same *maslak*. They might also, after returning to their homes, encourage boys in their own villages or towns to enrol in the madrasa where they studied or collect funds to support it. Some of the larger madrasas have formal old boys' associations which organize regular meetings and projects to expand or improve the facilities in their madrasas.

Teachers

In almost all 'traditional' madrasas, teachers (*ustad*s) are appointed through personal networks. Almost without exception, teachers at a particular madrasa belong to the particular *maslak* with which the madrasa is affiliated, thus reinforcing the madrasa's own identity as a representative of a particular school of thought. Few madrasas have any trained teachers. Generally, graduates are appointed as teachers after completing the *'alim* or *fazil* course, without having undergone any specialized training that the profession of teaching demands in 'modern' schools. Salaries vary, from Rs 500 a month in smaller towns and villages to Rs 5000 for a senior teacher in a large madrasa. According to one estimate, the average monthly income of a madrasa teacher is roughly Rs 1600.[19] Given their meagre salaries, many teachers are forced to supplement their income through other means, such as giving tuitions, lecturing in religious meetings (*wa'az*), preparing amulets (*ta'wiz*), or working as commission agents to collect donations for madrasas. Madrasas are not governed by any laws for employing or dismissing their teachers, who can be dismissed at will. Often, personal clashes between the management of the madrasa and a teacher can lead to the latter losing his job without notice. This naturally acts to promote a rigid conformity and stifle all dissent.[20] The poor service conditions and the low salaries means that many madrasas fail to attract the best teachers, having to remain content with mediocre 'ulama who are unable to obtain any other form of gainful employment. It is also often alleged that managers of several madrasas deliberately do not appoint good teachers for fear that they might challenge their authority. Many madrasa teachers are said to feel resentful of the high-handedness of the managers of madrasas but are forced to remain silent. As one writer angrily protests in the columns of the Urdu daily *Qaumi Awaz*:

> Agricultural and *bidi* workers have a minimum wage set by the government, but why don't madrasa teachers, although imparting education is the most valuable service one can render to the community? Religion does not permit the sort of exploitation that madrasa teachers have to suffer. Their meagre salaries are a

> violation of human rights. The relation between the madrasa managers and teachers now resembles that between mill owners and labourers.[21]

In a similar vein, three Muslims, in a joint letter published in the same paper, appealed to the government to take action against madrasas that continued to 'exploit' their teachers. Painting a pathetic picture of the situation of teachers in many madrasas, they explained:

> They are made to work like animals, in return for which they receive a measly 400 to 500 rupees a month. They force them to teach from 6 a.m. till 11 p.m., with only an hour's break. They make them go around the streets collecting donations for the madrasa, in the process having to suffer the taunts of people. They interfere in the teachers' personal lives, asking them why they send their children to modern schools and universities and rebuking them for this; scolding them for allowing their wives to go out shopping; admonishing them for keeping televisions at home and warning them to choose between all this and working at the madrasa.

Appealing to the government to pass a law fixing a basic minimum salary for madrasa teachers, they argued:

> It is not that the madrasas lack money, because the community liberally finances them. However, the managers generally use the money for their own comfort, or spend it on useless things like grand buildings. There should also be a proper, fixed time schedule for their work. A law should be passed making it compulsory for all madrasas to have unions of employees. The managers of the madrasas are bound to be opposed to this and they would accuse the government of interfering in minority-run institutions, in order to protect their own hegemony. However, the employees of the madrasa would fully support the government [if it did so].[22]

The relationship between teachers and students in 'traditional' madrasas is generally authoritarian, while at the same time being deeply personal, somewhat like between a father and son. It also often resembles the hierarchical yet close bond between a spiritual preceptor and his disciples. The teacher is considered to be a model for the student to emulate, faithfully representing the tradition established by the pious elders (*buzurg*s). Students are taught to hold their teachers in awe and reverence, for through them they acquire the knowledge that they believe holds the key to their salvation in this world and the next. Intricate rules of proper conduct governing relations between teachers and students are elaborated upon in special texts on madrasa pedagogy which are often part of the madrasa syllabus. Students even serve their teachers in their homes, performing domestic chores for them, to the extent of washing their clothes and massaging their tired bodies. In turn, teachers are expected to treat their students as their own children. In practice, however, relations between madrasa teachers and students can often be excessively hierarchical and even exploitative. Teachers favour some students, including their own relatives, over others, rewarding them with good grades or jobs even if they are not truly deserving. Personal, family, caste and ethnic factors all play a role in this. Cases of sexual abuse of students by their teachers are not unknown, despite the Islamic abhorrence of homosexuality. A former madrasa student describes the relations between students and teachers in many madrasas:

> In many madrasas teachers really love the students and look after them as their own sons. However, other teachers often treat students as their personal servants, and act like petty dictators. For every small thing they expect students to come and bow and scrape before them. They insist on controlling every act of the

students, even what they think! If they come to know that a student is reading a book by an '*alim* of another *maslak*, leave alone of another religion, they lose their tempers and sometimes even expel the student from the madrasa.

Methods of Teaching

Teaching methods have remained largely unchanged over the centuries in most 'traditional' madrasas. Typically, the teacher sits on a low platform, reclining against a bolster, while the students sit below him on mats spread on the floor, placing their books on low tables in front of them. The teacher reads out from the text or else asks the students to take turns in reading aloud, and then explains the content of the portions read out. The text is usually in Arabic, and the teacher comments and elaborates on it in Urdu. While questioning is not frowned upon, students rarely do so, and debate and dissent are certainly not encouraged. Blackboards are rarely used, except in junior classes. The traditional pedagogical methods and the distinct absence of a culture of criticism and questioning, added to the fact that almost all the books used in the madrasa are in Arabic in which few students are fluent, means that, as one '*alim* puts it, 'Most madrasa students have little enthusiasm for intellectual research and hardly any have expertise in any discipline.'[23] Rote learning is generally the rule in most madrasas. In the sections devoted to *hifz* or memorization of the Qur'an this is natural, but in other departments as well students are made to commit to memory large portions of their lessons, including the sayings attributed to the Prophet and leading 'ulama. They are also encouraged to memorize entire speeches on a range of subjects that they occasionally deliver to public congregations or to gatherings at mosques. Some higher-level madrasas have begun arranging for extension lectures to which they invite noted Islamic scholars or Muslim lecturers in colleges or universities to speak to their students on a range of issues of contemporary concern. In larger madrasas, such as Nadwa and Deoband, students' organizations, carefully controlled by the management, arrange for weekly lectures and debates among the students themselves, essay writing competitions, and publication of annual students' journals and monthly wall magazines, for which students are encouraged to write.

Management of the Madrasa

Larger 'traditional' madrasas such as Deoband are run by an elaborate hierarchy of functionaries. At the apex is the *sarparast* (chancellor), who is also often the founder (*bani*) of the madrasa or his successor, in which case he is generally a direct descendant of the founder. Below him is the *muhtamim* (vice-chancellor), who is followed by the dean (*sadr mudarris*) and teachers of various subjects. The seniormost teacher is the *shaikh ul-hadith*, who teaches the books of Hadith to senior students. The rector of the madrasa is assisted in his work by a committee of elders (*shur'a*), consisting of senior 'ulama and teachers and, sometimes, of notable Muslims including rich traders, philanthropists and important donors. The members of the *shur'a* are generally appointed by the senior 'ulama, which, leaves considerable room for nepotism. Although in theory staff appointments are made strictly on the basis of merit and piety, often the management of madrasas is in the hands of the families of their founders. In many cases, the founder of the madrasa appoints his own son or close male relative as his successor. Likewise, madrasa rectors often select their own relatives or other members of their own caste as senior teachers. Thus, many madrasas come to be seen as family ventures, with plum posts and access to funds being limited to a narrow circle of friends and relatives, many of whom may not have the religious or intellectual skills needed for the important posts that they handle.

In theory, elaborate rules of *adab* govern the management of the madrasa, and all decisions are supposed to be taken through discussion, consensus and in accordance with Islamic principles. In practice, however, things might be very different. According to a Nadwi '*alim*, himself the founder and manager of a leading madrasa in Azamgarh, most madrasas today have become like any ordinary business, and their managers are no different from commercial entrepreneurs. For many of those in control of the madrasas, they are simply a means for advancing their own personal, material and political interests, for which they are willing to use 'every acceptable and unacceptable means'. 'Instead of looking towards the true giver of wealth [God],' he complains, 'they seek the favour of wealthy donors.'[24] He accuses them of generally lacking in piety and 'bereft of any great ideals', so much so that they send their own sons to 'modern' schools to study instead of enrolling them in their own madrasas, regarding this as 'a source of great pride'. Because of their obsession with 'power and wealth', many madrasas, he claims, have degenerated into dens of corruption, nepotism and dirty politics.[25]

Madrasa Finances

'Traditional' madrasas rely on a variety of sources to meet their expenses. The vast majority depend on local funds which are generated from within the community. Many madrasas have land or property endowed to them as *waqf*s, from which they earn some income. Appeals are regularly issued by madrasa authorities to Muslims to contribute in cash or kind to the madrasa as a religious duty, in the form of *zakat* or *sadqa*. Such appeals appear in the publications of the madrasas, in posters put up on boards outside mosques and on walls in Muslim localities, and in advertisements placed in newspapers and magazines. After the festival of Bakra-i Eid, students are sometimes sent out to the houses of local Muslims to collect the skins of slaughtered animals (*charam qurbani*), which are then auctioned to leather merchants and the money given to the madrasa. Pious believers often make donations to madrasas in kind. Thus, a man might construct a room in a madrasa or donate a fan or cooler in memory of a deceased relative. A peasant family might contribute a sack of wheat after the harvest. Poor Muslims might form a committee in their localities and contribute a small jar of rice every day to a common fund which is then sent to the madrasa every week. A major responsibility of the staff of many madrasas is to arrange for sufficient funds for covering their expenses. In smaller madrasas, teachers and even students are sent to neighbouring towns and villages to collect donations in cash as well as in kind, particularly in the holy month of Ramzan. In some madrasas teachers' salaries are provided out of the donations for the madrasa that they themselves manage to collect.[26] Larger madrasas sometimes appoint special staff, called *vakil*s or *safir*s (lit. ambassadors), whose sole responsibility is to collect funds from the general public. This they often do on a commission basis, although some madrasas pay their agents fixed salaries.

Some larger madrasas with international contacts receive funds from generous donors from Arab states, both expatriate Indians as well as locals. Contrary to widely held assumptions of petrodollars flowing in to finance madrasas all over the country, in actual fact relatively few madrasas receive foreign money.[27] Many such madrasas have the appropriate government licences and permission from the state authorities to receive money from abroad, but some others are said to rely on what are technically illegal means, such as the *hawala* network. The largest beneficiaries of Arab largesse are probably the madrasas associated with the Ahl-i Hadith school, who share a similar understanding of Islam with the 'Wahhabis' of Saudi Arabia. Access to Arab money has led in some places to fierce competition between rival groups of 'ulama who have contacts with foreign benefactors, further exacerbating already deeply rooted inter-*maslak* conflicts.[28]

Foreign funds to Muslim institutions, as indeed to institutions run by Hindus and Christians for that matter, have opened the doors to corruption. Thus, according to one '*alim* who chooses to remain anonymous, a report was received by an Arab embassy in Delhi claiming that there were 114 madrasas in Deoband, while actually the town boasts of no more than four. The rest, he says, exist simply on paper for the purposes of attracting foreign money. Likewise, he says, some unscrupulous managers of madrasas pocket a sizeable portion of the money that they receive from foreign donors, spending only a little on the madrasas and their students. A Muslim advocate, writing in the columns of a leading Urdu daily, argues that certain wealthy Arab states are now funding madrasas and other Muslim institutions in poor countries, including India, in order to pursue their own political interests. Taking advantage of this, he writes, many Indian 'ulama have set up their own madrasas, and this has emerged as a virtual 'industry' in itself, attracting large sums of money from abroad. He goes on to claim:

> Any clever person who looks like a *maulvi*, and who knows some Islamic terms and can pronounce some difficult Arabic words,

> sets up his own madrasa and then dispatches commission agents to collect donations. During Ramzan they travel to Arab countries to collect money themselves. In Saharanpur town alone there are three madrasas whose principals did not study at any school or madrasa and are not trained 'ulama, but who have now become very rich, running madrasas of their own. They travel abroad every Ramzan and collect petrodollars in the name of the poor Muslim masses.[29]

In a similar vein, another Muslim critic of the madrasas, in an article titled 'Madrasas Have Become Profitable Business Centres', claims:

> Many madrasas are set up by racketeers who collect money from the community in the name of serving the 'guests of the Prophet', but provide the students with a very low standard of education and very limited facilities. They have very few trained teachers [. . .] They claim that they provide the students with free clothes and food, but this is often a lie. Students are often treated worse than animals and are sometimes used as beggars in order to procure money from the community, which the managers themselves pocket. Some Muslims say that the government must step in and ensure that the madrasas are regulated by the Children's Welfare Act and must punish offenders. Some madrasas are, in actual fact, like shops and factories and are a mafia running in the name of religion.[30]

Such views are surprisingly widely shared, even by several 'ulama themselves. For instance, Waris Mazhari, editor of the official organ of the old boys' association of the Dar ul-'Ulum, Deoband, argues that the system of collecting donations from the public is being widely misused:

> Many donors think that they are obliging those who ask for money [for the madrasas]. Those who take money from them lose their self-respect or sometimes do not even bother to see if

> the money they take is rightful (*ja'iz*) or not. Sometimes, even if they know that the money has been wrongly earned (*haram*), they take it. Many irreligious Muslims give them money simply to earn merit in the hereafter, or for worldly aims, and give it in a way that is insulting to the recipient. Today, there's fierce competition to collect donations for madrasas and religious projects, using strategies used by traders to attract customers [. . .] This goes against the tradition of our forebears, who relied only on God (*tawakkul*), but today people make pilgrimages to the houses of the rich to win their favour and flatter them. All this causes the 'ulama to fall in the eyes of the public.[31]

Other Activities of the Madrasa

The madrasa is not simply an educational institution, and the work of the 'ulama who serve there is not limited to teaching their students. Madrasas are linked to the wider community through a complex web of ties, playing a variety of important functions. A major role of the madrasa is to provide guidance to the general Muslim public. 'Ulama connected with the madrasas closely interact with Muslims outside the madrasa in their capacity as specialists in Islamic law and theology. They are regularly invited to preside over community functions and their names often figure on the boards of various community organizations. They might be requested to solemnize weddings and lead prayers during important festivals, marriages and burials. They might travel, along with teams of students, to nearby towns and villages, instructing Muslims in matters of faith and ritual.

A particularly important function of many madrasas is to deliver *fatwa*s in response to specific requests from the public. Several madrasas have arrangements for separate *dar ul-'ifta*s, offices where resident *mufti*s and higher-level students training under them deliver *fatwa*s. Requests for *fatwa*s come from all over the country and even abroad. Generally, they deal with questions related to marriage, divorce and inheritance, or the proper methods of performing various rituals, seeking proper 'Islamic' solutions. Very rarely, requests for *fatwa*s might seek advice on which candidate or political party to vote for. Sometimes, dramatic events involving Muslims occasion a flurry of *fatwa*s, such as those delivered by 'ulama of different madrasas in 2001 following the American attacks on Afghanistan, declaring it forbidden for Muslims to purchase American products. *Fatwa*s are given free, and are generally sent by post or else delivered personally. They are not binding, though for many Muslims they carry great prestige as authoritative statements claiming to represent the 'authentic' Islamic position on a particular matter. Often, however, if one is not satisfied with a particular *fatwa*, one can turn to another *mufti* to give a more favourable opinion, based on different methods of legal reasoning and often on different legal sources. Indeed, instances of purchasing a *fatwa* in one's favour through ingenious interpretations of the *shari'ah* are not unknown. Some madrasas regularly publish their collections of *fatwa*s in the form of voluminous compendia, which are then made available for sale to the general Muslim public.

In some of the larger madrasas special courts or *dar ul-qaza*s exist, where 'ulama handle cases in accordance with their own understanding of Islamic jurisprudence. Generally, these cases deal with issues related to divorce and inheritance, but the judgements delivered are not legally binding. *Shari'ah* courts often represent a cheaper and more expeditious form of justice than the regular Indian courts, where litigation is often expensive and long drawn out. Repeatedly stressed in the writings of the 'ulama, who favour such courts, is the need for

Muslims to have their personal disputes judged, as far as possible, by Muslim judges and in accordance with Islamic law, instead of by non-Muslim judges in what are sometimes seen as 'un-Islamic' courts.

Another important role of the madrasas is the publication of Islamic literature. Indian 'ulama have written on a range of subjects and many among them are widely read abroad as well. Several leading 'ulama combine teaching with literary pursuits, and some are credited with literally hundreds of works. Some madrasas bring out regular religious magazines that enjoy a wide circulation among the general public, while still others have separate publication departments, and publish books in a number of languages, including Arabic, Urdu, English, Hindi and various vernacular languages. Larger madrasas even have their own printing presses and, now, also websites. Through their writings, the 'ulama of the madrasas play an important role in the preservation of the Urdu language which is now largely bereft of state patronage and increasingly abandoned by Muslims themselves.

Madrasas and Arabic Colleges in Contemporary Kerala

The system of Islamic education in Kerala is in contrast to its counterparts elsewhere in India. India's first contact with Islam was in Kerala, where for centuries before the rise of Islam Arab traders visited local ports to trade. Legend has it that a group of Muhammad's companions visited Kerala on their way back from a pilgrimage to Adam's Peak in Ceylon, where Adam is said to have lived. Just then, it is said, Cheruman Perumal, the Chera ruler of the principality of Kodangallur, or Cranganore, in coastal Kerala, witnessed a miraculous occurrence, the sudden splitting of the moon. The visiting Arab traders explained to the king that the miracle was a sign that a prophet had been sent by God to Arabia. Soon after, Cheruman Perumal travelled to Arabia and accepted Islam. On his way back to India he died at the port of Zafar in Yemen, where his tomb later became a popular centre of pilgrimage. On his deathbed he is said to have authorized some of his Arab companions to go back to his kingdom to spread Islam. Accordingly, a group of Arabs led by Malik bin Dinar and Malik bin Habib arrived in north Kerala and set up several mosques there. The historical veracity of the story is disputable, although Muslim tradition does speak of an 'Indian king' who presented Muhammad with a bottle of pickle as a gift.[32] Whatever the truth of the story may be, ample evidence exists of Muslim merchants from Arabia settling along the Malabar coast not long after the Prophet's death, where they were welcomed by local kings for the valuable role that they played in the lucrative foreign trade. It was largely through the peaceful missionary efforts of Arab merchants that Islam spread in the region, particularly among the oppressed 'low' castes. Today, Muslims account for around a fourth of Kerala's population.

Traditional Islamic education in Kerala, like elsewhere, was largely mosque based. Students would gather in learning circles or *othupally*s to read a text or a set of texts from a particular teacher. The *othupally* system was almost entirely based on oral learning, and often students were not able to write despite several years of study. The curriculum originally consisted of a range of disciplines, including the 'transmitted' sciences as well as subjects like geometry, mathematics, astronomy, logic, history and medicine. Later, however, it was largely reduced to the Qur'an, Hadith and *fiqh*.

The early twentieth century witnessed the emergence of a number of powerful reformist movements among the Muslims in Kerala, and one of their aims was the reform of the Islamic education system. One of the pioneers in the field of Islamic educational reform in Kerala was Moulavi Chalilakath Munmuhammad Haji. In 1909 he was appointed headmaster of the Tanmiyath ul-'Ulum madrasa at Vazhakkad in British-ruled Malabar in north Kerala. He renamed the madrasa the Dar ul-'Ulum Arabic College, seeking to turn it into a modern institution for the teaching of both Islamic as well as modern subjects. As the new name of the institution suggests, it was sought to be modelled on the system of colleges that British rule had brought about in its wake. The Haji arranged for the preparation of textbooks for the new subjects and also introduced the use of tables, chairs and blackboards in the classrooms, a radical innovation for his times. Several graduates of the college went on to launch similar experiments in other parts of Malabar. At roughly the same time, efforts to reform the traditional *othupally* system were launched in southern Kerala. Vakkam Muhammad 'Abdul Qadir Moulavi (1873–1932) established a chain of modern madrasas in the princely state of Travancore and also arranged for government schools to teach Arabic to Muslim students. Likewise, in Cochin, Sanaullah Makti Thangal and Shaikh Muhammad Mahin Thangal opened a number of schools where Islamic subjects were taught along with modern disciplines. The work of these reformers was carried further with the establishment of organizations to reform the traditional Muslim educational system, including the Malabar Muslim Educational Association (1911), the Lajnat ul-Muhammadiya Sangham (1915), the Muslim Mahajana Sabha (1920), the Kerala Aikya Sangham (1922), the Kerala Jami'at ul-'Ulama (1924) and the Hidayat ul-Muslimin Sangham.

A central message of these reformist movements was that

Muslims must study the Qur'an for themselves, rather than be dependent on a professional class of religious specialists. They argued that the Qur'an was a book of divine instruction that must be properly understood by every Muslim. It was not, they stressed, a book of esoteric mantras to be chanted or simply a monopoly of the professional 'ulama, as was then widely believed. Naturally, the conservative 'ulama saw in the reformist project a major threat to their position as religious leaders. The reformists' bitter critique of popular customs associated with the cults of the Sufis and their advocacy of *ijtihad* also directly undermined the authority of many 'ulama who were quick to brand the reformists as 'anti-Islamic' Wahhabis. At several places reformist Muslims were socially boycotted, and some conservative 'ulama even went to the extent of issuing *fatwa*s of infidelity against them, discouraging marriages with them and even denying them the right to be buried in Muslim graveyards. Yet, the reformist cause gradually began to gather in strength, so much so that, not long after, the conservatives started to establish similar educational centres to meet the reformist challenge, setting up their own organization, the Samastha Kerala Jami'at ul-Ulama, for the purpose.

Interestingly, one of the important causes for the success of the reformists was the support that some of them received from the British in Malabar and the Hindu princely states of Travancore and Cochin in southern Kerala. In 1904, the British colonial administration deployed some *mullah*s from traditional *othupally*s to teach Arabic in selected government schools in Malabar. Later, the colonial authorities set up a few Muslim high schools in the region, where facilities were provided for the teaching of Arabic and Islam. Shortly after, in 1914, the government of Travancore began employing Qur'anic and Arabic teachers in several primary and high schools in the state and appointed a Mohammedan inspector of schools to supervise their work. The government later constituted an Arabic Examination Board which was responsible for the training of the teachers and for preparing a fixed syllabus and textbooks for the schools. In 1920 the government of Cochin began appointing Arabic teachers in schools with a large number of Muslim students. The introduction of Arabic and Islamic education in the government schools in Kerala, in both the areas under British and princely rule, thus played a major role in helping to bridge the divide between the *othupally* and the modern systems of education.

In the post-1947 period Arabic was introduced in several more government schools. In 1957, a year after the merger of Malabar, Cochin and Travancore into the newly created state of Kerala, Arabic was introduced in seventeen additional government high schools in the state. In 1958 Arabic began to be taught in primary government schools in Malabar, where, unlike Travancore and Cochin, it had earlier been taught only at the high-school level. Today, there are an estimated 6000 Arabic teachers working in government schools all over Kerala, with some 500,000 students, mostly Muslims, learning the language. The State Council of Educational Research and Training and the Directorate of Public Instruction both have separate sections to supervise Arabic education in government schools in the state. Expert committees appointed by the state government, consisting of leading Arabic scholars, have prepared modern textbooks for the teaching of Arabic, and these are regularly updated.

At the higher levels of education, too, the government has worked closely with Muslim organizations to reform the system of Arabic teaching. Today, the universities of Calicut (Kozhikode) and Cannanore (Kannur) have eleven affiliated

Arabic colleges, almost all located in the Malabar region, that provide facilities for higher-level Arabic learning. Several Arabic colleges are coeducational and it is not uncommon to find women teaching male students. They offer a five-year *afzal ul-'ulama* degree, for which the basic qualification is completion of high school. Some of them also have facilities for a two-year, post-*afzal ul-'ulama* course. The curriculum focuses on Arabic grammar and literature, along with general Islamic studies. Many Arabic colleges now have computer departments as well as a range of extra-curricular activities, including cultural programmes and social work conducted through local units of the National Service Scheme. In 1980, the syllabus was considerably restructured and modernized and English was made compulsory at all levels. Since the syllabus is set by an expert committee appointed by the state government, it is free of intra-sectarian polemics and disputations that are so central to the madrasa system in north India.

Besides the affiliated Arabic colleges, where staff salaries are paid for by the state, there are a large number of other privately run and funded colleges for the study of Arabic and Islamic studies. They are independent in setting their own syllabus, but they generally follow the curriculum prescribed for the *afzal ul-'ulama* degree by the universities of Calicut and Cannanore. In addition, they teach various Islamic disciplines such as Islamic law and Qur'anic commentary, which are either not taught at all or else receive little attention in the *afzal ul-'ulama* course. These colleges have their own system of examinations, but encourage their students to appear as private candidates for the *afzal ul-'ulama* degree as well.

Government recognition of the *afzal-ul-'ulama* degree has worked to help integrate the system of Islamic and Arabic education in the state with the 'mainstream'. In 1980, this course was accepted at par with a regular BA, and the post-*afzal ul-'ulama* with an MA. This has helped increase the number of occupations that graduates can aspire for. Graduates of Arabic colleges in Kerala are qualified to appear for a range of examinations for various government jobs or to go in for higher education in regular universities. Many graduates now work as translators and office workers in Arab countries, and several are studying or teaching abroad. A large number are also employed as Arabic teachers in government schools.[33]

Kerala's system of higher Arabic education is the most well organized in the country today. So, too, is its system of madrasa education. Full-time madrasas, such as in north India, are today a rarity in Kerala, although they are still to be found among 'traditionalist' groups, labelled as 'Sunnis' in popular parlance. What are called madrasas in Kerala correspond to the *maktab*s in the north. Students, both boys and girls, attend a madrasa for two hours daily, early in the morning or late in the evening, which allows them to study at regular school as well. Far from being discouraged to study at regular schools in addition to the madrasa, they are encouraged to do so in the belief that all forms of legitimate education are 'Islamic'. This has made for a close integration of traditional and modern education in Kerala unparalleled in the rest of India.

In contrast to madrasas in much of India, most Kerala madrasas are affiliated to and run by centralized organizations, which has made for a uniformity of standards and more efficient management. The most important of these organizations are the Kerala Nadwat ul-Mujahidin, the Jama'at-i Islami and the Samastha Kerala Sunni Jami'at ul-'Ulama. The Nadwat ul-Mujahidin corresponds to the Ahl-i Hadith of north India. They do not recognize any of the schools of *fiqh* as binding. They argue that one should follow only the Qur'an and the

Hadith, and if the schools of *fiqh* diverge on any matter from these two primary sources they are to be rejected. They are also opposed to popular customs that they see as having no sanction in the *shari'ah*. The Jama'at-i Islami shares a broadly similar orientation, although, unlike the Nadwat ul-Mujahidin, it has a clearly political orientation and sees the Islamic state as an essential pillar of Islam. Those who are known as the 'Sunnis' in Kerala, that is, generally speaking, Muslims not affiliated to either the Nadwat ul-Mujahidin or the Jama'at-i Islami, insist on the need for strict compliance with the schools of *fiqh* which in the case of most Muslims in Kerala, is the Shafi'i school.

The Nadwat ul-Mujahidin, now divided into two rival factions, the Jama'at-i Islami and the various groups of 'Sunnis', have their own Islamic education boards to administer the madrasas under their control. In 2003 it was estimated that the Nadwat ul-Mujahidin's Madrasa Vidyabhyasa Board administered some 500 madrasas, the Jama'at-i Islami's Majlis ut-Ta'lim al-Islami about 200, the Samastha Kerala Islam Matha Vidyabhyasa Board of the 'Sunnis' roughly 6000, and the Sunni Dakshina Kerala Jami'at ul-'Ulama some 1000.[34] Generally, a local community owing affiliation to one of these various groups decides to set up a madrasa and approaches the concerned education board for permission. The community provides a small building for the purpose and collects money to pay for a teacher. The education board then sends an inspector, and after it approves of the scheme formally affiliates the madrasa to it. Each board has a fixed curriculum and set of textbooks specially prepared for the different grades, and these are sent to the affiliated madrasas. They consist of lessons in Arabic and basic Islamic studies, reflecting the particular understanding of Islam of the school of thought with which the madrasa is affiliated. By the time the students pass the final grade they have a sound grounding in the faith and a good understanding of elementary Arabic. Examination papers are sent out by the boards, thereby ensuring certain minimum standards, a major problem with 'traditional' madrasas in other parts of India that are autonomous of any higher controlling authority.

In addition to the network of madrasas and Arabic colleges that they run, each of the three major Muslim groups in Kerala has also established a number of regular schools. They are like any other private school, following the state government syllabus, but also make arrangements for the teaching of Arabic and Islamic studies for their Muslim students. They are generally open to all communities, and some of them have a large number of non-Muslim students for whom religious education is not compulsory. As this suggests, the gulf between 'religious' and 'modern' knowledge and between traditional 'ulama and modern educated Muslims, so stark in large parts of north India, has thus considerably narrowed down in Kerala today.

Bridging Din *and* Duniya*: The Kerala Nadwat ul-Mujahidin*

Among the many Muslim organizations and movements in Kerala involved in promoting modern as well as Islamic education is the Kerala Nadwat ul-Mujahidin, commonly referred to simply as the Mujahid movement. Established in 1950, the movement grew out of the reformist efforts of the Kerala Muslim Aikya Sangha, formed in 1922, and then the Kerala Jami'at ul-'Ulama, set up in 1924. Several early leaders of the movement, such as K.M. Moulavi, E. Moidumoulavi and Muhammad 'Abdur Rahman, were also involved in the anti-colonial struggle. The Mujahids admittedly represent only a minority of the state's Muslims, but they have played a leading role in promoting educational awareness and social reform, influencing other Muslim groups in Kerala in turn. The Mujahids are, as mentioned earlier, the Kerala counterpart of the Ahl-i Hadith in north India, but are rather more moderate, sharing an understanding of Islam somewhere between the 'Wahhabis' of Saudi Arabia and the nineteenth century modernizing Salafis of Egypt, such as Muhammad 'Abduh and Rashid Rida. They believe that Muslims need to go back to the basic sources of the faith, the Qur'an and the Hadith, bypassing centuries of tradition as represented by medieval *fiqh* and Sufism. Followers of the movement call themselves *mujahid*s since they believe that they are engaged, not in a physical *jihad* or war, but, rather, in a spiritual *jihad* against superstition and corrupt practices that have crept into Muslim society.

Today, the Mujahid movement has 1000 units all over Kerala, with roughly 50,000 members, many of whom are highly educated professionals and businessmen. It runs scores of madrasas, schools and colleges in the state, in addition to a number of social work centres. It sees modern forms of knowledge as compatible with Islam, arguing for an Islamic understanding of modernity that willingly embraces new developments in the world but remains firmly embedded in the Islamic world-view. Husain Aboobacker Koya, general secretary of one branch of the Kerala Nadwat ul-Mujahidin, explains:

> The Qur'an stresses the importance of *'ilm*, or knowledge, and this includes both knowledge of Islam as well as of the world, there being no rigid distinction between the two. The Qur'an repeatedly asks us to ponder on the mysteries of creation,

> exhorting us to acquire knowledge of it. Thus, an '*alim* is anyone who has specialized '*ilm* in any particular field. The true 'ulama are those who are learned in any branch of knowledge and at the same time are God-fearing. Hence, we are opposed to the notion of professional priesthood, although we believe that there should be specialization in different branches of learning, because of which we have the separate Kerala Jami'at ul-'Ulama.

Although the Mujahids do not deny the need for specialized religious scholars, they insist that 'traditional' madrasa-trained 'ulama do not have a monopoly over performing religious functions. In fact, in several Mujahid mosques, trained doctors and other such professionals lead the congregational prayers and read the Friday *khutba* or sermon. Unlike the conservative 'Sunni' mosques in Kerala, in Mujahid-controlled mosques, numbering about 600, the *khutba* is delivered in Arabic as well as in Malayalam, so that the people can comprehend it. For the Mujahids, the *khutba* is an important means for promoting education and awareness in the community. Often, their *khutba*s relate to contemporary issues in the light of the Qur'an and Hadith. This is in marked contrast to mosques run by the 'Sunnis', where the *khutba* is almost always in Arabic only, and is often simply a rehashed version of sermons written several centuries ago. Again in contrast to the 'Sunnis', women are allowed and, in fact, encouraged, to pray in Mujahid mosques. Defending this practice, Koya argues:

> At the time of the Prophet women used to pray in the mosques and so we don't see any reason why they should not now, although we do not say it is compulsory. However, there are some people who believe that women must not pray in the mosques, and they find legitimacy for this in the books of medieval *fiqh*, which depart considerably from the Prophetic practice in this regard. They

allow women to come to Sufi shrines or to travel in buses and shop in market, but they resist them coming to mosques!

'Engaging in social work is a form of *jihad*,' Koya explains. As a grassroots movement inspired by an activist understanding of Islam, the Nadwat ul-Mujahidin runs several social work projects all over Kerala. In addition to its madrasas and Arabic colleges it has a number of high schools that use the state government syllabus, but also provide Islamic education. Many of these schools have a number of non-Muslim students as well. It administers about thirty orphanages, 300 Qur'an learning centres, a major scholarship scheme for poor children, and several blood banks, medical centres and vocational training centres. Its Yuvatha Book House has published over 200 titles on a range of religious and social issues, including translations of works by modern Arab scholars, a five-volume Islamic encyclopaedia and a four-volume Malayalam translation of the Qur'an. It also publishes several magazines, including one for women and another that deals specifically with cultural issues. The Mujahid's Rachana Kala Samithi (Literary and Cultural Committee) organizes regular cultural festivals. The youth wing of the movement, Ittihadul Shubban il-Mujahidin, organizes regular anti-drug and anti-liquor programmes and coaching centres for students.

Funds for these projects are collected from Mujahid members who contribute their annual *zakat* and two days' income. Mosque committees collect this money, which is then used to sponsor particular projects such as building houses for the poor or providing craftsmen with tools. Koya explains how the Mujahid's system of community self-help is organized, turning *zakat* from mere charity into a means for community development:

> We believe that *zakat* should be used to help people come out of poverty so that they, too, can in future give *zakat*, so we don't distribute little amounts of money to the poor, which would not help them out of the trap of poverty. In several parts of India poor Muslims go from house to house during Ramzan and people give them small amounts as *zakat*. I think this system is wrong as it makes the poor feel small. So, I feel our system of productive assets being given by a mosque committee is much better. Rather than giving small amounts of money to large numbers of poor people, we use the money to sponsor a small number of projects every year that can help the poor improve their earning power. The Qur'an says *zakat* should be spent on the poor, and does not specify that they must be only Muslims. So, last year we decided that we should also use our *zakat* funds for non-Muslims as well. In this way, given our limited resources, we have been engaged in promoting a socially engaged understanding of religion.[35]

The Mujahids are also engaged in inter-faith dialogue, through which they seek to promote inter-community harmony while at the same time presenting their own understanding of Islam to people of other faiths. In this regard, the movement has published a number of books in Malayalam on Islam and religious tolerance, and has held several inter-religious conferences to discuss issues of common concern for people of different faiths. Among the participants have been Christian and Hindu priests as well as Dalit and leftist activists. At the Mujahid's annual meetings scholars are often invited to present papers on issues of current concern, including communalism and inter-faith relations.

Kerala enjoys the highest levels of female literacy in India, and the Muslim women of the state are among the most educated in the country. The Mujahid movement has been at the forefront of Muslim women's education in Kerala, stressing the need for both Islamic as well as modern education for girls. Mujahid intellectuals have written extensively on women's rights from an Islamic perspective, although, because these writings are almost entirely in Malayalam and have not been translated into other languages, they remain largely unknown to Muslims in other parts of India. By denying the need to follow the established schools of *fiqh*, they argue that Muslims must rely only on the Qur'an and the Hadith, where they find ample justification for their cause of women's rights. Thus, 'Abdul Qadir, a senior Mujahid leader, approvingly cites the case of Ayesha, wife of the Prophet, from whom the Prophet is said to have instructed his companions to seek 'half the knowledge of the faith'. This, he says, strikingly suggests that women can be teachers of men. He sees no problem in women working outside their homes along with men, provided that they are never alone with a single man.[36]

Today, in several Mujahid madrasas and Arabic colleges girls outnumber boys by a considerable margin. All Mujahid madrasas and some of its Arabic colleges are coeducational, although girls and boys sit apart. The movement also runs a number of Arabic colleges exclusively for girls. A good example is the Mujahid's Anwar ul-'Ulum Women's Arabic College (AUWAC) in the village of Mongam in the Mallapuram district of north Kerala, an hour's drive from Calicut. Although there are several other women's Arabic colleges in south India, the AUWAC is the only such institution to be affiliated to a university, in this case the Calicut University. There are 300 girls here, a third of whom live in the college hostel. Several come from poor families, and some of them receive scholarships.

The girls here are not simply fed on a diet of Arabic tomes. Besides their regular studies, they are encouraged to busy themselves with some sort of social work, and the college has two wings of the National Service Scheme functioning on campus. Pictures of students in the college's album show neatly attired girls in black *hijab*s and spotlessly white cloaks, cleaning a village pond, running a medical camp and building a road in a neighbouring Dalit settlement with shovels and spades. 'In this way,' explains Zohra Bi, the principal of the college, 'we are training our children to become good citizens and also to show to ourselves and to others that true Islam means working for the betterment of society.'

Graduates of the college have gone on to take up a range of careers, for, as the Mujahids believe, Muslim women can indeed work outside their homes as long as certain restrictions are observed. Several graduates of the AUWAC teach Arabic in government schools, and a few are even elected members of local and district level panchayats. Many teachers of the college, some of them graduates from the same college, are also pursuing higher research. Zohra Bi, mother of seven, has an impressive list of degrees and certificates to her credit. After doing an MA from Aligarh Muslim University, she earned a Ph.D. from Calicut where she worked on the subject of women's rights in Islam. She is the recipient of the prestigious M.M. Ghani award for the best teacher in all Arabic colleges affiliated to Calicut University, of the Bharat Jyoti award, granted by the Delhi-based India International Friendship Society for community work, and of an award from Kerala's leading newspaper, *Malayalam Manorama*, in tandem with Air-India. Zohra Bi and her colleagues are presenting new role models for pious Muslim women, and she sees her work simply as 'service of the faith'. 'Islam,' she says, 'is wrongly thought of as a religion of women's oppression. Through our work in the college we want to show that Islam actually empowers Muslim women to work for the community at large.'[37]

*

As this account suggests, Islamic educational institutions in large parts of Kerala offer a remarkable contrast to their counterparts in other regions of India. The considerable success of these madrasas in integrating modern and Islamic education is due to to a number of historical, social, economic and political factors. To begin with, unlike in much of India, Islam came to Kerala through traders, not invaders. They were welcomed by the local kings who granted them land to establish mosques and the freedom to propagate their faith. The early Arab settlers played an important role in the local economy, controlling the region's foreign trade. The Arabs inter-married with local women, and adopted the local language and culture. Because Muslims are well integrated into Kerala society today, a legacy of their long history, they have been able to organize without major opposition from other communities, unlike, for instance, in much of north India. Kerala is still largely free of overt inter-communal strife (although the situation is now changing), and this has allowed Muslims to focus on constructive community work rather than on simply defending themselves or their identity. Again in contrast to north India, where madrasas were traditionally linked to ruling houses and large landlords, Kerala experienced only a brief period of Muslim rule. Hence, Muslim society here is remarkably free of what is often disparagingly referred to as the 'feudal' north Indian Muslim culture, to which the lack of enthusiasm for reform in many 'traditional' north Indian madrasas is generally attributed.

Further, from the late nineteenth century onwards Kerala has experienced waves of reformist movements, spearheaded by Christian missionaries, communists and 'low' caste activists, which have also profoundly affected the state's Muslim population. In addition, Muslims in Kerala, perhaps owing to their historical ties with the Arab heartlands, were among the earliest Muslim communities in India to accept the reformist impulses emanating from Muslim 'modernists' in countries such as Egypt and Syria. Then again, unlike north India, Kerala was not affected by partition. The bulk of the north Indian Muslim middle class, who could have been expected to take a lead in reformist efforts, left for Pakistan. This, in turn, had serious consequences for efforts to organize the community for modern education and to reform the madrasa system. In contrast, very few Malayali Muslims migrated to Pakistan. Today Kerala has a sizeable Muslim middle class which has played an important role in setting up new sorts of Islamic schools in the state. At the political level, the close integration of the Muslims into the state's political system has given them strong political leverage which has helped them to receive government assistance for numerous educational ventures, including schools and Arabic colleges. This explains in part why, in remarkable contrast to their counterparts in large parts of north India, many Muslim educationists in Kerala have not been averse to working along with the government.

The Kerala example is, however, not widely known among Muslims elsewhere in India. This is because, unlike in much of north India, Urdu is hardly understood in Kerala, being taught only in a very small number of madrasas and Arabic colleges in the state. Instead, almost all Malayali Muslim scholars and 'ulama write in Malayalam, which is not understood by Muslims elsewhere. This linguistic barrier has restricted communication between the 'ulama of Kerala and their counterparts in other parts of India. However, in recent years a number of 'ulama from north India have been working closely with their counterparts in Kerala. Some Arabic colleges in Kerala now have a few north Indian students, and some have even begun to teach Urdu. 'Ulama from Kerala regularly meet their colleagues from other parts of the country at gatherings and conferences. Delegations of 'ulama from other states visit Kerala to gain a first-hand understanding of the Islamic education system there, and some of them have gone back to their homes to launch similar experiments. However, this has been largely an unplanned exercise, because of which its influence has been limited. As a teacher at an Arabic college laments, 'Many north Indian Muslims are like the Brahmins, thinking that we in the south are inferior and that they have nothing to learn from us. Some even say that we cannot be good Muslims since we don't know Urdu!'

Old ways die hard, but increasingly madrasas elsewhere see in Kerala a model they could learn valuable lessons from. A growing number of Muslims in other parts of India, including several 'ulama, are today advocating reforms in the madrasa system following in the footsteps of their counterparts in Kerala.

{4}

Madrasas and the Agenda of Reform

Reforming the madrasas is a major cause for concern today. The governments of India, Pakistan, and countries in the West, particularly America, are now eagerly seeking to enforce changes in the madrasa system in the belief that 'unreformed' madrasas are rapidly emerging as major training grounds for 'terrorists'. In addition, many Muslims, including 'ulama themselves, are also at the forefront of demands for change in the madrasa system. The different actors in this complex political game have widely differing understandings of reform, each reflecting their own particular agendas. This chapter examines the different ways in which reform of the madrasas in contemporary India is imagined and advocated by a range of actors, including the 'ulama, Muslim social activists and the Indian state. While the practical efforts undertaken in this regard by selected madrasas and Muslim organizations are taken up in detail in the following chapter, this chapter also looks at some steps undertaken by both the central as well as various state governments to modernize the madrasa curriculum.

Before going any further, it is pertinent to keep in mind the role that the 'ulama and many, although not all, Muslims actually envisage for the madrasas. Arguments for madrasa reform often miss the point that, as many Muslims see it, the madrasa is not meant to be an institution for the general education of Muslims, training them for the job market. Rather, the madrasa is regarded as a specialized institution providing Muslims with specifically 'religious' education and transmitting the Islamic scholarly tradition. This being the case, the functioning of the madrasas must be judged, the 'ulama argue, in terms of the goals that the 'ulama set before them. As the former head of the Deoband madrasa, the late Qari Muhammad Tayyeb, insisted:

> When people criticize the madrasa syllabus, they forget that the aim of the madrasa is different from that of a modern school [. . .] The only way to pass judgment on the madrasas is to see how far they have been able to achieve their own aims, such as inculcating piety, promoting religious knowledge, control over the base self (*tahzib-i nafs*) and service of others. Therefore, no suggestion for reform of the syllabus that goes against these aims is acceptable.[1]

Critics of the madrasas tend to see them in stereotypical terms, often branding all madrasas as backward and reactionary. They are routinely described by their detractors, Muslims as well as others, as conservative and illiberal. They are looked upon as a major burden on Muslim society, consuming much of its meagre resources, and constituting an obstacle in the progress of the community. Much of what they teach is said to be 'useless' in the contemporary context, a complaint that reflects a view that 'useful' knowledge is that which helps equip a student to participate in the modern economy. A retired Muslim officer of the Indian Administrative Service sums up the modernist critique of the madrasas and their 'ulama somewhat crudely and tendentiously thus:

> The authorities [. . .] [of the] Indian madrasas are completely oblivious of the repeated directions in the Holy Qur'an regarding the need to acquire competence in study and reflection over [*sic*] scientific phenomenon [. . .] Madrasas have been promoting indifference towards modern and Western education, so graduates of madrasas find themselves unfit to breathe in the free air of the present age of science and technology. They would generally be suffering from inferiority complex [*sic*], hating everybody with modern education and themselves being hated by everybody with modern education [. . .] Islam cannot be defended by these 'misfits' who know nothing of modern knowledge.[2]

Such critiques, while not bereft of truth, appear somewhat exaggerated. The claim that all madrasas are impervious to change is misleading and is too sweeping a generalization to be taken seriously. As we have sought to show, madrasas today are considerably different in several respects from their counterparts in pre-colonial and colonial India, although there are significant continuities as well. As for the argument that madrasas are conservative, this is to state the obvious. For, as the madrasas generally see themselves, they are the guardians of Islamic 'orthodoxy' and they regard their principal role to be the conservation of Islamic 'orthodox' tradition which, although diversely understood, historically constructed and in a constant process of elaboration, is seen by the 'ulama as unchanging and fixed. Not surprisingly, therefore, many 'ulama regard the existing madrasa system to be in no need of any major reform. They argue that since in the past the madrasas produced great Islamic scholars there is no need for any change today.

As Maulana Sa'eed Ahmad Palanpuri, professor of Hadith at Deoband, argues:

> It appears that the products of the madrasas today do not come up to the standards expected of them. The cause of this is not the madrasa syllabus, but, rather, the lack of adequate experts in various disciplines, the carelessness of the students and their unwillingness to work hard.[3]

The argument that madrasas do not need any major reform is articulated by several ‘ulama in a fiercely defensive mode, and the intentions of advocates of reform are often dismissed as suspect and dubious. Thus, the principal of a Deobandi madrasa in Mewat, Haryana, insists:

> There is no need to change our syllabus at all. This demand, even if it is articulated by those who call themselves Muslims, is actually a plot hatched by the enemies of Islam. They know that madrasas are the backbone of Islamic identity, and using sweet words like ‘reform’ they want to destroy the madrasas and, thereby, destroy the Muslims as well and cause them to be absorbed into the Hindu fold. If the madrasas are not producing pious, God-fearing and socially engaged ‘ulama today the fault lies not in their syllabus but in lowering standards of piety and dedication, increasing materialism and our straying from the path of our pious elders. Let universities reform themselves, and that can only happen when they begin to teach religion to their students. Let those who pretend to be so concerned about reforming the madrasas turn their attention to universities instead. After all, universities are in much more need of reform. Universities are plagued with such problems as free sex, lawlessness and crime, not the madrasas.

While such voices undoubtedly reflect the stance of many madrasa teachers, it would be wrong to claim that they represent all shades of opinion among the contemporary Indian ‘ulama. As we shall see, several ‘ulama are themselves ardent advocates of reform, which they articulate in different forms and for different reasons.

Traditionalist 'Ulama and the Challenge of Reform

Debates on madrasa reform reflect different understandings of appropriate Islamic education and, indeed, of Islam itself. As many traditionalist 'ulama see it, since the 'pious elders' (*buzurgs*) have evolved a perfect system of education, and since they regard Islam as the ultimate truth, there is no need to learn anything from others. To try and do so is sometimes regarded as a sign of weak faith and as straying from the path that the 'elders' of the past have trodden. Change in the madrasa system is, therefore, often considered to be a threat to the identity and intensity of the faith. At the same time, and perhaps more importantly, it is recognized as threatening to undermine the power of the 'ulama as leaders of the community and their claims to speak authoritatively for Islam. Traditionalist 'ulama often see proposals for madrasa reform as interference in, or even invasion of, what they regard as their own territory. Since their claims to authority as spokesmen of Islam are based on their mastery of certain disciplines and texts, quite naturally any change in the syllabus, such as the introduction of new subjects or new books or the exclusion of existing ones, directly undermines their own claims. Besides, they fear that the introduction of modern disciplines in the curriculum might lead to a gradual secularization of the institution, tempting their students away from the path of religion and enticing them towards the snares of the world. Proposals for reform of the madrasas by incorporating modern subjects in the curriculum are sometimes seen as hidden ploys or even as grand conspiracies to dilute their religious character. This argument is repeatedly stressed in the writings of many 'ulama. Take, for instance, the statement of Ashraf 'Ali Thanwi, a leading Deobandi *'alim* of the early twentieth century:

> It is, in fact, a source of great pride for the religious madrasas not to impart any secular (*duniyavi*) education at all. For if this is done, the religious character of these madrasas would inevitably be grievously harmed. Some people say that madrasas should teach their students additional subjects that would help them earn a livelihood, but this is not the aim of the madrasa at all. The madrasa is actually meant for those who have gone mad with their concern for the hereafter (*jinko fikr-i akhirat ne divana kar diya hai*).[4]

Other traditionalist 'ulama may not go to such lengths to deny the need for the inclusion of modern subjects in the curriculum. However, while accepting the need for reform, they would argue that this should be strictly limited and must not threaten or dilute the 'religious' character of the madrasas. Madrasas, they assert, are geared to the training of religious specialists, and so it is important that 'worldly' subjects must not take the upper hand over religious instruction. Rather, it is enough, they stress, if students are able to read and speak elementary English, solve simple mathematical problems and are familiar with basic social sciences, albeit suitably 'Islamized'. To that extent, they welcome efforts for reform, and admit that madrasa students do need to gain a basic knowledge of these subjects so that they can function in the modern world. But they also insist that if 'excessive' stress were given to modern subjects in the madrasas the workload for the students would be simply too much to bear, because of which they would turn out to be 'of little use either for the faith or for the world' (*na din ke kam ka na duniya ka*).

While these arguments may not be entirely without merit, the opposition of some sections of the 'ulama to proposals for reform in the madrasas must be also seen as reflecting the fierce challenges that they perceive from Muslims articulating a different vision of Islam and Islamic knowledge. If all knowledge that is conducted within the limits set by the Qur'an and the Prophetic tradition is 'Islamic', as many reformists insist, the monopoly over the authoritative interpretation of Islam enjoyed by the traditionalist 'ulama is considerably undermined, if not done away with altogether. If, as some reformers say, a pious Muslim scientist researching the human cell or the stars in order to discover the laws of God is seen as much an '*alim* as one who has devoted his life to the study of the Hadith, the superior position that the traditionalist 'ulama claim for themselves based on their expert knowledge of certain classical texts and disciplines is effectively challenged.

Yet, madrasas are far from being completely immune to change and reform. Likewise, few 'ulama can claim to be completely satisfied with the madrasas as they are today. Indeed, leading 'ulama are themselves conscious of the need for change in the madrasa system. As their graduates go out and take up a range of new careers, in India and abroad, and as pressures for reform mount, from within the community as well as from the state and the media, madrasas, too, are changing. Change is, however, gradual, emerging out of sharply contested notions of appropriate Islamic education.

*

The dilemmas that accompany change are well illustrated in the case of the Dar ul-'Ulum at Deoband, often considered to be a major bastion of conservatism. The Deobandis, as noted earlier, stress conformity to traditional understandings of Hanafi *fiqh*, and tend to see the solution to all contemporary problems as lying in faithful adherence to past *fiqh* formulations. New ways of interpreting Islam are seen as akin to heresy and 'wrongful innovation'. As Maulana Mumshad 'Ali, himself a product of the Deoband madrasa, complains, 'the traditional 'ulama don't want to change. They are scared of the light because they have got used to darkness.'[5] Yet, today, there is mounting pressure from within the broader Deobandi fold for madrasa reform.

Faced with increasingly vocal demands that Deoband reform its syllabus, in October 1994 the madrasa organized a convention attended by a large number of teachers of Deobandi madrasas from all over India. The convention was ostensibly held to discuss the question of reform of the syllabus of the madrasas, but the inaugural lecture delivered by the rector of the Deoband madrasa, Maulana Marghub ur-Rahman, was a clear indication of how far the organizers were actually willing to go in allowing change. The Maulana insisted that there was no need at all to introduce modern education in the madrasas. There were thousands of schools in the country, he said, and Muslim children who wanted to study modern subjects could enrol there instead. Introducing modern subjects would, he claimed, 'destroy their [religious] character'. He argued that Islam had 'clearly divided' knowledge into two distinct categories of 'religious' and 'worldly'. 'The paths and destinations of these two branches of knowledge,' he insisted, 'were totally different', indeed mutually opposed. 'If one seeks to travel on both paths together', combining 'religious' and 'worldly' knowledge, one would 'get stuck in the middle', he declared. Hence, he argued, madrasas must remain 'purely religious', as the Deobandi elders had themselves all along insisted.[6]

Predictably, the convention concluded with a unanimous

decision not to make any concession at all to those who were clamouring for reform of the madrasa curriculum. It passed a resolution declaring that because Islam was a 'complete and perfect way of life' (*mukammil din*), it provided 'solutions to all problems'. Hence, it went on, in order to meet the challenges of modern life Muslims needed to rely 'only on the Qur'an, Hadith and *fiqh*', and there was no need for them to take the help of 'Western knowledge and culture'.[7] The only change in the madrasa syllabus that the convention agreed upon was cosmetic, i.e., to include new books in some subjects and to reduce the number of texts for others. As one critic, himself a graduate of the Deoband madrasa, caustically remarked:

> It seems that the convention had not been organized to seriously discuss the madrasa curriculum, to make suitable changes in it in accordance with changing social conditions, to meet modern demands and to improve the functioning of the madrasas. Rather, it appears to have been held simply to announce that all is well with the madrasas, and that because they worked well in the past they are doing so today, too, and to claim that those who are demanding reform have doubtful intentions. If this indeed was the intention of holding this convention, there was no need to do so. To prevent one's own weaknesses from being publicized and to proclaim the victories of the past is not a constructive approach.[8]

Despite the reluctance of the managers of Deoband to allow any significant reform in the madrasa system, the winds of change are being felt today even in the hallowed portals of the Dar ul-'Ulum. In fact, the convention was probably held, among other factors, due to the increasingly vocal insistence on the part of some Deobandis that the madrasas needed to change with the times. Not every Deobandi is a die-hard conservative, and not all of them are opposed to change in the madrasas. The growing pressure for change at the Dar ul-'Ulum owes, in part, to the influence of young Deobandi graduates who, after completing their studies at the madrasa, have gone on to regular universities for higher education or have taken up a range of occupations in India and abroad, but continue to maintain a link with their alma mater. Aware of the rapidly changing world around them, from which madrasa students are sought to be carefully insulated, they help transmit new ideas which, in turn, have given birth to new initiatives at Deoband itself. An important role in this regard is played by the Tanzim Abna ul-Qadim, the old boys' association of the Deoband madrasa, with its headquarters in Delhi. It has an ambitious list of aims and objectives:

1. To set up study centres and libraries to promote awareness about national and international affairs.
2. To promote the study of the Qur'an and Hadith, the movement of Shah Waliullah as well as of non-Islamic movements and to publish literature on these.
3. To publish articles in newspapers and journals on religious issues and on social reform.
4. To promote religious as well as modern education.
5. To establish *shari'ah* committees in Muslim localities, consisting of 'ulama and Imams of mosques to solve disputes in accordance with the *shari'ah*.
6. To promote social reform in accordance with the *shari'ah*, such as discouraging wasteful expense on celebrations, dowry, un-Islamic practices and unwarranted divorce.
7. To encourage Muslims to launch social work projects to help the poor.
8. To work along with people of other religions and castes for common social aims and for general relief and development of all, irrespective of religion and caste.

9. To promote interaction and good relations between people of different religions.
10. To resolve misunderstandings about Islam and Muslims among non-Muslims.[9]

The Association publishes a monthly magazine in Urdu, the *Tarjuman-i Dar ul-'Ulum*, which is widely read by graduates, students and teachers of the Deoband madrasa as well as madrasas affiliated to the Deobandi *maslak*. The magazine serves as an important vehicle for the transmission of new ideas, including issues related to madrasa reform. In contrast to many 'ulama at Deoband itself, it insists on the need for reform in the madrasa system if madrasas are to play a constructive role in society. It advocates a controlled modernization, seeing this as a return to, rather than a departure from, 'authentic' Islam and the vision of the founders of Deoband. Its appeal to Muslims to return to the 'authentic' Islamic tradition serves, in fact, to facilitate change and reform, rather than to oppose it wholly. Thus, for instance, in an article published in the magazine, Maulana Zain ul-Sajid bin Qasmi, a Deobandi graduate and now a teacher of Islamic studies at the Aligarh Muslim University, writes that madrasas can no longer ignore 'modern' challenges. 'We need 'ulama who are familiar with both religious as well as modern knowledge to serve the community and reply to the attacks on Islam from the West in the West's own language.'[10] While this proposal obviously suggests a defensive posture *vis-à-vis* the challenge of the West, it also signals a recognition of the importance of modern knowledge and might even represent an Islamic appropriation of modernity itself. In a similar vein, another contributor to the journal, the Deobandi graduate Maulana 'Abdur Rahim 'Abid, writes that many younger 'ulama today rightly feel that madrasas need to broaden their curriculum to include basic education in subjects such as mathematics, science, social sciences, Hindi and English. It is not necessary, he stresses, that students at madrasas be given detailed instruction in these modern subjects, but they should be familiarized with them on at least an elementary level. He recognizes that this might be construed by some as a betrayal of the Deobandi tradition, but assures his readers that in actual fact it is not so. He reveals that the founder of the madrasa, Maulana Qasim Nanotawi, arranged for Sanskrit to be taught at Deoband in its initial years, and that another leading reformist *'alim*, Maulana Ashraf 'Ali Thanwi, had, likewise, suggested the need to include Hindi as well as basic modern law in the madrasa curriculum.[11] In other words, he writes, the Deobandi elders felt that the madrasa syllabus should be dynamic in order to equip would-be 'ulama with knowledge of the changing conditions of the world around them so that they could provide answers to modern questions and challenges. Yet, he notes with distress that when a Muslim doctor based in America offered to send several computers to the Dar ul-'Ulum free of cost for the students, the authorities of the madrasa declined the offer, saying that they would be of no use to them. He laments that by opposing modern knowledge the madrasa authorities are actually working against the original vision of the founders of Deoband.[12]

Such critiques of the conservatives in Deoband are routine in the pages of the Association's magazine, and reflect an increasing dissatisfaction among several younger Deobandis with what they see as the inflexible, authoritarian conservatism of influential sections of the madrasa authorities.

Waris Mazhari is the editor of the *Tarjuman-i Dar-ul 'Ulum*. A graduate of the Deoband madrasa, he later studied at the Nadwat ul-'Ulama, Lucknow and then at the Jami'a Millia

Islamia, New Delhi. Besides editing the journal, he is involved in a number of projects promoting Islamic as well as modern education among Muslims, including madrasa graduates. His small office is located in an alley in the Muslim ghetto of Jogabai in south Delhi, and is a major hub of activity.

Mazhari clearly is a man with a mission, a complete contrast to the run-of-the-mill, stereotypical Deobandi '*alim*. He keeps a short, well-trimmed beard, does not wear a cap, and confesses to wearing 'Western' clothes on occasion. Some of his colleagues in his office, fellow Deobandi graduates and all in their late twenties and early thirties, dress in shirts and trousers and hardly fit the standard depiction of the Deobandi *mullah*. They well know, they confess, that numerous Deobandi 'ulama have devoted entire treatises denouncing such attire as 'Western ploys' to de-Islamize Muslims. Yet, they say, and Mazhari heartily agrees, that while they do indeed respect their Deobandi 'elders', they are not bound to accept all of what they have said or written as the final word. 'All of us, including the 'ulama, are, after all, human beings and are not infallible,' Mazhari explains. 'To take any human, no matter how pious, as perfect and to blindly accept whatever he says as the ultimate truth is to set up partners with God, which is the greatest sin in Islam,' he says.

Like many regular contributors to his journal, Mazhari too is critical of some aspects of the Deoband madrasa, particularly of its curriculum. 'In many respects,' he admits, 'the syllabus is irrelevant and is unable to meet the challenges of modern life.' He stresses the need for the introduction of new subjects as well as new books for teaching traditional disciplines. Many of the texts now being used in the madrasas, some of which are several centuries old, he says, need to be replaced by modern equivalents. He provides an interesting example to make his point:

> Take the case of the *Shara-i Aqa'id*, a treatise on theology written some six hundred years ago. This book continues to be taught in many Indian madrasas, including Deoband. It is written in an archaic style, and is full of references to antiquated Greek philosophy that students today can hardly comprehend. Rather than providing students with a firm understanding of the basic principles of Islamic theology, it deals with imaginary and hypothetical problems and verbal puzzles. It asks questions such as: Is there one sky or seven or nine? Or, can the sky be broken into parts? All this is irrelevant and completely unscientific. This book, like many other similar texts, is no longer being taught in schools in the Arab world, so why should it be taught at Indian madrasas any longer? I think we should remove such books at once from the syllabus, although I feel many conservative 'ulama at Deoband would vehemently disagree.

Mazhari advocates a thorough revision of the syllabus followed at Deoband, particularly for such core subjects as theology and jurisprudence. The books of theology still taught at Deoband are largely based on ancient Greek philosophy, having been written at a time when Greek philosophy posed a major challenge to Islam. They were also intended to combat various other rival schools and sects, such as the Kharijites and the Ismai'lis, and so they deal at great length with their doctrines in order to refute them. Today, however, he stresses, the challenge from Greek philosophy and the rival sects no longer exists, and so the traditional books of theology do not have relevance any longer. 'What madrasas need today,' instead, he passionately argues, 'are books of theology that also take into account the confirmed findings of modern science, and that seek to engage with contemporary ideological challenges, such as materialism atheism, Marxism, Hindutva and so on.'

For this purpose Mazhari suggests the introduction of new

commentaries on the Qur'an. He concedes that the medieval Qur'anic commentators, whose books are still used in the madrasas, did great service in the cause of the faith. That does not mean, however, that they should be idolized or their work considered sacrosanct. As he puts it:

> The 'ulama of the past, including the great Qur'anic commentators, were, after all, human beings, and no matter how pious they may have been they were certainly not infallible. When seeking to interpret the Qur'an they always insisted that theirs was a human effort, admitting that no human being could reveal fully or exactly the will of God as expressed in the Qur'an. To regard their commentaries as the last word on the Qur'an, as many conservative 'ulama seem to, is therefore wrong. Many medieval commentaries suffer from the influence of concocted *hadith* reports and from polemical debates and controversies that mar their credibility. Also, the commentators were naturally influenced in their thinking by their own social location, by the general prevailing social environment as well as by the then available stock of knowledge, and all this is reflected in the different commentaries that have been written down the ages. Hence, today, when social conditions have undergone such a radical transformation and when human knowledge has so vastly expanded, new interpretations of and commentaries on the Qur'an are needed. Since Muslims believe that the Qur'an is of eternal validity and provides guidance for all times, newer interpretations and commentaries of the text are needed as times change, in order to show the relevance of the Qur'an in every age.

Mazhari recognizes that his demands may not have many takers among the established 'ulama, particularly from the older generation. Reforms in the madrasa syllabus, he suggests, might be opposed because they would be seen as undermining the authority of the conservative 'ulama, whose claims as guides of the community rest on their knowledge of the classical texts. He finds hope, however, in the younger generation of Islamic scholars who increasingly are willing to articulate dissent.

Mazhari's vision for the reform of the madrasas is not limited simply to changes in their curriculum. He recommends that the madrasas which have the necessary funds should make arrangements for vocational training for those students who do not want to go on to become professional 'ulama. He also stresses the need for community leaders to give more attention to girls' education, Islamic as well as modern. He is critical of many 'ulama who are not in favour of higher education for girls, arguing that their stance is not in accordance with the Qur'an. He cites the instance of an article that he wrote in his journal lauding the achievement of a Muslim girl who stood second in the examinations for the Indian Police Service in 2001, presenting her as a model for other Muslim girls to follow. 'I received a flood of angry letters from many 'ulama protesting against the article,' he reflects amusedly, but adds, 'several graduates of Deoband wrote to me congratulating me for the piece.'[13]

The influence of the new thinking as represented by individual 'ulama such as those associated with the Old Boys' Association of the Dar ul-'Ulum madrasa, on the one hand, and the growing wave of attacks on madrasas, on the other, are today compelling the authorities at Deoband to consider introducing limited reforms in their syllabus and methods of administration. Thanks to the flood of journalists who flocked to Deoband in the wake of the events of 11 September 2001, looking out for material to make a 'good' story, Deoband now has two new departments—of English and of computer applications. The media hype about the Deobandi connections of the Taliban is said to have forced the authorities of the madrasa to finally relent and allow some of their students to learn English and computers so that they could answer the journalists and set at rest their fears of the madrasa's alleged involvement in terrorism.[14] Today, the madrasa has place for twenty-five students who have passed the *fazil* course to study in each of the two new departments. It has also launched a media cell to prepare reports and articles on issues related to the madrasas, document media reports on Islam and matters relating to Muslims, and to liaison with journalists. Several leading Deobandi authorities are now themselves calling for Muslims to take to both religious as well as modern education, exhorting them to set up both madrasas as well as regular schools in which arrangements should be made for the proper Islamic education of their children. Contrary to the image of all Deobandis as hardcore conservatives vehemently opposed to change, numerous Deobandis today would readily concur with Maulana Muhammad Aslam Qasmi, teacher of Hadith at Deoband, when he insists that Muslims must take to both modern as well as Islamic education, 'in a balanced way'.[15]

*

The interesting changes that are slowly making their presence felt in Deoband are not an isolated exception. In fact, voices for change in the madrasas, which have been gaining strength in recent years, are not in themselves particularly new. The urgent need for madrasas to reform has been consistently articulated by Muslim reformers, including many 'ulama themselves, from the late nineteenth century onwards, although the actual pace of reform has been slow and halting and the content and limits of the reform programme are still hotly debated.[16] In a recent survey, Siddiqui discovered that the majority of the over 450 madrasas that he studied in Delhi were in favour of curricular reform and the teaching of modern subjects, at least in the elementary classes.[17] Likewise, Qamruddin, in his survey of 576 madrasas across the country, estimated that over 96 per cent of the managers of madrasas felt the need to include modern subjects in order to ensure a better future for their students.[18] Yet, despite this widespread desire for reform, as Muhammad Qasim Zaman rightly notes, 'the significance of the initiatives towards reforming the madrasa itself remains to be appreciated'.[19]

In South Asia today, advocates for reform in the madrasa system include both trained 'ulama, products of madrasas, as well as men who have been educated in modern schools, including self-defined Islamists and Muslim modernists. Some of them have studied in madrasas and have then gone on to receive higher education in regular universities. Others are traditionally trained 'ulama, whose sons have studied in universities and have then joined them to help improve the functioning of their madrasas, a phenomenon increasingly common in India today. It is important, however, not to exaggerate the differences between the categories of traditionalists, Islamists and modernists. While these categories may be useful for heuristic purposes, in actual fact they do not exist as separate, neatly identifiable types. Rather, they represent a wide range of opinions, with one shading almost imperceptibly into the other. It is often the case, for instance, that an individual who could overall be defined as a traditionalist, might express modernist or Islamist sympathies in some significant respects.

Islamists, Muslim Modernists and Madrasa Reform

Voices for madrasa reform reflect a wide range of community agendas. Advocates of reform represent considerably different political positions—from those who see themselves as completely apolitical, to those who feel that reform is needed in order to integrate madrasa students into the wider society, and to those who insist on reform because they believe that it is only by combining Islamic with modern, particularly scientific, education can Muslims win political power and establish an Islamic state. In the absence of this, Muslims are believed to be incapable of leading truly Islamic lives.

Muslim scholars calling for the modernization of madrasas today share with their opponents a commitment to the Islamic tradition and present their schemes for modernized madrasas as a return to the 'authentic' tradition as represented by the Prophet and his companions, rather than as constituting a radical departure from it. The very notion of the 'authentic' Islamic tradition, being a social construct and an ongoing, constantly evolving project, is itself fiercely contested. Thus, different versions of what constitutes 'authentic' Islamic tradition are put forward and debated while appealing for madrasa reform.

Advocates for the introduction of modern subjects in the madrasa curriculum are also aware of the limits of reform, and there is considerable debate about how far reform should go. This tension centres on the perceived role and function of the madrasas. Those who see the madrasas as geared to the training of religious professionals argue that modern subjects should be allowed only in so far as they might help their students understand and interpret Islam in the light of modern knowledge. Others, recognizing that not all the graduates of the madrasas might be able or even want to become professional 'ulama, have suggested the creation of two streams of education in the madrasas. In the first stream, students who want only a modicum of religious education, preferring to then join regular schools, would be taught basic religious subjects along with modern disciplines. The second stream would cater to students wanting to train as professional 'ulama, and would focus on religious subjects, teaching modern disciplines only to the extent necessary for them to interpret Islam in the light of contemporary needs. A vocal minority insists, on the other hand, that an entirely new system of education must take the place of the traditional madrasas, employing a syllabus based on a blend of religious and modern subjects. Graduates of these schools could go on to train for a range of occupations, both religious as well as secular. Some go so far as to suggest that the larger madrasas, after being suitably reformed, should be converted into universities, with the smaller madrasas being affiliated to them. This, however, is not a widely shared view.[20] More acceptable is the suggestion that education be reformed in such a way that allows madrasa graduates to join regular universities after they finish their basic course of studies.

The reformists' rationale for introducing modern disciplines in the madrasas is framed in principally four ways. First, modernization is said to be a recovery of the 'authentic', holistic Islamic understanding of knowledge as all-embracing, covering worship as well as social relations and worldly pursuits, knowledge of God as well as of His creation. Second, it is said to be indispensable in order that the 'ulama may recover what is seen as their fast declining authority as spokespersons of Islam and as community leaders. Third, it is expressed as a necessary means for Muslims to prosper in this world and the next. Finally, it is seen as essential in order for the 'ulama to engage in *tabligh*, or Islamic missionary work. All these tie in with a new, more activist understanding of the role of the 'ulama. They are no longer to remain restricted to teaching in the madrasas. Rather, armed with modern, in addition to traditional, education, they are to play an important role as leaders of the community.

Modernization and 'Islamic Knowledge'

In the writings of the reformists, Islam's position on universal education is set apart from and above all other faiths. The alleged differences between Islam and other religions on this point are often exaggerated to the point of absurdity. For instance, religions such as Judaism and Hinduism are said to restrict access to knowledge, making it the preserve of the priestly elite. Islam, on the other hand, is said to stress the need for all people, men as well as women, to acquire knowledge. Christianity is depicted as being radically indifferent to worldly affairs, and as making a sharp distinction between what is Caesar's and what is God's, and thus between sacred and profane knowledge. The Church is accused of being fiercely hostile to science and reason, and is said to have a long history of persecuting scientists. Unlike Christianity, Islam, so it is argued, does not enjoin blind faith, but rather, faith based on reason. Further, in contrast to Christianity, Islam is said to be against monasticism and renunciation of the world. Islam is cited as striking a harmonious balance between this world and the next, and, consequently, as encouraging the cultivation of knowledge of the world and stressing both worldly as well as spiritual welfare.[21] Hence, it is argued, scientific development occurred on a grand scale at a time when Islamic civilization was at its zenith, because of, rather than despite (as in the Christian case), the deep-rooted influence of religion.[22] Thus, the great achievements of early medieval Muslim scientists in a range of fields including medicine, astronomy, physics, mathematics, biology and engineering, are seen to be a consequence of Islam's encouragement to explore the world as a 'sign' of God's majesty. These scientists are said to have been pious Muslims themselves, seeing their own scientific work as entirely in keeping with the teachings of Islam. It is argued that the great universities of the medieval Muslim world provided inspiration and knowledge to European scientists at a time when Europe was still in the clutches of the Dark Ages. In fact, many Muslim writers claim, modern science has its roots in the medieval Islamic tradition.[23] Hence, reformists argue, for present-day 'ulama to take to scientific education is not to abandon their faith or to embrace the alien. Rather, it is to reclaim what was once theirs, and constitutes a return to their 'authentic' roots. In fact, modern science, if cleansed of its 'un-Islamic' associations, can only help further strengthen Muslims' faith in Islam. On the other hand, if the 'ulama continue to ignore the importance of 'modern' knowledge, they would, they are warned, meet the same fate as the Church in Europe, and younger-generation Muslims would begin to turn away from Islam in the belief that it is opposed to reason and worldly progress.

For the reformists Islamic knowledge is a comprehensive whole. By denying the distinction between religious and secular knowledge, they advocate an alternative way of classifying knowledge, dividing all forms of it into two categories: 'useful' and 'harmful'. The former, consisting of all knowledge that leads to piety as well as worldly and social welfare, is to be willingly embraced. The latter, knowledge that leads to irreligiousness and immorality, is to be rejected. In support of this stance one *hadith* is often quoted. According to this tradition, Muhammad is said to have prayed to God, seeking 'beneficial knowledge from Him' and beseeching Him to protect him from 'such knowledge as is not beneficial'.[24] In this way of imagining the scope of Islamic knowledge, Islam is construed as covering every sphere of life, from personal relations to collective affairs. Accordingly, Islamic knowledge is regarded as holistic, this being presented as a logical outcome of the central Islamic notion of *tauhid*, the oneness of God.[25] If God is one, His creation is one, and so too are the various forms of knowledge needed to understand both the world and God. Since all spheres of legitimate knowledge are 'Islamic', it is argued, madrasas must not restrict themselves simply to the teaching of the Qur'an, Hadith, *fiqh* and so on. Rather, modern subjects must also be taught, albeit after suitably 'Islamizing' them, 'cleansing' them from the 'irreligious' underpinnings of Western epistemology and reconstituting them in a broad Islamic framework.[26] If Muslims were able to do this, claims Ghulam Yahya Anjum, teacher of Islamic studies at the Jami'a Hamdard, Delhi, they would produce leading Muslim philosophers, scientists and thinkers who would, as he puts it, be 'the envy of the world'. Such a system of education, he claims, would provide for the worldly as well as religious needs of Muslim students, training them to become 'perfect human beings' (*insan ul-kamil*).[27]

Similar views are articulated by Mohammad Aslam Parvaiz, editor of *Science*, India's only Urdu monthly popular science magazine, and reader in Botany at the Zakir Husain College, Delhi. Critical of many aspects of the madrasa curriculum, Parvaiz is actively engaged in promoting science education in several madrasas. He sees no contradiction between the confirmed facts of science and the Qur'an, and, on the basis of this claimed compatibility, argues for a holistic Islamic education including both what are narrowly described as 'religious' as well as 'secular' subjects. As he explains:

> The Qur'an repeatedly exhorts believers to acquire knowledge or '*ilm*, of both God as well as God's creation. '*Ilm*, as used in the Qur'an, is not restricted to knowledge of God or His attributes. The Qur'an describes the mysteries and wonders of nature as *ayat* or signs of God, and asks us to ponder on them because they reflect His glory. In the Qur'an God asks us to reflect on the cattle, the clouds, the mountains and so on, these being described as among His many signs. I take this to be an invitation to actively study genetics, atmospheric sciences and geology and so on. Appreciating the work of God as reflected in His creation, you are led to wonder at God's glory, and this, in turn, reinforces your faith in Him. In this way, the Qur'an exhorts us to study nature, and so positively encourages the promotion of science and a scientific attitude. I think this needs to be reflected in the madrasa curriculum as well.[28]

The holistic understanding of Islamic knowledge that reformists like Parvaiz advocate represents a creative effort to promote a specifically Islamic form of modernity. It also reflects an intense desire to define Islam in modern terms and to fortify the faith of Muslims faced with the unenviable reality of living in a world where they see themselves as increasingly marginalized and where Islam is widely regarded as a major obstacle to scientific thinking.[29] The assertion that Islamic knowledge is all-embracing in its scope, and that Islam governs all spheres of life, with a solution to every problem, serves as a powerful rhetorical device to defend the claim of the continuing relevance of Islam today as a comprehensive social system and to counter the appeal of alternative ways of imaging the world. At the same time, it also provides suitable 'Islamic' legitimacy for madrasa students who wish to acquire modern education.

Madrasa Reform and the Worldly Prospects of the 'Ulama

Advocates of reform see the present syllabus used in most South Asian madrasas, generally some variant of the *dars-i nizami*, as stagnant and in many respects no longer in tune with the demands of the times. While it is recognized that the *dars-i nizami* did indeed produce its share of brilliant scholars in the past, it is stressed that it was a product of a particular society, suited to the particular social and administrative needs of its time. Now that social conditions have changed drastically and human knowledge has expanded, the madrasa curriculum must correspondingly change in order that madrasas can provide a 'useful' and 'relevant' education.[30] This is regarded as particularly important for the future economic prospects of madrasa students.

This notion of 'useful' knowledge is itself novel, and one that can be traced to colonial discourse about what constituted appropriate learning. The classical 'ulama insisted, as many traditionalist 'ulama indeed still do, on the central importance of 'pure intention' (*sahih niyyat*) in the acquisition of knowledge. The quest for knowledge was, ideally, seen as being motivated simply to acquire God's favour, and students were sternly warned against any base or worldly motives. Knowledge, it was said, was a divine gift to be used only to do God's will, and not for worldly advancement. Yet, today, numerous Muslim scholars, including even some traditionalist 'ulama, are arguing precisely for the need for madrasas to seriously consider the worldly prospects of their students and to take these into account in framing their curricula.

The 'useful' knowledge that is sought to be included in the madrasa curriculum is variously described by different advocates of reform. Generally, it includes the basics of modern natural and physical sciences, as well as Hindi and English.

Often the need to include these subjects is justified as being in accordance with the classical notion of 'pure intention', and not motivated by worldly concerns on the part of the 'ulama. It is sometimes expressed as a means to help salvage the sagging prestige of the 'ulama and reinforce their moral authority. For instance, a Deobandi graduate writes that since the 'ulama lack a knowledge of basic Hindi or English, they often 'feel humiliated' when they 'step out of the four walls of their madrasas, having to depend on others for even such small things as filling out a train reservation form'. This, he says, leads to a 'loss of prestige on the part of the 'ulama', auguring ill for Islam.[31] It is thus forcefully asserted that unless modern subjects are added to the curriculum, thereby enabling madrasa students to remain abreast of contemporary developments, there is little to stop the growing irrelevance of the 'ulama in the eyes of the general Muslim public.[32]

For many advocates of madrasa reform modernization is proposed as a means to do away with or at least reduce the rigid dualism that sets modern-educated Muslims apart from the traditionalist 'ulama. If the madrasas were to incorporate modern subjects into their curriculum, it is suggested, they might also succeed in attracting students from better-off families to enrol, thereby helping to undermine the existing educational dualism, upgrade the standards of the madrasas and, as one '*alim* remarks, improve the moral standards of the students.[33] Incorporating modern subjects into the madrasa curriculum is also seen as particularly urgent given the increasingly visible and strident Hinduization of the 'secular' education system. In order to rescue Muslim children studying in modern schools from a subtle process of Hinduization and what is often termed as 'intellectual apostasy' (*zeheni irtidad*), it is suggested that madrasas should incorporate modern subjects so that their parents might be willing to send their children to study in such reformed madrasas, instead of regular schools, thereby preventing them from going astray. In this way, the appeal for madrasa reform is inextricably linked to broader concerns for maintenance of community boundaries and identities. It is also related to efforts on the part of the 'ulama to reach out to modern-educated Muslims who, they believe, have virtually abandoned the faith, and bring them back to Islam. It is recognized that it is only by familiarizing themselves with developments in the contemporary world can the 'ulama relate to and influence modern-educated Muslims and help them to lead a more proper 'Islamic' life. As some Islamist ideologues envisage it, this attempt at building bridges between the 'ulama and modern-educated Muslims will finally result in dissolving their separate identities, leading to the formation of a new class of 'ulama, firmly rooted in the Islamic tradition but at the same time better able to function in the modern world. As a Deobandi '*alim* puts it, it seeks to 'put an end to the war between the mister and the *maulvi*'.[34]

Introducing modern subjects in the madrasas is also seen as providing madrasa students with substantial real-world benefits. The fact that madrasa teachers are often poorly paid and that the career prospects of madrasa graduates are limited and not particularly lucrative, is a pressing concern for many advocates of reform. Reforming the madrasa curriculum is regarded as essential in order to deal with a central problem for many madrasa students, that of employment in an economy for which they have little or no training. The problem of suitable employment for madrasa graduates has now become a particularly serious one. With Independence in 1947, the absorption of Muslim-ruled princely states, and the eclipse of the Muslim feudal nobility, numerous madrasas and their 'ulama lost valuable sources of patronage. The problem has only worsened in the face of the general economic backwardness of the Muslims and the rapid increase in students graduating from the growing number of madrasas each year.

Many 'ulama have responded to the question by dismissing it altogether. Madrasas are meant, they say, for the training of religious specialists, not petty clerks. They insist that madrasa students should not worry about where and how they will earn their livelihood, for God, they are assured, shall provide for them. It also often argued that religious knowledge should be sought for its own sake, and not as a means for worldly advancement.[35] It is repeatedly stressed that the student's intention (*niyyat*) should be pure and unsullied by any worldly motives. His duty is simply to dedicate himself completely to the acquisition of knowledge of the faith and serve God. Following the pious ancestors (*salaf-i saleh*), he must lead a simple and austere life, and must depend solely on God for his livelihood, placing full trust in Him. Thus, Maulana Muhammad Taqi 'Usmani, a Pakistani Deobandi whose writings are still widely read in India, argues, 'The Creator of the world gives daily bread to dogs, donkeys and swine, so why won't He do the same to those who uphold His religion? So, madrasas need not worry about the employment problems of their students.'[36] Such 'ulama also often stridently claim that while thousands of unemployed university graduates roam the streets, there are almost no madrasa-trained scholars who are without jobs, no matter how humbly paid. In this way they have sought to ignore the question of the employment prospects of their students altogether.

Despite the widespread reluctance to discuss the issue, some writers, including many 'ulama themselves, today recognize that employment is indeed a fundamental concern for madrasa students, most of whom come from poor families and are sent to the madrasas by their parents in the hope that they will eventually be able to earn a livelihood as Imams in mosques or teachers in *maktab*s and madrasas. They see the introduction of modern education as important in helping to address the problem of acute unemployment among madrasa graduates, because, they argue, the existing avenues of employment for them are extremely limited. They say that were madrasas to include basic modern education in their curriculum, students would later be able to enrol in colleges and could then aspire to new avenues of employment.[37]

Related to the concern for shoring up the authority of the 'ulama and improving the economic conditions of madrasa students is the question of the empowerment of the Muslim community under the leadership of the 'ulama. Modernization of the madrasas is sometimes presented, by both Islamists as well as by many traditional 'ulama, as linked to the quest for political empowerment. This argument is expressed in terms of an overarching commitment to a world-view in which Islam is set irreconcilably against other religions in a desperate struggle for power, and it is asserted that Islam is destined to rule the world for it is the 'only true religion' in God's eyes. This obviously reflects a deep and painful consciousness among Muslims of their being marginalized in the global system as well as a yearning for an age long past when they were masters of much of the world. Sometimes this argument is framed in global terms in the form of an all-out struggle between Islam and the West for world domination. Thus, for instance, Sayyed Muhammad Rabe Hasni Nadwi, rector of the Nadwat ul-'Ulama, Lucknow, argues that Muslims need to acquire modern knowledge, of both the natural as well as social sciences, albeit suitably 'Islamized', in order to 'defeat the

West using the enemies' own instruments'.[38] Similar statements are often voiced by many other 'ulama as well as, of course, by Islamist ideologues.

Madrasa Reform and Muslim Missionary Activism

Introducing modern disciplines in the madrasa syllabus is also seen as central to the divinely ordained task of *tabligh* or Islamic missionary work. The 'ulama are deemed to have a special role in this, although *tabligh* is regarded as a duty that is binding on all Muslims. Islam is meant for the entire world and not just Muslims alone, it is stressed, and the 'ulama are reminded of their 'responsibility' towards their 'fellow countrymen', non-Muslim Indians, who are said to be 'in dire need of their guidance'.[39] The assumption here is that non-Muslims are doomed to perdition in hell if they do not accept Islam. In order to prepare themselves as effective missionaries, it is argued by several writers, the 'ulama must willingly take to new forms of knowledge. If Muslims were to lead the world in the development of knowledge, it is claimed, others would accept their leadership and follow them, and might even be inspired to convert to Islam. By mastering modern knowledge, the 'ulama would, it is believed, be able to impress upon the non-Muslims that Islam has the 'perfect solution' to all worldly problems, and this might inspire them to accept the faith.

Writings of advocates of reform highlight instances of noted 'ulama of the past who actively studied the languages, sciences and cultures of other peoples in order to carry on the task of *tabligh* more effectively. The figure of the eleventh century Imam Ghazali, the most accomplished Islamic scholar of his times, often comes up for discussion. Ghazali is said to have studied Greek philosophy in order to save those Muslims who had fallen prey to its 'snares' and had dismissed religion as a human creation. By mastering Greek philosophy he was able to refute its claims and establish the 'supremacy' of Islam. Likewise, it is stressed, present-day 'ulama must closely study, indeed master, 'un-Islamic' philosophies as well as modern subjects, not for their own sake, but, rather, in order to 'expose' them and assert the 'truth' of Islam. A new science of Islamic theology (*'ilm ul-kalam*) is thus called for, one that seeks to present Islam in contemporary terms in order to appeal to the modern mind. For this, it is stressed, the 'ulama must be familiar with various contemporary ideologies and knowledge systems that are 'opposed' to Islam.[40] To prepare effective missionaries of Islam and to rebut the claims of other faiths, numerous writers suggest the need for madrasas to teach comparative religions and English. Some also argue the need for madrasa students to be taught to use computers and the Internet in order to engage more fruitfully in *tabligh* work among people of other faiths.[41]

A Critique of the Existing Curriculum of Madrasas

Besides the 'rational' sciences of philosophy and logic, certain other subjects included in the present madrasa system are regarded by numerous advocates of madrasa reform as unnecessary and in urgent need of reform or removal. One of these is the teaching of ikhtilafiyat, the discipline of disproving other groups as 'un-Islamic'. *Ikhtilafiyat* forms a central component of the syllabus in several madrasas today, for each *maslak* and its associated madrasas regard as one of their primary functions the refutation of other Muslim groups, this serving to stress their own claims to Islamic authenticity. Those who see the teaching of *ikhtilafiyat* as unnecessary and even dangerous often complain that many madrasas play an inordinate role in promoting intra-Muslim conflicts by teaching their students to condemn all Muslim groups other than their own as virtually outside the pale of Islam. They argue that books that tend to promote hatred against other Muslim groups should be excised from the syllabus.

Another contentious issue that is repeatedly discussed in the writings of the advocates of reform is that of *fiqh*. *Fiqh* constitutes the core of the madrasa syllabus. It also forms the mainstay of the authority of the 'ulama, for they are experts of the subject. A number of reformists who plead for revision in the teaching of *fiqh* in the madrasas call for the inclusion of modern subjects in the madrasa curriculum in order to develop new *fiqh* perspectives attuned to the particular context of contemporary India. This is because the classical books of *fiqh*, they say, deal with many issues that are no longer relevant and are also silent on matters that modernity has forced people to deal with. Further, many of the books on *fiqh* as well as on other subjects that are still taught in the madrasas are said to consist only of innumerable commentaries or simply marginal footnotes, and are written in an archaic style and language. Many of these commentaries further complicate what the original books teach, rather than actually explain them. As a Deobandi graduate himself admits, they tend to promote 'heated verbal debates and quarrels and strife' and 'cannot open the minds of the students'.[42] Hence, it is stressed, new books on *fiqh* should take their place, books that are more easily comprehensible, dealing with issues of contemporary concern and relating to practical realities.[43]

Asghar 'Ali Engineer, director of the Mumbai-based Institute of Islamic Studies, is a vocal critic of the present madrasa curriculum, particularly for its obsession with medieval *fiqh*.

He sees the rigid insistence by most 'ulama on blindly following medieval jurisprudential opinions as a major hurdle in the path of Muslim progress. Thus, he argues:

> Today, most traditional 'ulama insist on the need to strictly follow medieval jurisprudential opinions, while ignoring what the many early 'ulama were so particular about—the need to exercise independent judgment or *ijtihad* based on a thorough understanding of the principles of *fiqh*. So, you have 'ulama today who talk about the great rewards of using a tooth-brush (*miswak*), because the Prophet used it to clean his teeth, and who write entire books on how long the tooth-brush should be and from which tree it should be made and so on, while they ignore the fact that the world has moved on to the age of toothpaste! Or, for that matter, many 'ulama pen tracts on the amount of *zakat* (poor due) that should be paid on a camel or a goat, while they forget that pastoral societies are fast disappearing from off the face of the earth! By remaining wedded to past jurisprudential opinions the traditionalist 'ulama ignore the need for developing understandings of Islam and Islamic jurisprudence that are relevant in today's context.[44]

A similar appeal for a dynamic, modernized critique is articulated by Waris Mazhari of the old boys' association of the Deoband madrasa:

> *Fiqh* must always evolve with the times, for as conditions change and new issues emerge new *fiqhi* or jurisprudential responses must be articulated. This calls for the need to exercise *ijtihad* to examine matters afresh and to take into account new developments. In matters of faith and worship and other areas that are specifically legislated for in the Qur'an there can be no *ijtihad*, for these are given for all time. But in large areas in the domain of social transactions (*mu'amilat*) one must be open to the possibilities of new interpretations. Unfortunately, this is

> strongly discouraged in most Indian madrasas. Thus, for example, they continue to teach about the laws governing trade, slavery, purchase and sale that were developed in medieval times and which were elaborated upon by the early 'ulama. They do not refer at all to modern developments, to the context of a now globalised economy. Although numerous 'ulama have written books dealing with *fiqhi* responses to new forms of commercial transactions and other modern developments, these books are, unfortunately, not included in the madrasa curriculum itself. Instead, they are often simply prescribed as optional readings for students to study on their own. We've been trying to get the authorities of the madrasas to radically overhaul the teaching of *fiqh* to include a range of modern issues, but, I must confess, most of them just don't seem to be willing to listen.[45]

Another passionate advocate of a modern, contextually relevant *fiqh* is Maqbool Ahmad Siraj, the executive editor of the Bangalore-based English monthly *Islamic Voice*. He is strongly critical of the reluctance of most traditional 'ulama to revise their understanding of *fiqh* in order to come to terms with the manifold challenges of contemporary life. As he explains:

> In the last four hundred years, Muslims have not made any significant contribution to the world. Every modern invention that we take for granted has come to us from the West. If at all Muslims do any scientific research they work on things like dates, camels, cumin seeds and *zam-zam* water, as the Prophet is said to have used these things. I think this narrow attitude is not just sickening, it is also profoundly un-Islamic. The Qur'an repeatedly exhorts us to exercise our reason, to use God's gifts for the benefit of all. But the traditional 'ulama of the madrasas turn a complete blind eye to all this, and are obsessed with the intricacies of jurisprudence and external rituals and symbols. I say there is no reason why Muslims should stick to the opinions of the established schools of Islamic jurisprudence. There could

> well be a thousand schools, for we need newer interpretations of the Qur'an and the Hadith as times change. Unfortunately, this is not happening today.

He goes on to lament what he sees as the lack of a culture of internal critique among the traditional 'ulama:

> There is such a climate of suffocation in the Muslim world today that we are not able to find solutions to even small things like the sighting of the moon for Eid. Decades after man has landed on the moon, the traditional 'ulama still insist that you cannot rely on the telescope for sighting the moon or use modern astronomical data for fixing the Islamic lunar calendar, while they don't hesitate to use spectacles to read their books! And so, as a result, you have Eid being celebrated on three different days by Muslims living in the same city. What I mean to say by this is that there is a pressing need to reinterpret many traditional concepts in the light of the times on a wide range of *fiqh*-related issues, on many of which the traditional 'ulama have totally outdated views. By this rigid approach to *fiqh* we have made ourselves the laughing stock of the world. At the risk of sounding pessimistic, let me say that Muslims, as a whole, are sticking to old, worn-out formulas, having forgotten the way to develop new formulas in accordance with the demands of the changing times.

Not surprisingly, the demand for a new *fiqh* attuned to the contemporary Indian context has been met with suspicion by many 'ulama. Such suggestions are often interpreted as 'hidden ploys' to 'destroy' Islam. This opposition must also be seen as emanating from the challenge that the traditionalist 'ulama face from critics of their authority to speak for Islam, which, for them, is seen largely through the lens of *fiqh*. This challenge is sometimes articulated subtly, but, on occasion, explicitly, denying that Islam has any place for the sort of religious specialists that the 'ulama have now been reduced to. As Maqbool Ahmad Siraj argues:

> Islam is one religion that does not recognize any priesthood, for it insists that there can be no intermediaries between the individual and God. The institution of quasi-priests entered Muslim societies only much later. And now respect for them has become so deeply ingrained in the Muslim psyche that many believe that by keeping the 'ulama happy they can earn for themselves a place in heaven, although this is totally against the teachings of the Qur'an. This feeling is further reinforced by the 'ulama themselves, who see their role as indispensable. While the misuse of science and technology for wrong purposes might account for some of the opposition on the part of the 'ulama to modern education, it is also the case that many among the 'ulama fear that with the spread of modern education among Muslims their own leadership positions would be threatened.[46]

In articulating a new, contextually relevant Islamic jurisprudence, advocates of reform such as Engineer, Mazhari and Siraj stress the need for a wide-ranging *ijtihad* in order to deduce rulings for new situations and problems from the Qur'an and Hadith. For this, it is suggested, the focus of the teaching of *fiqh* should shift from the details of jurisprudence (*fur'u*) to the principles of law ('*usul*).[47] One writer even suggests that madrasas should give their students some grounding in international law and comparative legal systems, in order, as he puts it, to 'meet modern challenges'.[48] Another leading '*alim*, associated with the Jama'at-i Islami, recommends that in order to break the stranglehold of *taqlid* and inter-*maslak* prejudices, madrasa students must be familiarized with the *fiqh* of other Muslim schools of jurisprudence. He insists on the need for *ijtihad* to deal with issues that the medieval compendia of *fiqh* either do not mention or do so in terms that are irrelevant today, including such subjects as religious pluralism, women's rights and social justice.[49] Engineer goes even beyond these somewhat limited suggestions of *ijtihad* within existing legal schools to argue that: 'There is no reason why there should be no new *mazhab*s and schools of thought attuned to today's conditions.'[50]

Those who are in favour of reforming madrasas have also written extensively on the need for a change in the teaching of the core subject of *tafsir* or Qur'anic commentary. The original *dars-i nizami* devoted little attention to Qur'anic commentary because it was envisaged principally as a syllabus to train government bureaucrats rather than religious specialists. Many Indian madrasas continue to pay scant attention to *tafsir*, limiting themselves to only a few texts by early medieval commentators that are now widely recognized as inadequate. Reform in the teaching of *tafsir* is articulated in two principal ways. First, it is argued that the Qur'an is a simple, easily understandable book of practical guidance. Hence, it must be approached directly, rather than with the help of 'outdated' commentaries. Second, it is often pointed out that all commentaries naturally bear the imprint of their authors and their own socio-historical location. While medieval *tafsir* literature is not dismissed as completely useless, it is argued that their authors were, after all, human beings and not infallible. Therefore no interpretation of God's word can be said to be absolute or to actually represent God's intention in its entirety. Conceding that every interpretation of the text is partial and limited, some writers suggest that new commentaries, written by modern-day scholars and taking cognizance of modern developments in knowledge, should take the place of outdated commentaries, although this does not mean that the medieval *tafsir*s must be totally neglected. This plea for reform is presented as a means of expressing the argument of the continuing relevance of the Qur'an in every age. It is also seen as 'proof' of the Qur'an's divine nature, for if the Qur'an provides suitable guidance for constantly changing conditions it must, so it is claimed, indeed be of divine provenance.

Coordination between Different Madrasas

Most madrasas function as independent bodies, run by their own management committees. Even in the case of the several thousand Deobandi madrasas in the country, each madrasa is autonomous in matters of administration, although the various madrasas share a similar ideology and commitment to what may be called a common Deobandi vision. Every madrasa is, in theory, free to formulate its own syllabus, select its own books, set its own standards, and conduct its own examinations. Because of this, and also because of fierce inter-*maslak* rivalries, there is no central coordinating body for all madrasas. This poses major problems in such matters as formulating policies for the reform of the madrasa syllabus, improving educational standards, student exchanges between madrasas, promoting unity among different Muslim groups, and combating various challenges that the madrasas see themselves as collectively faced with. Thus, all efforts to reform the madrasa system as a whole are doomed by the continued existence of sharp inter-*maslak* differences. As Tahir Mahmood, a leading Indian legal specialist, argues:

> It is naïve to expect [that] the 'ulama of India, having such tremendous differences, would unanimously agree on a single item of reform, if at all they agree to discuss it [. . .] In India, each group of 'ulama [. . .] has its own interpretation of the Qur'an

and Sunnah. They will take ages to express a unanimous opinion on any reform to be applied to all Muslims alike.[51]

A number of Muslim writers have called for efforts to build bridges between different madrasas as part of a broader programme of madrasa reform. Thus, Muhammad Zafiruddin Miftahi, a *mufti* associated with the Dar ul-'Ulum, Deoband, suggests that all Sunni madrasas, barring those run by the Barelwis, who are seen as vehemently opposed to other Muslim groups, should come together under one all-India madrasa board, with branches at the state, district and local levels. The proposed board would be charged with the responsibility of preparing a common syllabus for the 'transmitted' sciences, while each madrasa would be left free to choose which modern subjects it wants to teach. In order to gain general acceptance, the board would consist of 'ulama of various Sunni schools.[52] Another leading Sunni '*alim*, Maulana Muhammad Shams Tabrez, appeals to all Muslim *maslak*s, including the Barelwis, to set up a single madrasa federation which would frame a common syllabus for all madrasas and which could work for their collective welfare. The board would set common standards and conduct common examinations for the madrasas under it.[53]

Given the fierce rivalries between madrasas of different *maslak*s, efforts to unite the madrasas under a common board have proved unsuccessful. Madrasas, like other such institutions, cherish their autonomy, and many would regard control by an outside body as undue interference. Increasingly, however, leading madrasas of each *maslak* are moving towards setting up loose federations in order to streamline educational standards and examination procedures. In recent years, the growing fear and threat of interference by the state and attacks on the madrasas by extremist Hindu groups have further boosted this process, causing madrasas to seek to consolidate their ranks so as to more effectively respond to moves to control or regulate them. Separate federations have now been formed, among others, by the Dar ul-Ulum, Deoband, the Nadwat ul-'Ulama, Lucknow, the Ahl-i Hadith's Jami'at us-Salafiya, Varanasi, and the leading Barelwi madrasa in the country, the Jami'at ul-Ashrafiya, Mubarakpur. Each federation is headed by an *amir*, generally the principal of the apex madrasa, and member madrasas all belong to the same *maslak*. Regular meetings are organized to chalk out plans and projects and to discuss common problems and concerns.

Reforms in Teaching Methods

The need for suitable changes in methods of teaching employed in the madrasas has been written about extensively by advocates of madrasa reform. Reformists are critical of what they call the 'book-centred', as opposed to the 'student-centred', approach to education in the madrasas. The former is based on parroting entire sections of books without exercising reason or critical thought. This problem is exacerbated by the inordinate stress that most madrasas place on the study of particular books, as opposed to particular subjects, which generally means memorizing them.[54] As a result, few students can actually comprehend what they are taught. Even after years of poring over ancient Arabic tomes, hardly any madrasa graduates, laments Maulana Mumshad 'Ali Qasmi, a Deobandi '*alim*, are able to speak the language properly, having simply memorized a few sentences or chapters.[55] Many madrasa managers and teachers are said to sternly prohibit their students from reading books written by scholars of other *maslak*s and, indeed, any books outside the prescribed syllabus.[56]

While the merits of some aspects of the traditional

pedagogic styles and approaches are recognized, advocates of reform believe that madrasas must be open to learning new teaching methods from others, including from modern institutions. Such proposals are wide-ranging, and include the introduction of new methods of language learning that are used in universities, encouraging students to debate and discuss various issues, training them to write for newspapers and organizing cultural programmes in order to broaden the vision of the students. Some writers suggest the need for text-based learning to be combined with practical learning activities, such as various forms of social work and inter-faith dialogue programmes. Through such efforts, it is argued, madrasa students would be made more aware of the world around them, which, in turn, would help them to be more effective in their future work as religious leaders and missionaries. It would salvage the sagging prestige of the ‘ulama by making them more relevant to people's daily concerns. At the same time, it would help madrasa students develop a more contextually grounded and relevant understanding of the faith.[57]

In recent years a few madrasas have made some headway in reforming pedagogical methods. For instance, the Jami‘at ul-Falah, Azamgarh, now has a number of teachers, almost all madrasa graduates, with a bachelor's degree in education. At the Islamic Centre, Lucknow, the English teacher has a degree from the prestigious Central Institute for English and Foreign Languages, Hyderabad. Exposed to new teaching methods in such institutions, these teachers might be induced to reform traditional teaching methods, although this has, till date, been slow in happening. An innovative experiment that might prove a major catalyst in this regard is the madrasa teachers' training centre that the Jami‘at ul-Hidaya, Jaipur, proposes to start in the near future. So far no such institution exists, although organizations such as the Uttar Pradesh Falah-i 'Am Trust, Lucknow, the Ta'mir-i Millat, Hyderabad, the Samastha Kerala Sunni Vidyavasa Board, Calicut, the Hamdard Educational Society, New Delhi and the Centre for Promotion of Science, Aligarh, occasionally organize short-term training camps for madrasa teachers, where they are familiarized with new methods of teaching.[58] Likewise, the Jami'a Millia Islamia and the Aligarh Muslim University have organized similar courses in recent years.[59]

The Pace of Madrasa Reform

Given the world-view of the conservative 'ulama, and the vested interests involved in maintaining the madrasa system as it is, it is hardly surprising that the actual pace of reform of madrasa education in India has been slow and halting. In the absence of mechanisms to make the madrasas accountable to the community, change in the madrasa system has been piecemeal and ad hoc, rather than wide-ranging and well planned. Since each madrasa is an autonomous institution, its curriculum being set by its own management body, reform in the system has so far depended almost entirely on individual initiative. In most cases this is, if at all, done by the management body on its own, often on the personal whim of its principal or rector. Only a few madrasas have actively sought to involve academics from universities and trained educationists in reforming their curriculum. Typically, the involvement of outsiders in helping curricular reform is seen as opening the doors to 'irreligious' interference that would threaten the very 'religious' identity of the madrasa. Critics argue that this opposition actually has more to do with the threat that the managers of the madrasas perceive to their own positions of authority if they were to allow university-trained specialists, even if Muslims, a say in running their institutions.

The slow pace of change in the system might seem frustrating to advocates of reform. Yet, it needs to be understood with sensitivity for critics of the madrasa system often ignore the important positive contributions that many madrasas are actually making in the field of Muslim education today and the critical financial and other constraints that they face. Their contribution can be better appreciated when they are seen in contrast to the functioning of the government schools. For the poor in India often the only available and affordable form of education is provided by the government school system, where the standard of education, as numerous committees instituted by the state themselves concede, is quite pathetic. Teachers rarely make an appearance, and if they do they spend little time actually teaching. Although government schools provide, in theory, free education, poor families often find it difficult to meet the costs for clothing, books and food for their children. In many madrasas, on the other hand, these are provided free of cost.

Drawing an interesting contrast between government schools and madrasas, a Muslim journalist points out:

> A poor Muslim child has only two options to receive some sort of education. He could either go to a government school, where he would probably learn next to nothing, or else to a madrasa. At least in the madrasa he would receive free education, board and lodging, books and clothes. Classes in madrasas are held regularly and teachers generally take a keen interest in their students. At the madrasa the student would learn at least two languages, and probably a modicum of mathematics and other modern subjects. He would also learn the value of discipline, proper use of time, personal hygiene, respect for elders, honesty, good morals and hard work, all of which may be entirely new

> things for children coming from poor families. One cannot properly understand the role of the madrasas without taking all this into consideration. Yes, I admit that a lot needs to be done to reform the madrasas, but before criticizing them for their faults and for their slowness in changing, one must recognize the difficult conditions under which they work as well as the valuable services that they are rendering to poor children.

Likewise, an '*alim* at a Deobandi madrasa in Bangalore admits that there is much scope for reform in the madrasas:

> When talking about reform in the madrasas it is important to remember that had it not been for the madrasas thousands upon thousands of Muslim children would be roaming the streets, begging or doing no work, and turning into criminals. It is true that there is much that is wrong with the madrasa system, but who can deny that by educating so many poor Muslim children and training them to become good, responsible and law-abiding citizens they have made an immense contribution to the country and have also relieved the government of an immense burden that it would need to have shouldered in order to educate them? While madrasas should be thanked for this task, they are unfortunately being reviled as hideouts of terrorists today.

In seeking to evaluate the actual pace of reform in the madrasa system, it is important to bear in mind the considerable financial constraints under which most madrasas operate. Many of them might wish to provide a better education for their students and even to teach modern subjects, but are unable to do so for want of the necessary funds. Recruiting good teachers for modern subjects is often difficult because they cannot afford the high salaries that such teachers demand. Linked to this is the issue of the social background of the vast majority of the managers, teachers and students of the madrasas. Most come from poor or lower middle class families with little or no exposure to modern forms of knowledge and teaching methods. Being themselves products of traditional madrasas, they have been taught to believe that many aspects of modernity represent a revolt against Islam. Not surprisingly, reform is often seen as an invitation to treason and apostasy. Like most other religious specialists, the essential task of the 'ulama is to preserve a received tradition and not to innovate or experiment. Hence, to expect the 'ulama to wholeheartedly embrace reform is unrealistic and impractical.

In the case of most madrasa students, too, their social origins often inhibit any enthusiasm for making demands for reform. Most of them come from poor families and are wholly dependent on the madrasa for their education and living expenses. They too, have little exposure to alternative forms of education. To demand reforms in the madrasa system is a risky proposition that few students dare consider, for this would probably invite their expulsion. Modern-educated, middle class Muslims have themselves taken little interest in the reform of the madrasas, often viewing them as obscurantist and as beyond redemption. Few well-off families would choose to send their children to madrasas to train as professional 'ulama. Even among the poor, a noted '*alim* claims, it is generally those children who are either dull or quarrelsome who are sent to madrasas, the others being sent to government or private schools if the family can afford it.[60] Being thus characterized by a largely poor and deprived student composition, madrasas often remain insulated from the winds of change and reform that a more diverse student population might have engendered.

Further hampering efforts to reform the madrasa system is the widespread and growing perception among the 'ulama and the Muslim community in general of a grave threat to Islam and Muslims from militant, anti-Muslim Hindu chauvinist forces. This fear naturally dampens enthusiasm for reform and serves to further strengthen the forces of conservatism and reaction. In such a surcharged climate, suggestions for reform of madrasas are understood as hidden ploys by the 'enemies' of Islam to extirpate the faith by diluting the 'religious' character of the madrasas.

Although, as noted earlier, Muslim reformists, including several 'ulama themselves, advocate wide-ranging reforms in the madrasa system, in actual fact reform has been largely limited to the introduction of some new texts and subjects and the excision of others that are no longer seen as 'useful'. In other words, reform has so far been peripheral rather than structural or basic. Many madrasas have drastically reduced the number of books on antiquated Greek philosophy and logic in their syllabus, and have replaced them with more books on Hadith. In recent years, as is discussed in the following chapter, several madrasas have introduced the teaching of selected modern subjects, including basic English, and elementary social and natural sciences, along with Hindi and, in some cases, a regional language. However, in general the standard of teaching of these subjects leaves much to be desired. They are not taken seriously either by the teachers or the students and are considered relatively unimportant as compared to what are seen as 'Islamic' subjects. In many madrasas these subjects are taught by teachers who are themselves traditionally trained 'ulama, with little or no exposure to modern knowledge and teaching methods.

State-sponsored Efforts at Madrasa Reform

In recent years, demands have begun to be voiced for state regulation of the madrasas in the name of reform. Such calls were not unheard of in the past, but the rationale for government intervention through madrasa modernization was articulated in terms of helping the Muslims join the 'national mainstream', with madrasas being generally seen as 'backward', unconcerned with the world around them and resistant to change. Today, however, the rationale has shifted dramatically, with madrasas now seen as somehow too 'worldly' for 'proper' religious institutions, allegedly churning out militant activists charged with a burning mission to capture political power. Rather than representing a radical shift in the aims and methods of the madrasas as such, this changed rationale is more a reflection of the growing strength of Hindu chauvinism in India that is based on an abiding hatred of the Muslim 'other'.

Today, calls for state intervention in the madrasa system reflect a challenge perceived by the state from the autonomy of the madrasas. Most madrasas are not dependent on the state for funds. Their financial independence is seen by the state as giving the madrasas an influence over which it has little or no control. Their independence is generally viewed, particularly by government officials with a soft corner for Hindutva-brand nationalism, as a particularly potent challenge to the project of a monolithic Indian nationalism based on Brahminical Hinduism. As defenders of Islamic 'orthodoxy' and Muslim community identity, and as alleged advocates of pan-Islamism, madrasas are regarded by the Hindu chauvinists as particularly menacing. Hence, Hindutva leaders have insisted on the need for careful state monitoring and control of the madrasas, and some have even gone to the extent of demanding that the state close them all down. On the other hand, 'secular' political parties in power in some states have sought to extend assistance to a number of madrasas, aware of the considerable influence that the 'ulama wield over Muslim voters and appreciative of the efforts that madrasas are making in promoting literacy among Muslims. The state's relations with the madrasas are thus determined by a mixed set of motives.

Ostensibly, the state's case for modernizing madrasas rests on two premises: that such 'modernization' is needed in order to promote 'modern' and 'rational' thinking, and that it is only by 'modernizing' themselves that madrasa students can enter the educational 'mainstream' of the country.[61] It is also claimed that the modernization of madrasas is necessary for promoting 'national integration'.[62] The assumption, therefore, is that traditional madrasa education hampers such 'integration', causing Muslim children to be cut off from the 'mainstream'. The 'mainstream' and the 'nation' are viewed in hegemonic terms as represented by a distinctly 'upper' caste Hindu ethos. Joining the 'mainstream' might then be simply a euphemism for shedding a separate Muslim identity and merging it with a larger 'Indian' identity that is defined in 'upper' caste Hindu terms.

This suggests that the state's apparent concern for Muslim educational development through the modernization of madrasas needs to be carefully and critically interrogated. If promoting Muslim education were indeed a primary concern of the state, critics argue, it should have paid more attention to setting up modern schools in Muslim localities, something that it has clearly failed to do. In fact, it is pointed out, the level of educational provision by the state in Muslim areas is far below the average level, leaving the state open to charges of considerable discrimination against Muslims. Then again, proposals to legitimize state intervention in madrasas on the grounds of helping to promote 'modern' and 'rational' thinking appears dubious to many Muslims in the face of what is today a concerted effort on the part of the state to Hinduize the education system by introducing subjects such as astrology and Hindu rituals and mythology in the syllabus of schools and colleges. Not surprisingly, many Muslims view the state's efforts to interfere in the madrasas as motivated by ulterior motives. One prominent Muslim politician even suggests that the real purpose of the state's proposals for modernization is to 'monitor what goes on inside the madrasas through government-funded monitors in the form of teachers of English, Mathematics and Sciences'.[63] In response to a state-sponsored report that recommended that madrasas should teach 'Vedic Mathematics' as part of a proposed modernization scheme,[64] numerous 'ulama argued that this clearly showed that the state was attempting to dilute the Islamic identity of the madrasas through the back door while claiming to assist them.[65]

Broadly speaking, state efforts to reform the madrasas have taken three forms: (a) setting up by state governments of boards for madrasa education, (b) providing financial assistance to selected madrasas to teach secular subjects and (c) having some madrasas recognized by certain state-funded universities.

In India today, seven states (Assam, Bihar, Madhya Pradesh, Orissa, Rajasthan, Uttar Pradesh and West Bengal) have set up state-sponsored madrasa education boards to which a number of madrasas are affiliated. Only a relatively small number of the madrasas in these states are associated with these boards, although they are free to choose to join or not. Several of the affiliated madrasas receive some sort of assistance from state governments, such as for teachers' salaries. In turn, they have to abide by certain norms laid down by the state, including teaching some modern subjects. Graduates of most madrasas affiliated to the boards can go on to join regular colleges.[66]

In recent years, the Government of India and a few state governments have launched small schemes, ostensibly to assist some madrasas by assigning paid teachers to teach modern subjects. In 1986, the government issued a document on its new education policy, which included proposals for state intervention in madrasa education through what it called the 'Madrasa Modernization Programme'. The government's revised plan of action document issued in 1992 suggested the introduction of modern subjects such as science, mathematics, English and Hindi in the madrasas, the expenses for which would be borne partly by the state.

Despite its claims to be seriously committed to madrasa modernization, the government appears, in fact, to have done little in practical terms.[67] The funds sanctioned for the modernization scheme are said to be woefully limited. In actual fact, it has proved extremely difficult for many madrasas that wish to participate in the scheme to obtain financial assistance from the state. Under the rules of the scheme, madrasas are eligible to receive state funds only after getting security clearance from state governments, a condition that does not apply to Hindu institutions. This is said to entail long and complicated bureaucratic hurdles and, often, the added burden of paying bribes to petty government servants, which several madrasas either cannot afford or else simply refuse to do.[68] Further compounding the problem is the fact that some bureaucrats apparently do not wish the scheme to succeed. Thus, according to a report on the madrasa modernization project in Bihar, some government servants in the state 'with a communal bent of mind' effectively sabotaged the government's scheme of helping the madrasas by not disbursing the money allocated to them. Apparently the Ministry of Human Resources Development had sanctioned a sum of Rs 43 lakh to the Bihar government in 1999–2000 under the madrasa modernization scheme, which was to be implemented in the state by the Bihar State Madrasa Education Board. However, this money was not provided to the board, whose officials claimed they had no knowledge of how it was spent. B.P. Srivastava, Bihar's 'upper' caste Hindu education secretary and chairman of the committee dealing with the scheme, confessed that he had not sent a 'utilization certificate' to the central government explaining what happened to the money. He said that the money was not provided to the board because of 'preoccupation with other matters', a rather specious argument. Because Srivastava did not disburse the money, the Union government decided not to provide the Bihar government the sum of Rs 3.57 crore that it had allocated for the madrasa modernization scheme for the next year.[69]

On the other hand, in some other states the scheme seems to have achieved considerable results, and several madrasas have been keen to cooperate. In 2001, some 3500 out of a total of 6000 madrasas in Madhya Pradesh, with some 1,75,000 students on their rolls, received modest financial assistance from the state government through the Madhya Pradesh Madrasa Education Board to teach secular subjects.[70] By 1999, about 600 madrasas in Rajasthan out of 5000-odd in the state had received recognition from the state government, and several of them had also received some state funding. The state government allotted a sum of Rs 2 crore for madrasas in that financial year, but since the entire budget could not be utilized, it was cut down to Rs 78 lakh in 2001. Yet, despite the drastically reduced budget, state-recognized madrasas seem to have performed exceptionally well in Rajasthan. According to one report, 90 to 100 per cent of their students were successful in their examinations, as against 65 per cent in government schools situated in Muslim-dominated localities. Sixty per cent of the students of these madrasas secured a first division, while the corresponding figure for government schools was an abysmal 20 per cent. Half of the successful madrasa students were girls. Impressed with the progress that the madrasas were making, the state government, in cooperation with several madrasas, chalked out a plan to appoint 'education workers' (*shiksha karmis*) to teach secular subjects in select madrasas.[71] In addition, the government launched a scheme to distribute free science and other textbooks to some madrasas through the Rajasthan Waqf Board.[72] In a state where only 0.15 per cent of the students in colleges and universities are Muslim, well below the community's representation in the state's population, clearly the madrasas assisted by the government are playing a major role in promoting literacy.

Another way in which the state has sought to engage with the madrasas is by allowing some universities to recognize the degrees of certain madrasas, thereby enabling their graduates to go in for higher education and helping them join the educational 'mainstream'. Several larger madrasas have managed to get their degrees recognized by universities such as the Aligarh Muslim University, Osmania University, Lucknow University, Jami'a Millia Islamia and the Jami'a Hamdard. Graduates who join these universities generally enrol for courses in subjects such as Arabic, Urdu, Persian, Islamic studies and history, but increasingly a small number are going in for other disciplines such as English and mass communication. Some madrasas actively encourage their brighter students to enrol in universities in the hope that, equipped with modern knowledge, they would return to their madrasas to teach and help improve their standards. Indeed, a small though growing number of madrasas now include among their teachers former madrasa students who have also acquired degrees in regular universities.

Muslim Responses to State Assistance

For their part, the 'ulama and other Muslim leaders seem to be sharply divided on the matter of madrasas receiving state assistance. Some Muslim leaders have actually welcomed offers of financial assistance, provided it does not come with any strings attached. They see no harm in receiving funds from the state, claiming that the state has not yet linked its offer of financial assistance to any preconditions, such as radically changing the content of their curriculum or interfering in their administration. Responding to a question about state assistance to madrasas to 'modernize' their curricula, a leading Indian Muslim scholar, Zafrul Islam Khan, editor of the fortnightly *Milli Gazette*, asserts:

> I believe that the state does have the responsibility and the right to intervene and see that certain subjects are taught in the madrasas. The state should make it compulsory for madrasas to also teach modern subjects, and Muslims must obey this, for there is nothing in Islam that says that Muslims should not study these disciplines. And then, Muslims are also citizens of this country, and they have as much of a right and a duty to study these subjects as others do. Now, as for how these subjects should be introduced in the madrasas and how they should be taught, that is a separate question that needs to be debated. But, then, many madrasas might be opposed to this, because the managers of the madrasas have their own vested interests, which they think might be affected if the state steps in to intervene.[73]

In contrast to this, other 'ulama and Muslim leaders argue that accepting funds from the state will eventually lead to interference in the affairs of the madrasas, leaving them open to a subtle process of Hinduization. They claim that by linking assistance with modernization of the curriculum the religious content of the syllabus could be considerably watered down and, burdened with the need to learn both religious as well as modern subjects, the students would not do well in either. It is also pointed out that the standard of education in government-assisted madrasas is considerably lower than in independent madrasas, since the teachers in the former are paid by the government and are assured of a permanent job, and are not answerable to the madrasa management. They do not take their duties seriously, being concerned simply with getting a regular salary. Hence, it is stressed, madrasas should avoid taking any money from the state. A noted Deobandi '*alim*, Mufti Muhammad Sulaiman Mansurpuri, warns the 'ulama not to fall prey to the 'blandishments' of the state, asserting:

> To accept government aid from the state would lead to the death of the madrasas. It would be a gross violation of the aims of their founders, and would destroy their spirit of service to the faith [. . .] It would lead to the madrasas becoming graveyards of the sciences of religion [. . .] Because of this, no self-respecting '*alim* and servant of the faith can accept, even for a single moment, assistance from the state. We may suffer great financial hardships thereby, but we should reject government aid and rely only on Allah.[74]

Overall, then, the madrasas seem not to have been particularly enthusiastic about the state's offers of assistance, although there are notable exceptions. Rather than look to the state for assistance to promote reform, today some madrasas are seeking to help themselves by developing innovative forms of Islamic education. To these new experiments we turn in the chapter that follows.

{5}

Reformed Madrasas and New Forms of Islamic Education

Muslims are often accused of being fiercely opposed to modern education, being allegedly in the grips of a vicious set of clerics who are said to have a vested interest in keeping the community illiterate and backward. The non-Muslim press in India regularly carries sensational stories describing 'fanatic' and 'obscurantist' 'ulama railing against the modern world and demanding that Muslims go back a millennium to seventh century Arabia. The obvious educational backwardness of Muslims is recognized, but the blame for it is put firmly on the Muslims themselves. 'Muslims don't want to educate their children', 'They prefer to send their children to madrasas instead of modern schools', 'They think that modern knowledge is totally against their faith'—these and similar other views are routinely expressed in ordinary conversations by many non-Muslim Indians, and are articulated in less crude forms in 'sophisticated' analyses by newspapers and even government spokesmen.

That the conservative 'ulama have played a major role in perpetuating Muslim educational backwardness is undeniable. However, by placing the responsibility of Muslim educational backwardness solely on the Muslims themselves, their detractors conveniently absolve themselves of any complicity in the matter. It is as if the widespread discrimination by the state in recruiting Muslims to government jobs had absolutely nothing to do with the lack of Muslim enthusiasm for modern education. Or, for that matter, that the growing Hinduization of the government education system, with its clearly anti-Muslim stance, has no bearing at all on Muslim interest in such education.

This discourse on Muslim 'backwardness' completely ignores the fact that many Muslims are forced to send their children to madrasas not because they want to but for want of any other affordable alternative. Further, the denial that Muslims could at all possibly aspire to modern education completely ignores the creative efforts of numerous Muslims, including even some traditionally trained 'ulama, in evolving new forms of suitably modernized and, at the same time, culturally appropriate, Islamic education in India today.

Anyone who has lived among or closely interacted with Muslims in India would readily agree that like people of any other community, they indeed wish to see their children receive a proper, modern education. They too want to emerge from the throes of poverty and lead a decent and comfortable life. There can thus be no room for Muslim exceptionalism in this regard, as in any other. In recent years, particularly after the demolition of the Babri Masjid in 1992 and the ensuing anti-Muslim pogroms, Muslims are increasingly recognizing the need for modern education if they are not to be further marginalized and effectively consigned to the status of the 'new untouchables'. Today, this urge for modern education has taken the form of numerous schools set up by Muslims in various parts of the country that seek to combine religious with secular education.

It is also reflected in the increasing willingness on the part of many traditional madrasas to widen their curriculum and include the teaching of a range of modern subjects.

Bridging the Din *and* Duniya: *Islamist Educational Experiments*

Questioning the dualism that has developed between 'religious' and 'worldly' knowledge, Islamist activists, as we have seen in the previous chapter, see both forms of knowledge as part of a comprehensive whole. Accordingly, educational institutions run by Islamist groups in India have incorporated a range of modern subjects into their curriculum, thus helping to bridge the educational dualism that has characterized Muslim education for almost two centuries now. Among the most enthusiastic to embrace modern subjects and include them in their syllabi are schools associated with the Islamist organization Jama'at-i Islami Hind.

The Jama'at was founded in 1941 by the scholar-cum-activist Sayyed Abul 'Ala Maududi. Maududi saw the Jama'at as spearheading the struggle for the establishment of an Islamic state, strictly ruled in accordance with the *shari'ah*. A number of Muslims, including both madrasa-trained 'ulama as well as some who had received a modicum of modern education, were attracted to the Jama'at in its early years. One of Maududi's major concerns soon after founding the Jama'at was to formulate a new system of Islamic education which he presented as an alternative to both the traditional madrasas as well as regular schools. In 1944, he organized a meeting of top Jama'at functionaries at the organization's headquarters at Pathankot in Punjab. At the meeting he presented the outline of an ambitious educational programme based on a system of primary, secondary and high schools. Rather than produce professional 'ulama (a notion that Maududi seemed to view as un-Islamic and akin to a class of priests which Islam condemned), the proposed schools were to train a new generation of Muslims rooted in their faith but at the same time expert in various modern disciplines, capable of taking up a range of occupations, and, above all, leading the movement for the establishment of an Islamic state of Maududi's dreams. If committed and pious Muslims were to excel in every field of modern knowledge, Maududi claimed, they would be able to impress people of other faiths with the 'truth' of Islam. Consequently, the latter would either willingly become Muslim or else accept Muslim leadership.[1] This, in turn, Maududi believed, would help pave the way for the eventual establishment of an 'Islamic state'. Modern knowledge was thus regarded as indispensable for a very political purpose.

The partition in 1947 led to the division of the Jama'at, with the majority of its members, including Maududi himself, migrating to Pakistan, although Maududi had throughout opposed the Muslim League, regarding its agenda of Indian Muslim nationalism as a gross violation of the principle of universal Muslim brotherhood. The Jama'at now split into two separate wings, one each in Pakistan and India. In Pakistan the Jama'at registered itself as a regular political party, while in India, where Muslims were a beleaguered minority, the re-christened Jama'at-i Islami Hind functioned as a cultural and religious organization.

In September 1948 top Indian Jama'at leaders gathered at the movement's headquarters to discuss the setting up of a system of Muslim primary education. It was felt that if Muslim children were left to study at government schools they would slowly, yet inevitably, lose their distinct Muslim identity. Hence,

Jama'at leaders stressed the need for Muslims to set up their own schools, till at least the primary level, where their children could study modern as well as Islamic subjects in a 'proper' Islamic environment. At the meeting a provisional syllabus for Muslim school education was approved. The curriculum for the primary level consisted of general Islamic studies, recitation (*nazira*) of the Qur'an, and basic Arabic, Urdu, Hindi, English, mathematics, general knowledge, history and geography. For higher classes the syllabus included the Qur'an, Hadith, *fiqh*, principles of *fiqh* and Arabic, along with English, general knowledge, political science and economics.

Shortly after this meeting, the Jama'at set up its own publishing house, the Markazi Maktaba-i Islami, which was given the task of publishing suitable textbooks for teaching these various subjects. The books were prepared by a committee of Jama'at activists and supporters, including 'ulama who had received a madrasa education as well as men who had studied at regular schools. Some seventy-five textbooks, in English, Hindi, Urdu and Arabic, were published in subsequent years, and these were regularly revised and updated.[2] In line with Maududi's programme of the 'Islamization' of knowledge, modern subjects were presented in a suitable 'Islamic' framework. Thus, for instance, the mathematics texts contained sums related to the payment of *zakat* and intricate calculations related to the rules of division of inheritance according to the *shari'ah*. The natural science texts described the laws of nature as God-given, and referred to verses of the Qur'an that were said to pre-date significant scientific discoveries by centuries. In this way, the books sought to legitimize the acquisition of knowledge of modern subjects in Islamic terms.

In 1949 the Jama'at sought to put its educational programme into action by setting up the Markazi Darsgah (Central School) at Rampur. As its name suggests, it was envisaged as a regular school (*darsgah*) in contrast to a traditional madrasa. It aimed at training activists for the Islamist movement who were rooted in their faith but were also aware of developments in the world around them. It was seen as an alternative to state-run schools that were regarded as being opposed to Islamic beliefs and as teaching infidelity and irreligiousness.[3] The school functioned under the auspices of the Jama'at till 1960, when it was closed down due to administrative and financial problems. In 1986 it was restarted, managed now by a committee of nine persons, headed by Maulana Yusuf Islahi, senior member of the central committee (*majlis-i shura*) of the Jama'at. The Darsgah appears to have inspired the setting up of several other similar educational institutions in other parts of the country that also adopted its syllabus. According to a Jama'at source these included 1617 primary, sixty-five secondary and fifty-one high schools, as well as fifteen institutes for technical education.[4]

Today, the Darsgah provides education till the sixth grade, after which students generally join regular schools. Plans are being made to extend it to the higher secondary level in the near future. In line with the Jama'at's vision of Islam, students at the Darsgah are taught a combination of Islamic and modern subjects. The Islamic studies course includes several texts penned by Maududi himself. In contrast to traditional madrasas, it steers clear of *maslak* and *fiqh* divisions, seeking to promote an understanding of Islam that is based directly on the Qur'an and the Hadith. It thus stresses the unity of all Muslims, irrespective of *fiqh* differences, which, while recognized, are to be tolerated. Hence, admission is open to students irrespective of *mazhab* or *maslak*, and the school has had some non-Hanafi teachers on its rolls as well. The Darsgah has produced a number of students who have gone on to occupy leading positions in the Jama'at-i Islami and in various other Islamic organizations and movements. Other graduates have completed higher education at regular universities such as the Aligarh Muslim University and the Jami'a Millia Islamia, and now work as doctors, engineers and journalists.[5]

Another interesting Jama'at-sponsored educational initiative is the Jami'at ul-Falah, located at Bilariyaganj, near the town of Azamgarh in eastern Uttar Pradesh. It was set up in 1962 by a group of Jama'at activists and sympathizers. It was structured on the lines of a modern school, with a seven-year primary course and a higher course of another seven years, including a five-year '*alim* degree programme and a two-year *fazil* course. The *fazil* course included a number of optional subjects, such as journalism, calligraphy, comparative religion, Islamic missionary work, Hindi and elementary Sanskrit, social welfare and teacher's training.

Falah saw itself as training 'ulama as social activists to struggle for the cause of Islam as a 'complete system', as envisioned by Maududi himself, and to combat 'un-Islamic' ideologies as well as 'wrong' practices followed by many Muslims.[6] In this way, its students were trained, as its official publicity brochure puts it, to 'present Islam, with adequate proofs, before the world as the only means for success in the Hereafter'.[7] Furthermore, Falah saw as one of its principal tasks the creation of a class of 'ulama who, the brochure proudly announces, 'clearly understood the issues of their time'.[8] Hence, it included a number of modern subjects in its syllabus, believing that these were essential for preparing a class of educated Muslims who could lead the community in all spheres of life, and not simply as religious specialists as narrowly construed. It sought to provide its students with a broader outlook, free from the inter-*maslak* rivalry so characteristic of most madrasas.[9] Muslims of all sects and schools of thought were eligible for admission, and the school had a number of teachers from different *maslak*s, including from the Deobandi and Ahl-i Hadith traditions, besides the Jama'at-i Islami.[10] In contrast to most other madrasas, it did not promote any particular school of *fiqh*. Rather, it sought to cultivate an open attitude on matters of jurisprudence, seeking to take from each legal school what it thought to be in accordance with the primary sources of Islamic law, the Qur'an and Hadith, and insisting on the need for *ijtihad* to cope with modern issues and challenges.[11] In another significant departure from traditional madrasa education, it did not teach any of the medieval Qur'anic commentaries. Students were encouraged to try to understand the Qur'an on their own with the help of dictionaries, although they were free to study the medieval commentaries as well.

Today, Falah is one of the largest and better-organized madrasas in India. In 2003 it had an estimated 5000 students on its rolls, including around 2700 girls who study in a separate wing. It had more than 120 teachers, several of whom were graduates of the madrasa and had then gone on to regular universities for higher education in a range of disciplines. It has considerably restructured its course of study, extending it to the graduate and postgraduate levels. Till the junior high school level it uses the government-prescribed syllabus and textbooks prepared by the National Council for Educational Research and Training (NCERT), supplemented with selected books of its own choice. Thereafter, students do a seven-year specialized course in Islamic studies and Arabic, with English, geography, history, comparative religion, political science and sociology as additional subjects. The school also offers a two-year diploma course in Hindi. It has recently started a computer section, and computers are now a compulsory part of the curriculum.

Falah thus claims to provide a broad-based education, devised in such a way that its students receive a general grounding in both religious as well as modern subjects. This, in theory, enables them to choose, once they graduate, either to go on to regular universities or else to pursue further Islamic education. However, the quality of teaching of modern subjects leaves much to be desired, because of which the madrasa's claim of producing 'ulama well versed in modern disciplines seems somewhat far-fetched. Yet, the management and teachers at Falah actually welcome their students going on to enrol at regular universities once they graduate. Dismissing an oft-heard argument against madrasa students joining universities, a graduate from Falah, now a teacher in a college in a town in Uttar Pradesh, says:

> Some 'ulama argue that if madrasa students go to universities they would lose their Islamic character. They would begin to drink alcohol and smoke and wear Western clothes. They would stop saying their prayers and keeping the fast in Ramzan. I don't agree with this argument at all. If madrasa students are given proper intellectual and spiritual training and their faith is firm and secure, there is no reason why this should happen. In fact, I know of many madrasa students who are now studying and even teaching in universities in India and abroad. They are still as good Muslims as they were when studying in the madrasas. More than that, they are also setting a good example for the other students in the university, who admire them for their piety, simplicity, honesty, dedication and discipline. In this way they can play an important role in communicating the message of Islam to people of other faiths.

Likewise, a student presently studying at Falah, who hopes to enrol in a university after he graduates, says:

> One often hears this argument that if madrasa students begin to join universities and then train to become doctors or lawyers or anything other than a traditional maulvi, the very purpose of the madrasa system would itself be defeated. This, however, is completely false, because in Islam there is no contradiction between the demands of religion and the demands of the world. If a madrasa student becomes a doctor he can still remain a pious Muslim, and can even help the cause of Islam through his service to people of other faiths. After all, the Qur'an clearly says that there is no monasticism in Islam and that one's faith must be expressed in one's actions in all spheres of life. So, if you are a doctor and serve people in accordance with the teachings of Islam that is also a form of worship. Unfortunately, however, some misguided so-called 'ulama make a rigid distinction between religion and the world and wrongly claim that the two are opposed to each other, and that the only way one can serve Islam is by sitting in the mosque and counting beads.

Falah's degrees are now recognized by a growing number of universities in India and in Saudi Arabia and Egypt. This has allowed its graduates to seek further education in regular universities, opening up for them new job opportunities not available to products of traditional madrasas. Today, a growing number of Falah students, or 'Falahis' as they are called, work as college lecturers, journalists, translators, and as employees in business firms and Islamic institutions in India and in the Arab world. It is estimated that more than half of the students who pass the '*alimiyat* examination at Falah go on to take admission in regular universities, with less than a third staying on to complete the *fazilat* course.

In contrast to many smaller madrasas, Falah provides its students with facilities for a range of extra-curricular activities. It has a large sports field and students are encouraged to play a variety of games after school hours. The Jami'at ul-Tulaba,

Falah's students' association, organizes regular debates and essay competitions and brings out a college magazine containing articles written by the students themselves. The madrasa occasionally arranges for professors (almost all Muslim) from universities to lecture to the students on subjects of contemporary concern. Falah boasts of a library containing over 20,000 volumes, housed in a new three-storeyed building which also has a well-equipped computer centre, a large seminar hall and several reading rooms.

Similar educational experiments inspired by the Jama'at-i Islami have come up in other parts of India. In Kerala there are an estimated forty high schools associated with the Jama'at, where students train for the '*alim* course and simultaneously prepare for a bachelor's degree from a state university. Likewise, in other states too, a number of regular schools such as the Zikra High School (Hyderabad), the Millat High School (Jalgaon), the Iqra School (Aurangabad) and the Milli Model School (New Delhi) have been set up in by members or activists of the Jama'at. Some of these are English-medium schools and follow the regular government syllabus, with extra classes for Islamic studies for which they use textbooks prepared by the Markazi Maktaba-i Islami.

Although not affiliated to the Jama'at, the Islamic International School in the crowded Dongri district in Mumbai shares, in many ways, a similar vision of Islamic education. Founded in 2001, it is run by the Islamic Research Foundation, a missionary organization headed by the noted Islamic scholar Zakir Naik. Naik is India's most well-known Muslim polemicist. He specializes in debating with leading Christian theologians, and his admirers claim that he has worsted them all in numerous public rallies in India and abroad.

The International Islamic School is not a traditional

madrasa. In fact, it seeks to distinguish itself from a madrasa in significant ways. Its brightly painted classrooms are equipped with blackboards, tables and chairs, and colourful posters decorate the walls. In contrast to the simple classrooms in madrasas, which often do not even have fans, all the rooms in the school are air-conditioned, a luxury that only few schools in India can afford. Monthly fees amount to Rs 3000 which is well beyond the budget of an ordinary Indian Muslim family. Again, unlike most madrasas, the school is not affiliated to any particular Muslim *maslak*, being open, in theory, to Muslims of all sectarian backgrounds. In this way, it seeks to present an ecumenical image that transcends narrow sectarian barriers that are so deeply inscribed in the traditional madrasa system.

An employee of the Foundation explains the aims of the school, pointing out how it differs from traditional madrasas:

> We want to produce a class of pious Muslims, men as well as women, who will be able to represent Islam in all domains of life. We want to train good Muslim doctors, engineers, lawyers and scientists who would be able to show the world what Islam has to offer in all these spheres. Ours is not a madrasa in the traditional sense of the term. Unlike many traditional madrasas, where students have little or no understanding of the complexities of modern life, we want our students to be well aware of both Islam and the world around them. This is why we are not affiliated to any particular sect or school of *fiqh*. Instead, we go straight to the Qur'an and the Hadith for inspiration, because we see divisions based on *fiqh* and sect as inimical to Muslim unity.

The school aspires, as its name suggests, to 'international' status by providing English-medium education using modern teaching methods and aids, but in what is described in its publicity brochure as an 'Islamic' environment. The school is geared to a clientele of rich Muslims who seek a suitably 'Islamic' yet modern education for their children, for many of whom the education provided in general schools is culturally inappropriate and alienating. Students learn the usual subjects in addition to Islamic studies, which are taught with the help of primers published by Islamic organizations in the United Kingdom, the United States, Australia, South Africa and Saudi Arabia. The school is presently till the second standard, but it plans to shortly expand to the high school level.

Alternative Forms of Islamic Knowledge: Combining the Dini *and the* Duniyavi

Besides the new types of Muslim schools described here, there are growing numbers of madrasas which are incorporating modern subjects into their curriculum. A good example of a modernizing madrasa is the Markaz ul-Ma'arif Education and Research Centre, Mumbai. It was established in 1982 by Maulana Badruddin Ajmal, a graduate of the Deoband madrasa and a member of Deoband's central advisory committee. Originally from Assam, Ajmal is a prosperous Mumbai-based merchant and philanthropist. He represents a new, emerging breed of socially engaged 'ulama, setting up social work projects and also promoting religious education through innovative means. The Markaz runs a number of institutions in Assam and some other states in northeast India. These include ten English-medium schools, 550 part-time *maktab*s, three orphanages, a modern hospital and several vocational training centres. The Markaz claims to fund several small social work centres engaged in various developmental activities. It has a publishing wing which has produced a considerable amount of Islamic literature in various languages, including Assamese,

Bengali, Urdu and English.[12] It is also engaged in a limited form of inter-faith dialogue work, and has liberally contributed to various 'national' causes, making substantial donations to the Prime Minister's Relief Fund and the Army Central Welfare Fund with the purpose of helping the cause of 'martyrs who laid down their lives for the cause of the country'.[13]

In 1994, after consultation with the elders at Deoband, the Markaz decided to set up a centre in Delhi to train a selected number of madrasa graduates in English, computer applications and comparative religions. The principal objective of the programme was to enable madrasa graduates 'find a suitable place in the world' and also to 'reason scientifically and put forward convincing arguments before the masses about the positive teachings of Islam'.[14] Till it was recently closed and shifted to Mumbai, every year the Markaz selected about twenty students, mostly graduates from the Dar ul-'Ulum, Deoband, for a two-year course. The course involved intensive study of spoken and written English. Students were also taught various computer application techniques such as desktop publishing and web designing, skills they would need in their future profession as missionaries. In addition, they also learnt about the basic beliefs of other faiths which too would better equip them in missionary work.

Several graduates of the Markaz are now employed as English teachers at various madrasas, including two at the recently launched department of English at Deoband. A number of them teach Arabic in government schools in Assam, West Bengal and Bihar. Others work as journalists in Urdu as well as English papers brought out by different Muslim organizations. Yet others have found jobs as teachers and translators in Arab countries and in South Africa, which is home to a large and relatively prosperous Deobandi Muslim community. Two graduates from the centre manage the Markaz's website and on-line *fatwa*-dispensing unit based in Mumbai. Several of the centre's graduates are now studying at regular universities, pursuing research in Arabic, Urdu and Islamic studies.[15]

A similar experiment is the Dar ul-'Umoor, based at Srirangapatnam near Mysore in Karnataka. Founded as a registered trust in 1998, it is run under the auspices of the Tipu Sultan Advanced Study and Research Centre, the brainchild of Ziaullah Sheriff, one of the biggest architects and builders in Bangalore. It is located on a sprawling 40-acre campus adjacent to the tomb of the eighteenth century Muslim ruler of Mysore, Tipu Sultan. It takes its name from a similarly named institution set up by Tipu Sultan to promote scientific innovations. It sees itself as imparting what it describes as 'an integrated educational programme both in Islamic science and modern science and technology' so as to train a new class of socially involved 'ulama.[16]

In 2002 the Dar ul-'Umoor launched a one-year course, jointly prepared by university professors and 'ulama from the Nadwat ul-'Ulama, Lucknow. Till date most of its students have been drawn from the Nadwa itself. Education, board and lodging are provided free of cost, and each student is given a small monthly stipend. A major focus of the course is the learning of English and computer applications. Other subjects are also taught by visiting lecturers, including university professors, scientists, journalists, social activists, 'ulama, politicians and retired bureaucrats. They have spoken on a range of issues at the school, including inter-faith relations, modern *fiqh* issues, community development, conflict resolution, Indian history, personality development, information technology, mass media, and global politics. In addition, every Thursday the students are expected to engage in practical training, such as visiting schools, non-governmental agencies, scientific institutions and museums, as well as churches and temples to interact with Christian and Hindu priests. Students submit regular reports and articles, some of which have been published in local Urdu newspapers. All students are also simultaneously pursuing their master's degree in Urdu from the Karnataka Open University, Mysore.

'Abdur Rahman Kamaruddin, the amiable chairperson of the Dar ul-'Umoor, explains how the school seeks to promote a new breed of 'ulama who are cognizant of the world around them:

> Through the exposure that the students gain by interacting with experts in different fields, we want to prepare 'ulama who can play a constructive role in community affairs. If they are made aware of the problems and concerns of the world around them they would be in a better position to interpret Islam in order to meet new demands and challenges. They might also be able to influence the madrasas once they finish their studies here. In that way reforms can begin from within the madrasa system, instead of being imposed from the outside. Some students will return to madrasas to teach, sharing their knowledge and skills with other 'ulama. Others might be absorbed by various Muslim social welfare organizations or by Muslim magazines and newspapers as journalists. Yet others would work as preachers in mosques, and one of their principal tasks would be to deliver sermons on issues of contemporary relevance. In this way, we feel that the work that we are engaged in will have a multiplier effect and lead to a gradual transformation of the madrasa system as a whole.[17]

The Dar ul-'Umoor has made efforts to popularize its programme in different madrasas, seeking to make them aware of the need to reform their syllabus and methods of teaching. For this purpose, in 2001 it organized its first four-day orientation programme at the Nadwat ul-'Ulama, which was attended by a number of leading 'ulama and social activists. Speeches were delivered on issues of contemporary importance. The students and teachers at Nadwa apparently responded with enthusiasm, evincing interest in the future programmes of the centre. The centre has contacted several other madrasas and has offered to conduct similar workshops with their students.

Another experiment hailed as a unique and pioneering effort to combine Islamic and modern education is the Jami'at ul-Hidaya, located in a Muslim-dominated village on the outskirts of Jaipur. Established in 1986 by the Naqshbandi Sufi *shaikh* and '*alim*, Maulana 'Abdur Rahim Mujaddidi, it is affiliated to the Deobandi *maslak*, although it is open to Sunnis of all schools of thought.

Maulana Mujaddidi is a soft-spoken man, probably in his late sixties or early seventies. That he takes his Sufism seriously is evident from his humble, almost self-effacing, demeanour and his charming smile. He might appear as a simple '*alim* from the dress he wears, but he is one of India's most ardent champions of modern education in the madrasas. He was initially reluctant, in true Sufi fashion, to speak about the achievements of his madrasa, but on being prodded he explained:

> Our madrasa provides its estimated 700 students a traditional Islamic education. This is supplemented with compulsory modern education till the tenth grade level. For this we use textbooks published by the NCERT. Thereafter, we have a four-year '*alim* course, during which students learn a range of subjects, including the Qur'an, Hadith, *tafsir*, *fiqh*, and Arabic literature. Arrangements are also made for lectures by visiting 'ulama and university professors to speak on issues of contemporary concern. Students doing the '*alim* course must also learn a skill that would enable

> them to earn a gainful livelihood after they graduate. After all, we need to think about their future employment prospects as well. We don't want them to be a burden on the community. They need to stand on their own feet. Among the technical trades that we have arrangements for are computer applications, mechanical and electrical engineering, electronics and communications.

Several graduates of the madrasa, the Maulana explains, have now set up small businesses of their own, and some have even got jobs in companies in India and the Gulf countries. Other students of the madrasa, estimated at half the total number of graduates, have gone in for higher Islamic education, in India and abroad, and yet others have joined regular universities for higher studies.

The Maulana 'Abdur Rahim Education Trust, which runs the Jami'at ul-Hidaya, also manages three English-medium schools in Jaipur city, catering largely to boys and girls of poor Muslim families. In association with some professors of the Aligarh Muslim University the Trust recently set up the Al-Hidaya Study Centre at Aligarh in order to train Muslim students to appear for competitive examinations for various government services. The Trust has set a list of ambitious plans for itself, including launching a full-fledged faculty of commerce, as well as starting courses in refrigeration, air-conditioning, pharmacy, automobile engineering and journalism. It is also in the process of establishing a training centre for madrasa teachers, which would be the first of its kind in the country.

Reforms in Existing Madrasas

Stirrings of change have not left even madrasas, considered the bastions of Islamic 'orthodoxy', unaffected. Recently, as pointed out in the previous chapter, the Deoband madrasa launched two new departments, of English and computer courses. This was considered a particularly radical move, given the widespread perception of Deoband's hostility to 'Western' knowledge and culture. More open to change is the 200-year-old Jami'at us-Saifiya at Surat, the principal madrasa for the Bohra Shi'as, which conducts an eleven-year course for boys and girls, combining religious and modern subjects including natural and social sciences. Not all of its students go on to become professional 'ulama—several go on to universities for higher secular education while others are now successful traders and industrialists in India and abroad.[18] Numerous madrasas in Uttar Pradesh run by the Dini Ta'limi Council today teach both religious as well as secular subjects. Students then get a certificate that allows them to continue their education in regular schools.[19] Certain other madrasas may not be able to afford modern education for their students, but instead have facilities for training them in some craft or trade. This is the case, for instance, with the Jami'at ul-Islamia Khair ul-'Ulum at Domariaganj, in eastern Uttar Pradesh, which provides Islamic education till the *fazil* level, and also has a workshop where students can train to become welders, tailors and automobile mechanics.[20] Madrasas with few or no arrangements for modern education have modified their admission policies, timings and the structure of their courses in a way that allows their students to study in regular schools alongside their religious studies. Such is the case of the Jami'a Nazmia in Lucknow, one of the premier Ithna 'Ashari Shi'a madrasas in the country. It encourages its students to pursue education in regular universities simultaneously with their madrasa education. Almost all its students in the final year have done or are doing a graduation degree course at Lucknow University, mostly in the departments of Arabic, Urdu, Persian and Islamic studies.

Another Shi'a school in Lucknow, the Madrasa Imania Khadijat ul-Kubra, runs a two-year course for girls who are enrolled in regular colleges or universities.

Another way in which growing numbers of 'ulama are seeking to bridge the divide between religious and modern education is by setting up modern schools where basic Islamic education is also imparted, these being run along with traditional madrasas under a common management system. The Dar ul-'Ulum Deoband has spawned some interesting initiatives in this regard. Recently, one of its senior management committee members, Maulana 'Asad Madani, considered to be the man who actually holds the reins of power at the madrasa, inaugurated a polytechnic for girls in Deoband. His son runs the Madani Memorial English-medium School, also located at Deoband. Similarly, the Ahl-i Hadith's Jami'at us-Salafiya madrasa in Varanasi also runs the Ummahat al-Mu'minin Girls' Higher Secondary School, which it now plans to upgrade to a regular arts and science college providing education till the graduation level. In Srinagar, the Sayyed Mirak Shah Educational Trust runs a primary madrasa as well as a chain of regular primary and high schools which are affiliated to the educational board of the government of Jammu and Kashmir. In Kerala, the Markaz us-Shaqafat us-Sunniya runs one of the largest *shari'ah* colleges in the state, in addition to several modern schools, a technical training centre, a clinic and two orphanages.[21] The Delhi-based 'Abdul Kalam Islamic Awakening Centre, affiliated to the Ahl-i Hadith, runs a number of educational institutions, including two high schools (one each for girls and boys) and a large madrasa. In Kishanganj, Bihar, the All-India Ta'limi-o-Milli Foundation, established by a leading Deobandi '*alim*, runs a chain of *maktab*s, a girls' high school and an engineering college.[22]

Several other such examples can be cited. In these diverse ways, a small yet growing number of 'ulama and 'ulama-based groups are today making efforts to bridge the dualism between the madrasa and the modern school system.

Girls' Madrasas: A New Development

An interesting development in recent years is the setting up of a small, yet growing, number of madrasas specifically for girls by Muslim groups belonging to different *maslak*s. While schools for Muslim girls have been in existence since colonial times, the concept of separate higher-level madrasas for girls is relatively recent. Traditionally, well-off Muslim families would arrange for lady teachers (*ustani*s) or elderly men to come to their homes to teach their daughters the Qur'an, Arabic and Urdu. Often, as is still the case in large parts of India, girls from poorer families would be sent to *maktab*s to study the Qur'an from male teachers, along with boys of their age. After learning to read and recite the Qur'an and acquiring basic Islamic education, they were generally withdrawn from the *maktab*s with the onset of puberty (*balaghat*) and kept in their homes till their parents arranged for them to be married.

In the past, few girls, if any, actually went on to train to become religious specialists. They were provided with only a modicum of Islamic knowledge that was considered to be adequate for them to perform the basic Islamic rituals. Today, however, a number of girls' madrasas in various parts of India are engaged in training girls as '*alima*s, specialists in Islamic studies like their male 'ulama counterparts. The increasing awareness of the importance of girls' education, and a feeling that government schools, with their 'Hinduistic' syllabus and their coeducational system, are not suitable for their children, have combined to impress upon growing numbers of Muslims the need for separate girls' madrasas. By combining Islamic education with modern subjects to varying degrees, these schools are playing a major role in promoting literacy as well as Islamic awareness among Muslim girls, who are among the most educationally deprived sections of Indian society.

In the writings of Muslim advocates of special madrasas for girls, their education is seen as an essential Islamic duty for the Qur'an and the Hadith insist on the need for Muslims, men as well as women, to acquire knowledge. Girls' education is thus seen not as a novel development, but, instead, as a revival of a lost Prophetic tradition. An educated Muslim girl is said to be following in the footsteps of such role models as Ayesha, the youngest wife of the Prophet, who is said to have been a great *muhaddith*, relating a large number of *hadith* reports to several of the Prophet's male companions after his death.[23] Educated Muslim girls are, therefore, seen as figures to be admired and respected, with their own important functions to discharge in the preservation and promotion of the Islamic tradition.

The new agency that is provided to girls through these madrasas is generally circumscribed within the limits of the family. These madrasas see the sort of education that they provide as training girls to perform their domestic tasks in what they regard as a genuinely 'Islamic' manner. This does not necessarily mean a diminution in girls' status on all fronts. The language of rights is often used in arguing the case for girls' madrasas—it is claimed that if girls are taught the rights that Islam has granted them they will no longer be exploited by Muslim males. For instance, an educated Muslim woman who knows her rights in matters of inheritance and divorce, would, it is often argued, be able to challenge her husband if he acts in violation of the *shari'ah*. As educated mothers and wives, Muslim women might be able to play new roles and earn added respect within the household. As the brochure of a Deobandi girls' madrasa claims, through 'proper' Islamic education a Muslim woman can become an 'ideal' mother and wife and thereby earn the admiration of her family. She can also help educate her own children.[24] Education of girls is thus regarded as an essential Islamic duty not only because the Qur'an mandates it but also because it would help the community as a whole to lead a more 'Islamic' life.

The setting up of girls' madrasas has crucial implications for traditional understandings of gender relations and normative female behaviour. Arguments stressing the 'Islamicity' of girls' education that hark back to tradition and 'authenticity' might actually help pave the way for an inadvertent modernization, at least in some cases. Thus, a Deobandi '*alim* who passionately advocates the cause of girls' Islamic madrasas also suggests that these schools include a basic minimum of modern subjects in their curriculum, such as mathematics and social sciences, in order to create an 'enlightened mentality' (*roshan fikri*) so that the students can 'get to know about the affairs of the world as well'.[25] An educated Muslim girl is thus accorded a new agency as an active subject with an important role to play in social reform and in improving the conditions of her family. Empowered with the written word and with access to classical Islamic texts, girls educated in madrasas come to gain respect in a society where patriarchal biases are still often very acute. They can now function, at least in theory, as religious authorities in their own right. They might even be able to go on to contest patriarchal biases in the interpretation of the Islamic tradition, although this has not happened as yet on any significant scale. In actual fact, there seems to be no evidence of any major challenge emerging from these schools to patriarchal understandings of Islam, other than through highlighting some of the rights accorded to women in the Qur'an.

Overall, the rationale for special girls' madrasas is generally presented in conservative terms. Pious Muslim girls and women are depicted as symbols of Muslim community identity and as guardians of the purity of the faith in a world that is seen to be corrupt and licentious. In fact, it is often stressed by managers of these schools, most of whom happen to be men, that separate girls' madrasas are necessary in order to 'protect' Muslim women from the growing temptation to defy male authority, which they present as integral to their vision of Islam. It is argued that in the absence of 'proper' Islamic education, Muslim girls might be swayed by demands for women's liberation, consumerism and 'un-Islamic' ways of life that would threaten the integrity of the community itself. As an activist associated with the Jama'at-i Islami writes, in order to ward off this threat Muslim girls should be trained to combat 'irreligiousness' (*ilhad*) and 'immorality' (*be-hayayi*). In this way, he says, they would be able to protect the family, which he describes as the 'fort of sanctity' (*haram ka qila*).[26] The ideal Muslim woman is thus regarded as one who has a deep knowledge of her faith and uses that knowledge to help raise a truly Muslim family. In the writings of 'ulama who advocate Muslim girls' education, the sphere of the educated Muslim woman is generally seen as restricted to her home. Only a very small minority among them consider it permissible for Muslim women to work outside the domestic sphere.

Girls' madrasas in India today, like those for boys, display considerable variety. Some provide only a few years of general Islamic education, and when girls reach the age of puberty they are expected to discontinue their studies to get married. Others are more like regular schools that also make arrangements for

Islamic studies. Most major Muslim *maslak*s in India today, including those popularly seen as grossly misogynist, have set up girls' madrasas in different parts of the country.

Interestingly, despite their image as die-hard conservatives, the Deobandis have, in recent years, been among the more active in this regard. One of the largest girls' madrasas in India, the Jami'at us-Salihat in the town of Malegaon in Maharashtra, is linked to the Deoband tradition. It was established in 1973 by a Deobandi graduate, Maulana Muhammad 'Usman Qasmi. It has a large hostel where girls from various parts of India as well as abroad live together. Strict purdah is observed and the girls are generally not allowed out of the campus unless accompanied by a close male relative. The madrasa provides education till the *fazila* level. The syllabus is broadly similar to that employed in general Deobandi madrasas, with additional books on issues of *fiqh* that are related specifically to women. Over the years, the Jami'at has produced a large number of graduates, many of whom are now teaching in girls' madrasas in other parts of India as well as abroad. Several others have set up girls' madrasas of their own.[27]

Another example of a Deobandi girls' madrasa that has also incorporated a basic level of modern subjects in its curriculum is the Madrasa Jami'at ul-Banat in New Delhi. It is housed in an incomplete two-storeyed tenement on the periphery of a squalid slum in the Muslim-dominated Basti Nizamuddin, near the shrine of the renowned Chishti Sufi Hazrat Khwaja Nizamuddin Auliya. The area is characterized by considerable poverty and a high rate of unemployment. Like most other such Muslim localities, it lacks many basic facilities, suffering from acute neglect by the state authorities. The few state-run schools in the area, as is the case with their counterparts elsewhere, leave much to be desired. Teachers come to the school only occasionally, and the standard of education provided is dismal. Faced with such great odds, the Jami'at ul-Banat is bravely struggling to provide a modicum of education to Muslim girls, almost all of whom come from poor or lower middle class families from outside Delhi, the vast majority from Bihar, Bengal and Uttar Pradesh.

The madrasa was established as a registered society in 1996 by Maulana Ilyas Barabankvi, a graduate of the Deoband madrasa. It is said to be the only higher-level girls' madrasa in Delhi. Like many other madrasas, it is a family undertaking, managed by the founder's son-in-law, Maulana Muhammad Islam. The Maulana is a graduate of the Madrasa Kashf ul-'Ulum, Delhi, which is located at the global headquarters of the Tablighi Jama'at, the world's largest Islamic revivalist movement. The Tablighi Jama'at preaches a fiercely patriarchal understanding of Islam, and this is reflected in the syllabus and style of functioning of the Jami'at ul-Banat as well.[28]

The madrasa sees the education that it imparts as helping to train a class of Muslim girls who are committed to its understanding of Islam, and who can later go on to play a key role in the reform of Muslim society on 'Islamic' lines and combat what are seen as 'un-Islamic' ways of life. Thus, its official brochure stresses that one of its major purposes is to impress upon its students the 'dangers' of 'Western' culture, which is seen as being 'in total opposition' to Islam. 'Western' culture is said to be wholly decadent, and is believed to be in complete contrast to an idealized, indeed romanticized, understanding of the Islamic tradition, defending which the madrasa sees among its principal tasks. Students are taught, the brochure proudly announces, that the 'only reason for the rapid degeneration of the world' is because human beings have 'moved far from Islamic culture'. Thus, the only solution to the manifold problems of the world, the students must learn, is for people to strictly follow the path of the Prophet. The students of the madrasa are seen as 'practical models' for women in the rest of the world to emulate.[29]

The madrasa presently has 180 girls on its rolls, all of whom live in the madrasa in four small halls that also serve as classrooms. Admission is generally given to girls who have already studied till the seventh grade in a government or private school. Education is provided free, but a small sum is charged for food. For girls from very poor families even this amount is waived. The madrasa depends largely on public donations to cover its expenses.[30]

The madrasa's syllabus follows the basic structure of the *dars-i nizami*, while reducing sections of books of *fiqh* related to matters specific to males and replacing them with books detailing *fiqh* rules pertaining to women. The course is of a six-year duration, after which the students receive the '*alima* degree. Some modern subjects are also taught, although the standard of teaching is poor because the madrasa cannot afford the high salaries that qualified teachers of these subjects generally demand. Students are taught basic English with the help of NCERT readers, although their level of comprehension of the subject leaves much to be desired. They are also taught stitching, knitting and embroidery. Great stress is laid on regular observance of prayers, and students are expected to pray together five times a day.

A major focus of the teaching imparted at the madrasa is on the internalization of appropriate gender norms as defined in the Deobandi vision. Thus, purdah is rigidly enforced. Girls are not allowed to step outside the madrasa, not even for a walk or to make purchases in the local market. The only occasions on which they can leave the madrasa are when their male guardians come to pick them up before the annual holidays, or in case of a medical emergency when they must be accompanied by a close male relative. All their teachers, with one exception, are females, most of them graduates of the madrasa itself. The only male teacher, the Hadith *ustad*, is not allowed to see the students. He delivers his lecture into a microphone while seated in a room on the ground floor, and the girls sit in rooms on the first floor and listen to his discourse. If the girls have any questions they relay them to him through a microphone. While recognizing that in the Prophet's time Muslim women could appear in public, the manager of the madrasa justifies the strict purdah that is followed in his school on the grounds that 'today circumstances have changed and people are no longer as pious as they were in the past'. Hence, he insists, women need to be 'protected' from the ever-present threat of *fitna* or 'strife'.[31]

While the Deobandi girls' madrasas reflect one form of Muslim girls' religious education, there are other, somewhat less conservative, forms of girls' madrasas which have arrangements for Islamic as well as modern education. The most bold experiments in this regard have been made by girls' madrasas affiliated, either organizationally or ideologically, with the Jama'at-i Islami. A good example is the girls' wing of the Jami'at ul-Falah in Azamgarh, which now has some 2700 girls on its rolls. Students here train to become '*alima*s and *fazila*s, religious authorities in their own right. Besides Islamic subjects, they also study various modern disciplines till the high school level. Their course of studies is largely similar to that of boys, except in matters of *fiqh*, where greater attention is paid to matters particular to women. Home science is also taught as a regular discipline. While many female students of the madrasa marry soon after graduation, several have taken up independent occupations, such as teaching in girls' madrasas or setting up such madrasas on their own. Some have even gone on to enrol in courses to train as doctors of Unani medicine.

Another similar experiment is the Jami'at us-Salihat in Rampur in northern Uttar Pradesh. Established by a group of Jama'at-i Islami workers and sympathizers in 1972, some 4000 girls, mostly from middle class families, study in the school. Around a fourth of the students come from outside the town and live in hostels located on the campus. It provides religious education along with regular subjects, for which it follows the NCERT syllabus. All subjects are taught in the medium of Urdu, although English is a compulsory subject. From the fifth grade onwards, students are taught to use computers.[32]

Yet another modern girls' madrasa is the Siraj ul-Uloom Niswan College at Aligarh. Founded in 1948 by a lady philanthropist, Bilquis Sultana Begum, it is managed by a committee consisting of members associated with the Jama'at-i Islami. It provides a general education till the fifth grade, following the government-prescribed syllabus, along with basic Islamic studies. For higher Islamic studies it offers a six-year '*alima* course, which includes the Qur'an, Hadith, *fiqh* and *tafsir*, in addition to Urdu, Hindi, English, Persian, Arabic, mathematics, the natural and social sciences, and home science. '*Alima*s can go on to do a two-year *fazila* course, which consists of various standard traditional Islamic subjects, along with Islamic history and English. Among the school's various future plans are a course in Unani medicine, a girls' medical college and hospital, and a computer training centre. The school is affiliated to the government-run Arabic and Persian Education Board, Allahabad, which conducts examinations for the '*alim*, *maulvi* and *munshi* degrees.[33]

*

As these instances show, madrasas in India today are responding in diverse ways to the challenges of contemporary life, and cannot be said to be completely hostile to change. True, change may be slow in coming, and it may not always occur in expected or desired ways. Yet, inexorably, the pressure for reform and modernization is making its presence felt even in the secluded portals of the most traditional madrasas. However, the concerted campaign to discredit the madrasas as 'dens of terror', part of a larger anti-Muslim agenda that is becoming increasingly strident in India today, has posed major problems for madrasas that seriously wish to reform. Considering themselves under siege, appeals for reform are increasingly seen as representing hidden 'conspiracies' to destroy the religious character of the madrasas or even to uproot Islam from India. Naturally, this has worked to dampen enthusiasm for madrasa reform on the part of many 'ulama. We turn to this vexed issue of the alleged terrorist links of Indian madrasas in the chapter that follows.

{6}

Madrasas and Militancy

Recent events, particularly 9/11, have led to a growing concern with what are often loosely called Islamic 'fundamentalist' movements. These events have also seen an increasing interest in madrasas among government officials, policy planners as well as the general public, as very little is actually known about them. In the absence of any comprehensive knowledge of madrasas, and goaded by prejudice and preconceived notions, journalists and writers with their own agendas to pursue have been quick to link the madrasas with radical Islamist movements and to brand them indiscriminately as 'dens of terror' allegedly churning out legions of fanatic 'warriors of Islam'.

Before dealing with the alleged nexus between madrasas and terrorism, it is instructive to note that madrasas have been in existence in South Asia for centuries, and their syllabus has, by and large, remained the same for almost 200 years. Those who label madrasas as 'dens of terror' ignore the fact that politics is hardly ever explicitly taught in most Indian madrasas. The overwhelming focus of their syllabus is on religious beliefs and the nitty-gritty of *fiqh* rules governing 'proper' worship, dress, personal behaviour and appropriate gender codes. The curriculum is thus overwhelmingly conservative, literalist and legalist, but definitely not politically radical. Indeed, detractors of the madrasas, including radical Islamists, routinely accuse them of 'weakening' the community and playing into the hands of the 'enemies of Islam' by ignoring burning political issues, and focusing, instead, on discussions on issues such as the appropriate length of one's beard or the Prophetic method of purifying oneself after defecation.

Radical Islamist movements, as numerous studies have shown, enjoy little support in traditional madrasas. Rather, their main bases of support are regular colleges and universities, in particular faculties of hard sciences such as engineering and medicine. This is a phenomenon that has been observed not just in South Asia but in the Arab world and in the West as well. Not one among the Arabs accused of masterminding the attacks of September 11 had received a traditional madrasa education. Nor, for that matter, did the dreaded Osama bin Laden. They, like the leaders of almost all Islamist groups, had studied in regular universities, some of them in the West itself.

Radical Islamists are often bitterly critical of what they see as the stagnation of the 'ulama, of their apparent lack of concern for the affairs of this world, and of their willingness to serve the interests of ruling regimes in Muslim countries, which Islamists regard as slavish lackeys of the 'unbelieving' West and as Muslim only in name. In several Muslim countries, high-ranking 'ulama are actually paid employees of the state. Not surprisingly, many Muslim states have sought to use the 'ulama to undercut the influence of radical Islamists, by getting them to issue appropriate *fatwa*s against them and declaring their actions to be 'un-Islamic'. For many 'ulama, Islamists, who are often bereft of any formal Islamic training, have no authority to speak for Islam. Thus, for instance, in India, numerous Barelwi 'ulama have written voluminous tomes condemning Islamist groups such as the Jama'at-i Islami as 'enemies of the faith'. Likewise, in the Deobandi case, the leading ideologue of the Deobandi-inspired Tablighi Jama'at, Maulana Muhammad Zakariya, penned a voluminous treatise on the Jama'at-i Islami, declaring that what it preached was not Islam at all, but rather a new religion called 'Maududism', named after the Jama'at's founder, Sayyed Abul 'Ala Maududi. As rival claimants for the leadership of the community, Islamists present a grave challenge to the authority of the 'ulama, and the latter have sought to use every means possible to stave off that threat. To equate the two, therefore, is misleading.

Radical Islamism threatens the traditional 'ulama by bypassing the centuries-old tradition of *fiqh*, on which the power of the 'ulama rests, seeking, instead, to directly approach the Qur'an and the Hadith for inspiration and guidance. As many Islamists see it, Islam has no room for a quasi-priesthood that they regard the 'ulama as having transformed themselves into. In place of medieval *fiqh*, radical Islamists mouth the rhetoric of *ijtihad*, although there is little evidence to suggest that they have gone far enough in the quest for a new or more relevant understanding of Islamic jurisprudence. Then again, unlike many 'ulama, radical Islamists take politics very seriously. For them, Islam is centred around the notion of political power, and the Islamic state is seen as necessary for Muslims to lead their lives fully in accordance with the dictates of their faith. On the other hand, for many 'ulama of the madrasas the central core of Islam is *fiqh*, and they are often willing to acquiesce in the absence of an Islamic state as long as Muslims are allowed to freely practise their religion and observe their own personal laws. In other words, while radical Islamism has an inherent tendency to stress confrontation, whether ideological or physical, the Islam of the traditional madrasas tends towards an innate conservatism and pragmatic adjustment. True, exceptions exist in both cases. Some Islamists, in fact, are today key proponents of peaceful inter-faith dialogue, and some 'ulama associated with madrasas are enthusiastic spokesmen for armed *jihad*. On the whole, however, it can safely be said that, at least in India, madrasas have had nothing to do with active involvement in militancy, contrary to what is so often claimed.

The Indian 'Ulama and Politics: Changing Equations

The debate on the alleged links between Indian madrasas and militancy needs to be situated in a broader political context. For one thing, and this needs to be constantly borne in mind, religious militancy in India taking the form of large-scale violence and terror is much more characteristic of Hindu rather than Muslim groups. Scores of Hindu supremacist organizations openly call for violence against Muslims and other marginalized communities, and have been closely involved, often along with agencies of the state, in mass murders of Muslims in which thousands of innocent people have perished till date. Several thousand schools run by Hindutva groups exist across the country that carefully instruct their students in undying, relentless hatred of Muslims and other non-Hindu communities. In the garb of protectors of the 'Hindu nation', they claim a virtual monopoly of patriotism, and are often portrayed thus by the media. It is a sign of the extremely loaded discourse on nationalism in India today that while madrasas, the vast majority of which have nothing whatsoever to do with militant activism, are routinely described as 'dens of terror', schools and organizations run by Hindutva groups are generally seen as proudly 'nationalist', and as defending the honour of the country that is under constant threat from 'enemies' within and without. A comparative study needs to be done of madrasas and schools run by Hindu supremacist organizations. It would reveal surprising results, proving that obscurantism and militancy are by no means Muslim monopolies.

The question of the possible links of madrasas with militant activist groups must also be seen in a wider historical setting, tracing the complex ways in which madrasas have sought to relate to the Indian state. As shown earlier, prior to 1947 different Islamic groups had adopted a range of positions on the struggle between the Congress and the Muslim League. Several Barelwi 'ulama vociferously supported the League and its demand for a separate Muslim state of Pakistan. They argued that Islam forbade Muslims from befriending 'unbelievers', claiming that the Congress aimed at establishing a Hindu state and arguing, therefore, that the Muslims needed to have their own separate country. Likewise, the Islamist Jama'at-i Islami, led by Sayyed Abul 'Ala Maududi, stridently opposed the Congress, denouncing its call for a composite nationalism as a cover-up to Hinduize the Muslims or else to reduce them to utter subjugation under a Hindu majority. The Jama'at also castigated the 'Muslim nationalism' of the League, claiming that the notion of nationalism was completely foreign to Islam. All Muslims the world over, Maududi argued, were one nation, and hence there could be no room for a separate Indian Muslim nation in the form of a separate state of Pakistan. However, shortly after partition, Maududi left for Pakistan to continue the struggle for an 'Islamic' state. Following the partition, the Jama'at split, with separate units being set up in Pakistan and India. As for the Deobandis, leading 'ulama associated with the Dar ul-'Ulum were closely associated with the Congress party. They were critical of the 'two-nation' theory of the League, arguing that Islam did, in fact, allow for territorial nationalism. The Muslims and Hindus of India, they insisted, were members of the same nation. As they saw it, as long as Muslims were allowed to practise their religion and observe their own personal laws in a free India there could be no contradiction between Islam and Indian nationalism. Some Deobandis, such as Ashraf 'Ali Thanwi and Shabbir Ahmad 'Usmani, dissented from this view and supported the League, but they remained a small, albeit vocal, minority.

Partition reduced Indian Muslims to an even smaller minority, increasingly marginalized and threatened by the rise of aggressive, anti-Muslim Hindu militancy. This, in turn, led to growing pragmatism among various Muslim groups in India and a clear distancing from aggressive communal politics. The Barelwis turned their attention to attacking fellow Muslim groups, branding them, for all practical purposes, as non-Muslims, thereby seeking to establish for themselves a clear identity of their own. On the whole, the Barelwi 'ulama stayed away from overt political involvement, preferring to concentrate their attention and resources on undermining their Muslim rivals. The Jama'at-i Islami Hind, while not renouncing its commitment to an Islamic state in India, stressed the need to accept the fact of non-Muslim rule. This was regarded not as an abandonment of the long-term goal of the 'rule of Allah' (*hukumat-i ilahiya*), but, rather, as a sensible 'pious pragmatic policy' (*mukhlisana hikmat-i 'amali*), given the virtual impossibility of establishing an Islamic state in India as long as Muslims remained a relatively small minority. Thus, moving away from Maududi's insistence that secularism and democracy were wholly 'un-Islamic', Jama'at leaders argued that in the specific Indian context Muslims must work along with people of other faiths in order to promote secular democracy, for the only other alternative was a fascist Hindu state. Meanwhile, they stressed, Muslims needed to engage in missionary work among the Hindus and other non-Muslims of the country, in the hope that if the majority of Indians were won over by Islam, its goal of an Islamic state would be made much easier. The establishment of such a state was, however, postponed into the remote, unspecified future. The Jama'at also stressed the importance of working for inter-community harmony, for only in such a climate would at least some Hindus be receptive to its message. On the political front, the Jama'at gave up its rigid insistence that its members should desist from voting in a political system that Maududi had condemned as 'anti-Islamic'. Instead, the Jama'at argued that Muslims must seek to work closely with and support those political parties that were willing to serve Muslim interests as it envisaged them.

The Deobandis faced relatively little problem in coming to terms with the Congress-ruled Indian state, for most of them had remained closely allied with the Congress in the course of the freedom struggle. Leading Deobandi 'ulama were easily co-opted by the state, some of them even being nominated by the Congress as members of Parliament. The Deobandis, along with the pro-Congress Jami'at ul-'Ulama-i Hind, itself largely Deobandi in composition, appealed to the Muslims of India to shun the communal politics of the Muslim League, which had, they rightly argued, brought untold misery to the Muslims who had been left behind in India. Instead, they should work with secular political parties to establish genuine democracy and secularism. The Jami'at also focused its attention on promoting Muslim religious education, providing relief to riot victims and defending Muslim personal law.[1] Like other 'ulama groups, it also regularly protested against pogroms directed against Muslims that were sometimes orchestrated by the state, and against threats to Muslim identity.

For its part, the Indian state did not pursue a clear-cut strategy on madrasa education. The Constitution of independent India, promulgated in 1950, gave all religious and linguistic minorities the right to establish and run educational institutions of their choice, which meant that Muslims were free to set up *maktab*s and madrasas. However, the state actually did little to promote modern education among Muslims. Critics have argued that by deliberately paying scant attention to promoting modern education among Muslims the state actually strengthened, deliberately or otherwise, the influence of the madrasas and the conservative 'ulama. On the other hand, the state sought to use some of the leading madrasas, particularly Deoband, to 'showcase', as Mushirul Hasan puts it, India's claims to 'secularism'.[2] It even sought to project the madrasas abroad to serve its own foreign policy goals, to convince Middle Eastern countries that Muslims were safe and prospering in India and thereby tried to counter Pakistani claims to the contrary. Thus, in 1949, just two years after India's independence, officials from the home ministry and All India Radio visited Deoband and prepared a programme on the madrasa for the external radio service, lauding its various achievements.[3] Some state governments set up boards of madrasa education that provided financial assistance to a small number of madrasas. Larger madrasas, such as Deoband and Nadwa, were granted official permission to admit students from other countries, and the state provided visas to a number of such students.

The Dar ul-'Ulum at Deoband, today under attack for its alleged connections with the Afghan Taliban, received particular attention from the state in recognition of its powerful influence among Muslims in India and abroad. In 1957, the then president of India, Rajendra Prasad, visited the madrasa in his official capacity.[4] In his speech to the students and teachers of the madrasa he praised what he described as the great services of the institution in India's struggle for independence, expressing the hope that it would 'carry on in this tradition in the future as well' and 'expand its work'. He waxed eloquent about his close association with leading Deobandis in the course of the freedom movement.[5] He even went so far as to assert that by attracting students from many other countries, the madrasa had become a source of 'pride' for all Indians. He ended his speech with a prayer that the madrasa would expand and prosper 'in order to serve not just India but other countries as well'.[6] Expressing his delight at being at the madrasa, he declared, much to the joy of the 'ulama who gathered to hear him:

> I have been hearing about the Dar ul-'Ulum for a long time now, and have, ever since I first heard of it, wanted to come here, and today that wish has been fulfilled. The elders of the Dar ul-'Ulum acquire and impart knowledge for its own sake. There have been few people in the past that did this, and they were even more respected than kings. Today, the elders of the Dar ul-'Ulum are walking in this path, and I believe that this is a service not only to the Dar ul-'Ulum itself, nor only of the Muslims alone, but, in fact, of the entire country, and, indeed, of the whole world. Today, materialism has overwhelmed the world, leading people to despair and hopelessness. The only effective remedy for this is spiritualism, and I see that the elders of this institution are providing this to the world. I believe that if God wills this world to survive, the world must come back to this path. That is why the work of the elders of this Dar ul-'Ulum will progress. I am very happy having come here [. . .].[7]

Leaders of the Congress party kept up good relations with Deoband, acutely aware of the crucial importance of the madrasa and the influence that its 'ulama enjoyed among large sections of Muslim voters. In 1980, the then prime minister, Indira Gandhi, visited Deoband to participate in the madrasa's centenary celebrations, an occasion which caused a split in the madrasa between two rival groups contending for control. In her speech Mrs Gandhi lauded the efforts of the madrasa in India's freedom movement, and expressed the hope that it would continue in the tradition of its forebears.[8] Probably with an eye on the Muslim vote, she heaped praises on the 'ulama of Deoband for their scholarship and patriotism and their contribution to India's plural society. In the same year the Government of India issued a special 30 paise stamp in honour of the madrasa.[9]

Over the years, among other top non-Muslim Indian dignitaries who visited the Deoband madrasa and, predictably, lauded its work, were Jagdish Sahai, judge of the Allahabad High Court (1963), Ajit Prasad Jain, governor of Kerala (1965), Gopal Reddy, governor of Uttar Pradesh (1969), Vasudev Singh, speaker of the Uttar Pradesh Legislative Assembly (1976), Ram Naresh, deputy chief minister of Uttar Pradesh (1979) and Vir Bahadur Singh, chief minister of Uttar Pradesh (1985).[10] For their part, the authorities at Deoband seem to have warmly welcomed the prospect of hobnobbing with the highest authorities of the land, for it gave them a certain prestige in Muslim circles, reinforcing their claims against 'ulama of other Muslim groups to speak for the entire Muslim community. It also gave them an opportunity to stress their patriotic credentials and highlight the role of their elders in the freedom struggle, thus seeking to win the support of the Indian establishment and non-Muslim opinion in general.

Overall, then, after 1947 the Indian madrasas seem to have made a pragmatic adjustment to a situation of 'Hindu' rule, most of them consciously eschewing concern with the state and preaching a generally politically quiescent sort of Islam. Although many ‘ulama associated with the madrasas continued to insist (and teach) that Islam provided a comprehensive set of laws governing all aspects of personal as well as collective life, including the political sphere, they seem to have remained content with the limited applicability of Islamic law in the area of personal affairs as allowed for by the Indian state, as long as Muslims continued being in a minority. Muslim personal law thus emerged as the defining element of a separate Muslim identity in India. This was also reflected in the curriculum of most madrasas which continued to focus on matters of *fiqh* related to worship and personal affairs. Few madrasas actually taught the chapters on politics contained in the books of medieval *fiqh* in any great detail, although this did not mean that they regarded them as redundant. It was generally stressed that while the *fiqh* formulations on politics and public law were an integral part of Islam, as long as Muslims remained a minority in India it made little sense to talk in terms of an Islamic state ruled by the *shari‘ah*. Rather than the Islamization of the state or the capture of state power, the madrasas seem to have been particularly concerned about the need for the protection of Muslim religious identity, which was seen as threatened by a subtle process of Hinduization promoted by the state in the name of a homogeneous Indian nationalism that borrowed heavily from Hindu mythology. This explains, in part, the rapid spread of madrasas in various parts of India after 1947 that propagated an extremely apolitical form of Islam, focusing essentially on imparting knowledge of basic Islamic beliefs and rituals to Muslim children. Few, if any, madrasas taught anything overtly ‘political’, although in theological matters they remained for the most part extremely conservative.

The shift from the political to the personal did not, however, mean that madrasas had willingly embraced secularism as a principle, understood here as the complete separation of the state and religion. Secularism was generally seen as a matter of expediency. It made sense to talk about secularism in a situation where Muslims were a minority, although few 'ulama were willing to accept that principle in a Muslim-majority context. The acceptance of state neutrality in matters of religion represented, for most Indian 'ulama, a pragmatic adjustment to a situation of Muslim powerlessness which, while lamenting it, they could do little to redress. Faced with the obvious fact of Muslim marginalization, they sought solace in their conviction of the ultimate 'victory' of Islam over what were seen as 'false' (*batil*) ideologies. In God's eyes, they preached to their students, Islam alone represented the truth, and all other religions were either corruptions of earlier divinely revealed faiths or else mere human constructions. In either case, they were insufficient to qualify their followers for salvation in the Hereafter. If Muslims were persecuted and oppressed, they preached, they could take comfort in the belief that 'true' Muslims alone would enter heaven on the Day of Judgement. Further, many traditional 'ulama argued, if Muslims were to eschew political involvement and focus, instead, simply on cultivating their faith, God might be moved to grant them political power over the 'unbelievers' in the future, if He so willed.

'Ulama and Islamist Perceptions of the Contemporary Indian State

An indication of how several Indian madrasas have pragmatically come to terms with the Indian nation-state are the ways in which the Indian state is perceived and projected in the activities of the madrasas and in their curricula. Thus, several madrasas organize special functions on Independence Day and Republic Day, inviting local Muslims as well as non-Muslims to participate. The Indian flag is unfurled, and madrasa students sing patriotic songs extolling the greatness of India. Generally, senior madrasa teachers, and sometimes students, deliver speeches praising the country and stressing, in particular, the role of the 'ulama in the freedom struggle and the many contributions made by Muslims to Indian civilization. This is also often accompanied by a general lamentation of the fact of Muslim marginalization, the poor representation of Muslims in government services, the colossal loss of Muslim lives in frequent rounds of organized violence, and so on, these being presented as a cruel betrayal of the ideals of the freedom movement. An '*alim* who teaches at a Deobandi madrasa in Lucknow says:

> In general, non-Muslims have been taught, through the educational system and the mass media, that Muslims played no role at all in the freedom movement. They believe that all Muslims supported the Muslim League and its demand for Pakistan. That is why they still look at us with suspicion. In order to reach out to them, our madrasa has been regularly organising functions on Independence Day, to which we also invite local non-Muslims, including journalists, social workers and government officials. We tell them that it was actually under Muslim rule that India was unified—before that we Indians were all divided into hundreds of warring principalities. We tell them that Muslims produced a rich culture, which made India the envy of the world. Muslims built the Taj Mahal, the Red Fort, the Jami'a Masjid in Delhi and hundreds of other great monuments, in which every Indian takes such great pride. We also tell them that it was the Muslims who first lit the flame of revolt against the British. Hundreds of great 'ulama sacrificed their lives fighting the British,

> and this happened several decades before the Hindus ever thought of establishing the Indian National Congress.

A teacher at a Shi'a madrasa in Lucknow makes a similar point:

> The Prophet, peace be upon him, said, 'Love of the country is part of the faith'. We were born in this country, we live here and will die here. We will be buried in the soil of India. This means that our loyalties must be to our own country, and we must do all we can to serve it and work for its welfare. We stress this to our students, and we want to make them both good Muslims as well as good Indians. We see absolutely no contradiction between the two. To convey this message to our Hindu brothers we sometimes invite them to our madrasa on Independence Day and Republic Day, where we tell them about our work and the role that we can play in helping our country prosper.

The underlying message is that Muslims can hardly be considered aliens and enemies of the Indian state. Indeed, it is often suggested in the writings of the 'ulama that it is to Muslims that the Hindus owe a heavy debt for the freedom of the country as well as for their many contributions to Indian civilization. Islam and patriotism, it is stressed, are not opposed to each other. In fact, it is argued, Islam positively encourages Muslims to love their motherland and even to sacrifice their lives for it. This rereading of history and the Islamic tradition serves a very contemporary purpose. If India owes so much to the Muslims, then Muslims today must be allowed a status at least equal to that of the Hindus, and not just in theory, but in practice as well.

Explicit reference to politics is rare in classes at the madrasas. Some madrasas do, however, refer to debates on the legal status of the Indian state in their discussion of *fiqh*. The general understanding, despite exceptions, appears to be that although

India is not an Islamic state, and therefore not *dar ul-islam* ('abode of Islam'), neither is it *dar ul-harb* ('abode of war'). Some 'ulama choose to characterize it as a 'land of peace' (*dar ul-aman*) or a 'land of agreement' (*dar ul-ahad*), a domain where Muslims, although not the ruling class, are free to practise their faith. In the teaching of the books of medieval *fiqh*, often the chapters on politics dealing with the relations between the Caliphs and their subjects and based on the assumption of Muslim rule, are conveniently left out. In many cases this is not because it is believed that they are now redundant. For, as an '*alim* associated with a Deobandi madrasa in Delhi argues:

> Whatever is written in the books of *fiqh* about politics is important and we cannot reject it outright. The ideal state is one ruled by a Muslim Caliph in accordance with the *shari'ah*. Islam sets out detailed laws for this, specifying the rights and duties of the Caliph and his Muslim and non-Muslim subjects. But these laws can only be imposed in an Islamic state, not now. We familiarize our students with all these laws but do not treat them in any great detail.

As many 'ulama see it, a state governed in accordance with the *shari'ah* is the ideal political dispensation. The necessity of such a state, it is argued, follows from Islam's insistence on the need to follow what are said to be God's laws in every sphere of personal and collective life. The laws of God have, it is claimed, been revealed in the Qur'an and the Hadith and further clarified and detailed in the books of medieval *fiqh*. The project of establishing an Islamic state in India is recognized as a long-drawn-out process, and as only possible after Muslims overcome their minority status. Meanwhile, it is generally argued, Muslims must obey the laws of the land, as long as these do not contradict the provisions of the Qur'an and the Hadith.

On the other hand, a minority among the 'ulama would argue that Islam has nothing to do with matters of the state. As an '*alim* teaching at a madrasa in Lucknow, who is also a disciple of a Chishti Sufi, claims:

> The majority of the 'ulama say that Islam and politics are inseparable, but this is only because they are themselves hungry for political power. They have robbed Islam of its transcendental dimension, reducing it to a bundle of laws. No wonder, then, that so many people are repelled by their understanding of Islam. As I understand it, Islam simply means believing in the one God and doing good deeds, and for this you don't necessarily need political power. Some Muslims say that you need the state to impose the laws of the *shari'ah*, but I say that if you do not follow God in your own heart, how can the state compel you to do so?

However, the contradiction between accommodation to a theoretically secular state on the one hand, and a dogged commitment to the notion of a *shari'ah*-ruled state on the other, is not easily resolved. A small number of madrasas now teach Indian history and civics, including the principles of the Indian Constitution, for which, generally, textbooks published by the NCERT are used. This indicates a growing accommodation to a situation of the absence of Muslim political power that was hardly envisaged by the authors of the medieval books of *fiqh*. On the other hand, in these as well as other madrasas, arrangements are often made for the teaching of Islamic history. Students are taught about the life of the Prophet, including his role as the ruler of Medina, and the rule of the four 'Righteous Caliphs'. This brief period of Muslim political history is represented as the highest stage of humanity's evolution, as the 'Golden Age' of Islam, and one that Muslims must strive to reproduce. The belief is constantly sought to be stressed that the ideal state is one ruled by a pious Muslim Caliph in accordance with the laws of Islam. This represents an implicit critique of the contemporary nation-state, where Muslims are no longer the ruling class and where the role of the *shari'ah* is severely limited. Yet, this must not be taken to suggest that madrasas are actively involved in concerted political indoctrination. In fact, most madrasa rules prohibit their students from engaging in any overt political activities. Only in a few madrasas, particularly those associated with the Jama'at-i Islami, are Islamist student groups, such as the Students' Islamic Organization, allowed to recruit members.

As on the question of the state, the 'ulama belonging to different schools of thought display a remarkable diversity of understandings and positions on the crucial question of nationalism, citizenship and loyalty to the nation-state. On the one hand, many Deobandis, carrying on in the tradition of the Deobandi elders involved in the freedom movement, would argue that all Indians, irrespective of religion, belong to one nation. An '*alim* who teaches at a Deobandi madrasa in Bangalore says:

> In the Qur'an God says that He has made us into many different nations, so that we may know and recognize each other. When the Prophet established his state in Medina he included all the denizens of that city, Muslims, Jews as well as polytheists, as citizens of the state and as members of the same nation (*ummah*). This is why our elders insisted that all of us Indians, Hindus, Sikhs, Christians as well as Muslims, belong to the same nation. On the other hand, while an Indian Muslim shares the same religion as an Arab Muslim, their nationalities (*qaumiyat*) are different.

Composite nationalism, to this scholar, also means a common commitment to the welfare and defence of the country. He says:

> As citizens of this country we have our share of rights and responsibilities. Islam tells us that we are duty-bound to serve our country and to obey the laws of the land, provided we are allowed to freely practise our faith. As Muslims we must defend the country, even sacrifice our lives for it, even if it is wrongly attacked by fellow Muslims.

Like any text, the Qur'an can be interpreted diversely in order to read into it alternative political agendas. If many Deobandis argue that all the inhabitants of India share a common nationality, others, interpreting the Qur'an in strikingly different terms, offer different understandings of politics and nationalism. To some 'ulama, Islam has no place for nationalism, and Muslims and non-Muslims are seen to be polar opposites and eternal enemies. Nationalism might even be seen as an 'anti-Islamic conspiracy' to divide the worldwide Islamic *ummah*. Thus, a sympathizer of the Jama'at-i Islami, who teaches at a madrasa in a town in Uttar Pradesh, says:

> Islam and nationalism are two completely opposite ideologies, and they cannot co-exist. Islam insists that all Muslims, irrespective of colour, language, race or country, are members of the same *ummah*. They are all brothers and, hence, belong to the same nation. Conversely, all non-Muslims, no matter what their religion, belong to another, and opposed, nationality. The true believers belong to the party of Allah (*hizbullah*), while all others belong to the party of Satan (*hizb ul-shaitan*). Islam requires us to establish a single universal Islamic Caliphate. However, that can only come about in the future. As the Qur'an says, God does not wish to place any burdens on us more than what we can bear. That is why we must accept as a real fact the system of nation-states as they exist today, un-Islamic though this is, and then work gradually, through peaceful preaching and persuasion, for the establishment of the Caliphate.

Pan-Islamist commitment thus does not necessarily lead to militancy, although it does make for a certain rigid insularity and cultural separatism. Contemporary constructions of the Caliphate, while generally highly romanticized, also appear to take into account modern sensitivities as well as critiques of historical Islam. Thus, the Caliphate is presented as a unique political system that guarantees peace and prosperity for all peoples, Muslims as well as others. This represents, of course, an idealized image that bears little relation to the historical Caliphate. While sharing the same broad view of the Caliphate, Islamists differ on the methods that they advocate to establish it. While some Islamists call for armed uprising against existing states, others advocate peaceful and more diplomatic means. In the case of the latter, their advocacy of 'wise pragmatism' (*hikmat-i 'amali*) in pursuance of pan-Islamist goals might actually work to further integrate Muslims with people of other faiths. Thus, as the Jama'at-i Islami sympathizer quoted earlier adds:

> Although Hindus and Muslims thus belong to different nations, we live in the same country and share the same citizenship. As Muslims, we must seek to present the truth of Islam to our Hindu fellow countrymen. We must also serve all the inhabitants of this country, irrespective of religion, helping the poor and the needy. There is a saying of the Prophet, which says, 'Love of the country is half of the faith', and so we must be committed to work for India's welfare. Hence, as Muslims, we must love India, although we do not agree with those Hindus who insist that this love must take the form of nation-worship. If we can sincerely express our concern for our country through our deeds, our non-Muslim fellow Indians might be suitably impressed by Islam and might even take the step of accepting it. In this way, we will gradually move closer to the goal of establishing the global Islamic Caliphate.

The choice of means for working for the establishment of the Caliphate is seen to vary according to the context and is not a given. If militancy is seen as ineffective and as only threatening to further marginalize Muslims, it is to be discarded in favour of peaceful and more efficacious methods, this pragmatism being sought to be provided with appropriate 'Islamic' sanction. Thus, castigating militant Islamist groups in Pakistan who have called upon Muslims in India to declare armed *jihad* against the Indian state and struggle to establish the Caliphate (for which absorption of India into Muslim Pakistan is often presented as but the initial step), this Jama'at-i Islami sympathizer says:

> Like us, they, too, are struggling for the global supremacy of Islam and for the establishment of the Caliphate. However, the means that they have adopted are not just wrong but also, in some ways, un-Islamic. Islam says that when believers are faced with two evils, they must choose the lesser of the two evils so as to minimise the harm to the community. Now, as I see it, the Indian Muslims are faced with two grave dangers. On the one hand are the supporters of the secular, democratic state which rules according to the whims of the people, not according to the *shari'ah*. On the other hand you have the advocates of Hindu Rashtra, who have openly declared war on the Muslims. Now, Islam tells us that although both are un-Islamic, the latter are far more dangerous than the former. If Muslims were to rise up in armed *jihad* against the Indian state, it would only strengthen the hands of the Hindutva-walas, which would then further worsen the conditions of the Muslims living in India. If in the name of *jihad* Muslims get killed and we do not move any closer to the supremacy of Islam, as will certainly be the case if Muslims rise up against the Indian state, then it is better to accept the state as it is, and work for its transformation through peaceful means instead. Hence, Islam

> tells us that in such a context we must support those who are working for secularism and democracy and who are combating the Hindutva fascists. Yet, we must constantly bear in mind that this is simply a pragmatic strategy of survival, for secularism and democracy are anathema in Islam.

Overall, then, a remarkable diversity of positions and a distinct ambiguity characterize the ways in which the madrasas, the 'ulama and Islamist groups in India have sought to relate to the Indian nation-state. Despite their internal divergences, a general consensus seems to exist on the need to accept, albeit for some only as a temporary concession, the legitimacy of the Indian nation-state. Yet, along with this there remains a powerful nostalgia for the idealized 'Islamic' state and a firm belief that if 'true' Muslims were to rule India in accordance with Islam all the problems afflicting the country as a whole, and not just the Muslims alone, would somehow be miraculously solved.

Madrasas, the 'Ulama and Non-Muslims

Linked to the question of the nation-state in the world-view of the 'ulama is the perception of the non-Muslim 'other', a central issue in contemporary discussions of the Indian madrasas and their implications for national security. As has been pointed out earlier, a crucial concern of the madrasas is the maintenance and preservation of Muslim communal identity, which itself is often predicated on drawing a rigid distinction between Muslims as 'true' believers, and others as 'infidels'. Like all other processes of boundary maintenance, this entails the construction of dividing lines that clearly mark Muslims from others, setting 'true' believers apart from the rest.

The theological 'other' thus plays a central role in the

discourse of the contemporary Indian 'ulama. The 'other' serves as a crucial means of self-definition. In the process of constructing the 'other' as perverse, as an 'enemy of God' or as simply 'misguided', the self is imagined as the one truly guided community of faith, God's only trusted followers. For the contemporary Indian 'ulama the 'other' can take various forms. Often, the 'other' within is seen as more dangerous than the 'other' without, for its very familiarity threatens the integrity and faith of the community. Operating in a 'Muslim' guise and claiming to speak for Islam, the 'other' within is seen as possessing potent powers of seduction and as able to misguide 'true' Muslims in a manner that the 'other' without clearly cannot. This explains why for many 'ulama associated with the madrasas the 'other' within receives much greater attention, in the form of heated attack and censure, than the 'other' without. As a student at the Jami'at ul-Ashrafiya, Mubarakpur, the leading Barelwi madrasa in India, argues:

> At our madrasa we are taught to defend Islam from all its enemies, and today the fiercest enemies of Islam are not the Hindus or the Jews, as some people think, but the Wahhabis, the Deobandis, the Shi'as, the followers of Maududi and all those who say that Sufism is un-Islamic. Yes, the Hindus and the Jews refuse to accept Islam, but because of this ordinary Muslims know where they stand. On the other hand, the Wahhabis claim to be Muslims, they pray in the Muslim manner, grow their beards, keep Muslim names and say that they are working for Islam. That is why they are able to mislead innocent Muslims. Hence, at our madrasas, in our literature and speeches and in our interaction with the public, we give particular attention to combating groups like the Wahhabis. Some people say that in this way we are creating divisions among the Muslims, but this is not true. The Wahhabis are definitely not Muslims, so by attacking them how can we be said to be dividing the Muslim *ummah*?

If the 'other' within receives particular attention in the discourse of the 'ulama, the 'other' without is also employed as a device to shore up internal boundaries. Sometimes, the 'other' within is used as a metaphor for the 'other' without, for to openly refer to and condemn the latter might be seen as too politically sensitive and threatening. Thus, an Ahl-i Hadith '*alim*'s critique of the practices associated with the cults of the Sufis, which he condemns as 'un-Islamic' and as a product of an alleged 'Jewish conspiracy', might also be taken to imply an indirect critique of Hinduism because many of the practices associated with popular Sufism are seen by the Ahl-i Hadith as 'Hinduistic'. Likewise, when an Islamist activist insists that God forbids Muslims from 'imitating or befriending' Jews and Christians, he might actually wish to suggest that Muslims must limit their social relations with Hindus to the bare minimum. Such a means to relate to the 'other' without needs to be understood in the context of the rising influence of Hindu militancy, because of which open condemnation of Hindus or their faith would be regarded by many Muslims as dangerous and threatening.

The diverse ways in which the theological 'other' is understood by the 'ulama is also reflected in the depiction of other religions in the madrasa curriculum. Madrasas and their 'ulama, irrespective of *maslak* divisions, are convinced that Islam alone represents the truth, although, as we have seen, the ways in which they interpret Islam are diverse and often mutually contradictory. In the minds of the 'ulama it is only through Islam (as understood by each *maslak*) that one can attain salvation in paradise after death. Non-Muslims, no matter how pious and noble, are believed to be doomed to fierce punishment in the fires of hell. They are often described as 'misguided' (*gumrah*) and 'ignorant' (*jahil*). Harsher descriptions include 'unclean' (*napak*, *najis*), 'enemies of

Islam' (*dushmanan-i islam*) and 'friends of the devil' (*auliya-i shaitan*). Overall, for the non-Muslim 'other' there is no hope of redemption unless he or she converts to Islam.

Although comparative religions are generally not taught as a separate subject in most madrasas, reference to them is sometimes made in the course of teaching other subjects or in general conversation. Such references can be made in an extremely derogatory way in order to stress the claim of Islam's superiority. For instance, an '*alim* who teaches at an Ahl-i Hadith madrasa in Bihar says:

> Even if a Hindu or a Christian prays regularly and serves the poor and believes in one God, he will still be punished by God by being sent to Hell, where he will be forced to drink boiling water and will be constantly bitten by poisonous snakes and scorpions. Massive nails, many metres long, shall be driven into his body. This is because he does not believe in the Prophet Muhammad, God's last messenger. Hence, Muslims must not take non-Muslims for close friends, for they are actually friends of the Devil. Muslims must live in their own localities to insulate themselves from the poisonous cultural influences of the unbelievers.

Such shrill, combative voices do not, however, represent all shades of Muslim opinion. These understandings are based on selective readings of the Qur'an and the Hadith and the books of *fiqh*, and must not be thought of as shared by all Muslims or even by all 'ulama themselves. One '*alim* who has consistently spoken out against the negative portrayal of people of other faiths, within and outside the madrasas, is the Delhi-based Maulana Wahiduddin Khan. Author of several books, Khan is a controversial figure among Muslims, particularly for his allegedly close links with Hindutva leaders. Despite being routinely abused as a 'Hindutva agent', Khan continues to plead for inter-faith dialogue and for a more open and accepting attitude towards people of other faiths. Khan sees inter-faith dialogue as nothing less than an Islamic imperative. As he explains:

> Islam insists upon dialogue. After all, wherever progress has occurred in history it has been because of interaction between different peoples. Dialogue must start right from the school level. Some *maulvi*s say that if children are taught about other religions they will turn away from Islam. But is their faith in Islam so weak that if they learn about other religions they will renounce their own? We really must get to know the truth about each other's religions and clear up our mutual misunderstandings, because most prejudice is based upon simple ignorance or misrepresentation. As far as Islam is concerned, inter-religious dialogue is a binding duty. The early Muslims travelled to various countries to preach Islam, but that was only one aspect of their work. They also travelled in search of knowledge, interacting and openly discussing with people of other religions. So, for example, some of the early Muslims came to India. Here they studied Sanskrit and translated many Sanskrit texts into Arabic. Or, for that matter, when Spain was under Muslim rule many Christians would come there to study even the Bible from Muslim scholars.

Despite what he sees as the Islamic insistence on dialogue, Khan notes with despair that few madrasas, if any, have made any worthwhile efforts to build bridges with people of other faiths. Instead, he argues, many Muslim writers who claim to speak for Islam have only made the problem of inter-faith relations even more vexed and complicated by branding non-Muslims as sworn 'enemies of Islam'. He says:

> Muslim intellectuals of the last hundred years, and even today, generally saw, and continue to see, European and now American superiority in terms of a so-called grand anti-Islamic conspiracy. So, you have these seemingly never-ending cycles of violence in much of the Muslim world even today. This hatred of all others

that is filled into the minds of ordinary Muslims is really very scary. When I was a child I was taught to believe that the British were wholly evil and that nothing good could be attributed to them. It was only later that I discovered the many good things that they had done in India, such as building modern schools and the railways. If you look at the sort of so-called Islamic literature that has flooded the market you will see that many Muslim writers continue to propagate the so-called conspiracy theory, branding non-Muslims as evil enemies of Islam whose only mission in life is to destroy Islam and the Muslims. Just yesterday I got a letter from somebody in Kashmir, who wrote saying that till recently he had been exposed only to the writings of militant so-called Islamists, because of which he had been led to believe that all Hindus, and all non-Muslims in general, are sworn enemies of the Muslims. And then he said he had come across some of my books, which radically changed the way he saw the world. He said that he had had a complete change of heart and that he now realises that Hindus, too, are God's children who deserve to be loved.[11]

Another contemporary Indian advocate for inter-faith dialogue who argues his case from within the Islamic tradition is Hameed Nasim Rafiabadi. A doctorate from the Jawaharlal Nehru University, New Delhi, he now teaches at the Shah-i Hamadan Institute of Islamic Studies in Srinagar. Rafiabadi has written extensively on inter-faith issues and has attended numerous inter-faith dialogue conferences. He puts across his case for inter-faith dialogue as a duty that Muslims need to abide by if they are to be true to the demands that their faith makes on them:

I believe that there is ample evidence in the Qur'an of the need for Muslims to build bridges with people of other faiths. The Qur'an tells us that we should not abuse the idols or deities worshipped by others, for otherwise they would react and, in turn, abuse God out of ignorance. It commands us to tell others

> about Islam, but there is to be no compulsion at all involved. If someone listens to that call and decides to become a Muslim, well and good. If, on the other hand, he chooses not to accept Islam, that is his own concern, and then, as the Qur'an says, 'To them their religion and to you your religion'. The Qur'an very clearly tells us that we should communicate with others about our faith with 'wisdom' (*hikmat*) and words of 'beauty' (*hasanah*). Sadly, there is presently such a communication gap between Muslims and others that they cannot understand each other.

As Rafiabadi sees it, inter-faith dialogue must not remain restricted to mere theological exchange between religious specialists, confined to seminar rooms. Rather, it must also be translated into practical action, with people of different faiths, each inspired by their own faith commitments, coming to work together for common social purposes. For him the Prophet Muhammad is a role model in this regard:

> Explaining the teachings of one's own religion and understanding the beliefs of others is a central element of the dialogue process. But there is another level of dialogue that Islam also stresses—the need for people of different religious communities to act together to attain certain common social objectives. This is dialogue at the level of social action. Thus, when the Prophet Muhammad arrived in Medina, he entered into a pact with the Jews of the town. According to the terms of this treaty, the Muslims and the Jews were to help each other in times of need and in defending Medina from outside attack. It is on the basis of this pact that some Indian 'ulama called for a united struggle of Muslims, Hindus and others against British imperialism. What we learn from the example of the Treaty of Medina is that for the sake of common goals, Muslims can certainly cooperate with others. The Qur'an explicitly commands us that we should help each other in doing good and in pious deeds and in fighting oppression, but not in assisting each other in sin and oppression.

> We have an ideal model in this regard in the Prophet Muhammad, who, even before God had announced his prophethood, had set up an organisation of youth in Mecca, called the *half-i fizul*, to help the poor and the needy. Now, this was at a time before the announcement of Muhammad's prophethood, so the other members of the *half-i fizul* were all non-Muslims. That did not stand in the way of the Prophet helping them.[12]

Khan and Rafiabadi are no voices in the wilderness. Throughout Muslim history, numerous Sufis, for instance, as well as certain modernist Muslim writers from the late nineteenth century onwards, have sought to interpret the Qur'an to argue that salvation is open to people of all faiths. But the vast majority of the 'ulama of the madrasas would vehemently disagree. As one '*ālim*, who is also a disciple of a Sufi *shaikh*, says:

> Personally, I believe that all those who do good, no matter what their religion, can go to heaven. Heaven is not the physical place that most Muslims think it is. Rather, it is a state of being in the presence of God. Yet, I cannot say all these things openly. The 'ulama would collectively brand me as a *kafir* if I did that, and I might even be killed for my views. So, I prefer to keep quiet.

In recent years, some madrasas have begun teaching comparative religions to higher-level students as part of a specialized course after the regular *fazil* degree. Knowledge of other religions is seen as providing these students with the skills and information they would find useful in missionary work among people of other faiths. Tracts and books on various religions, mainly written from a polemical perspective by the 'ulama themselves, are used for these classes. Rather than trying to understand other religions dispassionately, and attempting to see them as their followers understand them, these texts set out to 'prove' them as 'false' or 'limited' and also aim to reinforce the belief in Islam as the ultimate truth. Almost no madrasa makes any arrangements for non-Muslim scholars and religious specialists to interact with their students and teach them about their religions on their own terms.

The teaching of other faiths, even if with the purpose of proving them 'false' and thereby stressing the inherent 'truth' of Islam, might sometimes have its share of unintended consequences. In at least some cases, it might inadvertently help to promote genuine efforts at building bridges between people of different faiths. Thus, a bookseller in Delhi, a graduate of a Deobandi madrasa and now active in a communist party, says:

> In the final year of my studies at my madrasa we were taught a book that described the principal beliefs of Hindus, Sikhs and Christians. The purpose, of course, was to argue the claim that Islam is superior to these religions. However, as I read the book I discovered that although these faiths differ from Islam in several respects they also pay great stress on morality and helping the poor. This made me interested to know more about these religions, and I managed to get some Hindu, Sikh and Christian literature from my non-Muslim friends. The more I read the more I understood that true religion consists not in rites and rituals but in serving God through serving the least of His creatures, irrespective of religion. That is how I got involved in the communist movement. People ask me, 'How can you, as a Muslim, and that too as a trained '*alim*, be associated with godless communists?' I tell them that a true Muslim is not one who prays a hundred times a day or grows a beard a metre long, but, rather, one who helps the poor, irrespective of religion.

On the whole, however, such cases are rare. Overall, the madrasas seek to instil in the minds of their students that Islam alone represents the truth and that non-Muslims are doomed to punishment in Hell. Often, the non-Muslims of the world are projected as being engaged in a global 'conspiracy' to destroy Islam, and all the problems that afflict the Muslims are attributed indiscriminately to this alleged plot. Muslims are thus warned not to befriend people of other faiths, and they are constantly reminded of the *hadith* that if they were to adopt the ways of people of other faiths they would be counted among them on the Day of Judgement, doomed to perdition in Hell along with them. This understanding of the world naturally does little to promote genuine dialogue and respect between Muslims and people of other faiths.

Yet, the belief that non-Muslims are 'enemies of God' and that infidelity (*kufr*) constitutes the gravest form of betrayal (*baghawat*) against Allah, does not necessarily mean that madrasas preach uncompromising hatred and violence against followers of other faiths, as is commonly imagined. On the contrary, the 'ulama often stress that Muslims must seek to cultivate good relations with people of other faiths, for only in that way would they be willing to lend a receptive ear to the message of Islam. Thus, an Ahl-i Hadith '*alim*, rounding off a long diatribe against Hinduism, says:

> Although non-Muslims shall certainly go to hell in the after-life, in this life Muslims should strive to live with them in harmony and co-operation as long as they do not place any restrictions on the free practise of Islam. Non-Muslims are enemies of God, but God tells us that we should try and win them over to Islam through peaceful preaching and good words. The Prophet Muhammad treated the Jews and Christians similarly, for as the Qur'an says, they, too, are God's creatures. By helping them when they are in distress, and living in peace with them as long as we are free to follow our faith, we can impress them with our noble example, because of which they might be attracted to Islam.

> The Qur'an explicitly allows us to befriend those non-Muslims who do not persecute us on account of our faith. Even if they choose not to accept Islam we should deal with them with civility.

In a somewhat similar vein, Maulana Asrar ul-Haq Qasmi, assistant general secretary of the All-India Milli Council and former general secretary of the Jami'at ul-'Ulama-i Hind, argues:

> We believe that Islam is the religion of God. In accordance with the teachings of Islam, we also believe that God is the Lord of all the worlds and of all creatures. God sent the Prophet Muhammad as the mercy for all. We certainly do not teach our students to hate Hindus, for that would be going against the teachings of our faith. In fact, the Qur'an says that God does not stop you from befriending people of other faiths if they have not persecuted you on account of your faith. It also explicitly lays down that Muslims must not let the enmity of others lead them to swerve from the path of justice.[13]

As the 'ulama see it, one of the principal tasks of the Muslim *ummah* is *da'wah*, 'inviting' non-Muslims to Islam. If Muslims fail in discharging that duty, the 'ulama stress, they will be severely chastised by God, in this world or in the next. *Da'wah* is thus a key means through which some 'ulama have sought to relate to followers of other faiths. In recent years, some madrasas, as well as a number of Islamic organizations, have set up their own *da'wah* departments, publishing literature on Islam in local languages meant specially for non-Muslims, and organizing seminars and conferences on Islam to which non-Muslims are regularly invited. Other, more engaged though less prominent, forms of *da'wah* include inter-faith dialogue initiatives as well as active involvement with non-Muslim groups in working for social welfare or communal harmony. Thus, reaching out to non-Muslims through a variety of *da'wah* ventures actually helps establish new points of contact between Muslims and others, which can, ironically, gradually undermine the separatism and insularity that the world-view of the traditional 'ulama is otherwise so carefully aimed at promoting.

Although in general the 'ulama fervently believe that other religions are false and inadequate for salvation, several 'ulama have been engaged in informal inter-faith dialogue initiatives. This usually takes the form of participating in local-level meetings where people of different faiths come together to reiterate the need for peace and harmony. The rapid deterioration of Hindu–Muslim relations in large parts of India has forced several 'ulama to take seriously the need to reach out to people of other faiths, seeking to work along with them for communal harmony while still remaining rooted in their own understandings of normative Islam. Sometimes the encounter with others provides a means for revising preconceived notions of other religions, making for a more positive appreciation of their teachings, particularly those which the different religions are seen to share in common.

One '*alim* who has sought to reach out to people of other faiths and work along with them for communal amity is Maulana Sayyed Hamid ul-Hasan, the principal of the Jami'a Nazmia, an Ithna 'Ashari Shi'a madrasa in Lucknow. He is one of the leading Shi'a 'ulama of India, having been educated at Najaf Ashraf in Iraq under the renowned Ayatollah Agha Khui. In a multi-religious society like India, the Maulana says, religious leaders must play a central role in promoting dialogue and actively seek to understand their own religions in such a way as to promote communal harmony. The Maulana regularly addresses non-Muslim gatherings, delivering lectures on religion and peace, highlighting, in particular, what he sees is the Qur'anic duty of promoting harmony and cooperation between people of different faiths. He also sometimes organizes special lectures during the month of Muharram to mark the martyrdom of Imam Husain, where he stresses the need for Muslims to work for the cause of all oppressed peoples and not just Muslims alone, following, as he puts it, in the path of the Imam himself. This, he says, is true *jihad*:

> I constantly stress in my addresses the true meaning of *jihad*, which is exertion in the path of Allah. *Jihad* does not mean killing innocent people, as is wrongly supposed. I often quote the Qur'an, which says that if a non-Muslim comes to you and seeks shelter, it is your duty to give God's message to him and then convey him to a safe place. The Qur'an also says that Muslims should struggle for the rights of all persecuted people, not just Muslims alone. I often cite the example of Hatim Tai's daughter. When, after a battle, she was arrested and brought before the Prophet, she told him that her father, who had died before the Prophet had declared his prophethood, used to help the poor and distressed, although, of course, he was not a Muslim. This so touched the Prophet that he ordered that she be immediately released. Then again, I often quote the story of the Christian priests of Najran, who came to Medina to debate with the Prophet. If the Prophet had ordered all non-Muslims to be killed, I say, how come the Christian delegation came to Medina? The Christians debated with the Prophet on various religious matters, but in the end did not accept Islam, and they returned home. If Islam really insisted on killing all non-Muslims how and why did the Prophet allow them to return?

While he regards it as important for Muslims to present a 'correct' picture of Islam to others, and in particular to clear their misunderstandings of Islam as an inherently violent faith, the Maulana also believes that Muslims must seek to understand other religions in a genuine quest for knowledge, not goaded by missionary or ulterior motives. As he puts it:

> When I interact with people of other faiths I don't do so with the intention of converting them or denigrating their religion. Rather, I interact with them in order to learn from them, to look at their good points. After all, everyone has the choice to follow the religion of his own choice. That's his own business and his affairs are with God. I feel that we need to study other religions because this will go a long way in promoting inter-communal harmony. Thus, when I say that I have studied some of the Hindu scriptures, and on the basis of that have come to the conclusion that Hinduism does stress moral values, I can come closer to my Hindu friends. But if I say that such values are found only in Islam, not only am I wrong, but I would also provoke hatred and conflict. So, I feel that there is a crucial need for us to study comparative religions, but this should be simply for the sake of promoting better relations with others, and not for refuting people of other faiths or creating conflicts with them. It is only through decent behaviour, not through heated debates, that we can actually resolve our differences. When you study other faiths you must first cleanse your mind of preconceived notions, or else you will not really learn anything at all.[14]

Militancy and the Madrasas: The Pakistani Case

Although madrasas have been in existence in India for centuries, it is only in the past decade or so that they have come to be associated with militancy and terrorism by many Indians. As Mushirul Hasan remarks, while earlier Deoband and other madrasas that had been closely involved in India's freedom struggle were projected by the state as symbols of India's commitment to secularism and as a strong rebuff to the 'two-nation' theory of the Muslim League, in recent years they have come to be routinely branded as 'the source of evil'. He argues that the propaganda against the Indian madrasas is based on 'misplaced suppositions and imaginary fear', adding that while radical Islamism might have found strong support in several Pakistani madrasas, this is certainly not the case with their Indian counterparts.[15]

As Hasan's comment suggests, the association of certain madrasas in neighbouring Pakistan and Afghanistan with militant, and often terrorist, activities in recent years has been used to argue the case that madrasas in India, too, have turned into 'dens of terror'. This argument, while lacking any firm evidence, is based on the assumption that madrasas in India are homogeneous in terms of orientation and political outlook, which is far from being the case. While the role of certain madrasas in Pakistan in terrorist activities in recent years is undeniable, to argue that all or most Indian madrasas are also treading the same path is misleading.

In discussing the growing radicalization of certain Pakistani madrasas in recent years it is important to bear in mind certain facts that are often ignored in popular discussions on the subject. To begin with, one must resist the temptation to exaggerate the strength of religious militancy in Pakistan. Some writers portray an image of Pakistan being under the untrammelled sway of fanatic *mullah*s baying for non-Muslim blood and exporting terrorism throughout the world. In actual fact, as Stephen Cohen points out, religious radicalism has only a limited support base in that country. Militant Pakistani Islamic groups, he remarks, have tended to derive their influence less from popular support than from active state patronage in order to counter secular opposition parties or to promote what are seen as Pakistan's interests vis-à-vis India and Afghanistan.[16] Although many Pakistanis would consider themselves as believing Muslims, they are not particularly radical in any sense of the term. Economic, linguistic and ethnic issues, rather than religion, have tended to dominate political discourse and conflict in Pakistan. Until recently, no single Pakistani Islamic party ever won more than 5 per cent of the national vote. In the elections held in October 2002, the Muttahida Majlis-i 'Amal (MMA), a six-member alliance of different Islamic parties, won 11 per cent of the total votes polled, earning 17 per cent of the seats in the national assembly, control over the government in the North-West Frontier Province and partnership in a coalition government in Baluchistan. This growth in the electoral strength of Islamic parties probably has less to do with the ideological appeal of radical Islamism than with growing anti-American feelings in the country, fuelled, in particular, by the American invasion of Afghanistan. In the North-West Frontier Province and Baluchistan, it might also reflect growing Pushtun nationalist sentiments.

Contrary to widespread stereotypical images of all Pakistani madrasas as 'dens of terror', it is also crucial to bear in mind that, as the leftist Pakistani scholar Mubarak 'Ali remarks, not all, or even most, madrasas in Pakistan have been involved in training militants.[17] Militant activism is not an inherent feature of the madrasa system as such, and for several decades after the creation of Pakistan madrasas in that country had no links with any militant outfits, the change coming about only later in the course of the American-backed *jihad* against the Soviets in Afghanistan. Then again, not all Muslim groups in the country seem to have gone along with the *jihad*ist agenda. The Barelwi 'ulama, for instance, who represent the majority of the Pakistani population, were not particularly active on the military front in Afghanistan, Kashmir and elsewhere, and have generally kept a low profile, although they have been involved in intra-Muslim rivalries inside Pakistan, particularly against the Deobandis and the Ahl-i Hadith, both of whom they consider as heretics and apostates. According to one source, only some 10 to 15 per cent of the madrasas in Pakistan promote 'extremist' ideologies.[18]

Interestingly, only a few of these madrasas are believed to have actually provided military training to their students in the course of the Afghan war, or even to have taught them specifically *jihad*ist texts, although they did play a supportive role by sowing the seeds of extremism in the minds of their students. Their role in promoting militant activism was more indirect. They concentrated on the careful indoctrination of their students in an extreme literalist form of Islam, one that set righteous Muslims against unbelieving 'hypocrites' and 'infidels' in an unrelenting struggle for world supremacy. These students were then motivated to join *jihad*ist groups engaged in actual fighting, first in Afghanistan, and then, after the Soviets were expelled from there, in other countries as well. It is important to stress that not all, or even most, Pakistani Islamist militants were madrasa students—many of them, as in the case of Jama'at-i Islami activists, were educated in regular schools and even in colleges and universities. The vast majority of the Muslim activists who took part in the Afghan *jihad*—estimated at between 35,000 and 40,000 from around forty countries—had no madrasa education at all. In fact, throughout the *jihad* against the Soviets, madrasa students seem to have played only a marginal role. The *jihad* was spearheaded not by traditionalist 'ulama but by Islamists, mostly influenced by the Jama'at-i Islami in Pakistan and the Muslim Brotherhood in Egypt. It was only later, after the Soviet withdrawal from Afghanistan, that Pakistan dumped the Islamists, seeing in the Deobandi Taliban a more pliable ally.

Journalists and even academics writing on the Afghan *jihad* and the Taliban often refer to the involvement in militant activities of what they describe as 'madrasas', located along Pakistan's border with Afghanistan. While several madrasas did engage in such work, it is important to remember that not all schools in the Pathan borderlands that took part in the Afghan *jihad* and later associated themselves with militant activism and terrorism elsewhere were actually established traditional madrasas. Several of them were simply makeshift schools intended to train fighters in the war against the Soviets, where a smattering of Islam was taught in order to strengthen the spirit of *jihad* against the Russians. These have been loosely and incorrectly described as 'madrasas'.[19] In actual fact, they were not even conceived of as religious schools. Rather, from their very inception they were intended as militant training camps, but were sought to be passed off as 'madrasas' in order to legitimate their operations and to solicit funds from Muslim states. The rapid growth and spread of such schools must be seen in the context of Cold War rivalries, and it is obvious that they had the blessings of the Americans, who, through the CIA, pumped in large amounts of weapons and cash to assist the *mujahidin*. If today for the Americans madrasas are synonymous with 'factories of terror', it is crucial to remember that at the height of the *jihad* against the Soviets the then American president, Ronald Reagan, had gone to the extent of blessing them as 'the moral equivalent of the Founding Fathers [of America]'.[20]

That said, one cannot ignore the significant role of certain established Pakistani madrasas in militant movements in recent years. This association goes back to the Islamic revolution in Iran in 1979 and the long and bloody war in Afghanistan following the Soviet invasion in the same year. On coming to power, Ayatollah Khomeini promised to export his brand of revolutionary Islam to other Muslim countries as well. He invited scores of Muslim activists from abroad for conferences and offered them money and military training in the hope that when they went back to their countries they would work to overthrow their corrupt, 'un-Islamic' and pro-Western regimes. Revolutionary rhetoric emanating from Iran had a powerful impact on Muslims in neighbouring Pakistan—not just on Shi'as, but on some Sunnis as well, including many madrasa students.

Although the Iranian revolution acted as a major catalyst in promoting radicalization of Muslim groups in Pakistan, it was the invasion of Afghanistan by the Russians in 1979 that led several Pakistani madrasas to train their students for *jihad* with the active assistance of the Pakistani state. Fleeing from Soviet terror, between two and five million Afghan refugees sought shelter across the border in Pakistan, setting up camps mainly in the Pathan-dominated North-West Frontier Province and Baluchistan. As part of its war against the Soviets, the United States helped channel arms and funds to the refugees to carry on a fierce resistance movement. Refugee camps, financed by the Americans and the Saudis, soon turned into centres for the preaching of radical Islam. A chain of ramshackle schools, incorrectly branded as 'madrasas' today, came up along Pakistan's border with Afghanistan, training war-worn refugee children in a *jihad*ist version of Islam. As long as the *mujahidin* were engrossed in fighting their Soviet enemy, the Americans saw in radical Islamism a convenient tool to pursue their own global hegemonic designs. As a Pakistani columnist, himself a bitter critic of the Islamists, writes, the Americans actively encouraged the growth of radical seminaries along the Afghanistan border in order to carry on their proxy war in

Afghanistan. Such schools, he argues, were 'part of Washington's policy to bleed the Soviet Union'.[21]

For America, these schools, which it now brands as 'factories of terror', were a powerful political resource in its war against the Russians. According to one source, America spent more than $50 million preparing special textbooks in Dari and Pushtu which were distributed to refugee children studying in these schools, exhorting them to join what the books blessed as a *jihad*. The texts, commissioned by the US Agency for International Development, and developed by the Centre for Afghanistan Studies at the University of Nebraska-Omaha, are said to have been 'filled with violent images and militant Islamic teachings', peppered with drawings of guns, bullets, soldiers and mines. An aid worker who examined one of these books found that almost half its pages contained violent images or passages. To cite an instance, one text showed a picture of a *mujahid* carrying a Kalashnikov but with his head missing. The picture was accompanied by a verse from the Qur'an, and a Pushtu tribute to the *mujahidin*, who were described as 'obedient to Allah': 'Such men will sacrifice their wealth and life itself to impose Islamic law on the government,' the book declared. Apparently, and not surprisingly, when the Taliban took over Afghanistan they found the books perfectly acceptable and in accordance with their own understanding of Islam. They are said to have allowed them to be used in the schools, although after effacing all the human representations that they contained.[22]

The radicalization of several Pakistani madrasas also had much to do with political developments inside Pakistan itself. Pakistan's military dictator, General Zia ul-Haq, who seized power in a coup in 1977, sought to actively use the Islamic card in order to bolster his regime. Acutely aware that he lacked any semblance of legitimate authority, he deliberately courted the Sunni 'ulama, hoping to win their support for his unpopular rule. As part of his 'mosque-military' alliance Zia lavishly patronized the 'ulama, appointing them as collectors of the *zakat* levy, granting vast amounts of money to various madrasas, and encouraging the 'ulama to enter politics as legislators and even as ministers.[23]

With the growing involvement of madrasas in the Afghan war the sophisticated arms that had flooded Pakistan following the Soviet invasion of Afghanistan soon made their way into many madrasas in the country, as they had into almost every Pakistani city and town. Dispatching their students for *jihad*, first in Afghanistan, and then to new trouble spots such as Kashmir, Central Asia, and even to countries as far as Bosnia and the Philippines, became a new means for madrasas of rival *maslak*s to assert claims to 'authentic' Islamicity, while also providing them access to new sources of patronage.[24] Several Pakistani 'ulama groups, particularly the Jama'at-i Islami, the Deobandis and the Ahl-i Hadith, set up armed militia units, composed mainly of products of their own madrasas.

This development must not be seen as an expression of some sort of logic inherent in the madrasa system as such. Rather, the phenomenon needs to be looked at in a more nuanced manner, placing it in the wider context of the changing contours of Pakistan's political economy. Social and economic inequalities and 'reforms' instituted under the dictates of the IMF and World Bank have only served to further widen the gulf that separates the country's Westernized and feudal elites from the poor. In a country where democratic channels to articulate dissent are choked, the mosque and the madrasa emerged as major centres of opposition, a phenomenon observed in many other Muslim countries as well. For scores of impoverished Pakistanis, radical Islamism became a vehicle for protest against inequality and marginalization. For many madrasa students, the bulk of whom come from poor and uprooted families, the increasing plight of the marginalized came to be seen as a result of a grand 'conspiracy' against Islam hatched by 'anti-Islamic' forces. Faced with a sense of being trapped and besieged, of being overwhelmed by powerful 'enemies' in the form of 'nominal Muslims', 'Jews', 'Christians', the 'West' and 'Hindus', appeals for militant *jihad*ist activism evoked a powerful response. Because the world seemed to have little or no place for them, they, in turn, saw it as waiting to be conquered and radically transformed in accordance with their own vision of Islam. In the 'Islamic' system of their dreams and hopes, the 'corrupt' Westernized and 'irreligious' elites would be swept away and replaced by God-fearing and *shari'ah*-abiding rulers. Even if that were not to happen, they were assured of abundant wealth and pleasures in heaven if they were to sacrifice their lives as martyrs for the cause of their faith.

The Pakistani authorities were all along fully aware of the growing involvement of some Pakistani madrasas in training militants, locals as well as foreigners. Yet, it turned a blind eye, for radical Islamists now had many sympathizers in the army and the bureaucracy. Further, militant madrasas were seen as a powerful tool to pursue Pakistan's strategic interests in the region. The ISI is said to have sponsored numerous armed Islamist outfits, such as the Lashkar-i Tayyeba, a terrorist organization owing allegiance to the Ahl-i Hadith, and the Deobandi-related Harkat ul-Ansar.[25] Such groups saw themselves as committed to a global *jihad* against what they described as non-Muslim 'enemies of God'.

Pakistan's policy of patronizing radical madrasas was also responsible for the emergence of the Taliban, who swept into power in Kabul with Pakistani support in 1996. The word *taliban* means 'students', and many Taliban were precisely that—students of Deobandi madrasas that had sprouted in recent years along the border between Pakistan and Afghanistan, catering particularly to impoverished Afghan refugees. Although the Deobandi tradition had been able to establish a significant presence in Afghanistan by the middle of the twentieth century, the military victories of the Taliban and the considerable popular support that they initially enjoyed had little to do with their specifically Deobandi doctrines and links as such. Rather, it appears that the ability of the Taliban to impose a degree of order and security in the areas under their control, combating the fiercely corrupt and warring *mujahidin* militia that had taken over in the wake of the Soviet withdrawal, largely accounted for their initial popularity. After all, and this is often forgotten, the Taliban were spawned as a movement when, in the spring of 1994, the one-eyed Mullah Omar gathered thirty of his fellow madrasa students to take revenge on a local *mujahid* commander who had earlier kidnapped and raped two girls from a village near Kandahar. Rather than simple religious considerations, it seems that the image of the Taliban as brutal and fierce warriors, but, at the same time, charged with a fiery moral zeal against corruption and lawlessness, determined Afghan support for the new regime.

The Taliban sought to create a state based on Deobandi extreme literalism, resulting in a further exacerbation of the Afghan civil war and untold suffering for millions of Afghans. Yet, one must remember that the United States did not, at least to begin with, see the Taliban as an enemy and as a grave threat to civilization, as it was to later insist. It is impossible that the Pakistanis and their Saudi backers could have arranged for the Taliban takeover of Afghanistan without American support. In fact, shortly after the Taliban came to power in Kabul, American petroleum companies were rushing to work out lucrative deals with them to allow for the building of pipelines that would transport Central Asian oil through Afghan territory. Pakistan enthusiastically embraced the Taliban, sensing that a pliable regime in Kabul would help it gain access to the vast oilfields and markets of Central Asia. The initial willingness of the Taliban to work along with the Americans suggests, as Barbara Metcalf rightly notes, that the regime was 'not ideologically driven' and was somewhat flexible in choosing whom it could work with. It was not 'abhorrence of Western culture' as such, Metcalf writes, that provided the driving force of the Taliban, but the specific goal of prevailing within Afghanistan and, in doing so, fostering its own conception of appropriate Islamic behaviour.[26]

*

The emergence of the Taliban, and the involvement of radical Islamist groups in Pakistan and Afghanistan and in the war in Kashmir helped create a climate of grave and widespread suspicion in India regarding Islamic organizations in general. Fiercely anti-Muslim groups among the Hindus, taking advantage of the growing fear of and hostility towards Islam, now stepped up their anti-Muslim propaganda. Muslim-bashing had all along been a favourite pastime for the Hindu right wing, and the growing suspicions about the madrasas gave them a further boost. It was now claimed that the Indian madrasas were hand in glove with Kashmiri militants and the

ISI as part of a wider conspiracy to destabilize India.[27] In 1995, Ashok Singhal, leader of the fiercely anti-Muslim Vishwa Hindu Parishad (VHP), angrily declared that his organization 'would not tolerate any *maktab*s and madrasas', on the grounds that they were allegedly teaching 'anti-Hindu ideas' to their students. He insisted that the madrasas must teach only 'Hindu culture', for that alone was 'Indian culture', adding that if they did not agree to this proposal Muslims should leave India.[28] His colleague, Praveen Togadia, general secretary of the VHP, echoed the same view, claiming that 'one hundred thousand' madrasas in India were all engaged in a sinister plot to train *jihad*ists to massacre the Hindus and establish Islamic rule all over the world.[29]

Virulent Hindutva propaganda against the madrasas as 'dens of terror' led to strident demands by leading right-wing Hindu politicians that madrasas be carefully monitored and controlled. Indian newspapers were filled with reports of alleged 'dens of terror' being run in various madrasas scattered all over the country. Hardly any Hindu-owned paper, not even the most 'secular', had anything positive to say about the madrasas. Carefully doctored 'investigative' stories about madrasas began to routinely appear in the Indian press, clearly calculated to defame Muslims as 'terrorists' and to fan the flames of anti-Muslim sentiments. The vernacular Hindu press, known for its pro-Hindutva slant, took a leading role in this campaign, but even the so-called 'national' English papers, thought of as being somewhat less imbalanced, did not remain uninfluenced. Interestingly, while lashing out at Muslim organizations for allegedly supporting militancy and threatening the unity of India, intelligence reports and many newspapers remained curiously silent on militant Hindu outfits that have been especially violent in recent decades.[30]

Madrasa-bashing rose to such feverish heights that even perfectly laudable patriotic acts by madrasas and their students could be twisted to press the charge of madrasas working as breeding grounds of terror. In one particularly bizarre incident, a group of students of a madrasa in a village near Meerut took out a procession to celebrate Independence Day, waving the Indian tri-colour and a green 'Islamic' flag embossed with a crescent and star, and raising slogans in support of Indian unity. Soon after, a certain Omkar Singh, the former *pradhan* of the village and an 'upper' caste Hindu who had been defeated in a recent election by a Muslim candidate supported by Muslim and Dalit voters, reported to the local police that the students were raising 'anti-India' slogans. This was said to be his way of taking revenge on the victorious Muslim *pradhan*. The police stepped in and arrested three 'ulama, including two teachers at the local madrasa. A day after the incident, two leading Delhi-based newspapers repeated Omkar Singh's story that the students had staged an anti-India demonstration, waving Pakistani flags and shouting slogans in support of Osama bin Laden. This provoked a reporter working for a Muslim magazine to visit the village and find out things for himself. He discovered that Omkar Singh's story was entirely fabricated. He interviewed the local police inspector, a Hindu, who told him that the report of an 'anti-India' demonstration in the village was completely false. All that the students had done, he said, was raise slogans in support of Hindu–Muslim amity, which, as he put it, 'would make any Indian proud'.[31] Predictably, no Hindu-owned newspaper chose to present the actual story, and the two dailies that had accused the students of parading in support of Pakistan did not have the courtesy to apologize or issue a rejoinder.

Like large sections of the Hindu-owned press and the

intelligence services, senior government officials and ministers from the right-wing Bharatiya Janata Party (BJP), which was then heading a coalition government at the Centre, joined in the witch-hunt against the madrasas. Wild, generally unsubstantiated, claims were made to the effect that the madrasas were in league with 'enemies' of the country and posed a grave danger to India's stability. Ministers spoke in contradictory voices, singing different tunes before different audiences, thus clearly suggesting that their allegations about the madrasas were largely unfounded. The then Union minister of state for home affairs, Vidyasagar Rao, for one, claimed that 'some' madrasas in Kerala were promoting 'terrorist activities' and that 'most' of the madrasas in the state were involved in 'shady dealings'. Predictably, the minister did not name any of the madrasas he had accused, and nor did he provide any reliable source for his claims. The media failed to point this out, and simply quoted his statement without any further clarification.[32] On the other hand, the then Union minister for human resources, the Hindutva hawk Murli Manohar Joshi, clarified that a statement issued by the acting president of the VHP Ashok Singhal, that madrasas in Uttar Pradesh were terrorist dens, was baseless.[33] While his own ministers, along with senior leaders of the Rashtriya Swayamsevak Sangh (RSS) and the VHP, both fiercely anti-Muslim 'nationalist' Hindu organizations, were lashing out at the madrasas as centres of the ISI, the then Prime Minister Atal Bihari Vajpayee chose to differ, while not directly contradicting his own colleagues. To a delegation of Muslims he claimed that he had no knowledge of any Indian madrasa that was engaged in anti-India activities on behalf of the ISI. Instead, he is said to have praised the madrasas as centres of learning and for their role in India's freedom struggle.[34]

Despite these conflicting statements by government officials, the state now began to take measures directed specifically at the madrasas. In 1998, the government decided to stop issuing visas to foreign students to study at several madrasas, including Deoband.[35] The next year, in the wake of the conflict in Kargil where Islamist militants and Pakistani regulars fought Indian soldiers in what threatened to break out into a full-fledged war between India and Pakistan, the Indian prime minister set up a four-member central ministerial group to suggest measures to scale up the country's security. The committee consisted of Home Minister L.K. Advani, Defence Minister George Fernandes, Finance Minister Yashwant Sinha and Foreign Minister Jaswant Singh. In February 2001 the group presented a 135-page report titled *Reforming the National Security System,* which received the approval of the government but was not made public. Yet, it was widely reported in the press, and led to a tremendous controversy, further heightening allegations against the madrasas.

Detailing various 'threats' to internal security, the report claimed:

> A recent phenomenon is the mushrooming of pan-Islamist militant outfits with links of radical orientation in Pakistan, Saudi Arabia, Sudan and some other West Asian countries. Funded by Saudi and Gulf sources, many new madrasas have come up all over the country in recent years.

The report went on to add that a chain of madrasas had been recently established in the country's sensitive border areas, claiming that they were engaged in 'systematic indoctrination of Muslims' in what it called 'fundamentalist ideology', and warning that this was 'detrimental to communal harmony'.[36] In short, it suggested that many madrasas had turned into threats to 'national security'. While making these claims, the report recommended that the government take appropriate measures against such madrasas, and advised that they should be carefully monitored. In order to wean madrasa students away from possible ISI-inspired propaganda, it suggested that steps be taken to arrange for madrasas to provide 'modern' education so as to bring them into the national 'mainstream'. For this purpose it suggested the setting up of a Central Advisory Board of Madrasa Education under the Ministry of Human Resources Development.[37] In other words, as the framers of the report appear to have seen it, madrasa reform and the promotion of Muslim education were not important in themselves. They were of concern only in so far as they allegedly seemed to impinge on 'national security'.

Predictably, the report led to considerable controversy. Hindutva groups claimed that it had only confirmed what they had been saying all along. Their critics, on the other hand, argued that the report had been carefully designed to promote the fiercely anti-Muslim Hindutva agenda.[38] Muslim groups and leaders saw the report as undeniably anti-Muslim. They pointed to what they saw as serious lacunae in the arguments put forward in the report. In claiming that many madrasas had been receiving external funds, allegedly from 'pan-Islamic' groups, the report, they insisted, had grossly exaggerated the magnitude of such support. Only a few, larger madrasas were said to have received such funds, while the vast majority of the madrasas in the country were entirely dependent on local resources, operating on minimal budgets. It was also argued that the madrasas which did accept foreign funding had done so after seeking the approval of the state authorities, and that this was perfectly legal.[39] Several Hindu and Christian organizations, too, they pointed out, received foreign money, and in fact on a considerably larger scale than Muslim organizations.

The report's suggestion that madrasas needed to be brought into the national 'mainstream' and the proposal to set up a central madrasa authority under close state supervision were seen as sinister moves on the part of the government and Hindutva groups to dilute the religious character of the madrasas and subject them to state control. The notion of the 'mainstream' that the government sought to impose was itself critically interrogated and dismissed. In defending the madrasas from the charge of keeping Muslims apart and away from the 'mainstream', Muslim leaders insisted that, far from encouraging separatism, the madrasas were actually deeply committed to 'national unity'. Thus, Maulana Ja'afar, senior leader of the Jama'at-i Islami Hind, argued that if by the 'mainstream' one meant 'national unity, patriotism and peace', then the madrasas needed no reform in that regard as they had been working precisely for these goals all along. Speaking for many Muslims, he implicitly suggested that the report had a rather different understanding of the 'mainstream' in mind, possibly one based on a Hindutva understanding of nationalism that brooked no space for non-Hindu identities. This, he stressed, was quite unacceptable to the Muslims. Likewise, Maulana Asrar ul-Haq Qasmi, assistant secretary general of the All-India Milli Council, dismissed allegations that madrasas prevented Muslims from joining the 'mainstream', and claimed that, in actual fact, the madrasas themselves represented the 'mainstream'. They were, he insisted, engaged in the onerous task of 'preparing noble-minded people and good citizens, teaching humanism, providing true guidance for all humankind, stressing universal equality and considering the Prophet Muhammad as a source of mercy for all'. If these values did not represent the 'mainstream', then, he asked in anguish, what did? Hence, he insisted, one simply could not question the credentials of the madrasas or seriously argue that they were an impediment to 'national integration'.[40]

Given the then government's clear pro-Hindutva leanings, it was quite natural that the report's proposals for the modernization of the madrasas was greeted with widespread scepticism and suspicion, being seen as a disguised effort to undermine the madrasas. Muslim leaders questioned the motives of the government; they asked why, if the government was really concerned about the educational plight of the Muslims, had it done virtually nothing to redress it all along? Was it not true that only now, in the wake of the Kargil conflict and the rise of the Taliban, that the issue was being raised? Several Muslim spokesmen recognized that the madrasa system was indeed in need of reform on several fronts, but decried the government's threats of intervention. It was for the Muslims themselves, particularly for the 'ulama of the madrasas, stressed Syed Shahabuddin, a noted Muslim politician, to undertake efforts to reform the madrasas. He claimed that in the name of modernizing the madrasas the government wanted to plant its own men in these schools. Gradually, this would open the way for the state to impose its curriculum in the madrasas, much of which might be opposed to Islamic teachings. The state might then seek to promote the teaching of secular subjects to such an extent that the place of Islamic disciplines would be drastically reduced, as a result of which the original purpose of the madrasas, the preservation and promotion of Islamic knowledge and the training of 'ulama, might be completely lost. Intervention by the state would, he claimed, allow the state to appoint non-Muslim teachers in the madrasas, thus interfering with or even controlling their administration. This would lead to a serious dilution of their Islamic identity, turning them, for all practical purposes, into state schools. In short, many Muslim leaders concluded, state intervention in the name of promoting reform, as the report had recommended, would make it far easier for the state to control the madrasas, thus helping Hindutva groups carry on with their agenda of absorbing the Muslims into the Hindu fold.[41]

The report's suggestion to the government recommending the setting up of a Central Advisory Board of Madrasa Education under the Ministry of Human Resources Development was also viewed with grave suspicion by many Muslim leaders. As in the case of proposals for the modernization of the madrasas, this suggestion was seen as a subtle means of putting an end to the independence of madrasas, of bringing them under state control, and undermining and ultimately destroying their Islamic character and identity. By providing funds to the madrasas, it was claimed that the proposed board would cause the madrasas to lose their organic bonds with the wider Muslim community, making them virtual appendages of the state instead. It was feared that the board would be used by the state to keep a close watch on the madrasas. It was claimed that the board might seek to regulate the madrasas by making a false and unconstitutional distinction between madrasas registered with the board on the one hand, which would be considered legal, and, on the other hand, other madrasas, the vast majority that wished to maintain their autonomy, which might then be branded as illegal and shut down.[42] This fear was not entirely unfounded, as the press and even senior politicians (including, surprisingly enough, the Marxist chief minister of West Bengal) had already begun talking of a large and growing number of 'illegal' madrasas which were not recognized by the state or affiliated to any of the state boards of madrasa education. Muslim critics argued that those who spoke alarmingly about the mushrooming of 'illegal' madrasas conveniently overlooked the fact that, from a strictly legal point of view, none of these were technically illegal because according to the law, they claimed, the state's permission was not required for setting up a school, whether secular or religious.

Charges about madrasas being involved in militant activities became even more shrill following the decision of the Taliban to give shelter to Osama bin Laden. With the incidents of 11 September 2001, rumours of the association between madrasas and terrorism grew into something of a national obsession in India. Right-wing Hindu groups and their ideologues, ever on the look-out for any opportunity to pick on Muslims, were quick to take advantage of the growing anti-Muslim sentiments in the West, going so far as to suggest that the time had come for India to join hands with America and Israel to combat what they called the monster of 'Islamic terrorism'. Militant Hindu groups declared that all madrasas should be banned forthwith. Soon, reports began pouring in of policemen and intelligence officers raiding various madrasas on the pretext of looking for 'militants', harassing teachers and students and generating a climate of terror and fear. In most cases the police found nothing incriminating, and several cases were reported of perfectly innocent madrasa students being arrested allegedly on the grounds of their being terrorists.[43] Hindu-owned newspapers were quick to accuse the madrasas from where these students were picked up as 'ISI dens', and even after the students were released with the charges against them being found to be false most papers refused to publish clarifications or apologies.

The Union and various state governments now began to plan new steps to control the madrasas. In early 2000, the Ministry of Human Resources Development announced plans to set up a committee to 'modernize' the madrasas. Meanwhile, the government was also said to be working on a 'secret project' to prepare a computerized database of madrasas and mosques all over the country.[44] In May 2002, the Union government suggested a new law to regulate and monitor foreign funding of madrasas.[45] Plans were afoot to set up a new, FBI-style intelligence agency, one of whose principal tasks would be to keep track of 'terrorists', including those alleged to be associated with various madrasas.[46] The government sent out a 'secret letter' to all chief secretaries and education secretaries of governments of states and union territories asking them to verify the antecedents of madrasas applying for financial assistance from the state, instructing them to ensure that none of the applicants was 'indulging [in], abetting or in any other way linked with anti-national activities'.[47] Madrasas along the Indo-Nepal border were ordered to furnish proof that they were not involved in 'activities that posed a threat to national security' and that they did not 'bear hatred towards any caste, creed or religion'.[48] No similar conditions were laid down for state assistance to Hindu educational institutions, critics noted. Orders were given forbidding the building of new mosques and madrasas in several areas along the border without prior permission of the district administration.[49] In March 2003, the BJP government in Gujarat, which had recently witnessed what some have called a state-sponsored genocide of Muslims, announced special measures targeted against the large number of madrasas in the state. The state's education minister, Anandiben Patel, revealed that the government had set up a task force to study the functioning of madrasas. She was commenting on a non-official resolution moved by Sunil Oza, senior BJP member of the state assembly, seeking de-recognition of religious institutions not imparting modern education, which many took to refer to madrasas alone. Conveniently ignoring the mushrooming growth of schools run by Hindu groups that could by no stretch of imagination be called 'modern', Patel argued that the government was 'dissatisfied' with the functioning of the madrasas, claiming that the education imparted therein was not consistent with the vision of 'modern Gujarat in the twenty-first century'. Without offering any firm evidence, she went so far as to claim that 'most' of the madrasas in the state had turned into breeding grounds for religious fundamentalists.[50]

The government in Gujarat could have been expected to embark on a witch-hunt of the madrasas, owing to the distinctly anti-Muslim stance of the BJP, but when the chief minister of communist West Bengal, Buddhadeb Bhattacharya, also made oblique references to certain madrasas in his state not affiliated with the state madrasa board as being allegedly involved in 'anti-national' activities, many eyebrows were raised, given that the ruling Communist Party of India (Marxist) enjoys considerable support among Muslims in the state, who account for almost a quarter of the population. Apparently, soon after the chief minister's statement, numerous madrasas in West Bengal faced the brunt of police harassment. Muslim organizations were quick to react, demanding that Bhattacharya supply proof to back his claim. The chief minister was unable to provide the name of any madrasa involved in 'anti-national' activity, and quickly sought to distance himself from the statement by claiming that he had been misquoted in the press.[51]

Despite the tirade against the madrasas launched by the government, the intelligence agencies and large sections of the press, little evidence seemed forthcoming to back the claim that the madrasas were engaged in any sort of overt militant activity or in an organized conspiracy against the country. In some places, activists said to be associated with militant groups were indeed apprehended, including some 'ulama and madrasa students.[52] Muslim leaders admitted that some of their co-religionists had engaged in violent activities to avenge the massacre of Muslims by Hindu mobs, often in league with agencies of the state, but claimed that almost none were madrasa students. Madrasa leaders themselves acknowledged that some madrasa students might have been associated with or sympathetic towards groups such as the now-banned Students' Islamic Movement of India,[53] but argued that this was an isolated phenomenon which did not have the approval of the madrasa authorities themselves. The possible involvement of a few madrasa students in criminal activities, they stressed, was part of a larger social problem that affected all educational institutions, and not madrasas alone. As a Barelwi '*alim* quipped, 'Criminals are found everywhere. For every criminal you find in a madrasa, you will probably find the same number in a Hindu *pathshala* and perhaps ten times the number in a regular university. Would you then demand that *pathshala*s and universities, too, be closed?'[54] In a similar vein, Zafrul Islam Khan, the editor of the Delhi-based English fortnightly *Milli Gazette*, remarked:

> Allegations of Indian madrasas promoting terrorism are utterly and totally fictitious. There is no evidence to suggest any such campaign on the part of a single madrasa. A *maulvi* here or a madrasa student there might have been arrested on some charges, but how can you blame the madrasa to which he belongs, or the madrasas as a whole, for that matter? Until now the authorities have not been able to identify a single madrasa in the country

providing any sort of military training. The newspapers or the authorities sometimes ambiguously claim, 'Some madrasas are spreading terror', but why don't they clearly name these madrasas if they have the evidence?[55]

Speaking for many Muslims, Ghatrif Shahbaz Nadwi, another Muslim journalist, remarked:

> It is simply a joke to claim that madrasas teach terrorism. The general environment of the madrasas, their curriculum and their teaching methods are such that their students become peace-loving to the point of even cowardice, and are cut off from the world around them [. . .] How can our students, who feel shy to ask even their teachers any questions, and live in a very restricted environment, ever become terrorists? The madrasa syllabus itself is so old, outdated and over-burdened that madrasa students are ignorant of the rapidly changing world around them [. . .] So, how could they even conceive of rebellion or taking to terrorism?[56]

Another Muslim writer, Khawar Hashmi, claimed that madrasas were actually playing a major role in combating terrorism, rather than promoting it. As he explained,

> The growth in the number of madrasas is because of the growing poverty among the Muslims. Remove poverty and the number of madrasas will automatically decline. But if you don't bother to address the problem of Muslim poverty and go ahead and close the madrasas the poor children who now study in them would be denied food and education. They would become beggars, dacoits, and criminals and might even take to terrorism.[57]

The 'ulama were among the most vociferous in condemning allegations of any association between the madrasas and terrorism, fearing that, if unchecked, the anti-madrasa propaganda could lead to state control or even the banning of madrasas. The rector of the Deoband madrasa, Maulana Marghub ur-Rahman, insisted, 'In our madrasas you will not even find a stick to beat anyone,'[58] adding that madrasas did not even train their students in self-defence techniques. Rather, he claimed, their concern was to produce 'simple, educated and law-abiding' citizens, for which they should actually be praised, rather than condemned.[59] He challenged the critics of the madrasas to name even one madrasa student who had been charged with rape, arson, killing innocent people, spying for other countries or attacking non-Muslim places of worship. He stressed that the gates of the madrasas were open twenty-four hours a day, and that anyone, Muslim or other, could come at any time to inspect them. As he declared:

> We're like an open book. I, as the rector of Dar ul-'Uloom Deoband, cordially invite anyone from the VHP to visit [the madrasa] without prior notice and attend all our classes, take rounds and inspect and assess if any terrorists are being sheltered here [or] if anyone is manufacturing weapons.[60]

In a similar vein, another leading '*alim*, the Barelwi Maulana Yasin Akhtar Misbahi asserted:

> I have repeatedly been stressing that if the government has any evidence that even a single madrasa is involved in anti-national activities it should present the evidence before the public, and we Muslims shall ourselves boycott such a madrasa and see that it is closed down. However, the government is spreading poisonous propaganda [about the madrasas] without any proof. Those who are spreading these canards are really enemies of the country [. . .] The Muslims are willing to participate in the progress of India, and the government should take stern action against all external as well as internal forces, be it the ISI or the RSS, who are spreading hatred and terrorism.[61]

Dismissing these allegations, Muslim leaders claimed that the madrasas were simply devoted to providing religious and moral education. Islam, they insisted, completely ignoring the activities of militant Islamists in neighbouring Pakistan and elsewhere, was a 'peace-loving' religion that stressed 'tolerance' and 'inter-communal harmony'. They argued that a 'true' Muslim could never be a terrorist, and that the term 'Muslim terrorist' was itself a contradiction in terms.[62] However, some of them willingly admitted that certain madrasas in Pakistan were indeed involved in terrorist activities, but claimed that the Indian madrasas had nothing to do with them.[63] Although some militant Pakistani madrasas did share a common ideological orientation with certain Indian madrasas, they insisted that allegiance to a shared *maslak* did not mean that the Indian madrasas had any organizational links with their Pakistani counterparts. The two were completely separate, and there was no coordination between them. They argued that the Pakistani context was completely different, and that the madrasas in the two countries had followed quite different paths. The Pakistani state had extended generous largesse to several madrasas in the country, and had in fact actually encouraged the politicization of the madrasas by enabling their 'ulama to enter politics and to serve Pakistani strategic interests by training their students to undertake militant activities in Afghanistan and Kashmir. This was in complete contrast to the situation in India, where not a single madrasa was involved in militant activity, not even in the troubled region of Kashmir. While numerous Pakistani madrasas had sent their students to fight in Afghanistan and elsewhere, no Indian madrasa student is said to have trodden that path, it was stressed. It was also pointed out that the madrasas which had the most militant bent in Pakistan were those that had been set up in areas inhabited essentially by 'warlike' and 'martial' peoples, such as the Pathans and the Punjabis. It was claimed that it was actually the 'martial racial spirit' of the Pathans and the Punjabis that had led the madrasas of the Pakistani Punjab and the North-West Frontier Province to the path of militant activism. In contrast, Indian Muslims were said to be 'docile' and 'peace-loving', as a result of which their madrasas stressed gradualism and accommodation, rather than confrontation and conflict. In other words, they argued, the circumstances in India had made the Indian madrasas adopt a clearly quietist stance *vis-à-vis* the state, and therefore it was completely misplaced to draw parallels between them and their Pakistani counterparts.[64]

That the government had no solid evidence to back its claim that madrasas were involved in training their students for disruptive activities was forcefully asserted by Muslim activists and 'ulama. It was pointed out that despite allegations of several madrasas along the Indo-Nepal[65] and Indo-Pakistan borders being used by the ISI, senior government officials, when asked, could not identify even one such school.[66] It was claimed that even in Kashmir, where Islamist groups were waging a bloody battle with the Indian army, madrasas were found to have no direct association with terrorism or militancy. Kashmir's inspector general of police, K. Rajendra, was quoted in Muslim papers as admitting that the police had 'never caught any militant with a madrasa background'. He is said to have stated that since the madrasas in Kashmir had clearly 'distanced themselves from extremism', focusing, instead, 'solely' on 'religious studies', he had 'no objection to their functioning'.[67] The fact that not a single case of questionable activities had been registered against any of the hundreds of madrasas and *maktab*s in Rajasthan's border districts adjoining

Pakistan was also widely highlighted in the Muslim press.[68] A senior police officer in Rajasthan admitted that madrasas in his state were not centres of the ISI and had not engaged in any 'anti-national' or 'criminal' activities.[69] A similar statement was issued by the director general of police of Uttar Pradesh,[70] and the same point was made by the chief minister of Assam.[71] A senior BJP leader was said to have admitted that most Indian agents of the ISI were Hindus, not Muslims.[72] In fact, some Muslim papers announced that Atal Bihari Vajpayee, the then prime minister, had himself declared 'in loud and clear terms' that madrasas were 'fountains of learning'. He recognized that they had played an important role in India's freedom movement, and also conceded that it was wrong to accuse them of being centres of the ISI.[73] Therefore, critics maintained, the propaganda against the madrasas was largely baseless. It was calculated to defame the Muslims, to terrorize them, to make them even more suspect in the eyes of the Hindus, and to stamp out the humble efforts that they were making to educate Muslim children.[74]

To many Muslim leaders, including 'ulama associated with the madrasas, the attacks on madrasas in India appeared to be part of a broader, American and Zionist-inspired 'conspiracy' against Islam in which the Indian government and right-wing Hindu groups were now seen as major actors, serving the interests of their American masters.[75] In putting forward this claim, they seemed to agree with the alarmist thesis of a 'clash of civilizations' between Islam and the West propounded by right-wing Western policy-makers. They claimed that since Islam had emerged as the main challenge to American global supremacy, America had launched a fierce war on Islam, thus tainting the madrasas as 'dens of terror' in order to give Islam a bad name.[76] Yet, it was also pointed out that America had not hesitated earlier to use *jihad*ist elements, including madrasa students, in its war against the Soviets in Afghanistan. Now, however, since its goal had been achieved and the *jihad*ists were seeking to challenge their former masters, America had launched a war against Islam, branding what it had earlier described as 'valiant freedom fighters' as 'bloodthirsty terrorists'. America, it was argued, was mortally afraid of Islam, considering it as the only force that could challenge its global hegemony. That is why, many Muslims claimed, the Americans had embarked on a war against Muslims. Since the 'enemies of Islam' had realized that madrasas were actually the 'powerhouse' and the 'forts' of Islam, they had launched a global campaign against them.[77] America wanted to exploit the entire world, it was argued, but found that the biggest hurdle in its path were the madrasas which were engaged in serving the poor and working for social equality and the promotion of moral values.[78] The calumny heaped on the Indian madrasas, it was alleged, was actually aimed at destroying Islam in the country, for once the madrasas, the real guarantors of Muslim identity and faith, had ceased to exist, nothing could prevent the absorption of Muslims into the Hindu fold. Accordingly, Muslims were appealed to to stand up and unite to face what was described as the gravest threat facing the community. If the campaign against the madrasas continued, Muslims were warned, the Indian Muslims would be sure to meet the same tragic fate as their co-religionists several centuries ago in Spain. As the editor of the official organ of the old boys' association of the Deoband madrasa put it, the vilification campaign directed against the madrasas was 'in reality, the fiercest challenge faced by the Indian Muslims in the fifty years of independent India, and responding to it is the most urgent need of the hour'.[79]

Interestingly, the heated debate on the alleged terrorist links of the madrasas led to numerous 'ulama openly expressing their commitment to 'true' patriotism and allegiance to the Indian constitution, branding their detractors as the 'enemies' of the nation. They argued that while the madrasas trained their students to become 'good, law-abiding citizens' and had absolutely no links with terrorism, those most furiously and vociferously opposed to them—Hindutva chauvinists—were terrorists and bloodthirsty fascists themselves. They were bent on inciting civil war and were responsible for the massacre of Muslims and other marginalized communities, besides also being behind the murder of the 'father of the nation', M.K. Gandhi.[80] In other words, it was repeatedly stressed, it was not the madrasas but rather their opponents who were the greatest 'enemies' of the unity and prosperity of India.[81]

The Indian nation and its supposed foundational values of democracy and secularism thus became the ground of fierce contestation, with rival parties to the debate furiously battling one another, each claiming the mantle of nationalism and love for the country. A Muslim journalist revealed that the majority of Indians arrested for spying for Pakistan were Hindus, not Muslims, and of the latter almost none had been a madrasa student or graduate.[82] Likewise, Mufti Ahmed Devlavi, a noted Deobandi *'alim*, and head of the Council for the Protection of Madrasas in Gujarat, argued that while madrasas had all along supported the freedom and unity of India, those opposed to the madrasas, by which he meant right-wing Hindu groups, had played no role at all in the freedom movement, serving instead as lackeys of their British colonial masters. While the madrasas had never challenged the Indian Constitution, he pointed out that the proponents of Hindutva had openly condemned the founding document of the republic, and were demanding a new 'Hindu' constitution to replace it. While madrasas taught their students 'civilized manners', their opponents preached hatred and terror, and were responsible for the mass murder of thousands of innocent Indians. While madrasas stressed inter-communal harmony, 'mutual trust', 'public order' and the 'honouring of different religions, their followers, their holy books and their religious leaders and institutions', their detractors were vehemently opposed to secularism and inter-communal amity, and, therefore, to the unity of the country. In short, he insisted, their critics were 'communal fascists', while the madrasas and their 'ulama were true 'patriots'.[83]

Anti-Madrasa Propaganda: Changing Roles of the Madrasas

The persistent propaganda campaign against madrasas as 'dens of terror' forced Muslim leaders, including the 'ulama associated with leading madrasas, to consider measures to defend the madrasas from attack. Interestingly, going by their public statements, many of them are now calling for greater engagement with non-Muslims, seeking to build bridges of understanding with people of other faiths and with agencies of the state in an effort to clear the madrasas of the charges levelled against them. This envisions new roles for more socially involved 'ulama seeking to interact with the wider society that many madrasas have hitherto deliberately sought to remain insulated from. This shifting stance entails an apologetic defence of traditional doctrines which, in the process of being sought to be defended, are interpreted in ways that might be more acceptable to a non-Muslim audience.

In the face of the attacks on the madrasas, not a single

madrasa, it is important to note, is known to have called for retaliatory violence or even for armed *jihad*. Rather, the overall trend seems to be in precisely the other direction, suggesting a growing realization on the part of the 'ulama that there is a need to reach out to people of other faiths if madrasas are to be allowed to function freely. A Deobandi '*alim* echoed the mood of numerous 'ulama when he suggested that in the face of the campaign against the madrasas the 'ulama must not 'take any step that will play into the hands of those opposed to the madrasas'. Instead, he argued, madrasas should follow the Qur'anic dictum of repelling evil with good, as a result of which their most inveterate foes might turn into their greatest allies and supporters.[84] This is no exceptional voice. In January 1995, shortly after a police raid on the Nadwat ul-'Ulama, Lucknow, the All-India Muslim Personal Law Board, the apex body of Indian 'ulama belonging to almost all the *maslak*s, met in Lucknow to discuss, among other issues, the growing wave of attacks on madrasas. Among the resolutions passed at the meeting was one that stressed the need for madrasas to arrange regular meetings with non-Muslim intellectuals, social activists, journalists, government officials and political workers in order to explain to them the curriculum, methods of functioning and aims of the madrasas. The resolution also called for madrasas to seek to combat the organized campaign against them through 'wisdom' (*hikmat*) and by eschewing 'emotionalism' (*jazbatiyat*).[85] The same sentiment was expressed seven years later when the campaign against the madrasas had reached new heights in the aftermath of the attacks of September 2001. At a meeting of various madrasa heads held in October 2002 near Lucknow, Maulana Muhammad Rabey Hasni Nadwi, rector of the Nadwat ul-'Ulama madrasa and president of the All-India Muslim Personal Law Board, argued that in this 'age of democracy', when 'no community could seek to eliminate all others through force', the only way to combat the concerted 'campaign' against Islam and the madrasas was through the use of the mass media.[86] At the same meeting, a carefully worded resolution was passed, appealing to the Muslims to rebut anti-madrasa propaganda, but only through peaceful means. Madrasas were advised to abide by the principles of 'seriousness, justice, tolerance and love for humanity', and Muslims were cautioned against taking to violence and thereby playing into the hands of 'anti-Muslim' forces.[87]

Similar suggestions have come from 'ulama from different parts of the country. Since one of the major charges levelled against the madrasas is their alleged involvement in 'anti-national' activities, many 'ulama have now begun to argue for the urgent need for madrasas to highlight before the non-Muslim public the role of the madrasas and the 'ulama in the freedom struggle in order to stress their patriotic credentials. Influential sections of the Indian 'ulama today feel the necessity of addressing multiple constituencies, Hindus as well as Muslims, if the madrasas are to be left unharmed. This entails actively reaching out to the wider non-Muslim public in order to convince them of the services that madrasas are said to be rendering, not just to Muslims alone but to the country as a whole, and to provide them with a more objective understanding of Islam and the madrasa system. One '*alim* suggests that madrasas must actively seek to counter the widespread conviction among non-Muslims that Islam sanctions the indiscriminate killing of others and is vehemently opposed to secularism and democracy.[88] Another '*alim* argues that in the face of the attacks on the madrasas the 'ulama must seek to convince the Hindu public that, far from preaching rebellion against India and hatred against other communities, the madrasas instil in their students such noble values as 'love for the country', 'unity and oneness' and 'good morals'.[89] Madrasas must seek to promote inter-communal harmony, says a leading Deobandi '*alim*, as this would help clear people's misconceptions of Islam as a violent religion.[90]

In order to communicate with their non-Muslim fellow countrymen and disabuse them of misconceptions that they might have concerning the madrasas, senior 'ulama are today increasingly advocating that madrasas should open their doors to welcome non-Muslims and allow them to freely meet and interact with the students and teachers so that they can discover for themselves what madrasas are really about. As part of this effort to reach out to others, some madrasas have begun organizing functions on special occasions such as festivals, Independence Day, Republic Day, to which they invite local non-Muslims to participate. Often these events become forums for the 'ulama to stress the patriotic credentials of the madrasas and their commitment to inter-communal harmony. In addition, some madrasas have begun limited efforts at promoting inter-faith dialogue with religious heads of other communities. In mid-2002 a newspaper reported that some 800 madrasas in and around the city of Hyderabad were planning to introduce patriotism as a separate subject in their syllabus in order to highlight the role of the madrasas in India's freedom struggle and the 'Islamic concept of love for the country'.[91] In early March 2003 a film commissioned by the Special Service Bureau, a hitherto 'secret organization' under the home ministry, discovered numerous madrasas along the Indo-Nepal border whose 'ulama were preaching the importance of patriotism to their students, thus contradicting reports by the Intelligence

Bureau that spoke of many of these madrasas as being actively engaged in 'anti-national' activities.[92]

As part of this broader effort to reach out to the non-Muslim public in order to combat the propaganda against them, numerous madrasas have brought out booklets, mainly in Urdu, but also in Hindi, English and various regional languages, stressing the constructive role of the madrasas and denying any association with terrorism. Some larger madrasas have organized press conferences and have issued press statements dissociating themselves from terrorism. Muslim-owned newspapers publish such statements of the 'ulama enthusiastically, but the 'ulama complain that, in general, non-Muslim papers show little interest in highlighting their views.

The campaign against the madrasas seems to have goaded Muslim leaders, including leading 'ulama, to take seriously at least some of the arguments of their critics. That all was not well with the madrasas themselves was widely recognized, and it was felt that although the calumny heaped on the madrasas as alleged dens of 'anti-national' elements and 'terrorists' was baseless, there was indeed an urgent need for curricular reform. As Asghar 'Ali Engineer noted, although the propaganda against the madrasas was 'unfair and unsubstantiated' and the Indian madrasas could hardly be accused of 'engaging in any sort of political activity', the time had come to seriously consider efforts to modernize their curricula and methods of teaching.[93] In a sense, then, the growing attacks on the madrasas came as a blessing in disguise for advocates of madrasa reform. Recognizing that the rhetoric of reform could give the state powerful justification to interfere in the madrasa system, Muslim leaders, including numerous 'ulama, argued for the need for madrasas to modernize, even if simply to stave off what was seen as the threat of government-imposed modernization programmes. Proposals for reform were limited, yet in many ways significant, suggesting a growing realization among sections of the ‘ulama of the need to take seriously the charge that the madrasas had remained stagnant and out of tune with the demands of the times, which had also left them open to accusations of being hand in glove with ‘enemies’ of the country.

This growing internal demand for curricular reform is today visible in even the most conservative of Indian madrasas, and, as we have seen, has not left the great Dar ul-‘Ulum at Deoband, considered to be the centre of Islamic ‘orthodoxy’ in South Asia, unaffected. In 2002, the newly founded Rabita-i Madaris-i Islamiya (Federation of Islamic Schools), an apex body of Deobandi madrasas, appealed to the heads of madrasas to introduce, ‘to the extent required’ (*hasb-i zarurat*), subjects such as mathematics, social science, Hindi, English and computers in their curriculum. The ‘extent required’ was deliberately not specified but was left to each madrasa to interpret on its own, thus affording a convenient way out for madrasas that did not feel the need to teach such subjects at all.[94] Although, as critics have pointed out, not much has happened on this front so far, the Rabita’s appeal did seem to suggest a growing awareness among even the most conservative sections of the Deobandi ‘ulama of the need for madrasa curricular reform.

An issue that received particular attention from ‘ulama in the wake of the growing attacks on the madrasas was the question of registration with state authorities. Many madrasas are not registered societies or trusts but, instead, are run as informal organizations. Although legally such institutions need not be registered with the state, there is today a growing realization that registration might help, rather than hinder, them. A senior Deobandi '*alim* advised madrasas to register themselves to prevent possible harassment by the state, which was said to be considering passing a law to control non-registered madrasas.[95] In 2002, the Deobandi Rabita-i Madaris-i Islamiya issued a statement suggesting that madrasas should register themselves with the government, keep written records of all income and expenditure, get their accounts audited annually, open and maintain bank accounts, and procure a licence under the Foreign Exchange Regulation Act (FCRA) if they sought foreign funds. In this way, the anti-madrasa propaganda seemed to be leading to an awareness of the need for better management and financial accountability on the part of the madrasa authorities, something that their critics have long been pressing for.

Faced with mounting anti-madrasa propaganda, madrasa leaders are now also being forced to consider the demand for careful monitoring of their students. In response to the attacks on the madrasas, a widely respected Deobandi scholar, Maulana Asrar ul-Haq Qasmi, suggested that in order to weed out possible unwanted elements the madrasas must properly scrutinize their prospective students before giving them admission, and should preferably get them to supply letters of recommendation from reliable persons. Madrasas, he advised, should maintain a list of people visiting their campuses and not allow anyone in who could be suspected of disruptive activities. He also suggested that madrasas should ensure proper discipline of their students and see that they did not unwittingly fall prey to any 'conspiracy'.[96]

The need to establish links with the state administration is also being stressed by several 'ulama in order to protect the madrasas from harassment. Recognizing that a distinct lack of communication between madrasas and the state was responsible for much misunderstanding on the part of the latter about the activities of the madrasas, the rector of the Nadwat ul-'Ulama advised madrasas to regularly interact with government officials and supply them with the information that they needed.[97] Similarly, a leading Sunni *'alim*, Maulana Abu Bakr Qadri of the al-Sunnah Cultural Centre, Calicut, called for 'frequent interaction' between madrasas, Muslim educational boards and government officials in order to discuss Muslim educational problems and concerns.[98] In this way, the anti-madrasa propaganda seems to have led at least some 'ulama to recognize the need for greater dialogue between madrasas and the wider, including Hindu, public, as well as agencies of the state.

*

As has been suggested during the course of our discussion here, there is no firm evidence to support the charge that madrasas in India are engaged in a concerted or organized campaign of training terrorists. In fact, there is probably no madrasa in India that, as an institution, is actively engaged in such activities. True, there may well be certain individuals associated with some madrasas, students as well as teachers, who might support militant forms of activism, not so much to forcibly establish an Islamic state, because that is recognized as impracticable in the immediate future, but, rather, as a response to or as a means of defence against organized Hindu militancy. Some leaders and activists of the now banned Students' Islamic Movement of India, accused of promoting terrorism, were graduates of the Jami'at ul-Falah madrasa in Azamgarh. They justified their call for *jihad* as a response to the massacre of Muslims at the hands of Hindutva groups in league with the state. Likewise, students and teachers in many madrasas, particularly those affiliated to the Deoband school, did support the Taliban regime and its policies, largely as a response to American aggression. However, and this point needs to be borne in mind, hardly any Indian madrasa students, even in war-torn Kashmir, have actually been involved in any militant sort of activity. There is no Muslim counterpart in India to armed Hindutva groups who have been responsible for the murder of thousands of Muslims in recent years. This owes much to the fact of Muslims being a relatively powerless minority, and the acute consciousness that violence committed by Muslim groups will invite severe reprisals from Hindus and what is largely seen as the 'Hindu' Indian state.

In such a situation, opposition might take symbolic, instead of physical, forms. What might be seen as a substitute for actual armed *jihad* is the belief that although Muslims might be persecuted in this world, they will be granted eternal solace and joy in heaven, and their 'disbelieving' oppressors will be dispatched to hell. Preaching hostility towards other religions or insisting that the ultimate goal of Islam is the establishment of a state ruled by pious Muslims in accordance with the *shari'ah* might not, technically, be considered akin to militancy. Yet, this does undeniably help cultivate a Manichean mentality that can easily be exploited by militant demagogues, as, for instance, in the case of numerous madrasas in Pakistan. It is possible that if fiercely anti-Muslim Hindutva groups gather further strength, whipping up anti-Muslim hatred and inciting violence against Muslims, as happened in Gujarat, the halting efforts that madrasas have been making in recent years towards reform and openness to the wider society will make little headway. In such a situation, many Muslims, finding themselves even more beleaguered and oppressed, might see in militant reaction the only means of defending themselves. This might easily affect the madrasas as well. The widespread negative stereotypes of non-Muslims as 'disbelievers' or 'enemies of God', which today encourage cultural insularity and exclusivism, could, in the face of growing attacks on the community, be used to mobilize support for militant struggle against oppression.

In other words, if militancy in the madrasas is not to turn into a self-fulfilling prophecy, the problem of Hindu–Muslim relations needs to be urgently tackled. Islamist and Hindu militancies feed on each other, and one cannot expect to counter one without also consistently opposing the other. Yet, to see the madrasas solely in terms of a potential security threat, as the state and much of the Indian media seem to, is obviously not the best way to relate to them. Madrasas, as this book has tried to show, serve several valuable functions, particularly catering to the poorer classes of Muslims, victims of governmental neglect and discrimination. These significant contributions are often ignored in debates about the madrasa system. As many Muslims themselves recognize, madrasas are in need of considerable reform, and today many madrasas are increasingly willing to consider such proposals. To subject the madrasas to unrelenting attack and demonization is the surest way of putting an end to the process of reform, driving the 'ulama to turn their backs on change. The actions and shrill rhetoric of Hindutva militants and aggressive Western powers that brand all madrasas as a 'terrorist' threat thus work to further diminish the prospects of madrasa reform. Clearly, reform cannot be imposed on the madrasas from without, contrary to what Hindutva ideologues and their American neo-conservative counterparts insist. Rather, the initiative for change has to come from within the madrasas themselves, by dialoguing with, rather than by hounding, the 'ulama. Such a dialogue can only succeed in a climate of trust and tolerably good inter-community relations. This, in turn, requires a consistent struggle against all forms of religious chauvinism, Hindu, Muslim, and other, as well as against the menace of Western imperialism that now sees Islam as its new global ideological rival.

Conclusion

As institutions for the preservation and transmission of the Islamic tradition, madrasas continue to play an important role in the lives of millions of Muslims in India. Given the significant Muslim population in the country, madrasas cannot be simply wished away, and nor can they be ignored. The role of madrasas has been hotly debated by their defenders and critics, Muslims and non-Muslims alike. As this book has sought to show, even among the 'ulama there is considerable dissatisfaction with the functioning of madrasas. Many Muslims themselves complain that the sort of education students receive in madrasas hardly equips them to function in a modern, plural society. This suggests the urgent need for reform in the madrasas, but in a manner that does not dilute what is seen as their religious identity.

The task of madrasa reform is best left to the Muslim community itself, although the state and well-meaning non-Muslims, including secular non-governmental organizations, do have a role to play in this regard. The greatest hope for reform lies in sections of the younger 'ulama and socially engaged Muslim activists who are increasingly offering more relevant perspectives of Islamic theology and jurisprudence and are today demanding to be heard. These voices of reform, although still not widely known, are beginning to articulate alternative understandings of Islam that seek to creatively engage with the manifold challenges of contemporary life. Some of them offer new views on a range of issues, from women's rights and inter-faith relations to the state and international relations. In doing so, they critically interrogate the historical *fiqh* tradition, seeking to reinstate a progressive *ijtihad* that seriously takes into account modern concerns. In their own ways they critique the traditionalist 'ulama and radical Islamists, on the one hand, and Western imperialists and their Indian Hindutva counterparts, on the other, regarding them all as a major challenge to what they portray as the 'authentic' Islamic tradition.

A critical task before progressive Muslims is the struggle to gain wider acceptance for alternative ways of imagining Islam within the wider Muslim community, particularly among the 'ulama and students of the madrasas. Such voices are as yet almost completely unheard in the portals of most Indian madrasas, for many 'ulama see them as little short of blasphemous and as a major challenge to their authority and hegemonic claims. Powerful and growing anti-Muslim sentiments, in the West, in India, and elsewhere, make the task of the proponents of Islamic reform doubly difficult. In times such as these, many Muslims are tempted to imagine that calls for a radical reappraisal of what passes off as tradition constitute a cruel betrayal of their faith and heritage and play into the hands of what are seen as the 'enemies' of the faith.

In a religiously plural society like India, inter-faith dialogue assumes a particular urgency, for it is indispensable for peace and progress of the community as a whole. Given this, the lack of enthusiasm for genuine dialogue on the part of the majority of the Indian 'ulama (as in the case of most Hindu priests, one could argue) is a major source of concern. Madrasas, like their Hindu counterparts, need to be sensitized to the crucial importance of building bridges of understanding with people of other faiths. In this regard, a central question that needs to be addressed is the ways in which the religious 'other' is understood and portrayed in the madrasas. Negative stereotypes of people of other faiths are deeply ingrained in established theologies, irrespective of religious label, and are reinforced by literally thousands of Muslim and Hindu religious schools throughout the country. Countering these images can only be possible in a climate of reasonably peaceful inter-communal relations. In the case of the madrasas, it is obvious that peace on the communal front is indispensable for them to be willing to open up to the wider society, through which new and more accommodative notions of the religious 'other' might find more general acceptance. Creative interaction between Muslims and followers of other faiths might, in turn, help develop understandings of Islam that are relevant to the particular context of contemporary India. While the task of fashioning bold restatements of Islamic theology and law is principally for Muslims to undertake, others too have a vital role to play. Obscurantisms and competing forms of religious militancy feed on each other—the rigidity of large sections of the Indian 'ulama cannot be understood without taking into account Hindu militancy and the role of the state in supporting it. If madrasas are to be enabled to play a constructive role in India's nation-building project, the growing threat of Hindu militancy needs to be seriously addressed, particularly by Hindus themselves.

All religions can be interpreted in diverse ways to suit different political agendas, and it is for believers—Hindus, Muslims and others—who are serious about their faith commitments as well as their concern for the future of India to choose and promote progressive understandings of their own religions that generously accept people of other communities despite their differences. This, to my mind, is the only way that India can survive, for there is simply no other way. And in this regard, madrasas, as a major factor in moulding Muslim opinions, have a central role to play.

Notes

Preface

1. <www.islaminterfaith.org>
2. Thus, Maulana Muhammad Taqi Usmani, a leading Pakistani Deobandi *'alim*, claims that because the traditional madrasas still survive in South Asia, unlike in many other parts of the Muslim world, 'there is more zeal for the faith in the subcontinent than anywhere else in the world' (Muhammad Taqi Usmani, *Fazilat-i 'Ilm-o-'Ulama*, Delhi: Farid Book Depot, 1999, p. 9).
3. Francis Robinson, *The 'Ulama of Farangi Mahall and Islamic Culture in South Asia*, New Delhi: Permanent Black, 2001.
4. Barbara D. Metcalf, *Islamic Revival in British India, 1860-1900*, New Delhi: Oxford University Press, 2002.
5. Muhammad Qasim Zaman, *The 'Ulama in Contemporary Islam: Custodians of Change*, Princeton & Oxford: Princeton University Press, 2002.

Chapter 1: 'Ilm *and Islam: The Early Islamic Scholarly Tradition*

1. Thus, madrasas are often referred to as *madaris-i diniya* ('religious madrasas') or *madaris-i islamiya* ('Islamic madrasas').
2. See Zafar 'Alam, *Education in Early Muslim Period*, Delhi: Markazi Maktaba-i Islami, 1997.
3. Qazi Athar Mubarakpuri, *Khair al-Qarun Ki Darsgahe Aur Unka Nizam-i Ta'lim*, Deoband: Shaikh ul-Hind Academy, 1996, p. 87.

4. G.M.D. Sufi, *Al-Minhaj: Being the Evolution of Curriculum in the Muslim Educational Institutions of India*, Lahore: Shaikh Muhammad Ashraf, 1941, p. 80.
5. Munawwar Jahan Rashid, *Qadim Islami Madaris*, Lahore: Majlis-i Taraqqi-i Adab, 1975, pp. 35–36.
6. These were the four immediate successors of the Prophet: Abu Bakr (632–634), 'Umar (634–644), 'Uthman (644–656) and 'Ali (656–661).
7. Abu Ameenah Bilal Philips, *The Evolution of Islamic Law and the Maddhabs*, Riyadh: Tawheed Publications, 1988, pp. 41–42.
8. Niyaz Ahmad Fatehpuri, *'Ilm: Ek Shari' Zarurat*, New Delhi: al-Kitab, 1999, pp. 24–47.
9. Ahmad Hasan, *The Early Development of Islamic Jurisprudence*, Islamabad: Islamic Research Institute, 1994, pp. 2–4.
10. Philips, op. cit., pp. 93–98.
11. Cited in 'Abdur Rauf Jhandanagari, *al-'Ilm wa'l 'Ulama*, Maunath Bhanjan: Idara Da'wat ul-Islam, n.d., p. 22.
12. Sayyed Riyasat 'Ali Nadwi, *Islami Nizam-i Ta'lim*, Azamgarh: Dar ul-Musannifin, 1992, pp. 35–37.
13. Bernard Lewis, *What Went Wrong? The Clash Between Islam and Modernity in the Middle East*, London: Weidenfeld & Nicolson, 2002, pp. 6–7.
14. Manzoor Ahmed, *Islamic Education: Redefinition of Aims and Methodology*, New Delhi: Genuine Publications & Media, 2002, p. 8.
15. Rashid, op. cit., p. 186.
16. Rashid, op. cit., pp. 272–98.
17. Named after the founder of the school of thought, the ninth-century Abu Hasan al-'Ashari of Iraq (874–935).
18. Eqbal Ahmed, 'Islam and Politics', in Asghar Khan (ed.), *Islam, Politics and the State: The Pakistan Experience*, London: Zed Books, 1985, p. 21.
19. Khaled Abou El Fadl, *Rebellion and Violence in Islamic Law*, Cambridge: Cambridge University Press, 2001, pp. 118–19.
20. Moinuddin Ahmad, *'Ulama: The Boon and Bane of Islamic*

Society, New Delhi: Kitab Bhavan, 1990, p. 88. For an interesting discussion of 'Asharism and its opposition to the Mu'tazilites, see Pervez Hoodbhoy, *Islam and Science: Religious Orthodoxy and the Battle for Rationality*, Kuala Lumpur: S.Abdul Majeed & Co., 1992.

21. Zia ul-Hasan Faruqi, *Islam Mai Rasikh ul-Ayteqadi: Bich Ki Rah*, New Delhi: Maktaba-i Jami'a, 1990, pp. 11–20.
22. Ziauddin Islahi, 'Qadim Murawaj Nizam-i Ta'lim Ka Ja'iza', *Nizam ul-Qur'an*, vol. 1, no. 2, January–March 2001, p. 34.
23. Philips remarks that today, when traditional 'ulama are confronted with a reliable *hadith* that appears to conflict with the position of their *mazhab*, they generally seek to interpret it in such a way so as to support their *mazhab* or else offer weak *hadith* reports to counter it (Philips, op. cit., p. 116).
24. Philips, op. cit., p. 107. Thus, al-Khatib collected a forged *hadith* attributed to Muhammad through Abu Hurairah, according to which Muhammad allegedly predicted, 'There will be among my *ummah* a man called Abu Hanifa. He will be the lamp of my *ummah*' (Philips, op. cit., p. 133).
25. Moinuddin Ahmed, *The Urgency of Ijtihad*, New Delhi: Kitab Bhavan, 1992, p. 45.
26. Philips, op. cit., p. 65.
27. Thus, for instance, in Nishapur the Shafi'is and the Hanafis are said to have 'engaged in rioting', being two 'warring factions' (Richard W. Bulliet, *The Patricians of Nishapur: A Study in Medieval Islamic Social History*, Cambridge, Massachusetts: Harvard University Press, 1972, pp. 30–33).
28. Daphna Ephrat, *A Learned Society in a Period of Transition: The Sunni 'Ulama of Eleventh Century Baghdad*, Albany: State University of New York, 2000, pp. 1–2.
29. Sayyed Muhammad Salim, *Dini Madaris Ki Rivayat Aur Nisab-i Ta'lim Ki Khususiyat*, Lahore: Idara Ta'limi Tahqiq Tanzim-i Asatiza-i Pakistan, 1987, p. 12.
30. For biographical details, see Sayyed Rizvan 'Ali Rizvi, *Nizam*

ul-Mulk Tusi: Ek 'Azim Muffakir, Mudabbir, Muntazim Aur Mahir-i Siyasat, Karachi: Karachi University, 1995.

31. Of him the noted scholar of Isma'ilism W. Ivanow writes, 'The talented vezier Nizam ul-Mulk was the man who served the invaders who had enslaved his people and his mother country, the man who amassed immense wealth, surely not by incorruptibility, and who had beaten all records in nepotism, so that even his contemporaries, with their rather specious standards with regard to such matters, were horrified' (W. Ivanow, *Brief Survey of the Evolution of Isma'ilism*, Bombay: Isma'ili Society, 1952, p. 73).
32. George Makdisi, *The Rise of Colleges: Institutions of Learning in Islam and the West*, Edinburgh: Edinburgh University Press, 1981, p. 281.
33. Rashid, op. cit., p. 114–25.
34. A. Ghafur Chawdhri, *Some Aspects of Islamic Education*, Delhi: Adam Publishers, 1999, p. 4.
35. S.M.W. Rashid al-Nadwi and Syed Ghulam Mohiuddin, *Survey of Muslim Education: India*, Cambridge: The Islamic Academy, 1985, p. 14.
36. Sayyed Riyasat 'Ali Nadwi, op. cit., pp. 27–29. See also Mansoor A. Quraishi, *Some Aspects of Muslim Education*, Baroda: Centre of Advanced Study in Education, M.S. University, 1970, pp. 4–5.

Chapter 2: Madrasas in India: Historical Evolution

1. Kuldip Kaur, *Madrasa Education in India: A Study of its Past and Present*, Chandigarh: Centre for Research in Rural and Industrial Development, 1990, p. 17.
2. Qamruddin, *Hindustan Ki Dini Darsgahe: Kul Hind Survey*, New Delhi: Hamdard Educational Society, 1996, p. 34. See also Sayyed Naushad 'Ali, *Musalmanan-i Hind-o-Pakistan Ki Tarikh-i Ta'lim*, Karachi: Salman Academy, 1963.

3. Ibid., p. 4.
4. For a detailed treatment, see Narendra Nath Law, *Promotion of Learning in India during Muhammadan Rule (By Muhammadans)*, Delhi: Idara-i Adabiyat-i Dehli, 1973.
5. For details, see Muhammad Hafizullah, *Salatin-i Hind Ki 'Ilm Parvari*, Patna: Muslim Academy, 1956.
6. Zafar ul-Islam Islahi, 'Ahad-i Wusta Ke Hindustan Mai 'Ala Ta'lim', in *Mulk-o-Millat Ki Ta'mir Aur Dini Madaris*, Bilariyaganj: Jam'iat ul-Falah, 1994, p. 123.
7. Sufi, op. cit., p. 8.
8. Sayyed Manazir Ahsan Gilani, *Hindustan Mai Musalmano Ka Nizam-i Ta'lim-o-Tarbiyat* (vol. 1), Delhi: Nadwat ul-Musannifin, 1987, p. 183.
9. Imdadul Hasan Azad Faruqi, 'Introduction', in Imdadul Hasan Azad Faruqi (ed.), *Hindustan Mai Islami 'Ulum-o-Adabiyat*, op. cit., p. 7.
10. Sufi, op. cit., pp. 81–82.
11. Zafar ul-Islam Islahi, op. cit., p. 75.
12. S.M.Wazeh Rashid Nadwi and Syed Ghulam Mohiuddin, *Survey of Muslim Education: India*, Cambridge: The Islamic Academy, Cambridge, 1985, p. 6.
13. Zafar ul-Islam Islahi, *Salatin-i Dehli Aur Shari'at-i Islamiya: Ek Mukhtasar Ja'iza*, Aligarh: Rehan Khan, 2002, pp. 75–80.
14. Thus, for instance, some 'ulama in Akbar's court sought to prove that the emperor was the Promised Mahdi or religious guide, who Muslims expected would arrive at the end of time. One '*alim* associated with Akbar's court even went so far as to bestow on Akbar the lofty titles of 'The Perfect Man', 'The Caliph of the Times' and the 'Reflection of God on Earth'. Another '*alim*, 'Abdullah Sultanpuri, issued a *fatwa*, probably at the emperor's request, claiming that the pilgrimage to Mecca was no longer binding. When he died a sum of *three* crore rupees was found in his treasury (Moinuddin Ahmed, *'Ulama...*, op. cit., pp. 75–78).
15. Zia ul-Hasan Faruqi, *Islam Mai Rasikh ul-Ayteqadi*, op. cit., p. 22.

16. Zafar ul-Islam Islahi, op. cit., pp. 16–17.
17. Zia ul-Hasan Faruqi, *Islam Mai Rasikh ul-Ayteqadi*, op. cit., p. 21.
18. Muhammad Sharif Khan, *Education, Religion and Modern Age*, New Delhi: Ashish Publishing House, 1990, pp. 84–102.
19. Zafar ul-Islam Islahi, op. cit., pp. 12–16.
20. Zia ul-Hasan Faruqi, 'Hindustan Mai Islami Rasikh ul-Aqa'id Ki Rivayat', in Imdadul Hasan Azad Faruqi (ed.), *Hindustan Mai Islami 'Ulum-o-Adabiyat*, New Delhi: 1986, p. 13.
21. Yohannan Friedmann, 'Islamic Thought in Relation to the Indian Context', in Marc Gaboreiau (ed.), *Islam et Societe en Asia du Sud*, Paris: Ecole des Hautes Etudes en Sciences Sociales, 1986, p. 80. The Shafi'i and Hanbali 'ulama considered only Jews, Christians and Zoroastrians as *zimmis*.
22. Kunwar Muhammad Ashraf, *An Overview of Indian Muslim Politics (1920–1947)* (translated by Jaweed Ashraf), New Delhi: Manak Publications, 2001, p. 28. Several other Muslim rulers refused to act on the advice of the 'ulama to embark on a full-scale massacre of Hindus. Thus, Iltutmish refused to do so, and his minister, Junaid, explained to the 'ulama that, 'If we in India practiced such a policy then persons like you should remember that in this country we are like salt in the dough. If we behaved in the manner suggested by you, even the small number of remaining reciters of the *kalima* shall be put under the sword' (ibid., pp. 170–71).
23. Sayyed 'Abdul Haye, *Hindustan Ka Nisabi Dars Aur Uskey Taghirat*, Lucknow, n.d., pp. 7–8.
24. Mujeeb Ashraf, 'Distinctive Madrasah-i Rahimiyah: Growth and Pattern of Educational Curriculum', *The Fragrance of the East*, vol.v, no. 1, January–March 2003, p. 34.
25. Abul 'Irfan Nadwi, '*Ma'qulat Ke Maidan Mai Hindustani Musalmano Ki Khidmat*', in Imdadul Hasan Azad Faruqi (ed.), *Hindustan Mai Islami 'Ulum-o-Adabiyat*, op. cit., p. 70.
26. Qamruddin, op. cit., p. 102.
27. Cited in Kaur, op. cit., p. 35.

28. Muhammad Sohrab, 'Mazi Mai Dini Madaris Ki Nisabi Rivayat', *Zindagi-i Nau*, September 1994, pp. 18–22.
29. For more details on the family, see Francis Robinson, *The 'Ulama of Farangi Mahall and Islamic Culture in South Asia*, New Delhi: Permanent Black, 2001, pp. 1–2. See also Muhammad Wali ul-Haq Ansari, 'Bani-i Dars-i Nizami Mulla Nizamuddin Aur Unka Khanvada Firangi Mahal' (part 1), *Tarjuman-i Dar ul-'Ulum*, December 1997, pp. 5–8.
30. Sayyed Muhammad Miyan, *'Ulama-i Hind Ka Shandar Mazi* (vol. 1), Delhi: Kitabistan, n.d., p. 364. See also Muhammad Raza Ansari Firangi Mahali, *Bani-i Dars-i Nizami Ustad ul-Hind Mullah Nizamuddin Muhammad Firangi Mahali*, Lucknow, 1973.
31. For a history of the Firangi Mahali family, see Inayatullah Ansari, *'Ulama-i Firangi Mahal*, Lucknow, 1988.
32. Robinson, op. cit., p. 71.
33. 'Alim Saba Navedi, *Nawab Wala Jah Aur Hazrat Allama 'Abdul 'Ala Bahr ul-'Ulum Firangi Mahali*, Chennai: Tamil Nadu Publications, 1995, p. 32.
34. Shariq 'Alavi, 'Madrasas in India', *The Fragrance of the East*, vol. v, no. 1, January–March 2003, p. 6.
35. Mullah Nizamuddin was himself a Sufi, a disciple (*murid*) of Shah 'Abdul Razaq Banswi.
36. Muhammad Wali ul-Haq Ansari, 'Bani-i Dars-i Nizami Mulla Nizamuddin Aur Unka Khanvada Firangi Mahal' (part 2), *Tarjuman-i Dar ul-'Ulum*, January 1988, pp. 5–16.
37. For details, see Mumshad 'Ali Qasmi, *Tarikh-i Dars-i Nizami*, Bilaspur, Muzaffarnagar: Majm'a al-Bahath al-'Ilmiya, 1994.
38. Thus, Zaman writes that it was only in the latter half of the nineteenth century, perhaps because of the influence of Western styles and institutions of education in British India, that the *dars-i nizami* acquired 'a more or less standardized form' (Muhammad Qasim Zaman, 'Religious Education and the Rhetoric of Reform: The Madrasa in British India and Pakistan', *Comparative Studies in Society and History*, vol. 41, no. 2, April 1999, p. 303).

39. Tirmizi, op. cit., p. 164.
40. Muhammad Raza Ansari Firangi Mahali, op. cit., pp. 265–77.
41. Thomas Metcalf, *Ideologies of the Raj*, Cambridge: Cambridge University Press, 1994, p. 133.
42. Muhammad Ishaq Jalis Nadwi, *Tarikh-i Nadwat ul-'Ulama* (vol. 1), Lucknow: Nadwat ul-'Ulama, 1983, pp. 26–31.
43. Mubarak Husain Misbahi, *Bar-i Saghir Mai Iritaq Bayn al-Muslimin Ke Asbab*, Mubarakpur: al-Jami'a al-Misbahi, 2001, pp. 119–34.
44. For a comprehensive study, see Usha Sanyal, *Devotional Islam and Politics in British India: Ahmed Riza Khan Barelwi and his Movement 1870–1920*, New Delhi: Oxford University Press, 2000.
45. Muhammad Amin Palanpuri, *Radd-i Raza Khaniyat*, Deoband: Dar ul-'Ulum, n.d., p. 13.
46. Yoginder Sikand, *The Indian 'Ulama*, Bangalore: 2002, p. 5.
47. Quoted in Zia ul-Hasan Faruqi, *The Deoband School and the Demand for Pakistan*, London: Asia Publishing House, 1963, p. 12.
48. Muhammad Hafizullah, *Salatin-i Hind Ki 'Ilm Parvari*, op. cit., pp. 25–26.
49. Quoted in Syed Ghulam Mohiuddin, 'Modern Education and the Educational Problems of Indian Muslims', in S.M. Wazeh Rashid al-Nadwi and Syed Ghulam Mohiuddin, op. cit., pp. 26–27.
50. 'Madrasa Education in West Bengal', *Muslim India*, August 1994, p. 367.
51. Quoted in Susanne H. Rudolph and Lloyd I. Rudolph, 'Living with Difference in India: Legal Pluralism and Legal Universalism in Historical Context', in Gerald James Larson (ed.), *Religion and Personal Law in Secular India: A Call for Judgment*, Bloomington: Indiana University Press, 2001, p. 390.
52. Sayyed Muhammad Salim, *Dini Madaris Ki Rivayat Aur Nisab Ki Khususiyat*, Lahore: Idara Ta'limi Tahqiq Tanzim-i Asatiza-i Pakistan, 1987, p. 16.
53. Sayyed 'Asad Madani, *Jang-i Azadi Mai Jami'at ul-'Ulama-i Hind Ki Khidmat*, New Delhi: Jami'at ul-'Ulama-i Hind, n.d., p. 6.

54. Sayyed Abul Hasan 'Ali Nadwi, *Madaris-i Islamiya Ka Muqam Aur Kam*, Khatauli: Mahad al-Imam Abul Hasan 'Ali Nadwi, 2002, pp. 26–32.
55. Qamruddin, op. cit., pp. 41–43.
56. Barbara D. Metcalf, *Islamic Revival in British India: 1860–1900*, New Delhi: Oxford University Press, 2002, p. xxvi.
57. Asghar 'Ali Salafi, 'Madaris-i Islamiya-i Hind Kya Haqiqi Islami Da'wat Ke Taqazey Purey Kar Rahe Hain?', *Muhhadith*, January–March 1994, vol. xii, nos.1–3, p. 105.
58. Sayyed Mahboob Rizvi, 'Ulama Ki Taraf Se Angrezi Ta'lim Ki Mukhalifat: Haqiqat Kya Hai?', *Tarjuman-i Dar ul-'Ulum*, July 1994, p. 261.
59. Muhammad Rizwan ul-Qasmi, *Dini Madaris Aur 'Asr-i Hazir*, Hyderabad: Markaz Da'wat-o-Tahqiqat, 1994, p. 8.
60. M. Mujeeb, *Islamic Influence on Indian Society*, Meerut: Meenakshi Prakashan, 1972, p. 140.
61. Habib ur-Rahman Qasmi, *Dar ul-'Ulum Deoband: Ek Maktaba-i Fikr, Ek Tehrik*, Deoband: Markazi Rabita-i Madaris-i Islamiya Arabiya, n.d., p. 38.
62. Mumshad 'Ali Qasmi, *Tarikh-i Dars-i Nizami*, Bilaspur, Muzaffarnagar: Majm'a al-Bahuth al-'Ilmiya, 1994, p. 146.
63. Ibid., p. 148.
64. Ibid., p. 159.
65. Sultan Ahmad Islahi, op. cit., p. 157.
66. Sultan Ahmad Islahi, *Hindustan Mai Madaris-i 'Arabiya Ke Masa'il*, Aligarh: Idara-i 'Ilm-o-Adab, n.d., p. 18.
67. Shaukat 'Ali Qasmi, *Rabita-i Madaris-i 'Arabia Dar ul-'Ulum: Qayyam, Ijtima'at, Sargarmiyan*, Deoband: Dar ul-'Ulum, 1998, pp. 12–14.
68. 'Aqidatullah Qasmi, 'Angrezi Ta'lim Ki Mukhalifat: Fasana Aur Haqiqat', *Tarjuman-i Dar ul-'Ulum*, February–March, 1998, p. 25. In the 1904 annual report of the madrasa a suggestion was made that students who had passed the entrance test of an English-medium high school and had taken admission at Deoband should be given a regular monthly stipend. Likewise, it

suggested that a similar stipend be given to graduates from the madrasa who wanted to go on to a regular school to study English and modern subjects. 'In both these cases', the report commented, 'there are many advantages for the Muslims'. However, these proposals were not implemented, apparently due to lack of sufficient funds (Sayyed Mahboob Rizvi, op. cit., p. 162).

69. Several 'ulama issued *fatwa*s of infidelity and apostasy against him, and some even went so far as to persuade leading 'ulama of Mecca to declare him to be an 'enemy of Islam' and 'worthy of being killed' (*wajib ul-qatl*) (Pervez Hoodbhoy, 'Ideological Problems for Science in Pakistan', in Asghar Khan [ed.], *Islam, Politics and the State: The Pakistan Experience*, London: Zed Books, 1985, p. 184).
70. *Ta'ruf-i Nadwat ul-'Ulama*, Lucknow: Nadwat ul-'Ulama, n.d., pp. 1–3.
71. Muhammad Ishaq Jalis Nadwi, op. cit., p. 171.
72. Muhammad Iqbal Ansari, 'Nadwat ul-'Ulama: Ek Dini-o-Ta'limi Tehrik' (part 1), *Islam Aur 'Asr-i Jadid*, vol. 7, no. 2, April 1975, p. 31.
73. Ibid., p. 33.
74. Ibid., p. 34.
75. Muhammad Ishaq Jalis Nadwi, op. cit., p. 173. Ahmad Riza Khan went on to attack the Nadwa for 'straying' from the path of Islam by bringing together what they saw as various 'un-Islamic' groups, such as the Shi'as, the 'Wahhabis' and the 'Necharis' (followers of Sayyed Ahmad Khan). He is said to have written an astounding 200 tracts against the Nadwa, as also *fatwa*s of infidelity against all these groups, claiming that if anyone married a follower of one of them he or she would be considered to be living in sin, and their children would be treated as illegitimate (*Paigham-i Mahmud* [Khidmat-i Dar ul-'Ulum Number], vol. 2, nos. 3 and 4, p. 129).
76. Muhammad Ishaq Jalis Nadwi, op. cit., p. 201.
77. Ibid., p. 95.
78. Ibid., p. 144.

79. Ibid., p. 95.
80. Shams Tabrez Khan, *Tarikh-i Nadwat ul-'Ulama* (vol. 2), Lucknow: Nadwat ul-'Ulama, 1984, pp. 80–81.
81. One of the reasons for Shibli's departure from Aligarh was his opposition to Sayyed Ahmad's religious views, in particular his 'rationalistic' interpretation of the Qur'an. He was also disappointed with the fact that students of Aligarh hardly learnt anything about their religion, while their understanding of 'modern' subjects was also 'shallow'. Further, he was also opposed to the Aligarh movement and its founder for their pro-British stance (Ghazanfar 'Ali Khan, 'Educational Views of Shibli Nomani', *Islam and the Modern Age*, vol. xxx, no. 2, May 1999, p. 154).
82. Ibid., p. 159.
83. Muhammad Ishaq Jalis Nadwi, op. cit., p. 67.
84. Ibid., p. 201.
85. For a general overview of Ahl-i Hadith madrasas in India, see Arshad ul-Haq 'Asri, *Pak-o-Hind Mai 'Ulama-i Ahl-i Hadith Ki Khidmat-i Hadith*, Maunath Bhanjan: Markazi Maktaba-i Ahl-i Hadith, 1995.
86. *Madrasat ul-Islah Ki Ibtida Aur Uska Nasb ul-'Ain*, Sara'i Mir: Madrasat ul-Islah, n.d.
87. For biographical details, see *Allama Hamiduddin Farahi: Ahl-i 'Ilm-o-Danish Ki Nazar Mai*, Sara'i Mir: Da'ira Hamidiya, n.d.
88. Nizamuddin Islahi, 'Ghalba-i Islam Ki Jad-o-Jehed Mai Madaris Ka Kirdar', in *Mulk-o-Millat Ki Ta'mir Aur Dini Madaris*, Bilariyaganj: Jami'at ul-Falah, 1994, p. 71.
89. Interview with Allauddin Khan Islahi, lecturer, Shibli National College, Azamgarh, 28 March 2003.
90. Nizamuddin Islahi, op. cit., p. 71.
91. Sultan Ahmad Islahi, op. cit., p. 167.
92. Sayyed 'Asad Madani, op. cit., pp. 7–9.
93. 'Adil Siddiqui, *Jami'at ul-'Ulama-i Hind: A'ina-i Ayyam Mai*, New Delhi: Jami'at ul-'Ulama-i Hind, n.d., pp. 4–5.
94. Zia ul-Hasan Faruqi, *The Deoband School and the Demand for Pakistan*, pp. 58–63.

95. Gilani, op. cit., pp. 18–19.
96. Husain Ahmad Madani was given the title of *shaikh ul-hind* or 'The Teacher of India' by Gandhi for his services to the freedom struggle (Muhammad Azfal ul-Haq Jauhar Qasmi, 'Dini Madaris Ke Khilaf Sazish', *Tarjuman-i Dar ul-'Ulum*, March 2002, p. 61).
97. Sayyed Husain Ahmad Madani, *Muttahida Qaumiyat Aur Islam*, New Delhi: al-Jami'at Book Depot, n.d.
98. Ghazanfar 'Ali Khan, op. cit., p. 202.
99. Jamal Malik, 'Between National Integration and Islamism: Lucknow's Nadwat al-'Ulama', in Mushirul Hasan (ed.), *Knowledge, Power and Politics: Educational Institutions in India*, New Delhi: Roli Books, 1998, p. 225.

Chapter 3: Madrasas in Independent India

1. Muhammad Badiuzzaman provides the following list for selected states of India, which does not, however, appear to be accurate:

State	*No. of madrasas*	*No. of teachers*	*No. of students*
1. Andhra Pradesh	721	2000	72,528
2. Assam	2002	4000	20,000
3. Delhi	1161	86	3722
4. Gujarat	1825	6000	1,20,000
5. Jammu and Kashmir	122	475	8515
6. Karnataka	961	1884	84.864
7. Kerala	9975	25,000	7,38,000
8. Madhya Pradesh	6000	12,000	4,00,000
9. Maharashtra	2435	4900	20,397
10. Rajasthan	1780	3600	25,000
11. West Bengal	2116	10,000	90,000

(Muhammad Badiuzzaman, 'Hindustan Ke Madrase Aur Masajid Markazi Hukukmat Ke Nishaney Par', in *Basat Zikr-o-Fikr*, May–June 2002).

2. Muhammad Akhtar Siddiqui, 'Development and Trends in

Madrasa Education', in A.W.B. Qadri, Riaz Shakir Khan and Mohammed Akhter Siddique, *Education and Muslims in India since Independence*, New Delhi: Institute of Objective Studies, 1998, p. 76.

A recent report provides the following figures for the number of madrasas in selected states: Assam (721), Bihar (3500), Gujarat (1825), Karnataka (961), Kerala (9975), Madhya Pradesh (6000), Rajasthan (1780), Uttar Pradesh (10,000) ('Modernisation of Madrasas in India', <www.bazaarchintan.net/pdfs/madrasas/pdf>).

3. 'Be Vigilant While Registering Madrasas, State Governments Told', *The Hindu*, Bangalore, 19 May 2002.
4. Comment by Maulana Muhammad Kaleem Siddiqui at the seminar on 'Islamic Madrasas: Services and Challenges', held on 24 August 2003 in New Delhi. Quoted in *Radiance Viewsweekly*, 7–13 September 2003.
5. See, for instance, Iqbal Husain, *Darsi Kitabon Ka Zeher Aur Musalman*, Lucknow: Dini Ta'limi Council, n.d. For an analysis and critique of the Hinduized and clearly anti-Muslim slant of government school textbooks, see Manzur 'Alam, *Khutba-i Isteqbaliya Rajasthan Dini Ta'limi Conference*, Jaipur, 1961. Also, *U.P. Sarkari Nisab-i Ta'lim Ka Mukhtasar Ja'iza*, Lucknow: Dini Ta'limi Council, n.d., and Akbar Rahmani, *Qaumi Yekjuhti Aur Nisabi Kitaben*, Jalgaon: Educational Academy, 1988.
6. Thus, madrasa managers, defending the system of madrasa education, often argue, 'You will not find a single unemployed madrasa graduate, while hundreds of thousands of university graduates roam the streets without jobs.'
7. Quoted in *Kul Hind Dini Madaris Convention Souvenir*, New Delhi: All-India Muslim Milli Council, 1994, p. 7.
8. For a detailed discussion of the curricula of 'traditional' north Indian madrasas, see Atiq ur-Rahman and Muhammad Shah Jahan Qasmi, 'Hindustan Ke Aham Dini Madaris Ke Nisab-i Ta'lim: Ek Taqabali Ja'iza', in *'Arabi Islami Madaris ka Nisab-o-Nizam-i Ta'lim Aur 'Asri Taqaze*, Patna: Khuda Bakhsh Oriental Public Library, 1995, pp. 187–205.

9. There are two separate wings of the Deoband madrasa now, following a split in the institution in 1980 as a result of a bitter leadership struggle that involved the police and the courts as well and threatened to take on violent overtones. Consequently, there are now two major madrasas in Deoband. Each claims to represent the 'authentic' Deobandi legacy: the Dar ul-'Ulum Waqf and the Dar ul-'Ulum Jadid, headed by rival 'ulama. In terms of theology, doctrine and *fiqh*, and in their relation to the Deobandi tradition as a whole, however, there is nothing to distinguish the two, and so it is in this sense that I speak of Deoband in the singular. For details of the split, see Qari Muhammad Tayyeb, *Ijlas-i Sadsalah Ke Bad Dar ul-'Ulum Mai Pesh Amida Afsosnak Hawadis-o-Waqiyat Ki Sahih Aur Mufassil Report*, Deoband: Dar ul-'Ulum, 1980.
10. Anis ur-Rahman Qasmi, 'Madaris-i Islamiya Ke Nisab-i Ta'lim Ka Ek Ja'iza', op. cit., p. 116.
11. 'Aur Ab Dar ul-'Ulum Bhi Nishane Par', *Tarjuman-i Dar ul-'Ulum*, June 1994, p. 31. Iqbal Ahmad Ansari puts the number at around eighty. See his 'Dini Madaris Ka Ta'limi Nizam', in *'Arabi Islami Madaris Ka Nisab-o-Nizam-i Ta'lim*, Patna: Khuda Bakhsh Oriental Public Library, 1995, p. 153. On the other hand, this source claims that the original *dars-i nizami* consisted of only thirty-five books. According to another source, the Deoband syllabus consists of twenty books on 'transmitted' sciences and forty-three on 'rational' sciences (Khalid Saifullah Rahmani, 'Nisab-i Ta'lim: Ek Ja'iza', in *Kul Hind Dini Madaris Convention Souvenir*, New Delhi: All-India Muslim Milli Council, 1994, p. 74).
12. A book of Hanafi *fiqh* prepared by Imam Badruddin Maini (AH 762–855). Legend has it that he wrote this book in one night.
13. A book of Hanafi *fiqh* authored by Allama 'Ubaidullah ibn Mas'ud.
14. A commentary on the Qur'an begun by Jalaluddin ul-Maljalli (1389–1459), and finished by Suyuti.
15. Habib ur-Rahman Qasmi, *Dar ul-'Ulum: Ek Ajmali Ta'ruf*, Deoband: Markazi Daftar Rabita-i Madaris-i Islamiya al-Arabiya, 1998, pp. 81–83.

16. Muhammad Rizvan ul-Qasmi, op. cit., p. 99. For a detailed examination of *Hidaya*, see Sufi, op. cit., pp. 21–22.The other books of Hanafi *fiqh* taught at Deoband and many other 'traditional' madrasas in India include the *Mukhtasar Qaduri* of Imam Abul Hasan Ahmad bin Muhammad Qaduri (d. AH 428), the *Sharah-i Waqayah* of Taj ul-Shari'ah Mahmud (d. AH 747) and the *Nur ul-'Izah* of Abul Ikhlas Hasan bin 'Amr Sharanbalali (d. AH 1069).
17. 'Ubaidullah Koti Nadwi, *'Allama Burhanuddin Mirghinani: Sahib-i Hidaya*, New Delhi: Nadwat ul-Mu'alifin, 2002, p. 45.
18. Mujibullah Nadwi, *Dini Madaris Aur Unki Zimmedariyan*, Azamgarh: Jami'at ul-Rishad, 2002, pp. 10–11.
19. Qamruddin, 'Status of Madrasa Education in India', *Radiance Viewsweekly*, 10–16 August 1997.
20. Sayyed Ghiyas ul-Hasan Mazhari, letter to the editor, *Qaumi Awaz*, 30 July 1993.
21. Nayyar Ja'fri, letter to the editor, *Qaumi Awaz*, 13 October 1993.
22. Muhammad Shahid, Faiz ul-Hasan and Muhammad Mustaqim, letter to the editor, *Qaumi Awaz*, 30 September 1993.
23. *Talaba-i Madaris Se Ek Khitab,* Lucknow: Jami'at us-Shabab il al-Islam, n.d., p. 13.
24. Mujibullah Nadwi, *Dini Madaris Aur Unki Zimmedariyan*, op. cit., pp. 12–13.
25. Ibid., pp. 30–32.
26. Waris Mazhari, 'Dini Idare Aur Chanda: Kuch Qabil-i Ghaur Pahlu', *Tarjuman-i Dar ul-'Ulum*, December 2002, p. 6.
27. One '*alim*, Maulana Muhammad Mu'azzam Nanotawi, teacher at a madrasa at Ambetha, writes that madrasas must stop taking foreign money as this has created the wrong impression of a flood of petrodollars coming in to finance Muslim institutions (Firoz Bakht Ahmed, 'Madrason Ki Islah Ke Beghayr Musalman Agey Nahin Badh Saktey', *Qaumi Awaz*, 14 June 1993).
28. Mubarak Husain Misbahi, op. cit., pp. 149–55.
29. Anwar 'Ali, 'Madaris-i Diniya Aur Hukumati Control' (Part ii), *Qaumi Awaz*, 19 June 2002.

30. 'Dini Madrase Munafa Bakhsh Tijarat Ke Adde Ban Gaye Hain', *Qaumi Awaz*, 26 July 1997.
31. Waris Mazhari, op. cit., pp. 4–7.
32. <http://merawatan.com/watan/perumalgift.htm>
33. For details, see Syed Ehtisham A. Nadwi, 'Reflections on Arabic College Education in Kerala', in E.K. Ahamed Kutty (ed.), *Arabic in South India*, Calicut: Department of Arabic, University of Calicut, 2003, pp. 56–76.
34. Ibid., p. 62.
35. Interview with Husain Aboobacker Koya, Calicut, 12 August 2003.
36. Interview with 'Abdul Qadir, Calicut, 11 August 2001.
37. Interview with Zohra Bi, principal, Anwar ul-'Ulum Women's Arabic College, Mongam, 13 August 2003.

Chapter 4: Madrasas and the Agenda of Reform

1. Quoted in Javed Ashraf Qasmi, *Faizan-i Dar ul-'Ulum Deoband*, Ghaseda: Madrasa Abi bin Ka'ab Tahaffuz al-Qur'an al-Karim, 2000, p. 92.
2. Moinuddin Ahmed, *'Ulama...*, op. cit., p. 105.
3. Quoted in Shaukat 'Ali Qasmi, op. cit., p. 22.
4. Quoted in Muhammad Zaid Mazhari Nadwi, *al-'Ilm wa'l 'Ulama*, Hathaura: Idara-i Ifadat-i Ashrafiya, 1996, p. 110.
5. Mumshad 'Ali Qasmi, op. cit., p. 71.
6. 'Dar ul-'Ulum Deoband Zer-i Ehtimam Ijtima-i Madaris-i Islamiya Ka Ineqad', *Tarjuman-i Dar ul-'Ulum*, November 1994, p. 11.
7. Ibid., p. 13.
8. Ibid., p. 12.
9. *'Amali Programme Tanzim Abna ul-Qadim Dar ul-'Ulum Deoband*, Delhi: Tanzim Abna ul-Qadim Dar ul-'Ulum Deoband, n.d., pp. 1–7.
10. Zain ul-Sajid bin Qasmi, 'Dars-i Nizami: Tarikhi Pas-i Manzar Aur Jadid Taqaze', *Tarjuman-i Dar ul-'Ulum*, November 1994.
11. Thanwi is said to have argued for the inclusion of Sanskrit in

the madrasa curriculum in order to 'spread Islam among the Hindus' and to 'rebut the Hindu scriptures'. Likewise, he is said to have recommended the learning of 'the languages and sciences of the infidels (*kuffar*) and the people of falsehood (*ahl-i batil*) in order to debate with them' (see 'Islah-i Nisab Ke Liye Maulana Thanwi Ki Chand Tajawiz', *Tarjuman-i Dar ul-'Ulum,* June 1994, pp. 14–15).

12. 'Abdur Rahim 'Abid, 'Madaris Ke Nisab Mai Tabdili Ka Masla: 'Ulama Kya Kahtey Hain?', *Tarjuman-i Dar ul-'Ulum*, October 1994, p. 20.
13. <http://www.islaminterfaith.org/august2003/interview.html#interview2>
14. This was finally made possible despite severe opposition from certain conservative 'ulama. Waris Mazhari says that they argued that it would lead the students astray from the path of religion, claiming that it was 'a cunning and sinister ploy to smuggle Zionism into the madrasa through the backdoor and thereby poison the minds of the students' <http://www.islaminterfaith.org/august2003/interview.html#interview2>.
15. 'Ilm-i Din Ke Sath Ma'ddi 'Ulum Bhi Zaruri', *Qaumi Awaz*, 11 April 1995.
16. See, for instance, the papers by 'ulama advocates of madrasa reform in *'Arabi Islami Madaris Ka Nisab-o-Nizam-i Ta'lim Aur 'Asri Taqaze*, Patna: Khuda Bakhsh Oriental Public Library, 1995.
17. Ehtashamuddin Khan, 'Madrasas Want to Modernise, But Not Too Much', *The Fragrance of the East*, vol. v, no. 1, January–March 2003, p. 59.
18. 'Modernising Madrasas', *The Times of India*, Bangalore, 8 July 2002.
19. Muhammad Qasim Zaman, 'Religious Education and the Rhetoric of Reform: The Madrasa in British India and Pakistan', *Comparative Studies in Society and History*, vol. 41, no. 2, April 1999, p. 295.
20. Sultan Ahmad Islahi, *Hindustan Mai Madaris-i-'Arabiya Ke Masa'il*, op. cit., p. 152.

21. Aslam Parvaiz, 'Madaris Ke Nisab Aur Science', in '*Arabi Islami Madaris*..., op. cit., p. 125.
22. Shahabuddin Nadwi, op. cit., p. 3.
23. Aftab Ahmad, 'Madaris-i-'Arabiya Ka Nisab Aur Waqt Ki Zarurat', in '*Arabi Islami Madaris* . . ., op. cit., p. 143.
24. Mufti Ahmad Yahya Devlavi, 'Madaris Mai 'Asri Ta'lim', *Da'wat*, 25 July 2003.
25. Ismail Raji al-Faruqi, *Tawhid: Its Implications for Thought and Life*, Herndon: International Institute of Islamic Thought, 1989.
26. Sayyed Abul Hasan 'Ali Nadwi, *'Ilm Ka Muqam Aur Ahl-i 'Ilm Ki Zimmedariyan*, Lucknow: Majlis Tahqiqat-o-Nashriyat ul-Islam, 1997, p. 7.
27. Ghulam Yahya Anjum, *Anwar-i Khyal*, New Delhi, 1991, pp. 123–30.
28. Interview with Mohammad Aslam Parvaiz, Editor, *Science*, New Delhi, 8 August 2004.
29. For a detailed discussion of the Islamization of knowledge project, see Leif Stenberg, *The Islamization of Science: Four Muslim Positions Developing an Islamic Modernity*, Lund: Lund University, 1996.
30. Khurshid Ahmad, *Nizam-i Ta'lim: Nazariya, Rivayat, Masa'il*, Islamabad: Institute of Policy Studies, 1996, p. 235.
31. Mumshad 'Ali Qasmi, op. cit., pp. 154–55.
32. Mujahid ul-Islam Qasmi, *Maqalat-i Sajjad*, Patna: Imarat-i Shari'ah, 1999, p. 72.
33. Muhammad Shahabuddin Nadwi, *Hamare Ta'limi Masa'il*, Bangalore: Furqania Academy, 1989, pp. 19–20.
34. Gilani, op. cit., p. 303.
35. Muhammad Wali Rahmani, *Dini Madaris Mai Sanati Ta'lim Ka Masla*, Munger: Jami'a Rahmani, 1981, p. 9.
36. Muhammad Taqi 'Usmani, op. cit., p. 22.
37. Muhammad Nejatullah Siddiqui, *Dini Madaris: Masa'il Aur Taqaze*, New Delhi: Markazi Maktaba-i Islami, 2001, p. 11.
38. Sayyed Muhammad Rabe Hasni Nadwi, *Musalman Aur Ta'lim*, Lucknow: Nadwat ul-'Ulama, 1997, p. 53.

39. Habib ur-Rahman 'Azmi 'Umri, 'Dini Madaris Ki Zimmedariyan Aur Biradiran-i Watan', in *Dini Madaris Aur Unkey Masa'il*, Bilariyaganj: Jami'at ul-Falah, 1990, p. 134.
40. Shihabuddin Nadwi, op. cit., p. 15.
41. Mohsin 'Usmani Nadwi, 'Madaris Ka Nizam-i-Ta'lim Aur Naya Challenge', *Islam Aur 'Asr-i Jadid*, vol. 32, no. 4, October 2000, pp. 107–08.
42. Mumshad 'Ali Qasmi, op. cit., p. 70.
43. Maqbul Ahmad Misbahi, 'Hindustan Aur 'Alam-i Arab Ke Nisab-i Ta'lim Ka Taqabli Ja'iza, *Islam Aur 'Asr-i Jadid*, vol. 32, no. 4, October 2000, p. 83.
44. Interview with Asghar 'Ali Engineer <http://www.islaminterfaith.org/oct2002/interview.html>.
45. Interview with Waris Mazhari, Editor, *Tarjuman Dar ul-'Ulum*, New Delhi, 22 August 2004.
46. Interview with Maqbool Ahmad Siraj, Executive Editor, *Islamic Voice*, Bangalore, 3 February 2003.
47. Abul 'Irfan Nadwi, 'Nisab-i Ta'lim Aur Tariqa-i Ta'lim: Maujuda Ahad Ke Taqaze', *Islam Aur 'Asr-i Jadid*, vol. 12, no. 4, October 1980, p. 36.
48. Muhammad Rizwan ul-Qasmi, op. cit., p. 29.
49. Fazlur Rahman Faridi, 'Dini Madaris Ka Nisab-i Ta'lim Aur 'Asri Challenge', in *Kul Hind Dini Madaris Convention Souvenir*, New Delhi: All-India Milli Council, n.d., p. 86.
50. Interview with Asghar 'Ali Engineer <http://www.islaminterfaith.org/oct2002/interview.html>.
51. Cited in Moinuddin Ahmed, *The Urgency of Ijtihad*, op. cit., p. 93.
52. Mufti Zahiruddin Miftahi, 'Madaris-i Diniya Aur Unke Masa'il', in *Dini Madaris Aur Unkey Masa'il*, Bilariyaganj: Jami'at ul-Falah, 1990, pp. 55–57. The Mufti writes that the Barelwis (whom he derisively refers to as 'Raza Khanis', followers of Imam Ahmad Raza Khan of Bareilly) dismiss all other Muslim groups as non-Muslim, and so cannot be expected to join the madrasa board.

53. Muhammad Shams Tabrez, ''Ilm-o-Taqwa Ki Buniyad Par Ta'lim-o-Tarbiyat', *Naqib*, Phulwari Sharif, 10–17 June 1996, p. 1.
54. Mumshad 'Ali Qasmi, op. cit., p. 82.
55. Ibid., p. 82.
56. Qamruddin, *Hindustan Ki Dini Darsgahe*, op. cit., p. 53.
57. Washim Ahmad, 'Psychology of Education: Madrasas of UP', *Economic and Political Weekly*, 25–31 March 2000 <http://www.epw.org.in/35-13/comm5.htm>.
58. The Centre for Promotion of Science functions under the Aligarh Muslim University, Aligarh. One of its principal aims is to promote the teaching of science in madrasas, for which it organizes workshops for designing appropriate teaching material as well as regular condensed courses on science for madrasa graduates. For details, see <http://www.angelfire.com/sc3/cps>.
59. Some madrasas have tried to introduce teachers' training courses but do not seem to have succeeded. The chief Barelwi madrasa in India, the Jami'a Ashrafiya, Mubarakpur, claims to have a two-year course, under which at present a mere four students are said to be undergoing some sort of training.
60. Shahabuddin Nadwi, op. cit., p. 20.
61. 'Prof. Joshi Has Designs on Madrasas', *The Milli Gazette*, 1–15 February 2000.
62. Nizam Elahi, *Modernisation of Madrasa Education Scheme in India*, New Delhi: State Council for Educational Research and Training, 2001, pp. 12–13.
63. Syed Shahabuddin, quoted in Madhav Godbole, 'Madrasas: Need for a Fresh Look', *Economic and Political Weekly*, 13 October 2001, p. 3890.
64. Nizam Elahi, op. cit., p. 21.
65. Comments of several 'ulama interviewed in the course of fieldwork.
66. According to a 1998 report, the figures for the number of madrasas affiliated to selected state boards of madrasa education

were as follows: Bihar (1600), Uttar Pradesh (375), Orissa (79) (quoted in Mohammad Akhtar Siddiqui, 'Development and Trends in Madrasa Education', op. cit., p. 78). In mid-2002, 507 madrasas in West Bengal were recognized by the state madrasa education board (*The Hindu*, 18 June 2002).

67. Thus, for instance, the scheme is said to have almost completely 'flopped' in Maharashtra (with only six madrasas joining the project). Amin Khandwani, chairman of the Maharashtra Minorities Commission, alleged that one of the main reasons for this was that the state government had sorely neglected the scheme (Shabnam Minwalla, 'Madrasas Need to Move With the Times', *The Times of India*, New Delhi, 3 December 2001).
68. Interview with Zafrul Islam Khan, Editor, *The Milli Gazette*, New Delhi, 2 January 2003.
69. Irshadul Haque, 'Bureaucrats Foil Madrasah Education Modernisation Programme', *The Milli Gazette*, 1–15 October 2002, p. 23.
70. 'Educational Awareness among Muslims: A Positive Step' <http://www.milligazette.com/Archives/15042001/Art11.htm>.
71. 'Madrasa Modernisation in Rajasthan', *Islamic Voice*, June 2001.
72. 'Winds of Change Sweep Rajasthan Madrasas', *Islamic Voice*, May 1997.
73. Interview with Zafrul Islam Khan, Editor, *The Milli Gazette* <http://www.islaminterfaith.org/may2003/interview.html>.
74. Mufti Muhammad Sulaiman Mansurpuri, 'Sarkari Imdad Dini Madaris Ke Liye Sitam Qatil', *Tarjuman-i Dar ul-'Ulum*, August 2003, pp. 19–22.

Chapter 5: Reformed Madrasas and New Forms of Islamic Education

1. For details, see Afzal Husain, *Jama'at-i Islami Hind Aur Dini Ta'limi Tehrik*, Delhi: Markazi Maktaba-i Islami, n.d., pp. 1–7.
2. Muhammad Ashfaq Ahmad, 'Jama'at-i Islami Ka Ta'limi Nizam',

in *Mulk-o-Millat Ki Ta'mir Aur Dini Madaris*, Bilariyaganj: 1994, pp. 137–39.

3. *Markazi Darsgah-i Islami, Rampur: Ek Ta'aruf*, Rampur: Markazi Darsgah-i Islami, n.d., p. 1.
4. Ibid., p. 141.
5. Interview with Salman Asad, Director, Islamic Studies and Research Academy, New Delhi, 4 January 2002.
6. *Jami'at ul-Falah: Ek Ta'aruf*, Bilariyaganj: Jami'at ul-Falah, n.d., p. 1.
7. *Jami'at ul-Falah: Aghraz-o-Maqasid*, Bilariyaganj: Jami'at ul-Falah, 1997, p. 1.
8. *Jami'at ul-Falah: An Introduction*, Bilariyaganj: Jami'at ul-Falah, n.d., p. 1.
9. *Nisab-i Ta'lim Jami'at ul-Falah*, Bilariyaganj: Jami'at ul-Falah, 2001, p. 3.
10. Interestingly, it had no Barelwi 'ulama as teachers, probably because of the insistence of the Barelwis that the Jama'at-i Islami was outside the pale of Islam.
11. Interview with Maulana Rahmatullah 'Asri, Principal, Jami'at ul-Falah, Bilariyaganj, 29 March 2003.
12. The Markaz has also published a few English books on various Deobandi 'ulama, stressing their role in India's freedom struggle and in opposing the Muslim League's 'two-nation' theory.
13. *Markaz ul-Ma'rif: Report on Activities Till March 2000*, Hojai: Markaz ul-Ma'rif, 2000.
14. Ibid., p. 11.
15. Interview with Maulana 'Atiq ur-Rahman, Assistant Manager, Markaz ul-Ma'rif, Mumbai, 2 October 2002.
16. *Dar ul-Umoor Tipu Sultan Advanced Study and Research Centre*, Bangalore: Dar ul-Umoor, n.d.
17. Interview with 'Abdur Rahman Kamaruddin, Chairman, Dar ul-'Umoor, Srirangapatanam, 6 October 2002.
18. Maqbool Ahmed Siraj, 'The Best of the Old and the New', *Islamic Voice*, February 2002.

19. H.U. 'Azmi, 'Contribution of Deeni Ta'limi Council to Muslim Education in Uttar Pradesh', in A.W. B. Qadri, Riaz Shakir Khan and Mohammed Akhtar Siddique, *Education and Muslims in India since Independence*, New Delhi: Institute of Objective Studies, 1988, pp. 147–50.
20. *Al-Jami'at ul-Islamia Khair ul-Ulum Educational and Technical Society*, Domariaganj: Al-Jami'at ul-Islamia Khair ul-'Ulum Educational and Technical Society, n.d.
21. K. Hamza, 'The Sunni Cultural Centre in Calicut' <http://www.milligazette.com/Archives/01-5-2000/the_sunni_cultural_centre.htm>.
22. *All-India Ta'limi-o-Milli Foundation*, Delhi: All-India Ta'limi-o-Milli Foundation, n.d.
23. Afzal Husain, *Jama'at-i Islami Ki Ta'limi Kavishey*, New Delhi: Markazi Maktaba-i Islami, 2002, p. 35.
24. *Jami'at ul-Banat al-Islamia Ka Mukhtasar Ta'aruf*, New Delhi: Jami'at ul-Banat al-Islamia, n.d., pp. 7–8.
25. Ibid., p. 7.
26. Afzal Husain, *Jama'at-i Islami Ki Ta'limi Kavishey*, op. cit., p. 35.
27. 'Abdul Halim Siddiqui, *Malegaon: Ek Shahr, Ek Jahan*, Malegaon: Misbah Educational and Welfare Sports and Research Society, 2000, p. 78.
28. For an analysis of the perception of the normative Muslim woman in *tablighi* discourse, see Yoginder Sikand, 'Women and the Tablighi Jama'at', *Islam and Christian–Muslim Relations*, vol. 10, no. 1, 1999.
29. *Jami'at ul-Banat al-Islamia Ka Mukhtasar Ta'aruf*, op. cit., pp. 40–41.
30. Ibid., pp. 66–67.
31. Interview with Maulana Muhammad Islam, Rector, Madrasa Jami'at ul-Banat, New Delhi, 28 October 2002.
32. S. 'Ubaidur Rahman, 'Jameatus Saliehat: Revolutionising Women's Education' <http://www.milligazette.com/Archives/01052001/Art04.htm>.

33. *Siraj ul-'Uloom Niswan College: An Introduction*, Aligarh: Siraj ul-'Uloom Niswan College, n.d.

Chapter 6: Madrasas and Militancy

1. Sa'eed Suhrawardy and 'Abdul Hamid Nu'mani, *A Glance at the Services of Jami'at ul-'Ulama-i Hind*, New Delhi: Jami'at ul-'Ulama-i Hind, n.d.
2. Mushirul Hasan, 'The Madrasas in India', *Daily Times*, 22 May 2003.
3. Sayyed Mahbub Rizvi, op. cit., p. 250.
4. Ibid., p. 31.
5. *Sadr-i Jumhuriya-i Hind Dar ul-'Ulum Deoband Mai*, Deoband: Dar ul-'Ulum, 1957, pp. 24–25.
6. Ibid., p. 27.
7. Ibid., p. 32.
8. Habib ur-Rahman Qasmi, *Dar ul-'Ulum Deoband: Ek Maktab-i Fikr, Ek Tehrik*, op. cit., p. 31.
9. Barbara D. Metcalf, *Islamic Revival in British India, 1860–1900*, op. cit., p. 15.
10. For details, see Habib ur-Rahman Qasmi, *Dar ul-'Ulum Deoband: Ek Maktab-i Fikr, Ek Tehrik*, op. cit., pp. 30–39.
11. Interview with Maulana Wahiduddin Khan <http://www.islaminterfaith.org/may2002/interview.html>.
12. Interview with Hamid Naseem Rafiabadi <http://www.islaminterfaith.org/sep2002/interview.html>.
13. Interview with Maulana Asrar ul-Haq Qasmi <http://www.islaminterfaith.org/july2004/interview-07-04.htm>.
14. Interview with Maulana Sayyed Hamid ul-Hasan, Principal, Jam'ia Nazmia, Lucknow, 21 March 2003.
15. Mushirul Hasan, 'Nipping Thought in the Bud?', *The Indian Express*, New Delhi, 20 February 2002.
16. Stephen Philip Cohen, 'The Jihadist Threat to Pakistan', *The Washington Quarterly*, Summer 2003, pp. 17–18.
17. <http://www.islaminterfaith.org/oct2002/interview.html>

18. Jessica Stern, 'Meeting with the Muj' <http://www.thebulletin.org/issues/2001/jf01/jf01sternhtml>.
19. Interview with Mubarak 'Ali <http://www.islaminterfaith.org/oct2002/interview.html>.
20. Pepe Escobar, 'The Roving Eye: Jihad, The Ultimate Thermonuclear Bomb' <http://www.atimes.com/ind-pak/CJ10Df01.html>.
21. Iqbal Khattak, 'US Allowed Growth of Seminaries as Part of Bleed-Russia Strategy', *The Friday Times*, 18 February 2002.
22. Joe Stephens and David Ottaway, 'From U.S., the ABC's of Jihad', *Washington Post*, 23 March 2002 <http://www.washingtonpost.com/ac2/wp-dyn/A5339-2002Mar22?language=printer>.
23. Musa Khan Jalalzai, *Sectarianism and Ethnic Violence in Pakistan*, Lahore: S.M.A. Anjum Rizvi, 1996, p. 415.
24. For a broad overview of the radicalization of various 'ulama-related organizations in Pakistan, see Musa Khan Jalalzai, *Sectarian Violence in Pakistan and Afghanistan*, Lahore: Systems Books, 1999.
25. The Harkat ul-Ansar, which later changed its name to Harkat ul-Mujahidin, is the single largest Pakistani Deobandi militant group involved in what it calls a *jihad* against India. Other Deobandi militias in Pakistan include the Sipah-i Sahaba, Lashkar-i Jhangvi, Tehrik-i Jihad, Ansar ul-Islam, Hizb ul-Jihad, Jami'at ul-'Ulama Mujahidin, and Jaish-i Muhammad.
26. Barbara D. Metcalf, *'Traditionalist' Islamic Activism: Deoband, Tablighis and Talibs*, Leiden: Institute for the Study of Islam in the Modern World, 2002, p. 14.
27. 'Abdul Qadir, 'Call to Ignore Singhal's Demand', *The Times of India*, New Delhi, 12 April 2003.
28. Quoted in Manjari Katju, *VHP and Indian Politics*, Delhi: Orient Longman, 2003, p. 110.
29. Habib ur-Rahman Qasmi, *Dar ul-'Ulum Deoband: Ek Maktab-i Fikr, Ek Tehrik*, op. cit., p. 57.
30. Yoginder Sikand, 'The ISI Bogey and the Not-So Intelligent Intelligence Reports' <http://www.milligazette.com/Archives/15-9-2000/Art4.htm>.

31. Muhammad Zeyaul Haque, '"Pakistani Flags" in Meerut Village', *The Milli Gazette*, 1–15 September 2002.
32. 'Madrasas Posing a Threat to Kerala's Security', *The Hindu*, 10 April 2002.
33. *Da'wat*, 4 October 2002.
34. 'Madrasa 'Ilm Ka Sarchashma: Vajpayee', *Rashtriya Sahara*, 9 August 2001.
35. Kartikeya Sharma, 'Deoband, The Second Largest Centre of Islamic Learning Fights off the Taliban Tag' <http://www.the-week.com/21jul01/life8/htm>.
36. Nasim Ahmad Qasmi, *Madaris-i Islamiya Ke Hifz-o-Baqa Ke Liye Imarat-i Shari'ah Ki Jad-o-Jehed*, Patna: Imarat-i Shari'ah, 2002, pp. 10–11.
37. Ghatrif Shahbaz Nadwi, 'Qaumi Hifazati Nizam Ke Barey Mai Vizarati Group Ki Report: Kya Kahtey Hain Akabirin-i Millat?', *Afkar-i Milli*, August 2001, p. 15.
38. Syed Shahabuddin, 'Throttling the Madrasas in the Name of Security' <http://www.milligazette.com/Archives/01072001/16.htm>.
39. Ghatrif Shahbaz Nadwi, op. cit., p. 14.
40. Ibid., p. 15.
41. Ibid., p. 15.
42. Ghatrif Shahbaz Nadwi, 'Madaris-i Islamiya Ko Darpesh Khatrat Aur Unka Tadrak', *Afkar-i Milli*, May 2002, pp. 18–19.
43. Thus, for instance, in April 2001 the police arrested a student of a madrasa at Hapur, accusing him of being linked to a Kashmiri militant group and of being involved in two cases of bombings. A few days later, the Bhopal court declared him innocent (Muhammad Manzur 'Alam, *Naqush-i Karavan: All-India Milli Council Ki Karkardagi Report,* New Delhi: All-India Milli Council, 2002, p. 26).
44. 'Prof. Joshi Has Designs on Madrasas' <http://www.milligazette.com/ Archives/01-2-2000/Art1.htm>.
45. This announcement was made in Parliament by the then minister of state for home, Vidyasagar Rao. Yet, Rao admitted that the government had not conducted any survey on the nature of funding

of the madrasas, particularly in the border areas. Without choosing to name any particular madrasa, he alleged that the ISI was 'trying to infiltrate the madrasas' in order to 'exploit and mislead' their students ('India to Monitor Foreign Funding of Muslim Seminaries', *Indo-Asian News Service*, 19 March 2002).

46. <http://www.silchar.com/news/news57.html>
47. Mushirul Hasan, 'The Madrasas in India', *Daily Times*, Lahore, 22 May 2003.
48. 'Muslims Unhappy With Laws to Monitor Madrasas', *Muslim India*, January–July 2003, p. 298.
49. 'No New Mosques and Madrasas in Indo-Nepal Border Areas', *Muslim India*, January–July, 2003, p. 298.
50. 'Gujarat Sets Up Task Force to Study Functioning of Madrasas', *The Hindu*, Chennai, 9 March 2003.
51. Muhammad Shahid Rafique, 'Madrasa Hunting: Buddhadeb Sends Wrong Signals', *Meantime*, 22 February–7 March 2002, p. 28. See also 'Bengal CM Bites Dust', *The Milli Gazette*, 16–28 February 2002, p. 1.
52. See, for instance, Leena Mishra, 'Madrasas Multiply on Gujarat Borders', *The Times of India*, New Delhi, 20 February 2002.
53. The Students' Islamic Movement of India (SIMI) counted among its leaders and several of its activists former students of the Jami'at ul-Falah, Bilariyaganj, a madrasa associated with the Jama'at-i Islami. Although the Jama'at had been instrumental in setting up SIMI, it later officially dissociated itself from it because of its growing militant posture although both the Jama'at and SIMI share a common commitment to the vision of the Jama'at's founder, Syed Abdul 'Ala Maududi.
54. Interview with Muhammad Shaukat Barkati, Islamic Education Board of India, New Delhi, 7 January 2003.
55. Interview with Zafrul Islam Khan <http://www.islaminterfaith.org/may2003/interview.html>.
56. Ghatrif Shahbaz Nadwi, 'Madaris-i Islamiya Ko Darpesh Khatrat Aur Unka Tadrak', op. cit., p. 19.

57. Khawar Hashmi, 'Dini Madaris Par Sarkari Control: Dusra Pahlu', *Qaumi Awaz*, 27 June 2002.
58. Quoted in Celia W. Dugger, 'Brothers in Islam, But Not in Politics' <http://www.milligazette.com/Archives/15072002/1507200219.htm>. This article originally appeared in the *New York Times*, 26 February 2002.
59. Firoz Bakht Ahmed, 'Defender of Faith', *The Times of India*, 24 March 2003.
60. Ibid.
61. Yasin Akhtar Misbahi, *Madaris-i Islamiya Aur Kashmir-o-Gujarat*, New Delhi: All-India Muslim Mushawarati Board, 2002, p. 7.
62. Habib ur-Rahman Qasmi, *Dar ul-'Ulum Deoband: Ek Tehrik*, op. cit., pp. 5–6.
63. Interview with Maqbool Ahmad Siraj, Executive Editor, *Islamic Voice*, Bangalore, 20 December 2002. Thus, one Deobandi '*alim* agreed that some madrasas in Pakistan had indeed taken to terrorism, but laid the blame for this on Pakistan's 'political instability' and the 'wrong policies' of its government (Waris Mazhari, 'Madaris Ke Khilaf Muhim: Ek Khamosh 'Amal Ki Zarurat', *Tarjuman-i Dar ul-'Ulum*, September 2002, p. 4).
64. Based on conversations with numerous 'ulama.
65. *Radiance Viewsweekly*, the official organ of the Jama'at-i Islami, quoted the deputy inspector general of Gorakhpur, H.S. Bilwaria, as saying, 'It is proved after the investigations by different agencies that the madrasas on the India–Nepal border are not the centre [*sic*] of ISI' ('Madrasas Are Not Centre of ISI', *Radiance Viewsweekly*, 23 February–1 March 2003, p. 22).
66. Yoginder Sikand, 'Targeting Muslim Religious Schools', *Economic and Political Weekly*, 1 September 2001, p. 3342.
67. Quoted in Meena Kandaswamy, op. cit., p. 21. See also 'Kashmir Madrasas Have Not Produced a Single Militant', *The Milli Gazette*, 1–15 June 2002, p. 16.
68. Andalib Akhtar, 'Defamatory Campaign Against Rajasthan Madrasas: Milli Council Plans Action', *Islamic Voice*, October

1998. Also, 'Milli Council Sees Conspiracy', *The Hindu*, 2 September 1998.

69. 'No ISI Activity in Rajasthan Border Madrasas' <http://www.milligazette.com/Archives/01022001/Art19.htm>.
70. 'Top U.P. Cop: No ISI-Presence in Madrasas' <www.milligazette.com/Archives/01-6-2000/n0_ISI_in_madrs.htm>.
71. 'Madrasas' Predicament' <http://www.milligazette.com/Archives/01032002/0203200212htm>.
72. 'BJP Leader: Hindus Are More Involved in ISI Activities' <http://www.milligazette.com/Archives/15-10-2000/Art9.htm>.
73. 'Madrasas Fountains of Learning: PM' <http://www.milligazette.com/Archives/01092001/02.htm>. A leading Deobandi '*alim* suggested that the contradictory statements issued by the government on the matter clearly suggested that the report's diatribe against the madrasas was based on false information. He noted that in February 2001 the Union home minister had issued a written statement in Parliament admitting that he had no evidence of any madrasa being involved in terrorist activity, but that in the same month he had contradicted himself in the report on national security, of whose preparatory committee he had been appointed chairman. Some months later, the '*alim* went on to reveal, the state minister for home affairs had issued a written statement in Parliament confessing that there were no specific charges or reports of terrorism against any particular madrasa, but in the same month the Union home minister had dispatched a circular to the state governments requesting them to keep a strict vigil over madrasas in their states (Interview with Maulana Wali Rahmani, *Bang-i Hira*, September–November 2002, pp. 19–20).
74. Thus, Mirwaiz 'Umar Farooq, former chairman of the Kashmir Hurriyat Conference, alleged that the state was 'systematically closing down madrasas all over the country', arguing that this suggested that the government 'does not want Muslims to become literate' ('Centre is Attacked for Targeting Madrasas', *The Asian Age*, New Delhi, 10 March 2003).

75. 'Dini Madaris Ko Registration Karne Ki Tajviz Naqabil-i Qubul', *Qaumi Awaz*, 2 July 2002.
76. H. 'Abdul Raqib, 'Dini Madaris Ki Mukhalifat Aur Hamari Zimmedari', *Da'wat*, 28 January 2003. See also Ibn ul-Hasan Abbasi, *Dini Madaris: Mazi, Hal, Mustaqbil*, Deoband: Idara-i Islamiyat, 2001, p. 74.
77. See, for instance, Khalid Nadwi Ghazipuri, 'Madaris-i Diniya Ka Tahaffuz: Milli-o-Dini Fariza', *Bang-i Hira*, July–August 2002, p. 7.
78. 'Report: Madrasa Convention', *Bang-i Hira*, September–November 2002, p. 17.
79. Waris Mazhari, 'Madaris Ke Khilaf Muhim: Ek Khamosh 'Amal Ki Zarurat', op. cit., p. 4.
80. Habib ur-Rahman Qasmi, *Dar ul-'Ulum Deoband: Ek Maktab-i Fikr, Ek Tehrik*, op. cit., p. 60.
81. Marghub ur-Rahman, 'Dar ul-'Ulum Ki Ta'limi, Milli Aur Difa'i Khidmat', in Habib ur-Rahman Qasmi (ed.), *Dar ul-'Ulum Deoband: Ek Maktab-i Fikr, Ek Tehrik*, Deoband: Markazi Daftar Rabita-i Madaris-i Islamiya 'Arabia, n.d., pp. 53–54.
82. Husam Siddiqui, 'Sangh Parivar Ki Madraso Aur Masjido Ke Khilaf Lambandi', *Bang-i Hira*, July–August 2002, p. 34.
83. Mufti Ahmed Devalvi, *Madressas: Where Civilised Manners Are Taught*, Jambusar: Jami'a Uloom ul-Qur'an, n.d., pp. 1–2.
84. Waris Mazhari, 'Madaris Ke Khilaf Muhim: Ek Khamosh 'Amal Ki Zarurat', op. cit., pp. 4–6.
85. 'Tahaffuz-i Madaris Ke Mauzu Par Zimmedaran-i Madaris Ka Ijtima', *Bang-i Dara*, January 1995.
86. 'Report: Madaris Convention', *Bang-i Hira*, September–November 2002, p. 16.
87. Ibid., p. 18.
88. Waris Mazhari, 'Madaris Ke Khilaf Muhim: Ek Khamosh 'Amal Ki Zarurat', op. cit., p. 5.
89. Nasim Ahmad Qasmi, op. cit., p. 4.
90. The late Qazi Mujahidul Islam Qasmi, former president of the All-India Muslim Personal Law Board, quoted in *Kul Hind*

Dini Madaris Convention Delhi: Pas-i Manzar, Rudad, op. cit., p. 16.

91. Shaik Ahmad 'Ali, 'Madrasas to Introduce Patriotism as a Subject', *The Times of India*, Bangalore, 11 June 2002.
92. 'SSB Film Contradicts IB Reports on Madrasas', *The Times of India*, Lucknow, 31 March 2003. The report quoted the director-general of the SSB as saying that while some madrasas along the Indo-Nepal border were 'suspected' of being funded by the ISI, 'the big danger to India on the Indo-Nepal border is from Maoist organisations'.
93. Interview with Asghar 'Ali Engineer <http://www.islaminterfaith.org/oct2002/interview.html>.
94. *Muhtamim-o-Muntazamin-i Madaris-i Islamiya Ke Liye Zaruri Ma'aruzat-o-Sifarishat*, New Delhi: Rabita-i Madaris-i Islamiya, Tanzim-i Abna ul-Qadim Dar ul-'Ulum Deoband, 2002, pp. 5–53. The statement added that the police and intelligence officers did have the right to investigate the madrasas, but only if they had the appropriate identity card and on the basis of a written complaint. In this case, the madrasas were told that they must cooperate with them, on the basis of the 'Islamic principles of good morality' and provide them with correct information (ibid., pp. 52–53).
95. Asrar ul-Haq Qasmi, 'Dini Madaris Ke Khilaf Hukumat Ki Nayi Muhim', op. cit., p. 35.
96. 'Report: Madaris Convention', op. cit., p. 18.
97. Sayyed Abul Hasan 'Ali Nadwi, 'Distinctive Features of Arabic Schools and Their Role in Indian History and Culture', *Fragrance of the East*, vol. 5, no. 1, January–March 2003, p. 29.
98. 'PM Asks Muslim Leaders to Evolve Consensus on Madrasa Reforms', *Muslim India*, January–July 2003, p. 298.

Glossary

ajlaf	'low' caste
'aqida (pl. aqa'id)	belief
'aql	reason, intellect
ashraf	'high' caste
dar ul-harb	abode of war
dar ul-Islam	abode of Islam
din	the primal religion
dini	religious
duniya	the world
duniyavi	related to the world; secular affairs
faqih (pl. fuqaha)	expert in Islamic jurisprudence
fatwa (pl. fatawa)	a legal opinion (in matters of Islamic jurisprudence)
fiqh	Islamic jurisprudence
ijtihad	derivation of rules for new situations from the principal sources of Islamic jurisprudence
'ilm	knowledge
khalifa	Caliph, deputy or successor
maktab	mosque-school
mazhab	school of jurisprudence
razil	'despicable' or 'low'
sahabi	companion (of the Prophet)
shaikh	elder; teacher; Sufi preceptor
sunnah	practice of the Prophet
tabligh	Islamic missionary work
tafsir	commentary (on the Qur'an)
taqlid	imitation (of past jurisprudential precedent)
ummah	the universal Muslim community
zimmi	protected non-Muslim citizen of an Islamic state

Sources

Interviews

'Abdul Qadir, Nadwat ul-Mujahidin, Calicut, 11 August 2001.
'Abdur Rahman Kamaruddin, Director, Dar ul-'Umoor, Srirangapatnam, 6 October 2002.
Allauddin Khan Islahi, Lecturer, Shibli National College, Azamgarh, 28 March 2003.
Ashfaq Husain, Head, Education Department, Jama'at-i Islami Hind, New Delhi, 23 October 2002.
'Atiq ur-Rahman, Assistant Manager, Markaz ul-Ma'arif, Mumbai, 2 October 2002.
Husain Aboobacker Koya, Nadwat ul-Mujahidin, Calicut, 12 August 2003.
Maqbool Ahmad Siraj, Executive Editor, *Islamic Voice*, Bangalore, 20 December 2002.
Mohammad Aslam Parvaiz, Editor, *Science*, New Delhi, 8 August 2004.
Muhammad Islam, Rector, Madrasa Jami'at ul-Banat, New Delhi, 28 October 2002.
Muhammad Shaukat Barkati, Islamic Education Board of India, New Delhi, 7 January 2003.
Muqtada Hasan, Principal, Jami'a Salafiya, Varanasi, 25 March 2003.
Rahmatullah 'Asri, Principal, Jami'at ul-Falah, Bilariyaganj, 29 March 2003.
Salman Asad, Director, Islamic Studies and Research Academy, New Delhi, 4 January 2002.
Sayyed Hamid ul-Hasan, Principal, Jam'ia Nazmia, Lucknow, 21 March 2003.
Siddiq Hasan 'Abdullah, *Amir*, Jama'at-i Islami, Kerala unit, Calicut, 10 August 2003.
Waris Mazhari, Editor, *Tarjuman Dar ul-'Ulum*, New Delhi, 22 August 2004.
Zafrul Islam Khan, Editor, *Milli Gazette*, New Delhi, 2 January 2003.
Zohra Bi, Principal, Anwar ul-'Ulum Women's Arabic College, Mongam, 13 August 2003.

Magazines and Newspapers

The Asian Age, Bangalore
Bang-i Hira, Lucknow
The Daily Times, Lahore

Da'wat, New Delhi
The Friday Times, Lahore
The Hindu, Bangalore
The Indian Express, Bangalore
Islamic Voice, Bangalore
Meantime, Calicut
The Milli Gazette, New Delhi
Muslim India, New Delhi
Qaumi Awaz, New Delhi
Rashtriya Sahara, New Delhi
The Statesman, Kolkata
The Times of India, Bangalore

Select Bibliography

Works in Urdu

'Abid, Abdur Rahim, 'Madaris Ke Nisab Mai Tabdili Ka Masla: 'Ulama Kya Kahtey Hain?', *Tarjuman-i Dar ul-'Ulum*, October 1994.

Ahmad, Khurshid, *Nizam-i Ta'lim: Nazariya, Rivayat, Masa'il*, Islamabad: Institute of Policy Studies, 1996.

Ahmad, Muhammad Ashfaq, 'Jama'at-i Islami Ka Ta'limi Nizam', in *Mulk-o-Millat Ki Ta'mir Aur Dini Madaris*, Bilariyaganj, 1994.

'Ali, Anwar, 'Madaris-i Diniya Aur Hukumati Control' (part ii), *Qaumi Awaz*, 19 June 2002.

'Ali, Sayyed Naushad, *Musalmanan-i Hind-o-Pakistan Ki Tarikh-i Ta'lim*, Karachi: Salman Academy, 1963.

Allama Hamiduddin Farahi: Ahl-i 'Ilm-o-Danish Ki Nazar Mai, Sara'i Mir: Da'ira Hamidiya, n.d.

All-India Ta'limi-o-Milli Foundation, Delhi: All-India Ta'limi-o-Milli Foundation, n.d.

'Amali Programme Tanzim Abna ul-Qadim Dar ul-'Ulum Deoband, Delhi: Tanzim Abna ul-Qadim Dar ul-'Ulum Deoband, n.d.

Amin, Muhammad, *Radd-i Raza Khaniyat*, Deoband: Dar ul-'Ulum, n.d.

Anjum, Ghulam Yahya, *Anwar-i Khyal*, New Delhi, 1991.

Ansari, Inayatullah, *'Ulama-i Firangi Mahal*, Lucknow, 1988.

Ansari, Muhammad Iqbal, 'Nadwat ul-'Ulama: Ek Dini-o-Ta'limi Tehrik' (part i), *Islam Aur 'Asr-i Jadid*, vol. 7, no. 2, April 1975.

Ansari, Muhammad Wali ul-Haq, 'Bani-i Dars-i Nizami Mulla Nizamuddin Aur Unka Khanvada Firangi Mahal' (part i), *Tarjuman-i Dar ul-'Ulum*, December 1997.

______, 'Bani-i Dars-i Nizami Mulla Nizamuddin Aur Unka Khanvada Firangi Mahal' (part ii), *Tarjuman-i Dar ul-'Ulum*, January 1988.

'Arabi Islami Madaris Ka Nisab-o-Nizam-i Ta'lim Aur 'Asri Taqaze, Patna: Khuda Bakhsh Oriental Public Library, 1995.

Argali, Faruq, 'Hamare Dini Madaris Mai Kya Ho Raha Hai?', *Qaumi Awaz*, 30 March 1994.

'Asri, Arshad ul-Haq, *Pak-o-Hind Mai 'Ulama-i Ahl-i Hadith Ki Khidmat-i Hadith*, Maunath Bhanjan: Markazi Maktaba-i Ahl-i Hadith, 1995.

'Aur Ab Dar ul-'Ulum Bhi Nishane Par', *Tarjuman-i Dar ul-'Ulum*, June 1994.

'Azmi, Sa'eed ur-Rahman, 'Nisab-i Ta'lim Aur Tehrik-i Nadwat ul-'Ulama', in *Kul Hind Dini Madaris Convention Souvenir*, New Delhi: All-India Milli Council, 1994.

Badiuzzaman, Muhammad, 'Hindustan Ke Madrase Aur Masajid Markazi Hukumat Ke Nishane Par', in *Basat Zikr-o-Fikr*, May–June 2002.

Dar ul-'Ulum Deoband Zer-i Ehtimam Ijtima-i Madaris-i Islamiya Ka Ineqad', *Tarjuman-i Dar ul-'Ulum*, November 1994.

Faridi, Fazlur Rahman, 'Dini Madaris Ka Nisab-i Ta'lim Aur 'Asri Challenge', in *Kul Hind Dini Madaris Convention Souvenir*, New Delhi: All-India Milli Council, n.d.

Faruqi, Imdadul Hasan Azad, 'Introduction', in Imdadul Hasan Azad Faruqi (ed.), *Hindustan Mai Islami 'Ulum-o-Adabiyat*, New Delhi, 1986.

Faruqi, Zia ul-Hasan, 'Hindustan Mai Islami Rasikh ul-Aqa'id Ki Rivayat', in Imdadul Hasan Azad Faruqi (ed.), *Hindustan Mai Islami 'Ulum-o-Adabiyat*, New Delhi, 1986.

———, *Islam Mai Rasikh ul-Ayteqadi: Bich Ki Rah*, New Delhi: Maktaba-i Jami'a, 1990.

Fatehpuri, Niyaz Ahmad, *'Ilm: Ek Shari' Zarurat*, New Delhi: al-Kitab, 1999.

Firangi Mahali, Muhammad Raza Ansari, *Bani-i Dars-i Nizami Ustad ul-Hind Mullah Nizamuddin Muhammad Firangi Mahali*, Lucknow, 1973.

Ghazipuri, Khalid Nadwi, 'Madaris-i Diniya Ka Tahaffuz: Milli-o-Dini Fariza', *Bang-i Hira*, July–August 2002.

Gilani, Sayyed Manazir Ahsan, *Hindustan Mai Musalmano Ka Nizam-i Ta'lim-o-Tarbiyat* (vol. 1), Delhi: Nadwat ul-Musannifin, 1987.

Hafizullah, Muhammad, *Salatin-i Hind Ki 'Ilm Parvari*, Patna: Muslim Academy, 1956.

Haye, Sayyed 'Abdul, *Hindustan Ka Nisabi Dars Aur Uskey Taghirat*, Lucknow, n.d.

Husain, Afzal, *Jama'at-i Islami Hind Aur Dini Ta'limi Tehrik*, New Delhi: Markazi Maktaba-i Islami, n.d.

———, *Jama'at-i Islami Ki Ta'limi Kavishey*, New Delhi: Markazi Maktaba-i Islami, 2002.

Islahi, Nizamuddin, 'Ghalba-i Islam Ki Jad-o-Jehed Mai Madaris Ka Kirdar', in *Mulk-o-Millat Ki Ta'mir Aur Dini Madaris*, Bilariyaganj: Jami'at ul-Falah, 1994.

Islahi, Sultan Ahmad, *Hindustan Mai Madaris-i 'Arabiya Ke Masa'il*, Aligarh: Idara-i 'Ilm-o-Adab, n.d.

Islahi, Zafar ul-Islam, 'Ahad-i Wusta Ke Hindustan Mai 'Ala Ta'lim', in *Mulk-o-Millat Ki Ta'mir Aur Dini Madaris*, Bilariyaganj: Jami'at ul-Falah, 1994.

Jami'at ul-Banat al-Islamiya Ka Mukhtasar Ta'aruf, New Delhi: Jami'at ul-Banat al-Islamiya, n.d.

Jami'at ul-Falah: Aghraz-o-Maqasid, Bilariyaganj: Jami'at ul-Falah, 1997.

Jami'at ul-Falah: Ek Ta'aruf, Bilariyaganj: Jami'at ul-Falah, n.d.

Jhandanagari, 'Abdur Rauf, *al-'Ilm wa'l 'Ulama*, Maunath Bhanjan: Idara Da'wat ul-Islam, n.d.

Khan, Salman 'Ali, *Jang-i Azadi Mai 'Ulama-i Kiram Ka Hissa*, Lucknow: Maulana Muhammad 'Ali Jauhar Foundation, 1998.

Khan, Shams Tabrez, *Tarikh-i Nadwat ul-'Ulama* (vol. 2), Lucknow: Nadwat ul-'Ulama, 1984.

Kul Hind Dini Madaris Convention Delhi: Pas-i Manzar, Rudad, Tajaviz-o-Faisle Aur Rabita-i Madaris-i Islamiya Ka Qayyam, New Delhi: All-India Milli Council, n.d.

Madani, Sayyed 'Asad, *Jang-i Azadi Mai Jami'at ul-'Ulama-i Hind Ki Khidmat*, New Delhi: Jami'at ul-'Ulama-i Hind, n.d.

Madani, Sayyed Husain Ahmad, *Muttahida Qaumiyat Aur Islam*, New Delhi: al-Jami'at Book Depot, n.d.

Madrasat ul-Islah Ki Ibtida Aur Uska Nasb ul-'Ain, Sara'i Mir: Madrasat ul-Islah, n.d..

Mansurpuri, Mufti Muhammad Sulaiman, 'Sarkari Imdad Dini Madaris Ke Liye Sitam Qatil', *Tarjuman-i Dar ul-'Ulum*, August 2003.

Markazi Darsgah-i Islami, Rampur: Ek Ta'aruf, Rampur: Markazi Darsgah-i Islami, n.d.

Mazhari, Waris, 'Dini Idare Aur Chanda: Kuch Qabil-i Ghaur Pahlu', *Tarjuman-i Dar ul-'Ulum*, December 2002.

______, 'Madaris Ke Khilaf Muhim: Ek Khamosh 'Amal Ki Zarurat', *Tarjuman-i Dar ul-'Ulum*, September 2002.

Miftahi, Mufti Zahiruddin, 'Madaris-i Diniya Aur Unke Masa'il', in *Dini Madaris Aur Unkey Masa'il*, Bilariyaganj: Jami'at ul-Falah, 1990.

Misbahi, Maqbul Ahmad, 'Hindustan Aur 'Alam-i Arab Ke Nisab-i Ta'lim Ka Taqabli Ja'iza, *Islam Aur 'Asr-i Jadid*, vol. 32, no. 4, October 2000.

Misbahi, Mubarak Husain, *Bar-i Saghir Mai Iritaq Bayn al-Muslimin Ke Asbab*, Mubarakpur: al-Jami'a al-Misbahi, 2001.

Misbahi, Yasin Akhtar, *Madaris-i Islamiya Aur Kashmir-o-Gujarat*, New Delhi: All-India Muslim Mushawarati Board, 2002.

Miyan, Sayyed Muhammad, *'Ulama-i Hind Ka Shandar Mazi* (vol. 1), Delhi: Kitabistan, n.d.

Mubarakpuri, Qazi Athar, *Khair al-Qarun Ki Darsgahe Aur Unka Nizam-i Ta'lim*, Deoband: Shaikh ul-Hind Academy, 1996.

Muhsin, Muhammad, 'Dini Madaris Ka Nisab', in '*Arabi Islami Madaris Ke Nisab-o-Nizam-i-Ta'lim*, Patna: Khuda Bakhsh Oriental Public Library, 1995.

Muhtamim-o-Muntazamin-i Madaris-i Islamiya Ke Liye Zaruri Ma'aruzat-o-Sifarishat, New Delhi: Rabita-i Madaris-i Islamiya, Tanzim-i Abna ul-Qadim Dar ul-'Ulum Deoband, 2002.

Nadwi, Abul Hasnat, *Hindustan Ke Qadim Islami Darsgahe*, Azamgarh: Dar ul-Musannifin, 1971.

Nadwi, Abul 'Irfan, 'Ma'qulat Ke Maidan Mai Hindustani Musalmano Ki Khidmat', in Imdadul Hasan Azad Faruqi (ed.), *Hindustan Mai Islami 'Ulum-o-Adabiyat*, New Delhi: 1986.

——— 'Nisab-i Ta'lim Aur Tariqa-i Ta'lim: Maujuda Ahad Ke Taqaze', *Islam Aur 'Asr-i Jadid*, vol. 12, no. 4, October 1980.

Nadwi, Ghatrif Shahbaz, 'Deoband Se Taliban Tak: Akabir-i Deoband Kya Kahtey Hain?', *Afkar-i Milli*, December 2001.

——— 'Madaris-i Islamiya Ko Darpesh Khatrat Aur Unka Tadrak', *Afkar-i Milli*, May 2002.

——— 'Qaumi Hifazati Nizam Ke Barey Mai Vizarati Group Ki Report: Kya Kahtey Hain Akabirin-i Millat?', *Afkar-i Milli*, August 2001.

Nadwi, Mohsin 'Usmani, 'Madaris Ka Nizam-i-Ta'lim Aur Naya Challenge', *Islam Aur 'Asr-i Jadid*, vol. 32, no. 4, October 2000.

Nadwi, Mujibullah, *Dini Madaris Aur Unki Zimmedariyan*, Azamgarh: Jami'at ul-Rishad, 2002.

Nadwi, Muhammad Ishaq Jalis, *Tarikh-i Nadwat ul-'Ulama* (vol. 1), Lucknow: Nadwat ul-'Ulama, 1983.

Nadwi, Muhammad Shahabuddin, *Hamare Ta'limi Masa'il*, Bangalore: Furqania Academy, 1989.

Nadwi, Muhammad Zaid Mazhari, *Al-'Ilm wa'l 'Ulama*, Hathaura: Idara-i Ifadat-i Ashrafiya, 1996.

Nadwi, 'Ubaidullah Koti, *'Allama Burhanuddin Mirghinani: Sahib-i Hidaya*, New Delhi: Nadwat ul-Mu'alifin, 2002.

Nadwi, Sayyed Abul Hasan 'Ali, *'Ilm Ka Muqam Aur Ahl-i 'Ilm Ki Zimmedariyan*, Majlis Tahqiqat-o-Nashriyat ul-Islam, Lucknow, 1997.

———, *Madaris-i Islamiya Ka Muqam Aur Kam*, Khatauli: Mahad al-Imam Abul Hasan 'Ali Nadwi, 2002.

Nadwi, Sayyed Muhammad Rabe Hasni, *Musalman Aur Ta'lim*, Lucknow: Nadwat ul-'Ulama, 1997.

Nadwi, Sayyed Riyasat 'Ali, *Islami Nizam-i Ta'lim*, Azamgarh: Dar ul-Musannifin, 1992.

Navedi, 'Alim Saba, *Nawab Wala Jah Aur Hazrat Allama 'Abdul 'Ala Bahr ul-'Ulum Firangi Mahali*, Chennai: Tamil Nadu Publications, 1995.

Nisab-i Ta'lim Jami'at ul-Falah, Bilariyaganj: Jami'at ul Falah, 2001.

Palanpuri, Muhammad Amin, *Radd-i Raza Khaniyat*, Deoband: Dar ul-'Ulum, n.d.

Parwez, Aslam, 'Madaris Ke Nisab Aur Science', in *'Arabi Islami Madaris Ka Nisab-o-Nizam-i Ta'lim*, Patna: Khuda Bakhsh Oriental Public Library, 1995.

Qamruddin, *Hindustan Ki Dini Darsgahe: Kul Hind Survey*, New Delhi: Hamdard Educational Society, 1996.

Qasmi, 'Aqidatullah, 'Angrezi Ta'lim Ki Mukhalifat: Fasana Aur Haqiqat', *Tarjuman-i Dar ul-'Ulum*, February–March 1998.

Qasmi, Habib ur-Rahman, *Dar ul-'Ulum: Ek Ajmali Ta'ruf*, Deoband: Markazi Daftar Rabita-i Madaris-i Islamiya al-Arabiya, 1998.

Qasmi, Javed Ashraf, *Faizan-i Dar ul-'Ulum Deoband*, Ghaseda: Madrasa Abi bin Ka'ab Tahaffuz al-Qur'an al-Karim, 2000.

Qasmi, Muhammad Afzal ul-Haq Jauhar, 'Dini Madaris Ke Khilaf Sazish', *Tarjuman-i Dar ul-'Ulum*, March 2002.

Qasmi, Muhammad Rizwan ul-, *Dini Madaris Aur 'Asr-i Hazir*, Hyderabad: Markaz Da'wat-o-Tahqiqat, 1994.

Qasmi, Mujahid ul-Islam (ed.), *Maqalat-i Sajjad*, Patna: Imarat-i Shari'ah, 1999.

Qasmi, Mumshad 'Ali, *Tarikh-i Dars-i Nizami*, Bilaspur, Muzaffarnagar: Majm'a al-Bahath al-'Ilmiya, 1994.

Qasmi, Nasim Ahmad, *Madaris-i Islamiya Ke Hifz-o-Baqa Ke Liye Imarat-i Shari'ah Ki Jad-o-Jehed*, Patna: Imarat-i Shari'ah, 2002.

Qasmi, Shaukat 'Ali, *Rabita-i Madaris-i 'Arabia Dar ul-'Ulum: Qayyam, Ijtima'at, Sargarmiyan*, Deoband: Dar ul-'Ulum, 1998.

Qasmi, Zain ul-Sajid bin, 'Dars-i Nizami: Tarikhi Pas-i Manzar Aur Jadid Taqaze', *Tarjuman-i Dar ul-'Ulum*, November 1994.

Rahmani, Khalid Saifullah, 'Nisab-i Ta'lim: Ek Ja'iza', in *Kul Hind Dini Madaris Convention Souvenir*, New Delhi: All-India Muslim Milli Council, 1994.

Rahmani, Muhammad Wali, *Dini Madaris Mai Sanati Ta'lim Ka Masla*, Munger: Jami'a Rahmani, 1981.

Rashid, Munawwar Jahan, *Qadim Islami Madaris*, Lahore: Majlis-i Taraqqi-i Adab, 1975.

Rizvi, Sayyed Mahbub, ' 'Ulama Ki Taraf Se Angrezi Ta'lim Ki Mukhalifat: Haqiqat Kya Hai?', *Tarjuman-i Dar ul-'Ulum*, July 1994.

Rizvi, Sayyed Rizvan 'Ali Rizvi, *Nizam ul-Mulk Tusi: Ek 'Azim Muffakir, Mudabbir, Muntazim Aur Mahir-i Siyasat*, Karachi: Karachi University, 1995.

Sadr-i Jumhuriya-i Hind Dar ul-'Ulum Deoband Mai, Deoband: Dar ul-'Ulum, 1957.

Salafi, Asghar 'Ali, 'Madaris-i Islamiya-i Hind Kya Haqiqi Islami Da'wat Ke Taqazey Purey Kar Rahe Hain?', *Muhhadith*, January–March 1994.

Salim, Sayyed Muhammad, *Dini Madaris Ke Liye Nisab-i Nau Ki Tajwiz*, Lahore: Idara Ta'limi Tahqiq, n.d.

______ *Dini Madaris Ki Rivayat Aur Nisab-i Ta'lim Ki Khususiyat*, Lahore: Idara Ta'limi Tahqiq Tanzim-i Asatiza-i Pakistan, 1987

Siddiqui, 'Abdul Halim, *Malegaon: Ek Shahr, Ek Jahan*, Malegaon: Misbah Educational and Welfare Sports and Research Society, 2000.

Siddiqui, 'Adil, *Jami'at ul-'Ulama-i Hind: A'ina-i Ayyam Mai*, New Delhi: Jami'at ul-'Ulama-i Hind, n.d.

Siddiqui, Husam, 'Sangh Parivar Ki Madraso Aur Masjido Ke Khilaf Lambandi', *Bang-i Hira*, July–August 2002.

Siddiqui, Muhammad Jamiluddin, *Musalmano Ke Ahad-i Zawal Mai 'Ulama Ka Role-o-Hissa*, Hyderabad: Rahman Publishers, 1990.

Siddiqui, Muhammad Nejatullah, *Dini Madaris: Masa'il Aur Taqaze*, New Delhi: Markazi Maktaba-i Islami, 2001.

Sohrab, Muhammad, 'Mazi Mai Dini Madaris Ki Nisabi Rivayat', *Zindagi-i Nau*, September 1994.

Tabrez, Muhammad Shams, ' 'Ilm-o-Taqwa Ki Buniyad Par Ta'lim-o-Tarbiyat', *Naqib*, Phulwari Sharif, 10–17 June 1996.

Talaba-i Madaris Se Ek Khitab, Lucknow: Jami'at us-Shabab il al-Islam, n.d.

Ta'ruf-i Nadwat ul-'Ulama, Lucknow: Nadwat ul-'Ulama, n.d.

Tayyeb, Qari Muhammad, *Ijlas-i Sadsalah Ke Bad Dar ul-'Ulum Mai Pesh Amida Afsosnak Hawadis-o-Waqiyat Ki Sahih Aur Mufassil Report*, Deoband: Dar ul-'Ulum, 1980.

Tirmizi, Shamim Haider, *Islam Ka Nizam-i Ta'lim*, Lahore: Karavan-i Adab, 1993.

'Umri, Habib ur-Rahman 'Azmi, 'Dini Madaris Ki Zimmedariyan Aur Biradiran-i Watan', in *Dini Madaris Aur Unkey Masa'il*, Bilariyaganj: Jami'at ul-Falah, 1990.

U.P. Sarkari Nisab-i Ta'lim Ka Mukhtasar Ja'iza, Lucknow: Dini Ta'limi Council, n.d.

Usmani, Muhammad Taqi, *Fazilat-i 'Ilm-o-'Ulama*, Delhi: Farid Book Depot, 1999.

Works in English

Ahmad, Moinuddin, *The Urgency of Ijtihad*, New Delhi: Kitab Bhavan, 1992.

———, *'Ulama: The Boon and Bane of Islamic Society*, New Delhi: Kitab Bhavan, 1990.

Ahmad, Washim, 'Psychology of Education: Madrasas of UP', *Economic and Political Weekly*, 25–31 March 2000.

Ahmed, Eqbal, 'Islam and Politics', in Asghar Khan (ed.) *Islam, Politics and the State: The Pakistan Experience*, London: Zed Books, 1985.

Ahmed, Manzoor, *Islamic Education: Redefinition of Aims and Methodology*, New Delhi: Genuine Publications & Media, 2002.

'Alam, Zafar, *Education in Early Muslim Period*, Delhi: Markazi Maktaba-i Islami, 1997.

Ashraf, Kunwar Muhammad, *An Overview of Indian Muslim Politics (1920–1947)* (translated by Jaweed Ashraf), New Delhi: Manak Publications, 2001.

Ashraf, Mujeeb, 'Distinctive Madrasah-i Rahimiyah: Growth and Pattern of Educational Curriculum', *The Fragrance of the East*, vol. v, no. 1, January–March 2003.

'Azmi, H.U., 'Contribution of Deeni Ta'limi Council to Muslim Education in Uttar Pradesh', in A.W. B.Qadri, Riaz Shakir Khan and Mohammed Akhtar Siddique, *Education and Muslims in India Since Independence*, New Delhi: Institute of Objective Studies, 1988.

Bulliet, Richard W., *The Patricians of Nishapur: A Study in Medieval Islamic Social History*, Cambridge, Massachusetts: Harvard University Press, 1972.

Chawdhri, A. Ghafur, *Some Aspects of Islamic Education*, Delhi: Adam Publishers, 1999.

Cohen, Stephen Philip, 'The Jihadist Threat to Pakistan', *The Washington Quarterly*, Summer, 2003.

Dar ul-Umoor Tipu Sultan Advanced Study and Research Centre, Bangalore: Dar ul-Umoor, n.d.

Devlavi, Mufti Ahmed, *Madressas: Where Civilised Manners Are Taught*, Jambusar: Jami'a Uloom ul-Qur'an, n.d.

Elahi, Nizam, *Modernisation of Madrasa Education Scheme in India*, New Delhi: State Council for Educational Research and Training, 2001.

Ephrat, Daphna, *A Learned Society in a Period of Transition: The Sunni 'Ulama of Eleventh Century Baghdad*, Albany: State University of New York, 2000.

Fadl, Khaled Abou El, *Rebellion and Violence in Islamic Law*, Cambridge: Cambridge University Press, 2001.

Faruqi, Ismail Raji al-, *Tawhid: Its Implications for Thought and Life*, Herndon, International Institute of Islamic Thought, 1989.

Faruqi, Zia ul-Hasan, *The Deoband School and the Demand for Pakistan*, London: Asia Publishing House, 1963.

Friedmann, Yohannan, 'Islamic Thought in Relation to the Indian Context', in Marc Gaboreiau (ed.) *Islam et Societe en Asia du Sud*, Paris: Ecole des Hautes Etudes en Sciences Sociales, 1986.

Godbole, Madhav, 'Madrasas: Need for a Fresh Look', *Economic and Political Weekly*, 13 October 2001.

Hardy, Peter, *Partners in Freedom—and True Muslims: The Political Thought of Some Muslim Scholars in British India 1912–1947*, Lund: Scandinavian Institute of Asian Studies, 1971.

Hasan, Ahmad, *The Early Development of Islamic Jurisprudence*, Islamabad: Islamic Research Institute, 1994.

Hoodbhoy, Pervez, 'Ideological Problems for Science in Pakistan', in Asghar Khan (ed.), *Islam, Politics and the State: The Pakistan Experience*, London: Zed Books, 1985.

Hoodbhoy, Pervez, *Islam and Science: Religious Orthodoxy and the Battle for Rationality*, Kuala Lumpur: S. Abdul Majeed & Co., 1992.

Ivanow, W., *Brief Survey of the Evolution of Isma'ilism*, Mumbai: Isma'ili Society, 1952.

Jalalzai, Musa Khan, *Sectarianism and Ethnic Violence in Pakistan*, Lahore: S.M.A. Anjum Rizvi, 1996.

______ *Sectarian Violence in Pakistan and Afghanistan*, Lahore: Systems Books, 1999.

Jami'at ul-Falah: An Introduction, Bilaryaganj: Jami'at ul-Falah, n.d.

Katju, Manjari, *VHP and Indian Politics*, New Delhi: Orient Longman, 2003.

Kaur, Kuldip, *Madrasa Education in India: A Study of its Past and Present*, Chandigarh: Centre for Research in Rural and Industrial Development, 1990.

Khan, Ehtashamuddin, 'Madrasas Want to Modernise, But Not Too Much', *The Fragrance of the East*, vol. v, no. 1, January–March 2003.

Khan, Ghazanfar 'Ali, 'Educational Views of Shibli Nomani', *Islam and the Modern Age*, vol. xxx, no. 2, May 1999.

Khan, Muhammad Sharif, *Education, Religion and Modern Age*, New Delhi: Ashish Publishing House, 1990.

Law, Narendra Nath, *Promotion of Learning in India During Muhammadan Rule (By Muhammadans)*, Delhi: Idara-i Adabiyat-i Dehli, 1973.

Lewis, Bernard, *What Went Wrong? The Clash Between Islam and Modernity in the Middle East*, London: Weidenfeld & Nicolson, 2002.

Makdisi, George, *The Rise of Colleges: Institutions of Learning in Islam and the West*, Edinburgh: Edinburgh University Press, 1981.

Malik, Jamal, 'Between National Integration and Islamism: Lucknow's Nadwat al-'Ulama', in Mushirul Hasan (ed.), *Knowledge, Power and Politics: Educational Institutions in India*, New Delhi, Roli Books, 1998.

Markaz ul-Ma'rif: Report on Activities Till March 2000, Hojai: Markaz ul-Ma'rif, 2000.

Metcalf, Barbara D., *Islamic Revival in British India, 1860–1900*, New Delhi: Oxford University Press, 2002.

———, *'Traditionalist' Islamic Activism: Deoband, Tablighis and Talibs*, Leiden: Institute for the Study of Islam in the Modern World, 2002.

Metcalf, Thomas, *Ideologies of the Raj*, Cambridge: Cambridge University Press, 1994

'Modernisation of Madrasas in India', <www.bazaarchintan.net/pdfs/madrasas/pdf>.

Mohiuddin, Syed Ghulam, 'Modern Education and the Educational Problems of Indian Muslims', in S.M. Wazeh Rashid Nadwi and Syed Ghulam Mohiuddin, *Survey of Muslim Education: India*, Cambridge: The Islamic Academy, 1985.

Mujeeb, M., *Islamic Influence on Indian Society*, Meerut: Meenakshi Prakashan, 1972.

Nadwi, Syed Ehtisham A., 'Reflections on Arabic College Education in Kerala', in E.K.Ahamed Kutty (ed.), *Arabic in South India*, Calicut: Department of Arabic, University of Calicut, 2003.

Philips, Abu Ameenah Bilal, *The Evolution of Islamic Law and the Maddhabs*, Riyadh: Tawheed Publications, 1988.

Quraishi, Mansoor A., *Some Aspects of Muslim Education*, Baroda: Centre of Advanced Study in Education, M.S. University, 1970.

Rizvi, Sayyed Mahboob, *History of Dar ul-'Ulum Deoband* (vol. 1) (translated by Mumtaz Hussain F. Quraishi), Deoband: Dar ul-'Ulum, 1980.

Robinson, Francis, *The 'Ulama of Farangi Mahall and Islamic Culture in South Asia*, New Delhi: Permanent Black, 2001.

Rudolph, Susanne H. and Rudolph, Lloyd I., 'Living with Difference in India: Legal Pluralism and Legal Universalism in Historical Context', in Gerald James Larson (ed.), *Religion and Personal Law in Secular India: A Call for Judgment*, Bloomington: Indiana University Press, 2001.

Sanyal, Usha, *Devotional Islam and Politics in British India: Ahmed Riza Khan Barelwi and His Movement 1870–1920*, New Delhi: Oxford University Press, 2000.

Sardar, Ziauddin Sardar and Davies, Merryl Wyn, *Distorted Imagination: Lessons From the Rushdie Affair*, London: Grey Seal Books, 1990.

Siddiqui, Muhammad Akhtar, 'Development and Trends in Madrasa Education', in A.W.B. Qadri, Riaz Shakir Khan and Mohammed Akhter Siddique, *Education and Muslims in India Since Independence*, New Delhi: Institute of Objective Studies, 1998.

Sikand, Yoginder, 'Targeting Muslim Religious Schools', *Economic and Political Weekly*, 1 September 2001.

———, 'Women and the Tablighi Jama'at', *Islam and Christian–Muslim Relations*, vol. 10, no. 1, 1999.

———, *The Indian 'Ulama*, Bangalore, 2002.

Stenberg, Leif, *The Islamization of Science: Four Muslim Positions Developing an Islamic Modernity*, Lund: Lund University, 1996.

Sufi, G.M.D., *Al-Minhaj: Being the Evolution of the Curriculum in the Muslim Educational Institutions of India*, Lahore: Shaikh Muhammad Ashraf, 1941.

Suhrawardy, Sa'eed and Nu'mani 'Abdul Hamid, *A Glance at the Services of Jami'at ul-'Ulama-i Hind*, New Delhi, Jami'at ul-'Ulama-i Hind, n.d.

Zaman, Muhammad Qasim, 'Religious Education and the Rhetoric of Reform: The Madrasa in British India and Pakistan', *Comparative Studies in Society and History*, vol. 41, no. 2, April 1999.

______ 'Sectarianism in Pakistan: The Radicalisation of Shi'i and Sunni Identities', *Modern Asian Studies*, vol. 32, no. 3, 1998.

______ *The 'Ulama in Contemporary Islam: Custodians of Change*, Princeton and Oxford: Princeton University Press, 2002.

Index